D0074730

England Eats Out

England Eats Out:
A Social History of
Eating Out in England
from 1830 to the
Present

John Burnett

Harlow, England • London • New York • Boston • San Francisco • Toronto
Sydney • Tokyo • Singapore • Hong Kong • Seoul • Taipei • New Delhi
Cape Town • Madrid • Mexico City • Amsterdam • Munich • Paris • Milan

PEARSON EDUCATION LIMITED

Edinburgh Gate
Harlow CM20 2JE
Tel: +44 (0)1279 623623
Fax: +44 (0)1279 431059
Website: www.pearsoned.co.uk

First edition published in Great Britain in 2004

© Pearson Education Limited 2004

The right of John Burnett to be identified as author
of this work has been asserted by him in accordance
with the Copyright, Designs and Patents Act 1988.

ISBN 0 582 47266 0

British Library Cataloguing-in-Publication Data
A CIP catalogue record for this book can be obtained from the British Library

Library of Congress Cataloging-in-Publication Data
Burnett, John, 1925–
    England eats out : a social history of eating out in England from 1830 to the present /
    John Burnett. – 1st ed.
        p.cm.
    Includes bibliographical references and index.
    ISBN 0-582-47266-0
        1. Food habits – England – History. 2. England – Social life and customs. I Title.

GT2850.B87 2004
394.1′2--dc22

2004044547

10 9 8 7 6 5 4 3 2 1

Set by 3 in 9.5 pt Melior
Printed in China
PPLC/01
The Publishers' policy is to use paper manufactured from sustainable forests.

Contents

List of illustrations

Black and white plates

Colour plates

(In central plate section)

List of tables

Acknowledgements

When the first edition of my book *Plenty and Want: A Social History of Food in England from 1815 to the Present* was published in 1966, the subject was so unfamiliar that public libraries catalogued it under 'Cookery'. Eating out then received only brief notice, but in recent years the phenomenon has attracted the attention of scholars not only of social and economic history but of several social science disciplines. For the present book I have been able to draw on some of their illuminating researches, and I gratefully acknowledge my indebtedness to those who have worked on parts of the broad canvas I have hoped to cover. In particular, I wish to thank the following for their valuable contributions to the subject from whose work I gained both knowledge and insights: Peter Bird, the late Christopher Driver, Joanne Finkelstein, Christina Hardyment, Moira Johnston and staff of the Museum of London, Professor Stephen Mennell, Stephen Price, Colin Spencer, Harlan Walker and contributors to the Oxford Symposium on Food, Professor Alan Warde and Lydia Martens, and Professor John Walton. Professor Derek Oddy has given me constant support and encouragement, and suggested many helpful references from his own wide researches; I also wish to thank several market research agencies – $E = Mc^2$ (the Compass Group), MSI Market Research for Industry, Social Surveys (Gallup Poll) Ltd and Taylor Nelson Sofres Research – who generously provided statistical data not freely available to the general public. Finally, I especially thank Annemarie Maggs, who battled efficiently and uncomplainingly with my manuscripts and also saved me from numerous grammatical errors and infelicities: any that may remain are entirely my responsibility.

Publisher's acknowledgements

The publishers would like to thank the following for permission to reproduce copyright material:

Rural History Centre, University of Reading, for figure 1.1; Museum of London for figures 1.2, 3.2, 4.3 and plate 1; London Metropolitan Archives for figure 2.1; Mary Evans Picture Library for figures 3.1, 4.2 and plates 2, 3 and 4; Cadbury World for figure 4.1; Punch Ltd. for figure 5.1; Tower Hamlets Local History Library and Archives for figure 6.1; Hulton Archive for figures 7.1, 8.1 and 9.1; Associated Newspapers for figure 8.2; Topham Picturepoint for figure 9.2; Mitchells & Butlers Plc for figure 10.1; Kevin Walsh, the Oakwood Grange Collection for plate 5; The Advertising Archive for plate 6; The Travelsite/Neil Setchfield for plate 7; Le Manoir aux Quat' Saisons for plate 8.

HMSO for extracts from the reports 'Social Trends 9' 1979 edition; 'National Food Survey' 1996; 'Family Expenditure Surveys' 1957–9, 1975; 'Family Spending' 1994–5; and 'Consumers Expenditure on meals and other food eaten outside the home' The Social Survey, Central Statistical Office June 1956; the Gallup Organization for extracts from *Peoples favourite menu* © 1947, 1973 and *Briton's favourite foods* © 1989 The Gallup Organization, all rights reserved; and TNS UK Limited for three extracts from *MealTrak Out of Home 364/950,* 1999.

In some instances we have been unable to trace the owners of copyright material, and we would appreciate any information that would enable us to do so.

Preface

Eating out is a major economic, social and cultural phenomenon in modern Britain, part of the consumer revolution which has changed the ways we live now. In historical terms it is a very recent change. Before the Second World War few people in England visited a restaurant at all frequently: eating out for pleasure was mainly restricted to the better-off, but for the great majority it was a rare indulgence, usually occasioned by some celebratory event. Even in 1950 there were no burger bars in England, no pasta or pizza places and a mere handful of Indian and Chinese restaurants. The explosive growth of commercial catering dates from the mid-1950s when food restrictions finally ended and rising standards of living began to expand markets for new kinds of consumption, leisure and entertainment. By the 1990s catering sales, conducted through more than 300,000 outlets, reached £20 billion a year, one-third of total food expenditure.[1]

People eat out for many and varied reasons. In recent times more have been financially able, and have found it convenient to do so, especially when in many households today both partners are at work away from home and the traditional role of the housewife as food provider has changed to that of additional earner. But the fact that restaurants are busiest at weekends rather than during the working week suggests other, less practical reasons. Diners expect to derive pleasure from eating in the public sphere, not only, or even mainly, satisfaction of appetite, but social and psychological enjoyment. In the restaurant eating is transformed into an entertainment experience: relieved of the chores of preparing a meal and in a different environment where one chooses what to eat and is waited upon, diners are free to enjoy, converse and interact, so that even a simple family outing to a McDonald's can provide a sense of occasion.[2]

If we define eating out as any food consumed outside the household, there is clearly a difference between eating from necessity ('utility eating') and eating from choice ('pleasure eating'). Workers whose homes are too distant have always had to make provision for food during the day – sometimes eating out has meant literally eating in the open air – and as home and work became increasingly distanced in modern urban societies the need for regular refuelling of the body became as insistent as the requirements of the motor car. This distinction between eating from necessity and eating from choice is useful up to a point, but the two are not mutually exclusive: a hungry person may well take pleasure in the simplest meal, while an expensive one chosen at a famous restaurant may result in pain if badly cooked or served.

The broad definition of eating out suggested above is very broad indeed, and in this book certain categories are excluded. Food in total institutions such as hospitals, prisons, boarding schools or in the armed services where a complete daily diet is provided, is not included as this is not what is normally understood as 'eating out'.[3] Second, eating by invitation to another's home, for example to tea or dinner, is also omitted since 'eating out' usually implies a non-domestic setting in a public place where a commercial transaction is involved. And lastly, though many drinks are also foods in the sense of supplying nutriment, drinking is distinct from eating and will only be considered where it is integral to a meal.[4]

Eating out has existed since man first collected fruits and berries and cooked meat on an open fire, and on a commercial basis it dates from the earliest urban communities. This book is concerned with eating out in modern England, and for this a starting point around 1830 is chosen (the Introduction gives a brief survey of earlier history). By the 1830s England was rapidly passing from an agricultural society to an urban, industrial one where more people now depended for their food supplies on commercial producers and retailers. While an emerging working class struggled to exist on precarious earnings, a middle class was developing with greater spending power and ambitions for conspicuous consumption: for the aristocracy and the newly wealthy grand hotels and fashionable restaurants were beginning to appear in London and resort towns with new styles of cuisine and decor requisite for the pursuit of pleasure. Improvements in communications, especially by railways, would soon increase the mobility of people, ideas and tastes, while cheaper, imported foods would begin to replace regional differences and scarcities with more standardised, commodified products. In terms of food culture, England in the 1830s was on the threshold of modernity.

Eating out has increased and changed dramatically in recent times, and more especially since the 1970s when it began to take on its contemporary characteristics – a democratisation of public eating to all classes of society, the emergence of American-style fast food chains to a major share of the market, the remarkable spread of ethnic restaurants and the equally notable renaissance of the public house as a place to eat, not only drink. While many traditional forms of eating out have survived or revived, a continually expanding range of new catering facilities now confronts the consumer with choices unimaginable even a generation ago. In our relative affluence, eating from necessity is often less demanding than eating out for pleasure: like other forms of modern consumption it has become a constant search for novelty, for new foods, combinations and flavours, new ways of presentation and new environments to feed appetites driven by desires rather than hunger.

A note about monetary values

For the convenience of the reader I set out below the equivalent values of British coinage before and after the currency was decimalised in 1971.

Pre-decimal	Post-decimal
1d.	½p
2½d.	1p
6d.	2½p
1s.0d. or 1/-	5p
2s.0d. or 2/-	10p
2s.6d. or 2/6	12½p
5s.0d. or 5/-	25p
10s.0d. or 10/-	50p
£1.0s.0d. or £1	£1
£1.1s.0d. or one guinea	£1.05

Notes and references

In all Notes and references the place of publication is London unless otherwise stated.

1 Edward Collins and Derek J. Oddy, 'The Centenary of the British Food Journal, 1899–1999', *British Food Journal*, vol. 100 (10/11), 1998, p. 455.

2 Joanne Finkelstein, *Dining Out. A Sociology of Modern Manners*, Cambridge, Polity Press, 1989, p. 2.

3 Some of these are discussed in C. Anne Wilson (ed.), *Food For The Community. Special Diets for Special Groups*, Edinburgh, Edinburgh University Press, 1993.

4 For this see John Burnett, *Liquid Pleasures. A Social History of Drinks in Modern Britain*, Routledge, 1999.

Introduction: Beginnings

For most people in the past the utility aspects of eating out were more important than the pleasurable or symbolic. Although in royal and aristocratic circles there was much feasting and entertainment for guests, this took place within the private domains of courts and noble households: for the many, eating publicly was mainly associated with work, and what is now described as 'fast food' existed throughout the urbanised old world, sold at street and market stalls and by fixed shops which undertook varying amounts of specialist preparation. In classical Rome cookshops sold slices of roast pork, salt fish, goats' milk cheese, figs and olives, while in China the eating of snacks in public was an important part of the working day for bureaucrats and scholars. China was particularly well supplied with establishments for eating and drinking on or off the premises – noodle shops, tea-houses, taverns and restaurants where specialities like barbecued meats, won ton, chicken and fish soups and honeyed fritters were sold.[1]

In England the growth of towns and trade after the Norman Conquest created similar demands for commercial catering to provide for residents and travellers. The medieval cookshop combined both restaurant and take-away in that ready-made dishes could be eaten on the premises or taken home, an asset for people in crowded accommodation which lacked adequate cooking facilities. In 1183 a London cookshop was offering roast, boiled and fried meats, venison, fish and 'birds both big and little',[2] but pies of many varieties, savoury and sweet, were the mainstays of these businesses, their contents and prices controlled, in theory at least, by the Guild of Cooks and Pastelers (piemakers). A price list of 1378 included capon baked in a pasty (8d.), roast pig (8d.), goose (7d.), heron (18d.), mallards (3½d.–4½d.) and five roast larks (1½d.);[3] some of these were evidently luxury foods intended for home consumption at a festive occasion.

By Tudor times expanding urban populations of artisans, merchants and professionals increased the pressure on places to eat, and establishments formerly concerned with the sale of drink now also moved into catering. The three types – inns, taverns and alehouses – represented a hierarchy of social status and offered varying levels of provision and service. Inns were distinguished by having accommodation for travellers as well as more elaborate menus acceptable to persons of rank: taverns specialised in the sale of wine, provided meals but little lodging, while alehouses served ale and beer but only simple food to the lower orders. In Shakespeare's time many of these did not offer much more than cakes and ale or toasted bread steeped in the liquor, though some sold pies (mutton, conger eel, apple), salt fish and cheesecake, and allowed customers to bring their own meat to be cooked at the fire.[4] By the beginning of the seventeenth century a significant development in some taverns and cookshops was the introduction of the 'ordinary', a fixed-price menu or 'table d'hôte', usually served at midday and consisting of meat, vegetables and bread, though some offered more ambitious dishes and became fashionable eating-places for men. Wealth was now flowing from landed estates, from capitalist industries like woollen cloth and from the expansion of overseas trade: visitors to London were astonished by the rows of goldsmiths' and jewellers' shops, the new styles of architecture and the elaborate dress of men and women. In an increasingly materialistic age when it was said that men 'gaped for gain', wealth was to be displayed and enjoyed, especially by those who had not inherited it. According to Keynes, there had never been such rich opportunities for the businessman, the speculator and the profiteer.

The scale and popularity of eating out for pleasure ultimately reflected the state of the economy, the ability of consumers to pay for a commercial product and their desire to participate in a new form of fashionable entertainment. If the introduction of the 'ordinary' was an early precursor of the modern restaurant, the catering developments which were stimulated by the euphoria accompanying the restoration of the monarchy in 1660 were even more significant. By the seventeenth century the guilds had lost control over the catering trades, and entrepreneurs could exploit new tastes free from regulation of price and content. From the sixteenth century French chefs were employed in some English noble households, and the monotony of roast meats began to be varied by sauces, soups, ragouts and vegetables cooked in the French style: portions became smaller – cuts of meat more delicately prepared rather than huge joints and whole birds – part of a 'civilising process' which was transforming manners and behaviour in the upper levels of society. By the time of the Restoration French cuisine, or versions of it, was sometimes available in larger inns and taverns, though generally the fare offered was traditional and plentiful. Samuel Pepys, the rising civil servant at the Navy Office, was often entertained by friends and business associates to enjoyable dinners in taverns, some of which were large establishments like The Sun Tavern in Westminster which had 22 rooms: the practice was for the host to hire a private room for the occasion and choose the menu in advance rather than eat in the public rooms, which were mainly for drinking. Pepys often took his wife and their friends to dinner at an inn, and for a special occasion he brought a lobster and his friends a sturgeon to ennoble the meal, though normally there was a sufficiently wide choice – sirloin of beef, haunch of venison, chine of pork, mutton, veal, neat's (ox) tongue, ham, capons, many kinds of fish, pasties and sausages. This was still old-fashioned English fare, but at 'Monsieur' Robbins in Covent Garden Pepys paid 6/- for a dinner for his wife and himself cooked in the French style – potage, *pigeons à l'esteuve* (stewed) and *boeuf à la mode* (casseroled), all very well seasoned. Robbins, and Pontack's in Lombard Street, were evidently restaurants in all but name, offering novel dishes and cuisine for the gentry at high prices, and not without some complaints about small helpings: for regular, midday eating Pepys used an 'ordinary' at 12d.–18d., or even a cookshop where he could have a cut from the joint, vegetables, a roll and a pint of beer for 8d.[5] (the modern 'carvery'?).

Two other institutions appeared in the seventeenth century, which further familiarised people with eating in public. One was the Pleasure or Tea Garden. Since medieval times certain natural springs and wells had been endowed with curative properties, especially for rheumatism, gout and stomach complaints; some of these developed into inland spas (see later), but in the environs of London natural springs, often situated in scenic surroundings, became mainly pleasure-grounds for a crowded population. With the introduction of the new exotic drinks tea (*c.*1619) and coffee (the first London coffee-house 1652), both with medicinal claims and fashionable associations, opportunities arose for commercial exploitation. Pleasure Gardens were laid out at New Spring Gardens (later Vauxhall) in 1661, at Cuper's Gardens on the South Bank, at Ranelagh, Islington, Sadler's Wells, and ultimately, a dozen more. Concerts, dancing, fireworks and other entertainments were provided on summer evenings, displays of flowers and shrubs, avenues for parading and shady arbours for less public encounters, but food and drink were also attractions. At Ranelagh, the most exclusive, refreshments consisted merely of bread and butter, tea or coffee, included in the admission fee of 2/6d., but at Vauxhall and elsewhere cold meals of chicken, ham and so on were served in the supper boxes, or patrons could bring food from outside to eat as a picnic. Pleasure Gardens were a significant social development in that they were patronised by both sexes (though not by respectable unaccompanied ladies) and open to all classes who could pay the usual 1/- admission charge.

The other important innovation in the later seventeenth century was the coffee house. Coffee was popularised principally by these places rather than as a domestic drink, the first being opened in Oxford in 1650. The location was appropriate. From the beginning coffee-drinking was a social activity, associated with lively discussion, the dissemination of news and ideas: it attracted men of letters, scholars, wits and men of affairs, but in London and commercial cities also merchants, lawyers, stockbrokers and other professionals. Coffee-houses were meeting places for both business and pleasure: though exclusively male, they were otherwise egalitarian and sometimes described as 'the penny universities'. Their number spread rapidly after the Restoration in 1660: some attracted political clienteles of Tories, Whigs and Republicans, some like Lloyd's (1685) were business houses for shippers and insurers or Jonathan's for stockbrokers, while others hosted meetings of companies and Freemasons and acted as auction houses. Numbers are uncertain, since many had an ephemeral existence, but a fairly reliable figure derived from the London Directories gives 551 for 1739, 144 within the one square mile of the City. Their importance in the history of eating out is as places of refreshment where a morning coffee supplied a boost to mental activity from its caffeine content, and a lubricant to social intercourse: more acceptable to some than alcohol, coffee was the drink of seriousness and respectability. Most coffee-houses also served tea, which carried similar associations as 'the cup that cheers, but not inebriates', but initially they did not supply food beyond a cake or biscuit. By the 1730s, however, many coffee-houses were changing in one of two directions, either to become clubs open only to subscribers, or to chop-houses where substantial meals were available, though often using the designation of 'coffee rooms.' The coffee-house was therefore another strand in the development of both the modern café and the restaurant, though distinct from both by its masculine exclusivity. Tea, more favoured by women, was predominantly a domestic drink and either accompanied or followed meals. Leaf tea was sold by grocers, provision merchants, apothecaries, glass and china dealers, and by specialist tea merchants like Thomas Twining, who opened his Golden Lyon Shop off the Strand in 1717. Here, ladies of quality sent in their servants to make purchases while they waited outside in their carriages or sedan chairs: it was not, as has some-times been claimed, a 'tea-house' or teashop where ladies entertained in public.[6]

By the middle of the eighteenth century population was rising rap-idly, and revolutionary changes in agriculture and industry were placing England among the wealthiest of European nations. In what has been described as 'the birth of a consumer society',[7] demand was created for new styles in architecture, furnishing and a range of luxury goods, in leisure activities and, not least, in the quality, presentation and service of food. Gastronomy was becoming recognised as a fine art, and the presen-tation of a fashionable table, appropriately adorned with silver and chi-naware, a symbol of gentility, a mark of arrival into the ranks of good society. An indication of the importance now attached to food was the remarkable proliferation of cookery books intended to instruct the lady of the house (and her servants) on correct practices: they included Eliza Smith's *The Compleat Housewife* (1727), Hannah Glasse's *The Art of Cookery Made Plain and Easy* (1747), John Thacker's *The Art of Cookery* (1758), Elizabeth Raffald's *The Experienced English Housekeeper* (1769), John Townshend's *The Universal Cook* (1773), Richard Briggs' *The English Art of Cookery* (1785), besides translations of two celebrated French works by Menon, *The Art of Modern Cookery* (1767) and *The French Family Cook* (1793). Many of these works went through numer-ous editions (for example, Eliza Smith was in a sixteenth edition by 1758), and it is interesting that several were written by proprietors or cooks at London taverns – Townshend at The Greyhound, Greenwich and

Briggs at The White Hart, Holborn – who were proud to so describe themselves on the title pages.

Eating out at this time was encouraged by a major expansion in travel: people now journeyed more often and further afield than formerly, on business, on visits to friends and relatives and to the spa resorts which attracted the wealthy with the hope of health combined with pleasure. Travel was now quicker, safer and more comfortable on the surfaced roads built by Telford and Macadam, and in sprung coaches with scheduled times for stops and refreshment. Stagecoaches normally ran only by day, and long-distance travellers stayed overnight at the inns which dotted all the main roads: wealthier guests with ladies would be served in private suites in the larger inns rather than at the common table. Leisurely travel of this sort, punctuated by frequent stops to change horses, could be interesting and enjoyable, especially if the inn had a good reputation for its catering. Coaching familiarised numbers of people with travel and with eating out at coaching inns. Opinions varied considerably about the quality of food provided. At country posting inns the landlord always had the problem of trying to anticipate the number and time of arrival of guests, and often tended to rely on 'cold stands' of beef, ham, brawn and fillings for pies which could be quickly prepared; since similar fare would be offered along the road, cooks tried to enliven their cold meats with distinctive home-made sauces – Yorkshire Relish and Worcestershire Sauce so originated.[8] But it seems that some inns managed to supply a well-cooked and varied menu at short notice, for Dr Johnson believed that 'Nothing has yet been contrived by man by which so much happiness is produced as by a good tavern or inn'. During his Northern Tour of England in the 1760s Arthur Young visited many inns and recorded his opinions: 37 were listed as 'bad', 'very disagreeable', 'cheap and dirty', but others served a profusion of food at moderate prices – at Scarborough a supper of chicken, lobster, anchovies and cheese for 1/4d., at Carlisle broiled chicken with mushrooms, plover, sturgeon, tart, mince pies and jellies for 1/6d., while at other inns he enjoyed partridges, ducks, veal cutlets, potted trout, oysters, haddock, smelts and char. This was traditional English fare, hardly changed for centuries – no hint of French cuisine here – and this was evidently what most gentlemen preferred. Lord William Lennox praised country inns for their 'freshwater fish in every form, eels stewed, fried, boiled, baked and spitch-cocked, salmon, the earliest cucumbers, saddle of Southdown mutton done to a turn, Irish stew, rumpsteaks tender and juicy, veal-and-ham [?pie], plum pudding, fruit tarts, trifle and gooseberry fool'.[9] Most towns of any significance had a leading inn, with accommodation large enough for public banquets, meetings, balls and other social events, and among London's estimated 3,000 there were numerous fashionable places with a high reputation for their cuisine, such as the Bull Inn, Aldgate and the London Tavern, where the cook, John Farley, published his *London Art of Cookery* in 1783. More simply, Richard Steele wrote in *The Spectator* in 1712 that 'I dine at the chophouse three days a week', where he would have had a choice of roast or boiled meat, beefsteaks and chops, always ready to serve.

By the later eighteenth century some inns were beginning to describe themselves, rather pretentiously, as 'hotels'. They were usually distinguished by being larger, more elegantly furnished, and with more private rooms and suites suitable for longer residence than a night or two: some were strictly 'private', having no public dining-rooms and open only to private coach travellers. In London there was a German Hotel in Suffolk Street, and a French inn, La Sablonnière, the inference being that foreign visitors preferred to be boarded by their fellow countrymen rather than risk English catering. But it was particularly in the larger spa and resort towns that hotels developed to accommodate visitors for several weeks while taking the 'cure' and enjoying the social advantages of meeting important guests, their arrivals always reported by the local press. From being places of pilgrimage and health resorts, 'Spas became places of amusement, centres of social education, and then models for resorts of a new kind, seaside watering places.'[10] Bath, Buxton, Harrogate and Tunbridge Wells were already emerging in the sixteenth century, but it was after the Restoration that something approaching a spa mania developed under royal and aristocratic patronage. Queen Anne stayed at Bath in 1702 and large parts of the New Town were elegantly designed by the two John Woods: at Buxton the Duke of Devonshire commissioned John Carr to build the Crescent, with assembly rooms and two hotels. Meanwhile, therapeutic sea-bathing began at Scarborough in 1735, at Weymouth, patronised by George III, and Brighton was transformed from a fishing village to a highly fashionable resort by the visits of the Prince Regent. By 1815 there were at least 40 established spas besides many other small, often ephemeral ones, and 15 coastal resorts, now offering a challenge to the inland centres.[11] With their wealthy clienteles resorts presented the potential for a new leisure market and holiday industry which entrepreneurs quickly exploited. As existing inns proved insufficient, builders constructed terraces of lodging-houses for letting by the season, as well as the social amenities of pump-rooms, assembly-rooms, concert halls, coffee-houses and, ultimately, grand hotels of a new standard of luxury. Lodgings were usually let on a self-catering basis, guests bringing their own servants or hiring others locally, but resort life was more public than domestic, and it was common practice to dine publicly at a tavern before the evening's entertainment. By the later eighteenth century boarding-houses, which relieved visitors of the chores of housekeeping, were becoming popular, and the line between the larger of these and 'hotels' was a thin one. Probably the first purpose-built hotel was the York Hotel, Bath (1765–9), but Weymouth had one in 1772, Cheltenham in 1785 (Mrs Edward's Hotel), Buxton (1786), Matlock (The Great Hotel, 1789) and Leamington (The New Inn, 1790, later renamed Smith's Hotel). Here were large public dining-rooms, sometimes drawing-rooms and ballrooms as well as private suites, but guests in these surroundings generally wished to see and be seen and engage in social encounters. That the spa was now a holiday resort was clearly demonstrated by the Polygon Estate at Southampton, built around 1768: this was a leisure complex, including besides a hotel and several eating-places, houses, shops, a ballroom, and billiard-rooms set in landscaped gardens, a pioneer pleasure-dome close to the spa and the beach where Frederick, Prince of Wales, disported.

Spa hotels therefore led the way to a new form of residential catering institution, spreading the concept widely over England and opening up places formerly little known: for example, in 1829 a grand Spa Hotel with 70 bedrooms and costing £30,000, was built at Dinsdale, near Darlington, its size matched only by The York at Bath and The Clarence at Leamington. In London as yet hotels were developing on a different pattern, providing the privacy and personal attendance comparable with life in an aristocratic mansion, their separate territories of suites avoiding the embarrassment of chance encounters. Even the exiled King Louis XVIII could stay at such a hotel, Grillion's in Albemarle Street, while awaiting his return to France in 1814.[12]

By 1830 a hierarchy of eating-places existed, catering for a range of needs and incomes – from humble cook-shops and 'ordinaries', to better-class inns, chop-houses and dining-rooms, up to a few renowned taverns and hotels. What was largely missing at this time was the restaurant, still at an infant stage of development though destined to become a predominant type of catering establishment. Origins, dates, founders and terminology are all disputed, though there is agreement that restaurants began in Paris and that a 'restaurant' (or 'restaurateur', often at first applied to the premises rather than the patron) initially served a restorative bouillon (a soup made from meat extracts, chicken and barley), believed to be a health-giving, light refreshment for weak digestions and nervous dispositions. While in Paris the guild of 'traiteurs' still claimed control over cooks who prepared solid food, bouillons were exempt since they were regarded in the light of medicines. The traditional account runs that in 1765 a M. Boulanger expanded his soup offering by adding sheep's feet in a white sauce, and although the guild contended that this constituted a 'ragout' which came under their jurisdiction as a cooked meat dish, their action failed. Numerous 'restaurants' then opened in the 1770s under proprietor-chefs such as Beauvilliers, Robert, Bancelin and 'Les Trois Frères Provençaux' to become fashionable eating-places.[13]

A variant of this account has recently been suggested by Rebecca Spang, who finds no documentary evidence of the existence of Boulanger and claims Roze de Chantoiseau, proprietor of the Champ d'Oiseau, as the first restaurateur, though she does not dispute a date in the 1770s.[14] What is important is the character and style of these early restaurants. The menu soon developed from soups to light, natural foods, influenced by Rousseau's advocacy of fruit and vegetables, eggs and dairy produce, for health and strength: the decor was elegant but restrained, with much use of mirrors, and the meals served at small, marble-topped tables. By about 1780 the 'carte' (menu) had come into use, offering a choice of dishes at fixed prices, including at 'Les Trois Frères' provincial items such as bouillabaisse (an example of polite peasant food). Restaurants deliberately provided a refined atmosphere which attracted a discerning clientele appreciative of novelty, though not, it appears, always of the original, spartan regime. By the outbreak of the Revolution in 1789 some restaurants were serving expensive, luxury dishes, and during the Terror were closed down as undemocratic centres of privilege, one of the Véry brothers even being imprisoned. Subsequently, however, there was a rapid revival from an estimated 100 Parisian restaurants in 1789 to 500–600 in 1804 and more than 1,000 by 1835.[15]

According to the *Almanack des Gourmets* (1804) the reasons for their increase in popularity were: 1. the desire of Frenchmen before the Revolution to imitate the English habit of dining in public in inns and taverns (an interesting comparison of the extent of eating out in the two countries); 2. the influx to Paris of 'undomiciled legislators' during the Revolution seeking somewhere to eat; 3. the break-up of noble and clerical households whose chefs had to find public employment; and 4. possibly, the newly rich plunderers of property who feared to expose their wealth in luxurious houses, but could eat well in a public setting.[16] In this view, the 'culinary genius' of France was established in the Parisian restaurants.

In his pioneering work, *Physiologie du Goût* (1825), intended to elevate gastronomy into an acknowledged art and science, Brillat-Savarin described the 'numerous advantages [that] flow from the use of restaurants, an institution in which all Europe has imitated Paris'. Everyone may dine when and how they choose according to the demands of business or pleasure: they can make a hearty meal, or a refined, dainty one, according to their tastes and pockets: restaurants serve the best wines, coffee and liqueurs – in short, 'every man who has twenty francs at command may take a seat at the table of a first-class restaurant, and be at least as well served as at the table of a prince'. Like a modern social scientist, Brillat-Savarin observed the clienteles of the restaurant. Here are the regulars, who give their orders loudly, know all the waiters by name, eat hurriedly, pay and go: here a country family on a visit, who 'order some dishes which are quite new to them, and evidently greatly enjoy the sight of all that goes on around'; there an old couple who have had nothing to say to each other for a long time, so different from the young lovers with 'the anxious attentions of one and the sly coquetry of the other'. 'Finally, you may see here and there some foreigners, especially English, who stuff themselves with double portions of meat, order the most expensive dishes, drink the most heady wines and require assistance to leave the table.'[17] By now, any original austerity had long since gone. At restaurants like those of Beauvilliers, Les Trois Frères Provençeaux or the brothers Véry (who supplied the table of the allied monarchs in 1814 at

£120 a day, not including wine) the gastronome had a huge choice from 12 soups, 24 side dishes, 15–20 entrées each of beef and veal, 20 entrées of mutton, 30 of game or fowl, 24 of fish and 15 roasts, concluding with 50 desserts.[18]

French cuisine ultimately set the style in most English aristocratic circles, in many clubs and some hotels, but before 1830 its influence was mainly restricted to royal and noble households where numbers of leading French chefs had found employment during and after the Revolution. The great Carême (1784–1833) worked as an itinerant chef for Talleyrand, the Prince Regent, Czar Alexander I and Baron Rothschild, Louis Eustache Ude, former chef to Louis XVI, cooked for the Earl of Sefton before moving to Crockford's Club, Honoré was cook to Lord Holland, Florence to the Dukes of Buccleuch, Aberlin to the Duke of Devonshire and Durand to the Duke of Beaufort: of 27 of 'the most eminent cooks of the present time in England' cited by Hayward, only four had English names.[19] It is hard to say how far French 'haute cuisine' had yet penetrated beyond the private domains of the aristocracy, where competition to employ a great-name chef who could command up to 1,000 guineas a year and could be relied on to produce spectacular, novel dishes, was an important marker of taste and social standing. In public eating-places, however, the use and dating of the term 'restaurant' is doubtful. Around 1770 a Mr Horton, a confectioner, established a soup-room in Cornhill, elegantly decorated in Venetian style, where fashionable people took light refreshments,[20] evidently in the Parisian manner, and by the early nineteenth century there were several French eating-houses in London,[21] though it is not known whether they described themselves as 'restaurants'. Probably the best French cooking at this period was found in a few hotels like the Clarendon, where M. Jacquier presided and dinner in 1814 cost £3–4 without wine. As yet, a limited supply followed a limited demand.

The tastes of most English people of whatever rank except, perhaps, the very highest, remained stubbornly attached to roast meats, game, poultry and fish, with simple dressings and no elaborate sauces. In his weekly journal, *The Original* (1835–6), the gastronome Thomas Walker described some memorable dinners which he regarded as models of good taste. At Lovegrove's Tavern at Blackwall he gave a dinner for eight guests consisting of turtle soup, whitebait (a speciality here), grouse, apple fritters, jelly, ices and dessert: they drank punch, champagne, claret ('particularly well iced'), coffee and liqueurs. 'Such, reader, is my idea of a dinner.' On Christmas Day a simple meal for two guests consisted of crimped cod, woodcocks and plum pudding (no 'traditional' beef or turkey yet), and at the Temple he entertained six to spring soup, turbot with lobster sauce, cucumber, dressed crab, new potatoes, ribs of beef with French beans and salad: to drink there was champagne, port and claret. This was 'An example of the plain, easy style of entertaining'.[22]

Notes and references

1 Reay Tannahill, *Food in History*, Penguin Books, revised edn 1988, pp. 78, 138.

2 F. M. Stenton, *Norman London. An Essay*, G. Bell and Son, 1934, p. 28.

3 C. Anne Wilson, 'Eight Centuries of the English Restaurant', in *The Good Food Guide*, Hodder & Stoughton/Consumers' Association, 1986, p. 599.

4 Peter Clark, *The English Alehouse. A Social History, 1200–1830*, Longman, 1983, pp. 132–3.

5 For further references to catering in the time of Pepys see *London Eats Out. 500 Years of Capital Dining*, Moira Johnston (ed.), Philip Wilson and Museum of London, 1999, pp. 33–41.

6 For the history of coffee-houses, coffee- and tea-drinking, see John Burnett, 'Coffee in the British Diet, 1650–1990', in Daniela U. Ball (ed.), *Coffee in the Context of European Drinking Habits*, Zurich, Switzerland, Johann Jacobs Museum, 1991, pp. 35–53; John Burnett, *Liquid Pleasures. A Social History of Drinks in Modern Britain*, Routledge, 1999, chs 3 and 4.

7 N. McKendrick, J. Brewer and J. H. Plumb, *The Birth of a Consumer Society. The Commercialization of Eighteenth Century England*, Europa Publications, 1982.

8 Dorothy Hartley, *Food in England*, Little, Brown and Co., 1999, pp. 411–12 (1st edn, 1954).

9 Quoted Mary Cathcart Borer, *The British Hotel Through the Ages*, Guildford and London, Lutterworth Press, 1972, p. 134.

10 Geoffrey Martin, Introduction to A. B. Granville, *The Spas of England and Principal Sea-bathing Places*, 2 vols, 1841. Facsimile edn, Bath, Somerset, Adams and Dart, 1971, p. V.

11 For this, and the best modern account of spas, see Phyllis Hembry, *The English Spa, 1560–1815. A Social History*, Athlone Press, 1990, and the

sequel, *British Spas from 1815 to the Present. A Social History*, edited and completed by Leonard W. Cowie and Evelyn E. Cowie, Athlone Press, 1997.

12 Borer, op. cit., pp. 135, 157.

13 Stephen Mennell, *All Manners of Food. Eating and Taste in England and France from the Middle Ages to the Present*, Oxford, Basil Blackwell, 1985, pp. 138–40.

14 Rebecca L. Spang, *The Invention of the Restaurant. Paris and Modern Gastronomic Culture*, Harvard University Press, 2000.

15 A. Hayward, *The Art of Dining, or Gastronomy and Gastronomes*, John Murray, New edn, 1883, p. 23. The first edition was in 1852, but Hayward explains that the 'groundwork' was written in two articles in the *Quarterly Review* in July 1835 ('Gastronomy and Gastronomes') and Feb. 1836 (review of *The Original*, a weekly magazine written by Thomas Walker in 1835). Walker died in Jan. 1836.

16 Hayward, 1883, ibid., pp. 23–4.

17 R. E. Anderson, *Gastronomy as a Fine Art, or the Science of Good Living*, Chatto & Windus, New edn 1889, pp. 229–32. First English translation of J. A. Brillat-Savarin, *Physiologie du Goût* (1825). Brillat-Savarin, b.1755, d.1826.

18 ibid., p. 233.

19 A. Hayward, *The Art of Dining*, etc., 1st edn, 1852, p. 77.

20 Moira Johnston (ed.), *London Eats Out*, op. cit., p. 63.

21 C. Anne Wilson, 'Eight Centuries', etc., op. cit., pp. 603–4. Similar French eating-places were established in New Orleans in 1794 and in New York c.1800. Arthur White, *Palaces of the People. A Social History of Commercial Hospitality*, Rapp and Whiting, 1968, p. 135.

22 T. Walker, *The Original* (1835), quoted Hayward, op. cit., New edn, 1883, pp. 92–9.

PART ONE

1830–1880

CHAPTER 1

Eating to live

The rural poor

A social history of eating out properly begins with the many rather than the few, with those for whom food was necessity rather than pleasure and who strove to obtain enough to keep them at work rather than to stimulate jaded appetites. Ironically, those whose standard of living placed them at the bottom of the social pile in the nineteenth century, agricultural labourers, were those who ate out more than any other class. Moreover, despite England's gradual shift to an urban, industrial society, agricultural workers remained the largest occupational group in 1851 (965,000) and still in 1881 (871,000), easily outnumbering building, textile, metal or mining workers.

Those employed on the land necessarily ate 'out' in all but the most inclement weather since the various farming operations of ploughing, seeding, weeding and harvesting took them into the fields, often too far from home to return for meals. The food they took to sustain them was spread over several meal-breaks, since in summer work began at daybreak and continued until dusk — at hay and harvest-time until dark. At such busy times a first breakfast might be eaten in the fields before 6 am, a second breakfast or 'eight o'clock', a 'bever' (from the French 'beivre', a short break with drink) at around 10 am, the main meal or 'nuncheon' at midday and a second 'bever' in the afternoon before returning home for supper.[1] The food available for all these occasions naturally depended on

FIGURE 1.1 ◆ *Eating in the open. Harvesters at their 'bever' (a drink and snack, from the Old French beivre): this could be only one of four or five breaks for refreshment during a long day in the fields (late nineteenth century).*

Source: Rural History Centre, University of Reading.

the labourer's earnings, the size and ages of his family, the region of the country and, ultimately, the economic position of the agricultural economy of which he was an essential part. A fair generalisation, however, is that he was the lowest paid, the worst fed and housed of all regularly-employed workers: uneducated and unenfranchised, immobilised by poverty and the Poor Laws, he had almost no power to improve his position of deferential dependence on his farmer-employer. This had not always been so. His condition had first deteriorated in the later eighteenth century when enclosures deprived many of access to land and common rights: unable to grow food, he became solely dependent on wages which failed to keep pace with the cost of living in a period of rapid inflation. By 1795 a crisis in the southern and eastern counties led to the introduction of the Speenhamland System of poor relief, which added a subsistence allowance to wages according to the price of bread and the number of dependants.[2] That year in the parish of Barkham, Berkshire, bread and flour took 6/3d. out of the men's wage of 8/- a week: no fresh meat was eaten and few families could afford more than 1 lb. of bacon, 1 oz. of tea and tiny amounts of sugar and butter.[3] It has been calculated that these budgets collected by the Revd David Davies would have yielded an average of only 1990 kcals, and 49 g of protein per person per day,[4] quite inadequate for a man at heavy manual work, who would need at least half as much again. The explanation must be that he consumed much more than the average for his family, with the result that his wife and children received a good deal less, a point often made by contemporary observers who noted that the man, as chief breadwinner, always took the 'lion's share' of food, especially of any meat that might be available.

The distress of the labourer became, if possible, even worse during the long agricultural depression which followed the end of the Napoleonic Wars in 1815. In 1824 wages for a married man were as little as 4/6d. a week in some southern counties, 5/0d.–8/0d. in others, but up to 12/- in Lancashire where industrial employment pushed up the general level.[5] Touring the country at this time William Cobbett wrote his *Rural Rides* in a tone of passionate indignation. English peasants were 'the worst-used labouring people upon the face of the earth. Dogs and hogs and horses are treated with more civility, and as for food and lodging, how gladly would the labourers change with them!' Fortunately, there were exceptions even in the poorest areas. At Eastdean, Sussex, he encountered a young labourer sitting under a hedge at his breakfast:

> *He came running to me with his victuals in his hand, and I was glad to see that his food consisted of a good lump of household bread and not a very small piece of bacon. In parting with him I said, 'You do get some bacon then?' 'Oh yes, Sir,' said he, with an emphasis and a sway of the head which seemed to say, 'We must and will have that' ...What sort of breakfast would this man have had in a mess of cold potatoes? Could he have worked, and worked in the wet too, with such food? Monstrous! No society ought to exist where the labourers live in a hog-like sort of way.*[6]

Writing of his food in the 1840s, Charles Astridge of Midhurst remembered that

> *We mostly lived on bread, but 'twasn't bread like we get now; 'twas that heavy and doughy 'ee could pull long strips of it out of your mouth. They called it growy bread. But 'twas fine compared with the porridge we made out of bruised beans; that made your inside feel as if 'twas on fire, an' sort of choked 'ee.*[7]

Potatoes would have been better than this, despite Cobbett's hatred of them as 'pig-food' and 'the lazy root' (because they were easy to cultivate!). One of the most poignant of all accounts of eating out comes from Lincolnshire in the 1850s, where gangs of small children from the age of 5 upwards were employed in field labour: at 8 this witness was the eldest of a gang of 40 which worked for 14 hours a day in all weathers:

> *We were followed all day long by an old man carrying a long whip, which he did not forget to use.... In all the four years I worked in the fields I never worked one hour under cover of a barn, and only once did we have a meal in a house. And I shall never forget that one meal or the kind woman who gave us it. It was a most terrible day ... the sleet and snow which came every now and then in showers seemed almost to cut us to pieces. Dinner-time came, and we were preparing to sit down under a hedge and eat our cold dinner and drink our cold tea when we saw the shepherd's wife coming towards us, and she said to the ganger, 'Bring these children into my house and let them eat their dinner there.' We all sat in a ring upon the floor. She then placed in our midst a very*

large saucepan of hot, boiled potatoes, and bade us help ourselves.
Truly, although I have attended scores of grand parties and banquets
since that time, not one of them has seemed half as good to me as that
meal did.[8]

James Caird's enquiry into the state of English agriculture in 1850
showed that the average wage now stood at 9/6d. a week, but still 7/- or
8/- in many southern and eastern counties. He described the diet of a
Dorset labourer who earned only 6/- and paid 1/- a week for his cottage:

After doing up his horses he takes breakfast, which is made of flour and
a little butter and water 'from the tea-kettle' poured over it. He takes
with him to the field a piece of bread and (if he has not a growing
family, and can afford it) cheese to eat at midday. He returns home to a
few potatoes and possibly a little bacon, though only those who are
better-off can afford that.[9]

In the period of agricultural prosperity which followed between the
1850s and 1870s the poor condition of the labourer improved somewhat,
though his diet remained monotonous and restricted. In 1863 he consumed on average 12¼ lb of bread weekly, 6 lb of potatoes or 27 lb per
family (but up to twice as much as this where he had the privilege of an
allotment), 1 lb of meat or bacon per adult and small amounts of cheese,
butter, sugar or treacle: his family consumed 2½ oz of the now indispen-
sable tea. This diet yielded 2,760 kcals and 70 g of protein per person per
day, still inadequate for heavy work, for a pregnant woman or a growing
adolescent.[10]

In packing up food for a man – and, in many cases, also a son – much
depended on the wife's skill and ingenuity in making a little go a long
way and devising tasty 'relishes' to break the monotony of bread. In
Harpenden, Hertfordshire in the 1860s, where wages were between 11/-
and 13/- a week, few cottages had an oven or range, and most meals were
cooked in a large pot over an open fire: whatever meat was available,
flour dumplings, potatoes and greens were all boiled together, though in
separate nets which allowed their cooking time to be controlled. The
poorer labourers took with them for their food large 'door-steps' of bread,
cheese, an onion and, if possible, a pint of beer, and thought it 'A meal fit
for a king ter 'ev', but the better-off also had a dumpling with a filling of

meat chopped up small (flank of beef, streaky bacon, pickled pork or liver), potato, onion and parsley, the proportion of meat usually a quarter or less. These were eaten cold or sometimes heated over a gypsy fire, or a bloater would be wrapped in several layers of newspaper and cooked in the embers.[11] The dumpling was always the favourite, however, combining sustenance with portability: it fulfilled a similar role to the Cornish and West Country pasty which could provide a two-course meal in one, with meat, potato and onion at one end and apple at the other. In the Midlands and North of England local supplies of fuel allowed more home cooking, and the bread diet was varied by soups and oatmeal porridge, but the problem remained of providing suitably portable food for the field. In Staffordshire in the 1870s Tom Mullins found that little white bread was eaten:

> We lived mainly on oatmeal, which was made into flat, sour cakes like gramophone records. . . . Usually enough were made at one baking to last a week or ten days. By that time they would be covered with green, furry mould, which would be scraped off.[12]

At last by 1880 Francis Heath was able to report 'dawning improvement' even in the poor western counties. Wages were still low, but now they went further with the lower prices of bread, tea, sugar and other necessities. In Somerset the labourer's day began with breakfast of bread, bacon or dripping and fried potatoes, followed by a 'ten o'clock' in the field of bread, cheese and cider, dinner of bread, bacon or other cold meat and more cider, and another break for bread and cheese at four o'clock before a substantial supper at home of hot vegetables, meat or fish, bread and butter and tea, 'making a grand total of no inconsiderable amount, and which only fairly hard work and fresh air enable him to digest'. Field fare was necessarily governed by transportability, and bread or, in the north, bannocks or oatcakes, were always the staples, but now increasingly varied with meat of some sort, often in a pastry case. Edwin Grey described the mechanics of eating out in Hertfordshire in the 1870s. The men's food was packed up by the women overnight, and carried in a basket made of plaited rush with a flap and two handles, swung over the shoulders by a stout cord. The basket always contained some salt, for which the older men used a bullock's horn, also a can of cold tea and a tin mug for beer. The men sat in a circle under a tree or hedge, and made their bread into a thick sandwich with whatever filling they had, then cutting pieces from the 'thumb-bit' with the pocket knives they all carried. In winter they made a fire to heat their cans of tea, and fashioned toasting-forks of hazel wood to cook bloaters or other foods.

> *I used often to find these [alfresco meals] very cheerful and amusing times, with many a laugh at the jokes bandied about; for one thing, no one apparently suffered with indigestion, so far as I could see all seemed to have excellent appetites and enjoyed their homely fare to the utmost.*[13]

No doubt the conviviality of these occasions owed something to the 'allowance' of beer which many farmers gave, especially for heavy or tedious tasks. This was a long-standing custom, approved by employers as an encouragement to effort or reward for successful work, and by all labourers except the small minority who had 'taken the pledge' of teetotalism, and resented what was, in effect, a supplement to wages in which they did not share. The amount and strength of this perquisite varied greatly. In some areas 'small beer' (the second mashing of the malt) was given throughout the year, in some, strong beer during particular tasks – in Cambridgeshire at haymaking and harvest a pint at each of the five meal-breaks,[14] in Bedfordshire 4 or 5 pints during the strenuous work of sheep-shearing.[15] A similar practice existed in the west and south-west of England, where hundreds of farms made cider for home use. In eighteenth-century Herefordshire the allowance had been 6 pints a day and as much as 24 pints in the harvest-field,[16] but by now this form of part-payment of wages in kind was under attack from temperance reformers and philanthropists. In north Devon in the 1870s Canon Girdlestone was indignant that wages were still only 8/- or 9/- a week, plus 3 or 4 pints of cider a day, 'very washy and sour ... valued at 2/- a week, but much over-valued'.[17] The substitution of tea or proprietary temperance drinks such as 'stokos' (made from oatmeal and cocoa) was not greatly popular, however: beer provided around 200 kcals of energy per pint – perhaps up to 1,000 kcals in the harvest-field – while beer and cider helped to moisten and digest cold food and were effective thirst-quenchers.

On a few occasions in the rural calendar the labourer was allowed, even encouraged, to indulge his appetite to the full, to enjoy as much food and drink as he could carry without the obligation of returning to work. This eating out for pleasure was principally confined to 'Harvest Homes' and 'Club Days', with some minor celebrations for women and children such as Temperance Teas and Sunday School Treats. 'Harvest Home' was the culmination of the year's farming efforts, the time for an employer to reward his labourers while reasserting his authority and their dependency, but also for the men to claim their share in whatever prosperity the season had brought. In the small hamlet of 'Lark Rise' in north Oxfordshire everyone attended the festivities except the bedridden and Laura's father, an independent-minded tradesman who complained that the farmer paid his men starvation wages and tried to make up for it by giving them one good meal. Long tables were laid out in the shade of a barn, which would be used in case of bad weather. Some men went without breakfast on the day, better to prepare themselves for the feast.

> *And what a feast it was! Such a bustling in the farmhouse kitchen for days beforehand, such boiling of hams and roasting of sirloins, such a stacking of plum puddings, made by the Christmas recipe, such a tapping of eighteen-gallon casks and baking of plum loaves would astonish those accustomed to the appetites of today.*[18]

Unused to such plenty, some guests over-indulged, to the extent that 'Harvest Homes' often gained a reputation for drunkenness and licentiousness which local clergy and gentry tried to reform. Heavy drinking also often accompanied being hired for the harvest gang, in anticipation of the extra wages which would become due when all was gathered in. The Revd Stephen Fawcett, Vicar of Eaton Socon in Bedfordshire, was moved to publish a warning pamphlet:

> *To the Harvest Labourers of the Parish.*
> *I have been told that it is a custom among you to get drunk on the first day of being hired for harvest ... Can you possibly expect God's blessing on your labour by running wilfully at the first start into a deadly sin? ... Some of you may perhaps say, 'Oh it is only once in a way that I so far forget myself.' Suppose that at that very time God should call you to your last account, what would that excuse do for you?*[19]

The criticism was scarcely justified. The labourer had few opportunities for excess, and in isolated villages there was little amusement except what men made for themselves in the public house. Most were generally sober, if only because their wages did not permit them to be otherwise. In 'Lark Rise' wives usually allowed their husbands 1/- a week for pocket-money, mainly for beer and tobacco: nearly all went to the pub each evening, and made half a pint last an hour or more: they went for companionship as much as the drink. The other principal occasion for indulgence was Club Day, when the village Friendly Society or Benefit Club held its annual feast. Members typically paid 1/0d. or 1/6d. a month, which entitled them to beer at the regular meetings, the remainder going into a 'common box' for small payments in the event of sickness, death or other contingencies. Feast Day usually commemorated the patron saint of the church, and began with a parade with banners before the festivities at the inn. There would be stalls and even roundabouts in the larger places, but at 'Lark Rise' there was only one stall kept by an old woman who sold gingerbread babies, striped peppermint humbugs, sticks of rock and a few bottled sweets. It was a sign of changing times in the 1880s when a box of thin, brown slabs packed in pink paper appeared. A sophisticated visiting cousin told Laura that it was chocolate: 'But don't buy any. It's for drinking: they have it for breakfast in France.'[20] For the adults' feast there was the traditional roast beef and plum pudding together with a great deal of drink, and, as at Harvest Home, complaints by respectable inhabitants of drunkenness and disorder. According to Richard Heath, 'The evening of a Club Day presents a sad scene in many a cottage home.'[21]

The urban poor

Poverty and inadequate diets were not, of course, restricted to the countryside. If life in the rapidly growing towns gave some workers opportunities to acquire new skills, better earnings and standards of comfort, for others it brought levels of destitution and suffering unparalleled even in the poorest villages. Yet the towns continued to attract hordes of migrants from the land: while the population of England and Wales doubled between 1801 and 1851 from 9 million to 18 million, the new centres of industry like Manchester, Birmingham, Leeds and others trebled and quadrupled in size, causing immense problems of housing, public health and, not least, food supplies. Meanwhile, London's growth from 1.1 to 2.5 million, though less rapid, placed her as the world's greatest city, the capital of 'the first industrial nation'.

Yet the 'Industrial Revolution', whose origins were at least a century earlier, was a very incomplete process. In 1851 agriculture still headed the list of occupations and domestic service was in second place: cotton, the great new factory trade, came next in order, but was followed by building workers, general labourers, and hand trades such as milliners, shoemakers and tailors. While some traditional skills survived in the new climate, many old ones were now decaying in the face of competition – the saddest case of all the handloom weavers, once a proud craft earning high wages but reduced by 1830 to earnings of 5/6d. a week as factory production overtook them. At around 400,000 this was the largest domestic industry, but its dying fortunes were matched by the framework-knitters of Nottinghamshire and Leicestershire, the silk workers of Spitalfields, the ribbon-makers of Coventry, nail-makers, glove-stitchers, lace-makers and others – a vast army of 'new poor' who had no share in the benefits of industrialisation. Even for the beneficiaries, however, work in the new industries was often irregular, beset by cyclical depressions in trade and consequent periods of short time and unemployment.[22]

There was, then, no homogeneous 'working class' but a hierarchy of groups ranging from the highly skilled 'aristocrats' of labour (wages £1.50 a week and above), through to semi-skilled factory operatives (£1–£1.25), and down to the struggling hand trades, the labourers, the casual and seasonal workers whose earnings, when in work, probably averaged 50–75p a week but in bad times fell even below this. Contemporary observers in mid-century were unsure whether industrialisation had benefited or disadvantaged the majority of people, though most writers, not only of the political left like Engels, tended towards a pessimistic view. Samuel Laing believed that 'as wealth increases, poverty increases in a faster ratio', and that the working classes could be divided into three, roughly equal, groups:

> About one third, plunged in extreme misery, and hovering on the verge of actual starvation: another third, earning an income something better than that of the common agricultural labourer, but under circumstances very prejudicial to health, morality and domestic comfort [i.e. factory work of his family]: and finally a third earning high wages, amply sufficient to support them in respectability and comfort.[23]

This section is concerned with Laing's first, and part of his second group.

From a dietary viewpoint town life for the poor had advantages and disadvantages. In London and other large cities most lived in very crowded accommodation, often in only one or two rooms of a divided house formerly occupied by a middle-class family. Cooking was limited to what could be done on an open fire, mainly boiling or frying: in northern towns back-to-back cottages might have a cast-iron range, but fuel was expensive, and women who worked long hours in factories had little time or energy to develop culinary skills. The great advantage of the town over the countryside, however, was the ubiquity of little food shops where tiny quantities of bread, butter, cheese, tea, sugar and other basics could be bought on a day-to-day, even meal-to-meal, basis, and where credit was often given to known customers. These corner shops, and markets where perishable foods were sold off cheaply on Saturday evenings, were particular assets for the poor before the rise of multiple grocers in the later nineteenth century: so also were the specialist pork butchers selling local varieties of spiced meats such as faggots, haslet, black pudding and brawn, which were valued 'relishes' to the monotony of a mainly bread diet. When meat of this or other kind was available, it was almost always the prerogative of male earners: women and children were the least well-fed, practically living, as it was often reported, on bread and endless cups of weak tea.

The common sight of slum children sitting on the doorstep eating a piece of bread was not quite 'eating out', but poor children took every opportunity of escaping from overcrowded homes, not only for play but also in the hope of supplementing the family rations. Life on the streets offered various possibilities of acquiring food, legitimately or illegitimately. As a young girl, Kay Garrett took an early-morning job as a 'step-girl' (cleaner) for 2d. a day and a breakfast of dripping toast and cocoa,[24] but another girl who had begged for work at several houses was not so lucky:

> One lady asked me if I was hungry: she said she was sorry she could not have her step cleaned, but if I waited she would give me something to eat. Presently she came to the door with a parcel, telling me not to waste any, what I could not eat I was to take home to my mother.... The parcel contained some very dry pieces of bread and some crusts that

*looked as if they had been nibbled by mice, and a large piece of bacon
rind. I could not eat any of it . . . So I gave the rind to a hungry-looking
dog and carried the crusts to a man who kept a donkey.*[25]

One of her happiest childhood memories was in summer when the older
girls took the babies for a picnic in Victoria Park, their mothers having
hired prams (1d. an hour single, 1½d. double), always over-filled. 'We
would picnic on bread and treacle under the trees' (there was a magnificent water-fountain in the Park). At the age of 10 she went to work as a
baby-minder to a small shopkeeper, and observed what men bought for
their dinners – a pennyworth of bread with two ounces of German
sausage, or a pennyworth of bread with a hole made to take a halfpennyworth of treacle.[26] At age 9 William Luby of Hulme, near Manchester, was
selling newspapers and buying his dinner from a street soup-seller – a
halfpennyworth of soup and a chunk of bread, though he noticed that
when the man's trade was good, the soup became very thin.[27] At this level
'treats' were rare events, and when some children had a penny to spare it
often went on food rather than sweets. In Oldham, Jack Wood's favourite
eating-out experiences were either meat pies sold at the street-corner, a
hole for gravy stubbed by a bandaged finger, or 'penny dips' ('ducks')
which consisted of half a muffin covered with a mixture of minced liver,
pluck [beast's heart, liver and lungs] and 'various internal parts of a
pig'.[28] Children who had nothing to spare could always try begging, and
at the end of a day were often seen outside factory gates asking for any
left-overs from the men's midday meal – Monday was reckoned to be the
best for this, as many men did not eat so much after Sunday's food and
drink. Or a tour of fish-and-chip shops could sometimes yield a free
supply of 'cracklings' (batter scraps) to eat in the street or take home for
supper with bread.

At times of economic crisis the poor – and even some workers who
were not normally poor – often had to fall back on charitable feeding.
Gifts of soup and other food to the deserving poor was a long-standing
tradition in the countryside where the better-off classes were moved by a
combination of genuine Christian philanthropy and a desire to cement
deferential social relations. In the famine years at the beginning of the
nineteenth century soup kitchens were organised on a wider scale in
both town and country, and it appears that it was at this period that soup

FIGURE 1.2 ◆ *Eating in public. The North-West Public Soup Kitchen, Marylebone Road, London, 1858. This was first established as a charity for the poor during the economic crisis of 1846, providing beef or pea soup or rice milk, with bread. Alexis Soyer set up a similar one in Spitalfields.*

Source: © Museum of London.

became particularly associated with pauperism and unpopular with the English working classes as a symbol of dependency (later confirmed by workhouse 'skillee'). Under the influence of Count Rumford, charitable donors came to regard soup as the great panacea for hunger: it was cheap and simple to prepare in large quantities, could be easily distributed and was warming, if not very nutritious. In fact, Rumford's famous soup, consisting mainly of barley, peas and bread, would have yielded less than 1,000 calories per portion, about a third of that needed by a man at moderate work.[29] Some soups were admittedly better than this. In 1847 Alexis Soyer, the eminent chef of the Reform Club, was moved by the distress of the starving Irish during the Potato Famine, and at the request of the British government established a large soup kitchen in Dublin which could feed 1,000 people an hour. Conditions were little better in some parts of English towns during a deep depression in trade, and Soyer then opened a soup kitchen in Spitalfields, a centre of the decaying silk industry. His letter to *The Times* promoted a public subscription and included his own recipe for beef soup (¼ lb of leg of beef, vegetables and barley to 2 gallons of water) costing ¾d. a quart: it was tasted and approved by 'numerous noblemen, Members of Parliament and several ladies'.[30] In Spitalfields the poor were offered a choice of soup or rice curry for 1d. though most had free tickets from subscribers, a device obviating the use of money which might be spent elsewhere. Soyer also published *The Poor Man's Regenerator* in 1847 which aimed to popularise other cheap but nutritious dishes such as 'Cabbage Stirabout' and 'The Poor Man's Potato Pie' (assuming that potatoes were now available). Such recipes for the poor, which could be made either by charitable bodies or by the poor themselves, at home, became much publicised in mid-century as a means of demonstrating that a satisfying diet could be provided at very low cost – usually with the implication that current culinary practices of the poor were ignorant and wasteful. Shortly after Soyer's book, Charles Elmé Francatelli, formerly chief cook to Queen Victoria, published his *Plain Cookery Book for the Working Classes*, which also included recipes for making large quantities of soup for public distribution, suggesting that 'sheep's heads, plucks, shanks and scrag-ends might very well be spared towards making a good mess of soup for the poor'.[31]

A leading dietician of the day, Dr Edward Smith, worked out specimen menus costing 1½d. for breakfast, 2d. for dinner and 1d. for supper, consisting mainly of porridge, suet pudding, skimmed milk and a little bacon or faggot.[32] He had recently seen poverty at first hand when commissioned by the Privy Council to report on the condition of workers in industrial Lancashire during the so-called 'Cotton Famine'. In the American Civil War (1861–5) the Northern states blockaded Southern ports, preventing the export of raw cotton on which the Lancashire mills depended: the result was that many had to close or go on to short time, and workers who had formerly enjoyed a reasonable standard of living were suddenly plunged into severe privation through no fault of their own. The 'Cotton Famine' therefore presented a prime opportunity for organised charity and much public sympathy was shown to the unemployed, most of whom continued to support the anti-slavery states, whose action was the cause of their distress. In London the Lord Mayor opened a public subscription, and relief committees were quickly established in the depressed areas. Once again, soup kitchens were the great stand-by, though some tried to vary the offering throughout the week: at Blackburn men received bread and coffee on Mondays and Fridays, soup on Tuesdays and Thursdays and 'lobscous' (a kind of Irish stew) on Wednesdays, while on Saturdays their wives were given dinner and a quart of soup to take home. Other committees varied the menu with potato-hash and bread and cheese, and at Accrington a group known as 'The Liberal Women' boiled cauldrons over open fires in the market-place to feed hungry children. Some idea of the desperate need is suggested by the fact that at Preston, where the kitchen opened at 5 am, there were always huge crowds already waiting, and a strong wooden maze had to be erected to control them.[33]

In subsequent years soup-kitchens returned whenever economic depressions and high levels of unemployment revived public sympathy or threatened to disturb the social fabric. When in 1886 distress triggered mass demonstrations in Trafalgar Square and the breaking of windows in Pall Mall clubs, a Mansion House Fund quickly raised £72,000:[34] what was not distributed in small doles again went to soup-kitchens. The significance of these large-scale charitable endeavours in the history of eating out is that they familiarised large numbers of people with eating in public, many perhaps for the first time in their experience. They had to become accustomed to eating alongside strangers in public spaces, usually church or chapel halls, to queueing in orderly fashion and being served in a primitive form of canteen or 'cafeteria'. That this was not a happy experience for people suddenly thrust into the ranks of the 'submerged tenth', all too redolent of the institutional feeding in workhouses, may well have prejudiced sections of the working class against communal dining.

Poor children were also usually considered proper objects of charity since, except in the most severe view, it was not believed that they should suffer for the sins or omissions of their parents. Food as reward had long been associated with regular attendance and good conduct at Sunday School, the annual Treat regarded as a red-letter day in the calendar. But to go beyond this – to any idea of general public feeding of children, however poor and needy – was to raise a fundamental ideological issue about the responsibility of parents to fulfil their most basic duty, the feeding of their offspring. School meals therefore began as a provision for certain groups of children who fell outside the normal family circle – the products of slum life, drunken parents and broken marriages – whose behaviour, dress and manners made them unacceptable in the church schools of the mid-century, and who needed to be tempted into education and discipline with the promise of food. This was the plan of the Ragged School movement, another of Lord Shaftesbury's philanthropic endeavours, which began in London in 1844 and by 1861 had established 176 schools in the poorest parts of many cities.[35] Other voluntary initiatives followed later as awareness of child poverty increased – the Destitute Children's Dinner Society (1864), the London Schools Dinner Association (1889) and the Charity Organisation Society's Penny Dinner movement, by which parents were expected to contribute 1d. towards the cost of the meal, so preserving the Society's cardinal principle of family responsibility. What was usually provided by these bodies was a breakfast of porridge or bread and cocoa and a dinner of soup, but often only during winter months and then only on three or four days a week on the assumption that on Mondays children would be adequately fed at home on left-overs from Sunday. As in many other aspects of social policy, motives were partly humanitarian, partly instrumental. Religious leaders saw the education and feeding of poor children as complementary Christian virtues: teachers had long complained that hungry children did not benefit from their lessons: middle-class reformers viewed communal feeding as a way of instilling civilised behaviour and table manners, while early socialist groups such as the Social Democratic Federation (1884) established their own Socialist Dinners in the hope of promoting fraternal 'social feeling'. By the late 1880s there were some 300 voluntary feeding agencies in Britain, the London School Board alone estimating that 44,000 children (12.8 per cent of attenders) were habitually short of food, but that fewer than half of these were receiving school meals.[36] Voluntary provision had evidently not met the need, and in the first decade of the next century publicly funded school feeding, as well as the medical inspection of children, were introduced (see later).

Adults, however poor, were of course expected to provide for themselves during their working hours, and there was little development of factory or works canteens before the late nineteenth century. Some men brought food from home for their meal-breaks, but there is little mention of this in contemporary accounts, probably for good reason. In poor households little food would have been kept overnight for lack of means and safe storage: food was bought daily in the smallest quantities and quickly consumed. Also, most working men left home very early at around 6 am without breakfast, before wives were about to pack up a meal even if the ingredients were available. Thomas Wright explained that the workman's call comes at 5.30 am, 'and if you happen to live at any considerable distance from your place of employment, even earlier than that'. This was also especially true for casual workers such as dockers, who had to be first on the scene to be picked for a day's work. On cold, dark mornings, Wright continues:

> The gleam from the hot-coffee stall comes like a guiding star through the gloom, and the coffee itself is as welcome as water in the desert. Here you get warmth in your hands on the outside of the cup and for the inner man from the liquid, which you get piping hot [for 1d.].[37]

For many men in London and other cities this could be only the first of several encounters with street-sellers of food and drink during the day. Here was available a huge variety of 'fast foods' for eating while standing, walking, sitting in the open or under some cover, especially convenient for outdoor workers such as builders, labourers, dockers, carters and cabmen, as well as for the crowds of casuals, itinerants and unemployed. Henry Mayhew estimated that there were 41,000 street traders in London in 1850, a ratio of 1 to every 63 people: of this great number, about 30,000 were costermongers selling fruit, vegetables or fish, around 5,000 dealers in manufactured goods and the remaining 6,000 selling eatables and drinkables. He believed that the poor preferred to buy from these street-sellers:

> Such customers will not be driven to buy at the shops. They can't be persuaded that they can buy as cheap at the shops; and besides, they are apt to think that shopkeepers are rich and street-sellers are poor, and that they may as well encourage the poor.[38]

It is also likely that they preferred the anonymity and convenience of ready-to-eat food, much of it hot and tasty, and costing only 1d. or ½d. But Mayhew was probably right in remarking that 'Men whose lives are alternations of starvation and surfeit love some easily-swallowed and comfortable food better than the most approved substantiality of the dinner-table.'[39] This is what they got in the streets: we may imagine that many 'grazed' throughout the day as hunger dictated and resources permitted.

From his detailed survey of street-sellers the following are examples:

1 Hot eels and pea soup (usually combined), *c*.500 sellers. Eels are sold by the cupful for ½d., soup also ½d. for half a pint. Some boys have up to 6 cupfulls of eels on a Saturday night, and a gentleman's servant once had 16 cupfulls at one standing.

2 Pickled whelks, *c*.300 sellers on Saturdays, otherwise *c*.150. Sold at from 2–8 for 1d. depending on size. About half the traders work the pubs. 'People drinking there always want something to eat. They buy whelks, not to fill themselves, but for a relish.'

3 Fried fish, *c*.350 sellers of fried plaice, sole, 'dabs', haddock, whiting and flounders. They buy at Billingsgate or cheap left-overs from fishmongers. Most fry their own: they live in poor courts and alleys: a dealer told Mayhew that a gin-drinking neighbourhood was best, as 'people hasn't their smell so correct there.' The fried fish is sold by itinerants carrying trays holding from 2–5 dozen pieces; much is sold in pubs, with a slice of bread for 1d.

4 Sheep's trotters, *c*.300 sellers, mainly stationary at street corners. The feet of 20,000 sheep are consumed weekly, sold at ½d. each or 1d. for fine, large ones.

5 Baked potatoes, *c*.300 sellers in winter. They are baked at a baker's and kept hot in specially designed cans with charcoal burners – some are highly polished, brass mounted and decorated, costing 50/- or more. Usually ½d. for a large potato, served with butter and salt. A seller at Smithfield market has sold 1,000 in a day.

6 Ham sandwiches, *c*.70 men and boys: sold for ½d. and 1d., often outside theatres.

7 Pie-men, *c*.80. Sell meat, fish and fruit pies for 1d. Trade has declined because of competition from pie-shops.

8 Boiled puddings (meat or currants) and plum 'duff'. Round puddings ½d.; slices of 'duff' cut from a roly-poly 1d. Customers mainly children.

9 Cakes, tarts, gingerbread, *c*.300 sellers. The pastries are all made by *c*.12 Jewish pastrycooks, who sell wholesale at 4d. a dozen: the street traders sell at ½d. each.

10 Muffins and crumpets, *c.*500 in winter. The muffin-man is also a great convenience to ladies who do not have a servant, as he comes round at about tea-time. Muffins ½d., crumpets 4 for 1d.

11 Ice cream, *c.*20 sellers in summer. The street trade only introduced in 1850. Ices are wholesaled by a man who owns a Master's Freezing Apparatus and retailed from a jar which is set in a 'cooler' of cold water. Sold in a cup or glass with a spoon for 1d.: the best customers are servant-girls and children. At first, customers did not know how to eat them – a seller, 'I don't think they'll ever take greatly on in the streets, but there's no saying. Lord! How I've seen the people splutter when they've tasted them for the first time.'

12 Coffee stall keepers, *c.*300, mostly women. Grew greatly after 1842 when the coffee duty was lowered, and also since chicory has been much used as a cheap adulterant. Sells at 1d. a mug or ½d. per half-mug. Many stall-keepers also sell ham sandwiches, boiled eggs, cake and bread-and-butter. Some appear as early as 3 or 4 am for men on their way to work, others only begin at around midnight, 'for the accommodation of "night walkers", "fast gentlemen" and "loose girls"'.[40]

Workers with full-time employment for 10 or 12 hours a day in mid-century had to make other arrangements for meals. Those who had not brought food from home bought from a pie-shop or street-stall for their dinner or sent a young assistant with an order which might, surreptitiously, include beer. In the earlier part of the period meal breaks were often not scheduled, and workers had to snatch a bite when they could. Only a few 'model' employers permitted set breaks and even provided mess-rooms where food and drink could be heated, but most did not, especially at busy periods, as a witness before the Committee on Factory Children's Labour (1831–2) reported:

> Q. *At what time in the morning, in the brisk time, did those girls go to the mills?*
> A. *In the brisk time, for about six weeks, they have gone at 3 o'clock in the morning, and ended at 10, or nearly half-past at night.*
> Q. *What intervals were allowed for rest or refreshment during those nineteen hours of labour?*
> A. *Breakfast a quarter of an hour, and dinner a half an hour, and drinking a quarter of an hour.*

Q. Was any of that time taken up in cleaning the machinery?

A. They generally had to do what they call dry down; sometimes this took the whole of the time at breakfast or drinking, and they were to get their dinner or breakfast as they could, if not, it was brought home.[41]

Another witness deposed that at the age of 7 he had worked for 14½ hours a day. Half an hour was allowed for dinner at noon, but after that there was no rest or refreshment, and 'we had to eat our meals as we could, standing or otherwise... You cannot take food out of your basket or handkerchief but what it is covered with dust directly... The children are frequently sick because of the dust and dirt they eat with their meal.'[42]

The Factory Act passed in 1833 prohibited the employment of children under 9 in textile factories, limited the hours of those aged 9–13 to eight a day and specified additional times for meals, but the appointment of only four Inspectors to enforce the regulations in hundreds of mills seriously limited its effectiveness. In any case, coal mines remained unregulated until 1842 and other factories and workshops until the 1860s and 1870s. At the age of 7 in the 1840s Charles Shaw started work as a potter's 'runner' from 5 or 6 am till 6, 7 or 8 pm for 1/- a week.

These long hours were worked, too, on the poorest and most meagre fare. Bread and butter were made up in a handkerchief, with a sprinkling of tea and sugar. Sometimes there was a little potato pie, with a few pieces of fat bacon on it to represent beef.[43]

Occasionally, the younger men would arrange to stay on at the pot-bank all night, and would persuade some of the women to join them: 'The night was a revel of drink, lust and beastliness.'[44] At about the same time men, women and children were working underground in coal mines, when a Royal Commission in 1842 revealed that in the great majority of pits no regular time was set for meal breaks. The workers' 'snap' was taken down in a tin box for protection from the rats, together with water or cold tea in a tin can. Even at the end of the century, by which time miners in the Rhondda had won an eight-hour shift, only 20 minutes was allowed for food.

Eating out by the poor in the period did not usually extend to sitting for a meal in any sort of public eating-place. Along main roads there were simple cottages and shacks where travellers, drovers and others could obtain basic food, but public houses and the new beershops which opened after 1830 were the workman's principal social centres, and they did not provide substantial meals unless ordered for special occasions. The usual offering of bread and cheese, pickled onions and the like was more an encouragement to drink than the satisfaction of hunger, though Charles Shaw, the boy potter, remembered with a mixture of pain and pleasure the hot rolls and cheese which the local pub served on Saturday night pay-day while the landlord deliberately fumbled to find change:

> Men, women and children had to go there for their wages... Each one
> was expected to have a hot roll and cheese, to be paid for out of the
> wage, however small the pittance... These rolls and cheese were
> devoured with rare gusto. Such shiny crust, and such white, flaky
> insides were never seen in 'cottage loaves'... The boys would hold out
> the remainders of roll and cheese to show how much each one had left,
> and he was considered the hero of the hour who would seem to be
> eating all the time and yet be the last to finish.[45]

Notes and references

1 C. Anne Wilson, *Luncheon, Nuncheon and Other Meals. Eating with the Victorians*, Stroud, Gloucestershire, Alan Sutton Publishing Ltd, 1994, pp. 35–7.

2 Under this system, when a gallon loaf cost 1/- a single man's wage would be made up to 3/- a week, with an additional 1/6d. for a wife and each child.

3 David Davies, *The Case of Labourers in Husbandry, Stated and Considered* (1795), facsimile edn, Fairfield, New Jersey, Augustus M. Kelley, 1977, p. 8.

4 D. J. Oddy, 'Food, Drink and Nutrition', in F. M. L. Thompson (ed.), *The Cambridge Social History of Britain, 1750–1950*, 2 vols, Cambridge University Press, 1990, vol. 2, Table 5.5, p. 274.

5 Labourers' Wages. Report from the Select Committee on the Rate of Agricultural Wages, and on the Condition and Morals of Labourers in that Employment, P.P. 1024 (092), vol. II.

6 William Cobbett, *Rural Rides* (1st edn, 1830), edited and introduced by George Woodcock, Harmondsworth, Middlesex, Penguin Books, 1981, p. 126.

7 *The Hungry Forties. Life under the Bread Tax*, Descriptive letters and other testimonies from contemporary witnesses, Introduction by Mrs Cobden

Unwin, T. Fisher Unwin, People's Edn, 1905, p. 14.

8 'A Childhood in the Fens about 1850–1860', in *Life As We Have Known It, by Co-operative Working Women*, Margaret Llewelyn Davies (ed.), (1st edn, 1931), Virago, 1977, pp. 109–11.

9 James Caird, *English Agriculture in 1850–51*, Longman, Brown, Green and Longmans, 1852, pp. 84–5.

10 T. C. Barker, D. J. Oddy and John Yudkin, *The Dietary Surveys of Dr Edward Smith, 1862–3*, Queen Elizabeth College, University of London, Occasional Paper No. 1. Staples Press, 1970, pp. 43, 46.

11 Edwin Grey, *Cottage Life in a Hertfordshire Village* (1st edn, 1934), Harpenden, Herts, Harpenden and District Local History Society, 1977, pp. 101–3.

12 Tom Mullins, in *Useful Toil. Autobiographies of Working People from the 1820s to the 1920s*, edited and introduced by John Burnett (1st edn, 1974), Routledge, 1994, p. 51.

13 Grey, op. cit., pp. 101–7.

14 Pamela Horn, *The Rural World, 1780–1850. Social Change in the English Countryside*, Hutchinson, 1980, pp. 29–30.

15 Nigel E. Agar, *The Bedfordshire Farm Worker in the Nineteenth Century*, Bedford, Bedfordshire Historical Record Society, vol. 60, 1981, p. 113.

16 R. K. French, *The History and Virtues of Cyder*, London, Robert Hale, 1982, p. 17.

17 Quoted Francis George Heath, *The English Peasantry*, Frederick Warne, 1874, pp. 99–100.

18 Flora Thompson, *Lark Rise to Candleford* (1st edn, 1939), Harmondsworth, Middlesex, Penguin Books, 1976, p. 237.

19 Quoted Agar, op. cit., pp. 118–19.

20 Flora Thompson, op. cit., p. 231.

21 Richard Heath, *The English Peasant. Studies Historical, Local and Biographic*, T. Fisher Unwin, 1893, p. 128.

22 See John Burnett, *Idle Hands. The Experience of Unemployment, 1790–1990*, Routledge, 1994, especially chs 2 and 3.

23 Samuel Laing, *National Distress. Its Causes and Remedies*, Atlas Prize Essay, 1844, pp. 8, 27.

24 John Burnett (ed.), *Destiny Obscure. Autobiographies of Childhood, Education and Family from the 1820s to the 1920s*, Allen Lane, 1982, p. 57.

25 Mrs Layton, quoted in *Life As We Have Known It, by Co-Operative Women*, Margaret Llewelyn Davies (ed.), op. cit. p. 9. The author was born in Bethnal Green, London, in 1855, one of 14 children.

26 ibid., pp. 4, 20. After finishing work at 7 pm she attended a 'Ragged School' evening class twice a week.

27 William Luby, in John Burnett (ed.), *Useful Toil. Autobiographies of Working People from the 1820s to the 1920s*, op. cit., p. 93.

28 Jack Wood, 'The Good Old Days', Articles in *Oldham Chronicle*, 27 Jan. 1973. Quoted in John Burnett (ed.), *Destiny Obscure*, op. cit., p. 60.

29 J. C. Drummond and Anne Wilbraham, *The Englishman's Food. A History of Five Centuries of English Diet*. Jonathan Cape, 1939, pp. 306–7.

30 Andrew Langley, *The Selected Soyer. The Writings of the Legendary Victorian Chef, Alexis Soyer*, Bath, Absolute Press, 1987, pp. 31–4.

31 Charles Elmé Francatelli, *A Plain Cookery Book for the Working Classes* (1852), reprinted Scolar Press, 1977, p. 100.

32 Edward Smith, *Practical Dietaries for Families, Schools and the Labouring Classes*, Walton and Maberley, 1864, pp. 229ff.

33 Norman Longmate, *The Hungry Mills. The Story of the Lancashire Cotton Famine 1861–5*, Temple Smith, 1978, pp. 158–62.

34 Gareth Stedman Jones, *Outcast London. A Study in the Relationship between Classes in Victorian Society*, Harmondsworth, Middlesex, Penguin Books, 1976, pp. 291–6.

35 David Owen, *English Philanthropy, 1660–1960*, Cambridge, Mass., Harvard University Press, 1964, pp. 147–8.

36 M. E. Buckley, *The Feeding of School Children*, G. Bell and Sons, 1914, p. 16.

37 Journeyman Engineer (Thomas Wright), *The Great Unwashed* (1868), reprinted New York, Augustus M. Kelley, 1970, pp. 175, 185.

38 Henry Mayhew, *London Labour and the London Poor. Vol.1. The London Street-Folk*, Griffin, Bohn and Co., 1861, p. 60.

39 ibid., p. 158.

40 Descriptions and numbers of street-sellers are from Mayhew, ibid., pp. 160–207.

41 Report of the Select Committee on Factory Children's Labour, PP 1831–2, vol. XV. Evidence of Samuel Coulson.

42 ibid. Evidence of Joseph Haberjam.

43 Charles Shaw, *When I Was A Child* (1st edn, 1903), Introduction by John Burnett, Firle, Sussex, Caliban Books, 1980, p. 54.

44 ibid., p. 50.

45 ibid., pp. 67–8.

CHAPTER 2

Places of refreshment for the working classes

Eating for work

In 1840 contemporaries were unsure whether England's rapid growth in industry and wealth had brought more gains than losses to the majority of the working classes. By 1880 they had no doubts about the benefits of increased purchasing power, lower food prices and the general advance in standards of living. A. L. Bowley, the leading statistician, calculated that between 1860 and 1891 real wages (i.e. the purchasing power of money wages) rose by no less than 92 per cent, and that 'In so far as actual want is now only the lot of a small proportion of the nation (though intrinsically a large number) and comfort is within the reach of large masses of workmen, the greatest benefit of this prosperity has fallen to wage-earners; but this is only the righting of injustice and hardship'.[1] His optimistic assessment obscured the extent of poverty which still existed and would shortly be revealed by the researches of Charles Booth and Seebohm Rowntree, but it was undeniable that there had been a substantial filtering-up from the lower ranks of labourers towards steadier, better-paid employment, and that, in particular, more working-class families were beginning to enjoy an improved, more varied and nutritious diet. Some would even begin to think that eating was not only for necessity, but for pleasure.

As yet, only a handful of employers saw the provision of food for their workers as any part of their responsibility, despite the fact that in the few cases where such arrangements were made, a more efficient and contented workforce actually conduced to their profits as much as their social conscience. This had been demonstrated by Robert Owen during his management of the New Lanark cotton mills (1799–1824) where, in addition to decent housing, schools, a co-operative store and other amenities, he provided large kitchens and a dining-room where employees could, if they wished, eat all their meals at very moderate prices.[2] Owen believed that his social experiment had converted the labour force which he had inherited – 'a collection of the most ignorant and destitute from all parts of Scotland' – into 'conspicuously honest, industrious, sober and orderly' employees, though few employers followed the lead of a socialist and atheist. Where factories or mines were located in rural areas remote from shops, employers often supplied their workers with food and other necessities, deducting the cost from their wages: this gave some the opportunity to exploit a 'truck' system, providing poor quality goods at inflated prices, but it also encouraged others, like Samuel Oldknow at Mellor Mill and the Gregs at Styall, to organise supplies of flour, meat, milk and vegetables on a non-profit basis. The altogether more ambitious concept of building a new model town was initiated by Titus Salt, an alpaca wool manufacturer of Bradford. Begun in 1853, Saltaire, three miles distant, ultimately contained 850 'convenient cottages', churches and chapels, an assembly hall, art and reading-rooms and public baths, all designed in a neo-Victorian Gothic style: the inner man was served by a dining-hall where meals were supplied at cost, or the worker could have brought food cooked in public kitchens. Other pioneers of industrial feeding in this period include Hazell, Watson and Viney, printers and publishers of Aylesbury and London, who supplied light lunches and a tea or coffee break at 4 pm (3d. a week for a pint, with milk and sugar), and Thomas Adams, lace manufacturer of Nottingham, where 'the girls leave their counters and refresh themselves with a glass of milk and a bun, from four to half past six'.[3] Greater developments in industrial catering were to follow in the closing years of the century (see later).

Much of this early provision of canteens was in factories employing a high proportion of women and girls. The inference is, perhaps, that they were considered the most appropriate subjects for welfare in that their wages were much lower than men's, they were mainly engaged in very repetitive, monotonous work, and their early starting hours meant that they often left home with no more than a drink of tea. Men could fend for themselves, and even enlightened employers rarely provided more than a mess-room where food brought from home or bought locally could be heated and consumed. The North-Eastern Railway Co. at their Gateshead works thoughtfully provided long tables with a division ten inches high running down the centre so that no one could see what his opposite number was eating, 'and all can go home with the comforting hallucination that their neighbours supposed them to fare better than they did'. In respectable working-class households Sunday dinner, with roast meat, vegetables and a pudding, was both the culinary highlight of the week and a sensible economy, since the meat yielded dripping for several days' sandwiches: otherwise, bread and cheese, bacon, a small pie or some variety of pork-butcher's tasty meat were the usual stand-bys for packed lunches.

In London and other cities better-paid workers ate out on some days at a cookshop or 'ordinary', particularly in winter, where they could get a hot meal at low cost. The quality of the food usually tended to match the price, though criticisms by contemporary middle-class writers may well reflect what they considered to be a good meal rather than what was acceptable to a mainly proletarian clientele. The author of *The Food of London* (1856) described the great trade carried on by cookshops in thickly populated areas between 12 and 1 o'clock, but found them often dirty and unsavoury places which 'the black coat and the silk hat' avoid: the meat is frequently cheap and bad, the soups and puddings of 'questionable character'. Yet the fact that the trade is described as 'immense' suggests that they were very popular and met a real need for cheap eating-places.[4] Soups and stews could be had for 2d. or 3d., a plate of beef, potatoes and vegetables for around 6d.: there were also specialist hot eel, pie and mash cookshops which were beginning to take over from the street traders. Yet another lunch-time possibility was the porter-house, where one could bring a chop, steak or sausages to be cooked on a large gridiron for 1d. or 2d., including bread and salt: here the proprietor expected to make most of his profit from the sale of drink.

In the hierarchy of eating-places the 'ordinary' stood somewhat higher than the cookshop, though also of variable quality according to contemporary opinion. Here one was offered a set meal or 'table d'hôte' of a main course at modest price, with extras for a pudding, cheese or dessert. The better ones offered a choice of meats and fish and therefore resembled a cheap restaurant. In 1860 Charles Selby believed that:

> Until within the last few years a comfortable, well-served table d'hôte at a moderate cost was not to be found in all London. Shilling ordinaries at one or, at the latest, two o'clock, where the fare consisted of our proverbial 'gory joints' and badly cooked cheap fish, served on a second day's table-cloth ... in a dingy room with a sanded or sawdust-strewed floor garnished with a spittoon ... were the only attempts at social dinners in public, and their frequenters were nearly all coarse feeders of a vulgar stamp, careless of anything but the quantity of meat and pudding they could swallow for their shilling.[5]

It was usual for these critics to complain both about the premises – often situated not in main thoroughfares but in side streets and basements – as well as the quality of food and cooking, frequently compared unfavourably with French cuisine. The author of *The Memoirs of a Stomach* (*c.*1855) observed that there were many first-rate restaurants in Paris because the French appreciated good food and were prepared to pay much more for their dinners than the English: 'The Gallic gourmet is an artisan. Every dish has a chromatic relation with its antecedent: every condiment has a studied, specific purpose.' Compare this with 'The English system of cookery ... that huge round of parboiled ox flesh, with sodden dumplings floating in a saline, greasy mixture, surrounded by carrots looking red with disgust and turnips pale with dismay.' The author continued:

> I have dined in eating-houses the effluvium of which, steaming up through the iron grating, made me qualmish before eating and ill all the day after ... I have groped my way down hypocausts in Fleet Street, and dined in cavern-like taverns, wishing myself a thousand miles away the moment the eternal joint was uncovered.[6]

Such complaints long continued, though Charles Selby in 1860 believed that the 'shilling ordinary' had recently been reformed, the cooking had improved and the environment was now more polite and civil. Good meals at various grades and prices were now available in London, but the cheapest one he approved – 'Sawyer's London Dinner' in Fleet Street – cost 1/6d. for meat and vegetables, cheese and a salad, well beyond the budget of a working man.[7] The difficulty here and elsewhere in the contemporary literature is one of definition. Selby was evidently referring to what was more usually described as a 'dining-room' where standards of cuisine and comfort were more acceptable to 'the black coat and the silk hat'.

For a really cheap meal a new institution appeared in the 1860s and grew rapidly in popularity. This was the fish-and-chip shop, reviled by some but loved by the many as a fast-food convenience dear to the working class. Fish, especially fresh or smoked herring, had long been a staple of the poor, so much so that slum areas of London were said permanently to reek of their smell. According to Mayhew the poorer inhabitants of London were consuming 875 million herrings a year in 1850 at four for a penny, and, as previously noticed, the sale of fried plaice, haddock, sole and whiting was already supporting more than 300 street-sellers. There is mention of a fried fish 'warehouse' in Field Lane in *Oliver Twist* (serialised 1837–9) which, presumably, supplied them wholesale, and Alexis Soyer, the eminent chef of the Reform Club, was seen eating fried fish as he walked in the streets in the 1840s.[8] Fried potatoes, as well as baked, were also sold separately at this time, especially in the north of England, where potatoes were a valued article of diet. Soyer himself gave a recipe for them in his *Shilling Cookery for the People* (1855), but here the potato was to be 'cut into very thin slices, almost shavings',[9] i.e. into scallops. Precisely where and when the modern-shaped chip was sold with accompanying fish is disputed between Lancashire, where a Mr Lees of Mossley opened a pea soup and pig's trotter business in 1863 and added fish and chips a few years later, and London, where Mr Malin claimed to have opened the first shop in Old Ford Road in 1868. Their subsequent rapid growth depended importantly on increased supplies of cheap white fish: the development of steam trawlers and ice packing made it possible to fish much further afield in the central area of the North Sea and as far as Iceland and the Faroes; also, railways could now supply inland areas with fish cheaply and in good condition. In 1887, 553,000 tons of wet fish were landed in Britain; the all-time peak catch was 1,140,000 tons in 1911.[10] It is estimated that 20–25 per cent of these catches and around 10 per cent of the potato crop went to the fish-and-chip trade by the early twentieth century,[11] but these proportions would be considerably higher in northern industrial towns where fish and chips were by then a firmly established dinner or supper meal. Specialist frying equipment in the form of cast-iron ranges became available from the late 1860s, manufactured by firms like Faulkner of Hollinwood, near Manchester, and Nuttals of Rochdale, quickly followed by machines for potato peeling, washing and chipping. An estimate of 1888 suggests ten to twelve thousand fish-and-chip shops in Britain, rising to 25,000 by 1910.

The heavy concentration of shops in the north of England, especially in industrial Lancashire, reflects the uniquely high employment of women and girls in the cotton industry, and the great convenience of a cheap, warm and tasty meal available at lunchtime and in the evening. With portions of chips at ½d.–1d. and fish at 1d.–2d. this made a nutritious meal for people not yet concerned about the amount of fat in their diets. We do not know how much of this food was eaten 'out' in the shop itself or in the street compared with what was taken home, but almost certainly it was the majority. Many small shops had a few tables and chairs at the front or in the rear of their premises, charging a little extra for the use of plates, cutlery and condiments if needed, and at least as early as 1896 in London Sam Isaacs was developing a chain of restaurants where fish and chips, bread and butter and tea were sold for 9d. in superior 'palaces'.[12] In some mill-towns girls left basins on their way to work to collect at the dinner-break, or large orders would be delivered in a basket to the workplace. But despite some upgrading of quality and premises towards the end of the century, fish and chips generally continued to have a somewhat low image, especially on Saturday nights after closing-time of the pubs. Although they had become an integral part of the proletarian diet well before 1914, embedded in the cultural fabric of the working class almost as deeply as the pub itself, they were not quite respectable. As Robert Roberts observed in Salford,

> Good artisan families avoided bringing them home: a mother would have been insulted. Fried fish without chips she could already buy from cookshops. One could eat at these shops, or take out a fourpenny hot dinner in a basin. Many working women . . . took advantage of the basin meal.[13]

This was evidently one of the nice social divisions within the working class, though it probably did not prevent children of almost any level from surreptitiously eating a pennyworth of chips on the street.

It was an indication of a desire to civilise the working man, his manners and eating habits, that another institution appeared in the 1840s and developed strongly in the following decades – a revived and remodelled version of the coffee-house, which aimed to provide non-alcoholic drinks, simple food, comfort and respectable amusement as an alternative to the public house and its moral temptations. 'This type of coffee-house', wrote E. Hepple Hall in 1878, owed its existence to 'temperance advocates and social reformers' and was part of 'the growing sober sentiment' of the times. He continued that in order to be successful, however, the houses had to be as comfortable and attractive as the English public house or the Continental café: if this were achieved, they could become the working man's social centre, a club where he could refresh his body and improve his mind.[14]

The Temperance Movement began in Scotland in 1829 and crossed the border shortly afterwards. Its greatest enemies were spirits and beer and the gin-palaces and public houses which purveyed 'the demon drink', so corrupting, demoralising and often pauperising the working man. Estimates in mid-century suggested that around a quarter of working-class earnings, £15–£20 out of average yearly incomes of £60–£80, went on alcohol, more than enough to reduce heavy drinkers to poverty. The revived coffee-house movement was part of the attempt to redress this evil, and, from their proprietors' standpoint, to combine a moral crusade with modest, legitimate profit. Coffee had not challenged the popularity of tea as the main domestic drink of the working classes, but it had a following among men as a stronger, thicker and more satisfying beverage, especially when loaded with quantities of sugar and milk. A major stimulus to increased consumption was tariff reductions in 1825 and 1842 which lowered the price of a cheap grade of coffee to 1/- a pound, made to go further by mixing with chicory at half the price.[15] G. R. Porter noted in 1847 that

> Great numbers of houses have been opened for the sale of cups of coffee
> and tea at low prices. It is said that there are from 1600 to 1800 of these
> coffee houses in the metropolis alone, and that they are established and

FIGURE 2.1 ◆ *The Early Rambler's Coffee Bar, Old Ford Road, London, 1899. Many temperance coffee rooms (sometimes called Coffee Taverns or even Coffee Public Houses) were established as non-alcoholic places of refreshment, selling coffee, tea, cocoa and light meals at low prices for the working classes. This one was situated next door to a chimney sweep's premises.*

Source: © London Metropolitan Archives.

*rapidly increasing all over the country; about thirty years ago there were
not above a dozen.*[16]

The exact numbers must be uncertain since the description of a 'coffee-
house' was inexact and some were more like gentlemen's clubs where
patrons paid a shilling for admission, smoked a cigar and played a game
of chess. These looked back to the heyday of the coffee-house of the early
eighteenth century, but what now attracted public interest and approval
was the working man's coffee-house. Porter described one of these in the
Haymarket which opened at 5.30 am to provide for men on their way to
work, and closed at 10.30 pm: it sold coffee at 1½d. a cup and had
1,500–1,600 customers a day 'of all classes, from hackney-coachmen and
porters to the most respectable classes.' An article in *Household Words* in
1852 described them as frequented by

*swart artizans, burly coalheavers and grimy ballast-porters who are
content to come straight from the factory, the anvil or the wharf . . . and
content themselves with the moderate evening's amusement to be found
in cheap periodicals . . .* [17]

This was, perhaps, an optimistic assessment of places which came in
many forms, not all very clean or comfortable and selling very adulter-
ated coffee: some were 'little better than mere barns, where you may see
the navvy and the hodman importing their own food'.[18]

In fact, many coffee-houses soon developed from merely serving
coffee, tea, cocoa and soft drinks to supplying food, becoming another
type of eating-place. This made sound economic sense, for unless the sale
of drinks was very large they would not have yielded sufficient profit to
cover costs, rent and service. George Dodd noted in 1856 that many had
already progressed from serving breakfast to simple dinners, while in the
evening they became reading-rooms, with a bright fire, and a good supply
of newspapers, periodicals, and board games.[19] Their major expansion
into catering, however, dates from the 1870s, coinciding with the beginning of a long decline in alcohol consumption. Until now coffee-houses
had been owned and run by individual proprietors, but in the 1870s several new ventures were established on a corporate basis, using the limited
liability company legislation of 1862 to spread ownership to shareholders. In 1874 'The People's Café Company' was formed under the

presidency of no less than the famous philanthropist, the Earl of Shaftesbury. One of its houses in St Paul's Churchyard served 2,000 customers daily, the bill of fare offering soup, hot and cold joints, fish, entrées and confectionery: no gratuities were permitted. Unusually for this period, it claimed to be patronised by both sexes, young people and adults: cleanliness and good order were insisted on.[20] Similar groups were established in provincial towns, including Leeds, where 'The British Workman Coffee Houses', begun in 1867, served breakfast for 4d. (including ham or bacon) and a dinner of soup, beef and potatoes and a pudding for 8d. In London again, 'Coffee Palaces' were an attempt to improve the standard of decor and furnishing, which had usually consisted of box-benches as in many pubs of the period: the first 'palace' was apparently opened in Limehouse in 1872 on the initiative of Dr Barnardo, and the organisation also bought 'The Edinburgh Castle', a large gin-palace at Mile End, to convert to non-alcoholic purposes. But acknowledging the deep-seated loyalty of the working classes to the pub, 'The Coffee Tavern Company', incorporated in 1876, deliberately used a familiar term in its title: two years later it had branches in Nottingham, Portsmouth, Coventry, Huddersfield, Darlington, Oxford (where the first coffee-house in England had been opened in 1650) and, more surprisingly, Tunbridge Wells. This organisation was rivalled by the even more explicit 'Coffee Public House Association' of 1877 which quickly claimed 53 establishments.[21] By the end of the century coffee-houses of the new type, many of them on a corporate basis, had spread widely across England, not only in the hearts of manufacturing areas: the county of Sussex, for example, claimed 19 'Temperance Taverns' in 1900, mainly in the coastal regions and aimed partly at the growing numbers of holiday-makers. 'The Hope of Brighton' Coffee Palace owned the adjacent Phoenix Hall for temperance lectures and, no doubt, magic-lantern slide shows, a haven particularly for women and children.[22]

The significance of these corporate initiatives lies in their being early attempts to provide mass catering for working-class consumers at affordable prices in respectable surroundings. Their emergence in the 1870s was especially timely. They recognized that standards of living were demonstrably rising and that more working people could now afford to eat out in public and also needed to do so as home became more separated from workplace. For better-paid workers the move from crowded city centres to new suburbs was well under way, encouraged by low rents and cheap rail fares: this represented a new style of life, closer to the values of the lower middle class, a 'growing sober sentiment' which no longer looked to the public house as its natural social centre. The glowing testimonials of most contemporaries about the 'reformed' coffee houses should not, however, be taken at face value. They were limited in extent – 121 in London in 1884, the Liverpool Coffee Taverns Company 30, the Leeds British Workman Public Houses 17. Although they aimed to be open to both sexes and all ages – almost like a family café on the Parisian model – their custom was overwhelmingly adult male, women making up only 6 per cent of the clientele.[23] Some houses were quite short-lived, lacking professional management and financial control, and some of the companies paid little or no dividends until they were wound up. Fundamentally, the coffee-house did not seriously challenge the conviviality of the pub and the lubricating effects of alcohol – there was, after all, a limit to the number of cups of coffee or cocoa that could comfortably be consumed in an evening – while the spartan atmosphere of some houses did not conduce to animated social interaction. What was evidently lacking in many was sufficient amusement to tempt custom in the evening, and in 1880 'The Coffee Music Hall Company' was established in London to promote temperance music halls where men might take their wives and children 'without shaming or harming them'. The Royal Victoria Music Hall in south London was rented and extensively redecorated, but was in debt within seven months: it failed to attract top professional turns (partly because of its censorship), and even devout teetotallers were not greatly amused by the large diagram of the Liver of a Drunkard displayed between acts.[24] Charles Booth commented on similar lines about temperance coffee-houses in general: 'Good food might excuse the texts, but the texts do not excuse bad food.' Their real importance in the history of eating out is that they set a precedent and provided a lesson for the much more successful commercial enterprises in mass catering which shortly followed.

Eating for pleasure

So far, eating out by the working classes had been considered mainly as an adjunct to work, the necessary refuelling of the body for continued

labour. Food therefore usually took the form of a midday meal, sometimes of breakfast but rarely of an evening meal, as this would generally
be provided at home. But increasingly from mid-century onwards, eating
out also became associated with leisure, pleasure, entertainment and holidays in which food formed part of a wider enjoyable experience distinct
from workaday life. There were several determining reasons for this
major change in social habits. More workers were now beginning to enjoy
an income not wholly absorbed by necessities – food, clothing and shel-
ter: in particular, food, always the largest item in the budget, was becoming cheaper as a result of Free Trade policies, tariff reductions on articles
of mass consumption, and imports of cheap foreign wheat and meat.
Although the average earnings of adult male manual workers in 1885
were still only around £60 a year, this now went further than in the past,
and in any case, the average conceals the substantial gains that more
skilled workers were making. A little later, Seebohm Rowntree wrote of
the 'Class D' families in York, whose incomes were £1.50 a week or more:

> It is a growing practice ... to take a few days' summer holiday out of
> York. During the August Bank Holiday week working men crowd into
> Scarborough, and many of those who do not take such an extended
> holiday avail themselves of the cheap day and half-day excursions run
> by the N.E. Railway Company.[25]

This group constituted 52.6 per cent of the working-class population –
artisans, better-paid factory workers and railway employees who could
put a little money aside or use their co-operative society 'dividend' for an
annual seaside holiday. In response to this new spending power, a commercial leisure industry developed in the later nineteenth century,
specifically aimed at a new group of consumers who could afford to
engage in mass entertainment.

Equally important was the greater amount of free time for leisure
activity. Work itself had never been regarded as the be-all and end-all of
life in working-class culture, and as it became more intensive, more rou-
tinised and repetitive in the machine age, its psychological rewards continually diminished. Time away from work, at one's own disposal and
not the employer's bidding, was increasingly valued, sometimes at least
as much as the financial return for labour. Thus, the trade unions of
skilled workers during the mid-century boom devoted much effort to

negotiating shorter working hours, possibly at the expense of higher wages: the engineers, one of the founding 'New Model' unions, achieved a nine-hour day in 1871, followed soon by other craft workers though much more slowly by the less skilled. Long before that, workers in many trades had regulated their labour by unauthorised absenteeism, and the observance of 'Saint Monday' as an extended weekend holiday survived from pre-industrial times through much of the nineteenth century. The Royal Commission on Labour in 1892 estimated that coal-miners lost between 20 per cent and 25 per cent of time, and that absences from work on the Monday after the monthly pay-day were so common as to be recognised by the employers, while in some South Wales collieries the unofficial 'Mabon's Day' holiday often extended to almost a week. Also in the 1890s, Charles Booth found that in London absenteeism was common both among highly-paid piano-makers, whose pattern was 'hard work ... succeeded by idleness and hard drinking', and among poor, casual workers and women, like the girls at the Victoria Match Factory, who regularly took from half a day to two days off though their earnings were only 8/- to 10/- a week. In the London furniture trade it was said that men 'worked a ghost' (an extra shift) on Friday nights in order to keep 'Saint Monday'.[26] For some men this was merely the opportunity to recover from a weekend's heavy drinking – or to continue it – but for others it was a family holiday and, in fine weather, a day out.

The 'Journeyman Engineer' (Thomas Wright) in 1867 noted that many day-trips were run by railways and steamboats on Mondays 'during a great portion of the year' to the coast and to pleasure-grounds like Greenwich and Blackheath. Some visitors have their meals at eating-houses or tea gardens while others take the remains of the Sunday joint for sandwiches: wives bring packets of tea from home and have a kettle boiled for 2d., but smart, single workmen go in groups or with their girls and pay 1/6d. for dinner at an inn and 9d. for tea.[27]

Unauthorised absenteeism persisted partly because few employers granted official holidays until the late nineteenth century, thereby virtually obliging workers to take matters into their own hands. Before that, the position about official holidays was uncertain and complicated, though it clearly varied with region and occupation. The Factory Act of 1833 specified that textile workers under 18 'shall be entitled' to the traditional holy days, Christmas Day and Good Friday, though the ambiguity of the term made for evasion, and in any case the Act did not apply to adults. In some iron works Christmas Day was apparently the only recognised holiday, but in most industries in mid-century Good Friday or Easter Monday and Whitsuntide were added, together with occasional half-days for local fairs, race meetings or other sporting events. The Lancashire cotton industry was more fortunate than most, with its 'Wakes Week' which might extend from a day or two to a full week. An important step towards regularising the matter was the Bank Holidays Act of 1871 introduced by the Liberal MP John Lubbock, which by requiring banks to close on four days in the year – Boxing Day, Easter Monday, Whit Monday and the first Monday in August – in effect recogised them as public holidays. The revolutionary implication of the Act lay in treating the first three of these days no longer as part of religious festivals, and adding a purely secular holiday in August at a season when the weather might be expected to encourage outings – for some years after 1871 this was only half-humorously known as 'St. Lubbock's Day'. But for poorer workers the advent of compulsory holidays meant a loss of earnings: unlike civil servants, bank clerks and local government staff, who by now were beginning to enjoy a week or more of holidays with pay, manual workers sometimes had to decline the offer of a few days' unpaid leave. The first holidays with pay were apparently granted by a chemical firm in 1884, and in the 1890s Booth found that most railwaymen were receiving up to a week with pay, not yet as of right, but as a reward for good service.[28]

The other crucial determinant of the transformation of leisure for the masses was increased mobility. Places formerly limited to walking distance could now be reached by a variety of new transport facilities – in towns by regular services of vans, horse-buses and, later, trams, on the water by steamboats, and inland by the railways which spread after 1830. Before then, coach travel – slow, expensive and uncomfortable – had been limited to the middle and upper classes who had time and money for journeys costing 2½d.–4d. a mile: in the 1820s the fastest express coach from London to Brighton took 5¼ hours, hardly feasible for a day out. At first the new railways were not greatly cheaper, and in third class, open carriages little more comfortable, but the important development was the introduction of the 'Parliamentary Train' Act in 1844, by which the companies were obliged to run some trains each day at a maximum charge of 1d. a mile. Even before that, a Select Committee on Railways in

1840 had pointed to their potentialities for leisure, in that 'the health and enjoyment of the mechanics, artizans and poor inhabitants of the large towns would be promoted by the facility with which they would be enabled to remove themselves and their families into healthier districts'. Next year, 1841, a temperance advocate of Leicester, Thomas Cook, also saw the possibilities of railways for moral reformation when he hired a train at his own risk to convey supporters to a mass meeting in Loughborough at a cheap excursion fare. By 1845 he had developed a successful commercial excursion business and in 1851 conveyed hundreds of thousands of visitors to the Great Exhibition. Seaside resorts, inland towns, Switzerland and Egypt were soon within his programme, and in 1867 workers from Bolton were taken to visit the Paris Exhibition.

By 1850, 6,000 miles of railway had been built, and almost every town of any size was now connected by the iron way. A major blow to the coach trade came with the opening of the London to Birmingham line in 1839, when 22 coaches a day quickly fell to four. Stagecoach services survived in remoter rural areas and as feeders to main lines, but the last regular service, from Thurso to Wick, ended in 1874 with the construction of the Highland Railway.[29] Most coaching inns were now redundant and many were ruined, especially in country areas where, if they survived at all, they generally declined into mere pubs: those in towns and cities often fared better with the increase in traffic and need for accommodation that the railways brought. But apart from some dire warnings about the effects of speed on passengers' constitutions, the moral hazards of long, dark tunnels, and the milk yields of neighbouring cows, the railway was generally greeted with paeons of praise, wonder and admiration as another triumph of British ingenuity and achievement. 'I rejoice to see it,' enthused Dr Arnold, Headmaster of Rugby School, 'and think that feudality is gone for ever', while Macaulay believed that the abridgement of distance did more for civilisation than anything except the invention of the alphabet and the printing press. Railway travel would be the great liberator, emancipator, educator and moral improver of the masses, releasing them from the bondage of isolated villages and overcrowded, insanitary towns, leading them to wider interests, useful knowledge and healthy enjoyment. The early railway age coincided with the movement for 'rational recreation', led mainly by middle-class philanthropists and taking the form of providing public parks, arboretums and playing-fields, libraries, museums and art galleries, nourishment for the body and the mind. Such places were now within the reach as well as the pockets of the mass of the people. If some chose to take their leisure at the coast or in the countryside, the fact that six million people (a third of the population of England and Wales, and the same number that visited the Millennium Dome) attended the Great Exhibition in 1851 in only 144 days seemed to indicate a latent intelligence, a thirst for knowledge and culture previously unsuspected in the working classes. And as early as 1844, only two years after Edwin Chadwick's deeply disturbing *Report on the Sanitary Condition of the Labouring Population*, the health benefits of access to fresh air were stressed by *The Railway Chronicle*:

> *In the first three days of Easter Week hundreds of thousands were transported to the green fields, the smokeless heavens and the fresh, free beauties of Nature. The railways can boast a new and nobler characteristic in their almost universal adaptation to the wants and recreations of the masses. Railways are everywhere contributing to the recreation and health of all classes.*

Travel for a shorter or longer distance was almost inevitably required for the enjoyment of the new forms of leisure and entertainment. Almost necessarily also, attendance at such places involved the provision of food and drink: eating and drinking were integral to the pursuit of pleasure, whether indoor or outdoor, near at hand or distant. According to Thomas Wright ('Journeyman Engineer'):

> *The theatre is the most popular resort of pleasure-seeking workmen [on Saturday nights] and the gallery their favourite part of the house. Two or three mates generally go together, taking with them a joint-stock bottle of drink and a suitable supply of eatables. Or sometimes, two or three married couples . . . make up a party, the women carrying a plentiful supply of provisions.*

Wright believed that these were likely to be much better than the bad beer and porter, the rotten fruit and stale biscuits which the management offered at high prices.[30] By the 1860s the popularity of the theatre was being rivalled by the music hall, which was developing out of the informal 'free-and-easy' of the public house, with its comic songs and sketches to encourage the drinking, into a specialised, commercial institution, staging professional singers, dancers, comedians, acrobats and other turns. In 1860 the Panopticon of Science and Art in Leicester Square was converted into the Alhambra music hall, seating 3,500 and providing spectacular productions, while next year The Oxford opened in Oxford Street, the first purpose-built music hall, with lavish decor and a bevy of handsome barmaids. By 1866 there were 33 large halls in London, probably 200–300 smaller ones still closely associated with pubs, and they were also developing rapidly in the midlands and the north.[31] Unlike theatres, music halls did not normally allow food and drink to be brought in as these were sold by the proprietors and made up a substantial part of the profits, up to 25 per cent in some cases. In 1867 Wright described them as 'practically large public houses': the refreshments supplied were 'generally moderately good, but at the same time more than moderately dear'.

For many working men social life was also enlivened by membership of a Friendly Society, which as well as providing insurance benefits against sickness, funeral expenses and other contingencies, sought to promote fellowship and neighbourliness in what was often the anonymity of urban life. The very names of some of the larger societies, such as 'Foresters' and 'Ancient Order of Buffaloes' romantically evoked a past before communities were fragmented by industrialisation and urbanisation. Their social programmes of regular club meetings, entertainments and outings culminated in the grand annual Feast, when members and their families were regaled with copious quantities of roast beef and ale, the traditional fare of John Bull. In Bolton, the Lancashire milltown which grew from 13,000 in 1801 to 104,000 in 1851, Peter Bailey has noted that by the latter date there were more than 200 lodges of the various societies in the town, and that 30 or 40 Feasts might take place on the same night. In 1866 a national meeting of the Friendly Society of Ironfounders was held for 1,500 delegates in a large pavilion erected in Peel Park. Organised by a local publican, the feast included 1,000 lb of beef, 500 lb of lamb, 400 lb of mutton, and 300 lb of salmon, 150 plum puddings and hundreds of fruit tarts and cheesecakes, besides appropriate quantities of liquid refreshments of all kinds: the celebrations continued until dawn with songs, recitations and dancing.[32]

Less formal eating and drinking were customary practices closely associated with work, especially in the craft industries where men served apprenticeships of five or seven years. In 1839 John Dunlop identified 300 drinking usages in 98 trades, including payments for 'footings' on apprenticeship, completing the term of training, changing jobs, marriage, birth of a child, even learning a new skill, at which times the member of the shop was expected to celebrate by treating his colleagues. Dunlop thought it 'wonderful that there are any sober men in the mechanic class at all when such perpetual drinking dominates'.[33] These rites of passage usually involved the provision of a feast, or at least some food, making it a heavy expense for a young man who had existed on the small wages of an apprentice. In 1843 Thomas Wood of Bingley, Yorkshire, ended his seven-year term with a local engineering firm: his father, a poor hand-loom weaver with ten children, had made great sacrifices for Thomas to learn a trade (ironically, powerloom machinery) at a wage which slowly rose to only 8/- a week by the end of his apprenticeship.

> In due course I was twenty-one. I was called upon by the custom of the shop to provide a supper for the men to celebrate the occasion. In consideration of my poverty they agreed to have the supper in the shop instead of a public house. The master ... cooked it in his house hard by. It was a quiet, economical affair, but I had to borrow the money to defray the expense.[34]

Two months after starting work as a journeyman at 14/- a week he was dismissed, and went on a tramp through Lancashire, eventually finding good work at Platts Bros of Oldham, one of the largest textile-machinery manufacturers in the country. Here was a different world, where the men earned 32/- a week:

> Most of them gambled freely on horse- or dog-races. Numbers brought a day's food with them, and nearly all their breakfast, which they dispatched with celerity when betting books were produced ... Flesh meat, as they called it, must be on the table twice or thrice a day. A rough and rude plenty alone satisfied them. The least pinching, such as I had seen scores of times without a murmur, and they were loud in their complainings about 'clamming' [starving].[35]

The public house played a central role in the social lives of such men. Often described as their 'club house', it was usually the venue for meetings of trade union lodges, its name sometimes reflecting the associated trade –

'Masons' Arms', 'Bricklayers' Arms' and so on. Of some 700 pubs in 135 towns used by major unions in mid-century, 100 bore trade names,[36] but all had the important function of acting as 'houses of call' for unemployed members of the craft on tramp. Craft unions had developed an elaborate system by which men out of work could tramp from one town to another in daily distances of around 15–20 miles on defined circuits, sometimes extending to 1,000 miles or more. On presenting their membership card they would be informed of any vacancies by the local secretary, provided with a supper, beer, bed and breakfast the following morning, and a small allowance to take them on to the next stage if necessary.[37] In the context of eating out, the importance of this system lies in familiarising many workers with eating in a public place, probably previously unknown to them, and in the fact that these public houses could provide meals and accommodation, serving in effect as simple workingmen's hotels.

For many workers the most popular form of recreation which combined a change of scene with eating out was the day outing on a Sunday, a 'Saint Monday', Bank Holiday or local festival. Some fortunate families could even enjoy a weekly day out in summer in a garden or allotment, situated not far from their homes which, in crowded cities, often lacked any private open space. In Birmingham, Nottingham and other industrial towns there were 'Guinea Gardens', let at 21/- a year, often by philan-thropic landowners who wished to extend the benefits of fresh air and exercise to working people who could also profit from growing vegetables and fruit as well as flowers. Many plots contained a summer-house or even a small, brick-built room with a fireplace, where families could spend the day, picnic or cook a meal. By the 1840s many industrial towns had public parks, the gifts of local manufacturers like Peel and Strutt: arboretums with specimen trees, shrubs and flower-beds, bandstands for concerts, playing-fields for sports and zoological gardens were all approved as 'rational recreation' and health-giving lungs for city-dwellers. Londoners had long had access to royal parks and public heaths, and had used the Thames to escape upstream to Hampton Court and Richmond or downstream to Greenwich where, at the surviving Fair, they would be tempted by stalls selling oysters, gingerbread, oranges, nuts and cakes. Now it was an easy matter to take a day-trip to the coast at Margate, Ramsgate or other resorts by steamers, which began services in the 1820s, even before the railways. In 1829 ten steamboats were operating the

Margate run, conveying around 85,000 passengers a year: entertainments included a band, with dancing on deck (weather permitting) and the facility of a dining-saloon providing roast and boiled joints, vegetables in season, pastries and dessert 'served up in a style both pleasing and surprising when the limited size of the kitchen is considered'.[38] Less affluent passengers brought their own food and picnicked on board or on arrival, but at a return fare of 5/- from London to Margate or Ramsgate, and 3/- to Southend in 1846, a day's outing by steamer was an affordable occasional treat. From Liverpool pleasure-boats plied to the Lancashire coastal resorts, to North Wales (second-class return to Rhyl 2/6d.), and to the Isle of Man, creating there a holiday resort for the first time.[39]

Nevertheless, traditional types of day outings which did not involve the new forms of transport survived throughout the period. Employees of a workshop or small factory arranged 'sprees' or 'blow-outs' at a local pub or could include a preliminary drive into the countryside by horse-drawn van. In 1868 Thomas Wright described a fictitious, though probably not untypical, 'Saint Monday' outing in which 'Bill Banks' and his wife joined a party of friends to visit Hampton Court. They might have journeyed by train or steamboat, but chose a horse-drawn van for privacy. On arrival:

> The owner of the van had contracted to supply us with a good dinner at half-a-crown [2/6d.] a head, and was to have it all ready at three o'clock in a nice, quiet spot near the Wilderness ... The dinner was a first-rater – beef and mutton and ham and any quantity of rolls, and lots of fruit tarts in the way of eating, and bottled ale and a small cask of porter to wash 'em down.

On return, the outing ended with a visit to the famous Alhambra music hall and an unaccustomed ride home in a four-wheeler cab:

> As we went up the street I could see the women coming to the bedroom windows at the noise of the cab, and I could twig them taking stock of Bessie and me as we were getting out.[40]

This is likely to have been a more libidinous affair than the day outings organised by some employers for their workers as tokens of paternal concern and gratitude for effort. In the tradition of 'Harvest Homes', aristocratic landowners gave annual fêtes for the local community, one of the largest being that at Petworth in June 1836, when Lord Egremont invited 3,000 women and children to roast beef and plum pudding, men being excluded on this occasion on account of some 'irregularities' the previous year.[41] In the industrial environment employer-sponsored outings took the form of a day at the coast, at a beauty spot or, when sufficiently grand, at the owner's country house and gardens. Such events could be major feats of organization, requiring the hiring of special trains and professional caterers (in 1882 a Melton Mowbray firm advertised 'Provisions for Treats', including, of course, its famous pork pies). Until 1877 Mr Colman (of the mustard firm) took his employees to Carrow Abbey, but discontinued the outing when numbers became too vast, but Mr Ecroyd, a mill-owner, overcame the organisational difficulties by appointing 39 'Captains' to maintain order when he took 1,200 staff to his mansion and grounds at Arrowthwaite, Cumberland. A special train left Nelson at 5.15 am; on arrival tea or coffee and a bun were provided, and at 1 pm a dinner of cold roast beef, meat pies, beer or ginger-beer: the afternoon was spent in sports, boating, a cricket match and dancing before departure at 6 pm.[42]

Long before that, the Great Exhibition in Hyde Park in 1851 was outstandingly the greatest single day out for the British people as a whole. The dire warnings of critics of Prince Albert's scheme about the dangers of vast crowds to public health, morality, crime and political disorder (the last Chartist demonstration in London had taken place only three years before) proved to be totally unfounded. The masses who arrived by excursion trains from all parts of the Kingdom were orderly and respectable, eager to learn and take pride in Britain's achievements and the products of her great Empire. The Exhibition was a triumph for 'rational recreation': in many ways it heralded the incorporation of the working classes into the mainstream of society, no longer the dangerous poor, but people worthy of the vote, better education and housing and more opportunities for constructive leisure. The unexpected profits from the Crystal Palace would go to the construction of magnificent, permanent exhibitions in South Kensington for the future edification and enjoyment of the people. Meanwhile, the multitude required material sustenance before, during and after a tiring day through the galleries, providing major opportunities for catering initiatives. The streets leading to Hyde Park were lined with stalls selling 'fast' foods, tea and cold drinks: in the Exhibition, strictly non-alcoholic catering was let out to contractors who supplied mountains of sandwiches, pies, sausage rolls, cakes, pastries, jellies and the novel ice-cream, sold by Thomas Masters who claimed to be the machine's inventor. Contemporary statisticians delighted to calculate the prodigious quantities of eatables and drinkables consumed during the 144 days of the Exhibition, totalling £75,000 or an average of 3d. a day for each visitor, many of whom took advantage of the cheap 'shilling day' for admission. Britain's leading soft drinks manufacturers, Schweppes, sold more than a million bottles of soda water; 400,000 lb of meat were consumed, 2 million buns, 100,000 lb of paté, 100,000 loaves, 60,000 quarts of milk and 20,000 lb of tea, coffee and chocolate.[43] Visitors who could not return home during the day crowded into any available accommodation, usually boarding houses, though the Exhibition's organisers published a list of local residents willing to let rooms. One Thomas Harrison of Pimlico advertised 'The Mechanics Home', which boasted 1,000 separate bedrooms (or cubicles), dining-rooms, a smoking room, newsroom and a daily evening concert: lodging cost 1/3d. a night, breakfast 4d. or 6d. and a substantial dinner 8d.[44]

The lodging-house was also the key residential facility for the spread of the popular seaside holiday which gathered momentum after 1850. Before that, Brighton, Weymouth, Scarborough and a few more coastal towns had developed as aristocratic resorts, still retaining the atmosphere of spas with Masters of Ceremonies to organise the 'season' of fashionable entertainments. By mid-century the arrival of railways began to bring a new, middle-class clientele of families who rented lodgings for a few weeks in the summer, husbands returning to work in the city after the weekend and accommodated in their clubs. What were to become the great proletarian pleasure resorts were yet scarcely more than villages – in June 1841 Blackpool had 590 visitors, Skegness a mere 44.[45] But by the 1850s steadier, better-paid employment, the adoption of the Saturday half-holiday in many trades, and the advent of cheap excursion trains were beginning to establish the conditions for mass leisure. As yet, the seaside holiday might only be for a day or two, rarely for longer than a week before holidays with pay began to develop at the end of the century. Brighton became accessible for a day outing from London when the railway opened in 1841, but Bournemouth (population 695 in 1851) was not easily reached until the railway was extended from Poole in 1870, and even then was too far for most day 'trippers'. For industrial Lancashire Blackpool, Morecambe and Fleetwood were now within easy reach, North Wales and the Isle of Man for rather longer visits. Blackpool, the stereotypical playground of the people, swelled from a population of 6,000 in 1871 to 47,000 by 1901.

Whether short or long, a seaside holiday before 1880 was a novel, exciting experience for many working-class people, seeing the ocean for the first time, paddling and bathing, breathing the sea air and engaging with the crowds of fellow pleasure-seekers. Food and drink were essential parts of the enjoyment, whether a picnic on the sands or a meal in one of the many eating-houses which quickly appeared in resort towns. For a day-trip food was usually brought from home, perhaps supplemented by some local speciality such as pies or shell-fish: on the beaches were itinerant sellers of fruit, ice-cream and aerated drinks, while a kettle of water could be boiled for 1d. for those who brought their own tea equipment. The fried fish-and-chip shop was an early migrant from inland towns to the coast, with the obvious advantage in some places of locally landed supplies, while Blackpool in the late 1870s had many cheap eating-places with touts shouting the bill of fare and even gripping visitors to steer them towards their establishment.[46]

For longer-staying visitors requiring overnight accommodation there were broadly two alternatives. The cheaper was the lodging-house, or apartment system, where the guest hired a bed by the night and might have the use of a dining-room for some or all meals: in this case, guests brought their own food with them or bought it in local shops to be cooked by the landlady. Sometimes she provided basics like bread, milk and potatoes and hot water for tea at a small charge, and there might be 'extras' for the use of the cruet or sauces. Economies could be made by sharing bedrooms with children or renting a cheap attic room. The superior system was the boarding-house, mainly restricted before 1914 to the upper levels of the working class and the lower middle class. Here, as well as the bedroom, either all meals or breakfast and evening meal (half-board) were supplied, and residents could expect the use of a communal sitting-room.

By 1880, therefore, the social life and habits of many of the working classes were in process of transformation. If poverty was still the lot of some third of the people, the majority were notably better off than their parents and grandparents had been, better educated, clothed and housed and, above all, better fed. The benefits of Britain's industrialisation, formerly restricted to a minority, were now beginning to be more generally shared: work was increasingly seen not merely as the means for survival, but as bringing greater opportunities for personal freedom, leisure and enjoyment. In all the recreational activities this chapter has surveyed – trade and club festivities, day outings, visits to theatres, music halls and exhibitions and, now, the emerging annual holiday – eating and drinking outside the home were integral to the pleasure of the occasion. As yet, the catering trades had scarcely recognised the potential of a mass market for simple, affordable, well-cooked food served in pleasant surroundings. The growth of large-scale commercial catering was to become an important part of the wider 'retailing revolution' of the following years.

Notes and references

1 A. L. Bowley, 'Changes in Average Wages (Nominal and Real) in the United Kingdom between 1860 and 1891', *Journal of the Statistical Society*, vol. LVIII, 1895, pp. 225, 251–2.

2 Sir Noel Curtis-Bennett, *The Food of the People, being the History of Industrial Feeding*, Faber and Faber, 1949, pp. 156–7.

3 N. P. Gilman, *A Dividend to Labour*, Boston, Mass., Houghton Mifflin Co., 1899, quoted Curtis-Bennett, op. cit., p. 188.

4 George Dodd, *The Food of London*, Longman, Brown, Green and Longmans, 1856, p. 506.

5 Tabitha Tickletooth (Charles Selby), *The Dinner Question. Or How to Dine Well and Economically* (1st edn, 1860), facsimile edn, Totnes, Devon, Prospect Books, 1999, pp. 144–5.

6 *Memoirs of a Stomach. Written by Himself, That All Who Eat May Read: Edited by a Minister of the Interior*, Chapman and Hall, 5th edn, n.d., c.1855, pp. 97–8, 110–11.

7 Selby (Tickleworth), op. cit., pp. 143–6.

8 John K. Walton, *Fish and Chips and the British Working Class 1870–1940*, Leicester, Leicester University Press, 1992, p. 23.

9 Alexis Soyer, *A Shilling Cookery for the People*, Geo. Routledge and Co., 1855, p. 114.

10 D. J. Oddy, 'The Changing Techniques and Structure of the Fishing Industry',

in T.C. Barker and John Yudkin (eds), *Fish in Britain, Trends in the Supply, Distribution and Consumption during the Last Two Centuries*, Department of Nutrition, Queen Elizabeth College, University of London, Occasional Paper No. 2, 1971, Table 1, p. 17.

11 Walton, op. cit., p. 7.

12 ibid., p. 34.

13 Robert Roberts, *The Classic Slum. Salford Life in the First Quarter of the Century*, Manchester, Manchester University Press, 1971, p. 82.

14 E. Hepple Hall, *Coffee Taverns, Cocoa Houses and Coffee Palaces. Their Rise, Progress and Prospects*, S.W. Partridge, 1878, pp. 15–18.

15 John Burnett, *Liquid Pleasures. A Social History of Drinks in Modern Britain*, Routledge, 1999, pp.84ff.

16 G. R. Porter, *The Progress of the Nation in its Various Social and Economical Relations*, John Murray, 1847, p. 686.

17 'A Cup of Coffee', *Household Words*, 1852, p. 566.

18 'London Coffee Houses, Past and Present', *Leisure Hour*, vol. XII, March 1863, p. 187.

19 Dodd, op. cit., pp. 514–15.

20 Hall, op. cit., pp. 19–24.

21 ibid., p. 95.

22 John Lowerson and John Myerscough, *Time To Spare in Victorian England*, Hassocks, Sussex, Harvester Press, 1977, p. 69.

23 Robert Thorne, 'Places of Refreshment in the Nineteenth-Century City', in Anthony D. King (ed.), *Buildings and Society. Essays on the Social Development of the Built Environment*, Routledge & Kegan Paul, 1980, pp. 232, 245.

24 Peter Bailey, *Leisure and Class in Victorian England. Rational Recreation and the Contest for Control, 1830–1885*, Methuen University Paperbacks, 1987, pp. 169–70.

25 B. Seebohm Rowntree, *Poverty. A Study of Town Life*, Macmillan and Co. (1st edn, 1901), 4th edn, 1902, pp. 76–7.

26 Charles Booth, *Life and Labour of the People in London. Final Volume: Notes and Social Influences*, Macmillan, 1902, p. 73.

27 Journeyman Engineer (Thomas Wright), *Some Habits and Customs of the Working Classes* (1st edn, 1867), facsimile edn, New York, Augustus M. Kelley, 1967, pp. 116–21.

28 Details of the growth of holidays are from J. A. R. Pimlott, *The Englishman's Holiday. A Social History*, Faber and Faber, 1947, pp. 153–5.

29 Mary Cathcart Borer, *The British Hotel Through the Ages*, Guildford and London, Lutterworth Press, 1972, p. 170.

30 Journeyman Engineer (Wright), op. cit., pp. 196–8.

31 Bailey, op. cit., pp. 155–6.

32 ibid., pp. 23, 99–100.

33 John Dunlop, *The Philosophy of Artificial and Compulsory Drinking Usages in Great Britain and Ireland*, Houlston and Stoneman, 1839.

34 *The Autobiography of Thomas Wood, 1822–1880*, privately published, 1956. Extract in John Burnett (ed.), *Useful Toil. Autobiographies of Working People from the 1820s to the 1920s*, Allen Lane, 1974, pp. 308–9.

35 ibid., pp. 310–11.

36 R. A. Leeson, *Travelling Brothers. The six centuries' road from craft fellowship to trade unionism*, George Allen & Unwin, 1979, p. 135.

37 For a recent account of the tramping system see H. R. Southall, 'The Tramping Artisan Revisits: Labour Mobility and Economic Distress in Early Victorian England', *Economic History Review*, vol. 44, May 1991, pp. 727–96.

38 G. E. Mingay, *The Transformation of Britain, 1830–1939*, Routledge & Kegan Paul, 1986, p. 69.

39 Pimlott, op.cit., p. 78.

40 Journeyman Engineer (Thomas Wright), 'Bill Banks's Day Out', in Andrew Halliday (ed.), *The Savage Club Papers for 1868*, Tinsley Bros, 1868, pp. 222–30.

41 Lowerson and Myerscough, op. cit., p. 98.

42 For further details of firms' outings see Alan Delgado, *The Annual Outing and Other Excursions*, George Allen & Unwin, 1977, pp. 30, 60–70.

43 George Dodd, *The Food of London*, 1856, op. cit., p. 519.

44 Delgado, op. cit., pp. 122–3.

45 Pimlott, op. cit., p. 77.

46 John K. Walton, *The Blackpool Landlady: A Social History*, Manchester, Manchester University Press, 1978, p. 119.

CHAPTER 3
• • • • • • • • • • • • • • • •

The growth of gastronomy

The changing social structure

In his political novel, *Sybil* (1845), Benjamin Disraeli characterised English society as Two Nations, the Rich and the Poor,

> *Between whom there is no intercourse and no sympathy, who are as ignorant of each other's habits, thoughts and feelings as if they were dwellers in different zones or inhabitants of different planets, who are formed by a different breeding, are fed by a different food [and] ordered by different manners.*

It was a powerful, though over-simple, analysis of the social structure, since what was already significant was the growth in numbers and influence of an intermediate group of people of moderate means – a 'middle class' as they were now generally recognised. Their rise did not yet imply any great threat to the wealth and prestige of the traditional upper class whose incomes were drawn from landed estates and whose titles confirmed them as the accepted arbiters of taste and fashion.[1]

In a rapidly industrialising age a social order based on land not only survived but prospered until the onset of an agricultural depression in the 1880s when mass imports of cheap grain and meat began to undermine the profits of all but the most efficient English farmers. Until then, a growing urban population with generally rising standards of living created a strong demand for home-produced foods. In the 'Golden Age' between 1850 and the mid-1870s land was both profitable and desirable for the social status it conferred, and 'nouveaux riches' industrialists and entrepreneurs were keen to acquire it: in 1873 a 'New Domesday Survey' found that four-sevenths of the land of England and Wales was owned by only 4,000 persons.[2] The good times were soon about to change. 'Land', said Lady Bracknell in *The Importance of Being Earnest* (1895) 'has ceased to be either a profit or a pleasure. It gives one position, but prevents one from keeping it up.'

What was new in Victorian social structure was the growth in the size, wealth and power of the middle classes to a point where, by the end of the Queen's reign, it was *their* values, manners and codes of behaviour that set the patterns – England had become very largely *their* England. It was not, of course, an entirely new class. For centuries past on the land there had been rent-paying farmers, and in the towns merchants, shopkeepers and professionals, but industrialisation and urbanisation now swelled the existing occupations and created new ones. No single middle class emerged, but a series of sub-classes: at the summit some industrialists and bankers as rich as aristocrats, in the centre professions required to service the needs of expanding population, commerce and government, and, at the base and most numerously, more shopkeepers, clerks, schoolteachers and lower clergy, petty businessmen and dealers of all kinds. Because there was never a precise definition of who might be admitted to the class, there can be no exact estimate of its size. Clearly, occupation and income were important determining factors, as were education, dress, speech and manners, but income alone is an uncertain guide. Some historians have taken £160 a year as a minimum, the point at which income tax became payable after its reintroduction by Peel in 1842 and a level above that of even a very skilled worker, but £160 a year would exclude elementary schoolteachers, the lower clergy, clerks and bookkeepers who, in their own estimate, and probably that of others, were acceptable members of the class. Even £60 a year would be too high to admit Bob Cratchit of *A Christmas Carol* (1843) earning only 15/- a week.[3]

While accepting the hazards of precise quantification, we may suggest the size of the middle class in 1830 as around 10–12 per cent of the population, 15 per cent in 1850 and about 18–20 per cent in 1880. This would fit reasonably well with Dudley Baxter's estimate of the distribution of

TABLE 3.1 ◆ *Distribution of personal incomes, 1867*

Class	Income per annum	No. of recipients	
Upper class	Over £5,000	7,500	} 49,500
Upper class	£1,000–£5,000	42,000	
Middle classes	£300–£1,000	150,000	
Lower middle classes	£100–£300	850,500	} 2,003,500
Lower middle classes	Under £100	1,003,000	
Skilled labour class	" "	1,123,000	
Less skilled labour class	" "	3,819,000	} 7,785,000
Agricultural workers and unskilled labour class	" "	2,843,000	

Source: R. D. Baxter, 'The National Income of the United Kingdom', paper presented at the Royal Statistical Society, 1868.

personal incomes in 1867, which he based on 10 million persons in England and Wales receiving independent incomes, i.e. not including dependents (as shown in Table 3.1).

Baxter evidently included wealthy financiers and industrialists in his 'Upper class', no longer restricted to landed proprietors, and perhaps the 'true' middle class were those with incomes over £100 a year, i.e. numbering 1,005,000. An income of £150 a year normally allowed the employment of a maid-of-all-work, but Mrs Beeton in 1861 believed that £500 a year was necessary for the full conduct of gentility, employing a cook, a housemaid and a kitchenmaid or nursemaid.[4]

The growth of the middle classes was due not only to their own high reproduction rate (an average of 5.8 children per family until the 1870s), but also to additional recruitment from the classes above and, particularly, below them. Some younger sons of the landed interest who, because of the law of primogeniture, were unlikely to inherit estates, entered the church, the law and the army, but more men achieved upward mobility from the ranks of artisans, petty tradesmen and minor public servants. Many of these had imbibed the doctrine of self-help, believing with Samuel Smiles that success in life depended on hard work, and that 'the qualities necessary to secure success are not at all extraordinary. They may be summed up in these two – common sense and perseverance.' By these, together with the exercise of thrift and sobriety, a man could achieve freedom, independence and an income sufficient for a place in respectable society. By the 1860s a second or even third generation was forgetting its humble origins and feeling secure in the characteristics of the class it had largely created – home and family-centredness, privacy, respectability and religious observance, if not actual piety. But some of the class were beginning to divorce themselves from their heredity of thrift, frugality and seriousness, and, at least at the higher levels, were adopting more of the pleasure-seeking habits of the gentry: the sons of both classes now fraternised on the playing-fields of reformed public schools, while daughters might meet at the same balls and garden parties.

A major expansion of interest in leisure and pleasure is noticeable in the third quarter of the century, reflecting the strength and stability of the economy in the 'Golden Age' of prosperity. An article on 'Modern Amusements' in *The Times* in June 1876 characterised them as 'a mingled mass of perfectly legitimate pleasures',[5] the key word being 'legitimate'. Although much middle-class leisure was centred on the home – reading, music, children's games, adult entertaining and dinner-parties – the annual holiday 'en famille' was much approved as healthful and instructive, as were outdoor games and sports, in some of which both sexes participated. Lawn tennis, croquet and ice skating boomed in the 1870s, as did athletic clubs for football, cricket, rowing and swimming, often on the initiative of public school men. This was 'rational recreation', not mere pleasure seeking for its own sake or the despised, coarse amusements of the poor: true recreation revived the body and the mind, increasingly necessary to counteract the strains of modern living.

Precisely where food, whether eaten at home or 'out', fitted into this philosophy is not quite clear. Good food was one of God's gifts to mankind, to be received thankfully and enjoyed, though not to the point of gluttony. It was recognised that men needed to be well fed for their continued labour, especially now that the working day had been lengthened by longer journeys from the suburbs, later sittings of courts and Parliament, and the extension of office hours by gas lighting. Instead of the former biscuit and glass of wine at midday, a luncheon at club or restaurant was now requisite as well as providing the opportunity for informal business meetings. The postponement of the evening dinner hour until around 7 pm, or in elite society, 8 pm, in effect created the need for the Victorian luncheon as well as afternoon tea for ladies at home.

But if food was not yet acceptable as a subject for polite conversation at the dinner-table, middle-class women were offered a plethora of advice on the construction of menus for different occasions, table service and the duties of servants in cookery books, manuals of domestic economy and ladies' magazines. Throughout the period up to 1880 the dishes recommended in these writings were almost always English and traditional, not least because most 'plain' cooks in middle-class households would have had no knowledge of anything other. In *The Epicure's Almanac, or Diary of Good Living* (1841) Benson Hill provided 365 recipes, one for each day of the year, fewer than a dozen of which were Continental dishes, while a new edition of Eliza Acton's best-selling *Modern Cookery for Private Families* (1856) devoted only 15 of its 650 pages to 'Foreign and Jewish Cookery'. It was primarily in the sphere of eating outside the home – in hotels, clubs and restaurants where professional chefs were employed – that new tastes were formed and fashionable eating became legitimised as a mark of sophistication and social status.

The rise of grand hotels

For many middle- and upper-class people in this period a main experience of eating out was in a hotel, either for an overnight stay in the course of travel or for a longer residence in a city or resort. As noted in the Introduction, there was nothing new about visits to inland spas, which offered entertainment and the prospect of improved health, but what was new in the railway age was the increased speed and ease of travel which opened up formerly exclusive, aristocratic resorts to wider clienteles whose primary object was the pursuit of pleasure. In response to demand, a new accommodation industry developed, especially in the building of hotels of greatly improved standards of size, elegance and comfort which gradually set a pattern throughout the larger English cities. The intention of such places was not only to provide good food and accommodation, but to act as settings for social display or 'territories of snobbery' for aspiring patrons who wished to see and be seen. In the grand hotels it now became common for women to escape from private suites to eat in luxuriously furnished dining-rooms, many of which were not open to non-residents, so that social contacts could be strictly controlled.

In 1815 there were at least 40 functioning spas,[6] many of which survived well into the later nineteenth century. Although some earlier spas became challenged as centres of fashion by later arrivals like Cheltenham and Leamington, lavish new hotels were built at Bath (the Grand Pump Room Hotel, 1869; the Midland, 1886), at Harrogate (the Crown, 1847; the Queen, 1851; the Prince of Wales, 1860) and other well-established resorts. In many places the coming of the railway had a direct effect on hotel construction, as for instance at Buxton, where the monster Palace Hotel with 200 bedrooms was built in 1868, four years after the town was connected by rail to Derby and Manchester. Croft Spa, on the border of Yorkshire and Durham, owed its development largely to the London North-Eastern Railway, which built a station at the village in 1851, like the small Woodhall Spa in Lincolnshire which only expanded after the railway arrived in 1855. Here, at the Victoria Hotel, which had mainly middle-class patrons, the modest charge for board and lodging was only 5/- a day, very different from the Royal Hotel, Leamington, where the tariff for meals alone was £3-3-0d. a week, and accommodation could double this.

An illuminating account of a journey from London to Harrogate in 1840, when only a few main lines had yet been built, is provided by Dr A. B. Granville, who was compiling a hydropathic tour of English spas for the information of visitors. His train left Euston at 8.40 pm, arriving at Birmingham at 1.35 am: here there was a short halt for passengers continuing to Liverpool, and a vast tea-room where up to 300 were seated at long tables 'attacking and demolishing tea, coffee, chickens, tongue, ham and stale bread – beef, pork and stuffed pies – and all in ten minutes and for two shillings'. The train then proceeded to Liverpool, where he arrived at breakfast-time to find the best hotel, the Adelphi, full of people for the races. After a hearty meal he took a train to Manchester (1¼ hours), which was as far as the line then went: he therefore boarded 'the Earl of Harewood' coach to Harrogate, a ride of 7½ hours and a total journey of a day and a night. 'The railroad from Manchester to Leeds, about to be completed, will expedite, without increasing its fatigue, the journey to that Spa.'[7]

In two large volumes Granville described the topography, climate, medical properties of the waters and the types of accommodation available in all the principal spas and coastal resorts. At Harrogate about 20,000 visitors were registered during the season (June–October): the six or seven larger hotels each accommodated around 100 guests and provided good 'tables d'hôtes' with a band playing during dinner. The typical charge for board and bedroom was 2½ guineas a week, but at the 'crack' Granby Hotel a family with two or three children and their own servants would pay not less than £20. Formerly, merchants from Manchester, Leeds and Sheffield stayed at a modest hotel or boarding-house, and would not have dreamed of entering the Granby or the Dragon – those were 'sacred places'. But now

> Pretty little gauche misses and their snuff-coloured coated papas boldly stack into both houses; cutlers and cottonspinners aspire to great assembly-rooms and gigantic banquetting-saloons, and nothing pleases the wealthy townsmen of Bradford and Huddersfield, Halifax and Rochdale but . . . the well-stuffed sofas of red damask and the 'cuisine par excellence' of those two crack hotels.[8]

One clearly paid for style, for at nearby Scarborough Granville enjoyed an excellent breakfast at the Bell Inn of new-laid eggs, cold beef, raised pies, shrimps and other potted fish, tea-cakes and muffins, where the tariff was only 6/- a day for a room and four substantial meals served at 9 a.m., midday, 4 pm and 8 pm: boarding-houses charged 4/6d., 5/6d. and 6/6d. a day.[9] At the opposite end of the scale was the Royal Hotel at Leamington, where bed and breakfast alone cost 13/6d., and with dinner 18/-.

By mid-century the popularity of inland spas was being challenged by coastal resorts, which, as well as similar social amenities like theatres, concert halls and assembly rooms, had the attractions of sea-bathing, invigorating air, promenades, piers and scenic views. In many, bottled spa and 'tonic' waters were available for those who still favoured the claims of 'the cure', but the seaside resort really represented a new phase in the development of the holiday industry and the patronage of a different social clientele. While the tradition of the spa was aristocratic, the seaside resort was more popular: while the spa

catered primarily for adults the seaside appealed to families with children and fitted easily into the home- and family-centred concerns of the
middle classes. Seaside resorts therefore developed a wider hierarchy of
accommodation than spas, ranging from cheap lodging-houses to 'all-in'
boarding-houses and newly built hotels, some of great size and elegance. At Scarborough the gigantic Grand Hotel (1867) rose 13 storeys
from the beach in neo-Gothic splendour, Bournemouth had luxury
accommodation at the Bath Hotel. Brighton, already well established
since Regency times, had the Bedford, the St. Alban's, the Royal Cliff,
the Marine and the magnificent Bristol Hotel. Resorts became socially
differentiated at an early stage, mainly on the basis of their distance
from large, urban centres and their accessibility by rail: thus, Brighton
quickly lost its aristocratic image after the first excursion train from
London arrived in 1844 (Queen Victoria ceased visiting as the crowds
had become 'very indiscreet and troublesome'), but the more remote
Torquay long retained an upper-class clientele. Here a local landowner
and Member of Parliament formed the Torquay Hotel Co. in 1863 and
built the grand Imperial Hotel in 1864 in a highly decorative Italianate
style. At what became known as 'the English Riviera' because of the
mildness of its climate, the 'season' was from October to Easter, with
many guests staying for two or three months. In 1871 the ex-Emperor
Napoleon III stayed at the Imperial and congratulated the French chef
who had formerly worked at the Palace of the Tuileries: the new chef
had evidently arrived at a point of departure from the traditional
English menu (see menu from Imperial Hotel below) or may well have
been responsible for the change.[10] At the other end of the social scale,
Blackpool had boarding-houses and hotels 'suited to every class of persons' at from 3/- to 5/- a day for full board. Granville stayed at Nixon's
Hotel, where 50–60 guests, including children, sat down to dinner in
the banqueting room at a long table 'groaning under a double line of tin-
capped dishes': he believed that 'the highest in rank' there were an iron-
founder from Bradford and a retired Liverpool wine merchant, and the
way the guests fell upon the joints of meat and the chickens was
'appalling'.[11] He was referring to their table manners rather than the
quality of the offerings, but complaints in mid-century about the food
and service in seaside resorts were legion, and not confined to the
cheaper establishments. Of an expensive hotel in Ryde in 1843 Jane

THE IMPERIAL HOTEL, TORQUAY
* * *
Monday 25 March 1867
* * *
Table d'Hote.
* * *
BILL OF FARE
* * *

SOUPS
Mulligatawny
Shrimp
Oyster
* * *

FISH
Turbot & Lobster Sauce
Salmon
Fried Skate
Gurnet
* * *

ENTREES
Rissoles de Homard
Riz de Veau à l'Italienne
Poulet à la Meringo
Cotelette de Agneau aux Petit Pois
* * *

JOINTS
Saddle Mutton
Braised Beef a la Jardinere
Fore Quarter Lamb
Boiled Fowls
Tongue
Ducks
* * *

ENTREMETS
Poudin de Cabinet
Poudin St. Clair
Junket
Gellée au Pistache
Ices
* * *

DESSERT

Carlyle wrote that 'the cream was blue milk, the butter tasted of straw', and the 'cold fowl' was a lukewarm one and 'as tough as leather',[12] while at a Brighton hotel that year Macaulay commented that 'It was a dinner on yesterday's pease-soup and the day before yesterday's cutlets.'

In London around 1830 there was the inheritance of Regency hotels, usually adapted from terraces of fashionable town houses; many were 'private' in the sense of providing only suites and no public dining-rooms, meals being served in the guests' sitting-rooms. Mivart's Hotel in Vere Street was one of the most exclusive, containing an 'appartement des Princes' used by visiting royalty like the Grand Duke of Russia, later Czar Alexander II, when attending Queen Victoria's coronation in 1837. The reputation of these places depended on their proprietors, several of whom were former French chefs: at the Clarendon, M. Jacquier, one-time chef to Louis XVIII, prepared genuine French dinners costing up to £3 or £4, but other renowned hotels such as Fenton's, Stephens's, Grillion's, Limmer's, Clunn's and Ibbotson's were somewhat more moderate. French cuisine was now fashionable at many of these leading hotels, for example at the Pulteney where Escudier presided, and at the St. James's, run by Francatelli, formerly chef to Queen Victoria. Hotels frequently changed their names and proprietors – Osborne's Hotel became the Adelphi, Mivart's was bought by Claridges, former upper servants, in the 1850s, Miller's became the Cavendish in 1868, but before then a clutch of new hotels had appeared: Brown's Hotel in Vere Street was established in 1837 by a former gentleman's servant and his wife, a lady's maid to Lady Byron, Morley's Hotel followed in the 1850s and the Langham in 1865.[13]

Nevertheless, there appears to have been a shortage of good accommo-dation in London, especially at times of heavy demand such as the Great Exhibition in 1851. For the opening on 1 May, carriages had drawn up in Berkeley Square overnight, where the ladies and gentlemen slept in them: on the pavement at 6.30 am powdered footmen brewed tea and fried eggs and bacon.[14] It also seems that some old-established hotels traded on their former reputation. When Lady Paget stayed for the Princess Royal's wedding in 1858 at Fenton's, regarded as one of the fore-most establishments, she was given a small, dark room, no fire because the chimney smoked, and no table (she had to write letters on her knee): 'The dirt, the darkness of these rooms was most repulsive.'[15]

Improvement was at hand. Much of the best accommodation in Victorian cities was in the new, purpose-built railway companies' hotels situated at termini and main stations. The first was opened by the London and Birmingham Co. at Euston in 1839; built in two parts, it reflected the social division of travellers on the railway itself – a first-class section, managed by a former steward of the Athenaeum Club, and a second-class Victoria Hotel described as a 'dormitory and coffee-room'. Standards soon rose as companies vied with each other to advertise their visible assets. The Great Western Hotel at Paddington opened in 1854, the London Bridge Terminus Hotel 1862 (with a separate ladies' coffee-room) and the most magnificent, the Midland Grand Hotel at St. Pancras, 1873, designed in neo-Gothic splendour by George Gilbert Scott. Its first manager, Etzensberger, was lured from the Victoria Hotel, Venice, and no expense was spared on the decoration of the interior, the furniture by Gillows and the silver-plate by Elkington. Described as 'the most sumptuous and best-conducted hotel in the Empire', it contained many novel features such as electric bells, hydraulic lifts, dust-chutes and telephones to listen in to theatre and concert performances. Despite its magnificence, the hotel was able to offer a good 'table d'hôte' dinner for 5/-, presumably on the principle of economies of scale. The railway hotels, and company-financed hotels like the Westminster Palace (1858) and the Langham (1865) represented a new phase of scale and standards, with up to 700 bedrooms in some. Their rise reflected the new mobility of the population, the growth of middle-class travel and incomes, the expansion of overseas trade and visitors from Europe and America, and the attractions of London and provincial capitals for both domestic and foreign tourists – theatres, concerts, museums and art galleries as well as general sight-seeing.

It also seems probable that hotel developments in the United States, and in Continental capitals like Paris and Vienna, had significant, if belated, influence in England, which until the 1860s and 1870s had little to compare with the Tremont, opened in Boston, Massachusetts, in 1829, the Astor in New York (1836) or the St. Nicholas (1852) also in New York and the first to cost a million dollars. These were to be genuine 'Palaces of the People', appropriate for a democratic society which embraced modernity, and where status was measured by wealth and success rather than title. At the Tremont, where both Dickens and Thackeray stayed, there were public bars and a dining-room to seat 200, the innovation of printed menu cards, and room service of meals at the guest's choice: it claimed to be the first American hotel to have a French chef and French cuisine, a trend soon followed by other first-class American hotels. The St. Nicholas went further in an elegant design in marble and an interior with huge crystal chandeliers and much gold-leaf decoration, while an innovation in the bedrooms was spring mattresses.[16]

Why the wealthiest country in the world had lagged behind others in the provision of luxury hotels is difficult to explain. Part of the answer was probably the preference of the nobility for smaller, 'private' hotels which mirrored the characteristics of their domestic establishments: part was due to the rise of gentlemen's clubs which satisfied their need for exclusive eating-places at a time when English ladies did not normally dine in public. English entrepreneurs, perhaps more cautious than American, hesitated to invest in ambitious hotel schemes, at least until after the Limited Liability Acts of 1855–62 gave protection against claims on shareholders' estates. At all events there was a widespread opinion in mid-century that England was poorly supplied: as a *Times* leader in 1855 complained, everyone knew of Mivart's, the Clarendon and two or three more first-class places, 'but whose purse is equal to the expenditure?'; what was needed was moderately priced accommodation and good meals as on the Continent, where a 'table d'hôte' dinner superior to our sole, steak and cheese can be had at half the price. The railway hotels are good, but they are not in the heart of London, and so inconvenient for tourists.[17] Next year Albert Smith developed the theme in *The English Hotel Nuisance.* He argued that England still suffered from her inheritance of old coaching inns, shabby, dirty and decaying since the railways had left the roads deserted. Here the inevitable menu was 'Chop sir, steak, braised fowl?': bedrooms were filled with huge, four-poster beds with dirty hangings: one was expected to pay for wax candles, whether used or not, and to tip decrepit waiters, porters and chambermaids 'What you will, sir'. 'It was a blessed thing when the stage coaches were run off the roads by the winged engine of the rail, and therefore I think that the enterprising proprietor who heads his advertisement in *Bradshaw* "The Olden Time Revived" mistakes the public taste and offers anything but an attraction.'[18] His other main complaint was about over-charging in hotels which considered themselves first-class. In one such in Scarborough the author and his brother each ordered a plate of sandwiches and a bottle of Pale Ale.

> I was charged for this, and I paid, seven shillings (it was put down in the bill as two luncheons at three shillings each and the Bass at its usual price). The sandwich was not near so excellent as that I get with a glass of ale for fourpence in London.[19]

On the other hand, some looked back to the old coaching inns with nostalgia, comparing their warmth and friendliness with the impersonality of the new 'Magnifico' hotels. This was, characteristically, the line taken in *All the Year Round*, the journal 'conducted by Charles Dickens'.

> Today we have a warmer welcome at the first shop we enter to buy a pair of gloves than at the Grand Hotel of our time ... A wedding [reception] at an hotel – fashionable or otherwise – is rather a dismal business. There is a fatal air of insincerity over the banquet which has a 'baked-meats' air. The waiters eye the 'happy pair' hungrily ... they never lose sight of the happy man for a second, fearful lest he should be plotting to defraud them of expected 'backsheesh'. In these huge edifices of 'unpleasant-looking yellow brick, as if built of monster blocks of Stilton', the lifts frequently break down from fatigue, and 'there is no more dismal sight than to see strong men in the prime of life struggling and gasping up the eighteen or twenty flights of stairs'.[20]

A sign of the attractions of the capital as a tourist centre was the publication of Baedeker's *Handbook for Travellers to London and its Environs*, the first edition in 1877 and a fuller version two years later. By then, accommodation was more plentiful and varied, with railway hotels increased to include the Great Northern at King's Cross and the Charing Cross Hotel, and company-owned hotels like the Langham, the Alexandra, the Buckingham Palace and the Westminster Palace. The Guide acknowledged Claridge's as the first hotel in London, patronised by royalty and nobility, and very expensive, but listed around a hundred other good, more moderately priced establishments: at those in the West End, rooms cost from 3/6d. to 10/- a night, breakfast 3/- to 4/- and dinner 5/- to 10/- , but in cheaper areas one could find an acceptable 'pension' at 6/- a day. The listing of a number of hotels 'conducted in the

Continental fashion' was a significant sign of the times – De Keyser's Royal Hotel ('table d'hôte' 4/-), the Sablonnière, the Hotel de Paris, Bertolini's, the Solferino and others – suggesting the growing number of foreign visitors and, perhaps, a changing taste of English guests for Continental cuisine. Baedeker noted that the Leicester Square area was much frequented by French visitors, but warned that here there were 'several houses of doubtful reputation', and one should be careful not to seek accommodation without recommendation.[21]

The diffusion of French cuisine

'I regard the discovery of a dish as a far more interesting event than the discovery of a star, for we have always stars enough, but we can never have too many dishes'. Abraham Hayward in 1852 was quoting the French gourmet, Henrion de Pensey, with evident approval.[22] Hayward was writing at a time when food was becoming elevated from the mundane to the aesthetic, when it was becoming polite to discuss gastronomy as a fine art and when a group of celebrity chefs had appeared in England with the aim of educating national taste and raising the appreciation of fine food. The origins and personalities of this cultural change were, of course, French. It was in France during the Napoleonic and Restoration period after 1815 that 'haute' or 'Grande cuisine' reached its heights of innovation and luxury in extravagant royal and noble courts, especially under the influence of the chef Carême and his disciples. But it is not immediately clear why an alien gastronomy, the product of a traditional enemy with whom England had recently fought a long and costly war, should have become adopted as the exemplar of ultimate fashion. Partly it was simply a desire for the new and different, a change from the heavy, meat-based English diet which however excellent the quality might be, tended towards repetitious monotony. Many new and imaginative dishes and sauces had already originated in Parisian restaurants,[23] and, as previously noticed, many leading French chefs had emigrated to England during the Revolution to adorn and reform the kitchens of the nobility. After the restoration of the monarchy in 1815, Paris again became a mecca for tourists, especially English and German, so furthering the diffusion of a different culinary culture. But contemporary opinion, not only in France, believed that by the 1830s and 1840s French hegemony in gastronomy was in decline, and that the crown had now passed to England. Hayward offered an economic determinist theory for this:

> It is allowed by competent judges that a first-rate dinner in England is out of all comparison better than a dinner of the same class in any other country; for we get the best cooks, as we get the best singers and dancers, by bidding higher for them.[24]

This opinion that leadership in gastronomy went with leadership in national wealth and prestige was echoed by the well-known gourmet, Count d'Orsay, in 1852 who believed that standards in Parisian restaurants had badly fallen off:

> The culinary art ... has emigrated to England and has no wish to return. We do not absolutely die of hunger here, and that is all that can be said. [25]

The invention and diffusion of 'haute cuisine' is particularly associated with four celebrated chefs, Carême, Ude, Soyer and Francatelli. Their influence was greater than that of other, perhaps equally talented practitioners, because their abilities were not hidden in private households: three of them worked at some time in public places, notably gentlemen's clubs and hotels, and all four published cookery books which became classics in their time. Antonin Carême (1784–1833) is described by Stephen Mennell as 'the chef who more than any other ... codified French cuisine for most of the nineteenth century'.[26] Beginning as a *pâtissier*, he worked only briefly in England for the Prince Regent, but as a peripatetic chef to Czar Nicholas I, Baron Rothschild and the Austrian court, creating dishes of the most costly ingredients and elaborate design. His characteristic was presentation, often in architectural forms with temples, pillars and statuary moulded from spun sugar, marzipan and lard and usually inedible, but his meats and fish were of superb quality, flavoured and garnished with some of the hundred and more sauces which he originated. In a short life, he published five books, two on pâtisserie and three on the art of French cuisine. His ascendancy was overlapped by that of Louis Eustache Ude, who after a varied career in France, including a short spell on the stage, became chef to Mme. Letitia Bonaparte. After migrating to England he worked as maître d'hôtel to the Duke of York, for twenty years as chef to the Earl of Sefton, and then at the aristocratic gaming club in St. James's, Crockford's. Here, at the enormous salary of £1,200 a year, he produced the finest dinners and late suppers for many of the greatest in the land, derived from his book *The French Chef* (1813). Ude was much concerned to raise the status of the chef in England from that of an upper servant to what he believed it should be – an artist comparable to the genius of a Raphael or a Rubens.[27]

In 1841 a leader in *The Globe* wrote, 'The impression grows on us that the man of the age is neither Sir Robert Peel [the Prime Minister] nor Lord John Russell [the leader of the Opposition] . . . but Alexis Soyer.'[28]

Soyer (1809–58) was the best-known chef in England in mid-century, though perhaps not the best: his contemporary, Hayward, thought that 'he is a very clever man, of inventive genius and inexhaustable resource, but his execution is hardly on a par with his conception, and he is most likely to earn his immortality by his soup-kitchen [for the poor] than by his soup'.[29] In fact, his reputation derived first from his period as chef to the Reform Club from 1837, and then more widely, from his famine relief works in Ireland (1847) and his reforms of army and hospital catering in the Crimean War (1855). Like Carême, whose style of cooking he followed, he also published five books, one on the history of gastronomy, the others cookery books aimed at different social levels. A brilliant kitchen designer and administrator, he could produce generally excellent, moderately priced daily meals at the Reform but, for a special occasion, a dinner costing a hundred guineas or a vast banquet like one for the Prince Consort and all the mayors in England. From becoming leading chef in a famous Paris restaurant at the age of 17, he migrated to England during the Revolution of 1830 and worked for several private employers before being appointed 'chef de cuisine' at the recently-formed Reform Club, with authority to plan the kitchens in collaboration with the architect, Charles Barry. When completed in 1841 they were regarded as the most advanced in England, using many of Soyer's own inventions such as a huge range, gas and steam cookers, water heaters, hotplates, mixers and other labour-saving devices: on most days in the week he conducted parties of admiring members and guests through the wonders of modern gastronomic technology. Soyer delighted in showmanship, in art (his wife was a painter), music, the theatre and ballet, and, like Ude, he wished to raise the status of the chef to that of an artist and scientist. With his health impaired after his 'Culinary Campaign' in the Crimea, he never recovered from a fall when his horse threw him in

FIGURE 3.1 ◆ *The kitchens at the Reform Club, c. 1840. Alexis Soyer was appointed chef de cuisine in 1837 and collaborated with the architect of the new clubhouse, Charles Barry, to design the most technologically advanced kitchens of the time; innovations included gas and steam cookers, heated plate cupboards and ice drawers.*

Source: Mary Evans Picture Library.

Kensington (he was on the way to a picnic at Virginia Water), and he died two years later. He had achieved a fame beyond that of other chefs of his time, and far beyond the portals of the Reform Club – for his work with the poor in Ireland and London, his contributions to military and hospital diets, and for his celebrated 'Soyer's Sauce', marketed by his friend Thomas Blackwell (of Crosse and Blackwell). Florence Nightingale wrote of his death as

> *A great disaster. Others have studied cooking for the purposes of gourmandising, some for show, but none but he for the purpose of cooking large quantities of food in the most nutritious manner for great numbers of men. He has no successor.*[30]

He had, however, a distinguished contemporary. Charles Elmé Francatelli was of Italian origin, but born in London and trained in Paris under Carême. After working for several peers, he followed Ude at Crockford's, then, for two years, became head chef to Queen Victoria until dismissed for striking a kitchenmaid. After succeeding Soyer at the Reform Club, he went to the fashionable St. James's Hotel (later, the Berkeley). Ude, Soyer and Francatelli therefore all moved in intersecting circles of noble households and leading London clubs, and all extended their reputations and influence by their writings, but Soyer and Francatelli also vied with each other in demonstrating that their skills and concerns were not restricted to the palates of the wealthy but applicable to all levels of society. Francatelli's *The Modern Cook* (1846) was closely followed by Soyer's *The Modern Housewife* (1849), both books aimed mainly at a middle-class readership, while Francatelli's *Plain Cookery Book for the Working Classes* (1852) was paralleled by Soyer's *Shilling Cookery for the People* (1854). Gastronomy had gained a social conscience.

Gentlemen's clubs

Clubs composed of like-minded men had begun in Elizabethan times, but developed strongly in the eighteenth century. Several originated in coffee-houses (White's, the Cocoa Tree), others in taverns (the Kit-Kat, the Dilletanti): their founders were often aristocrats who met to further the interests of a political party, literature or science, but some were primarily gaming clubs (Brookes's, Boodle's) and some merely social. The consumption of good food and wine was always an important element, and some clubs existed for no other purpose – the Sublime Society of Beefsteaks (1732–1869) met merely to eat steaks of great size and the finest quality. In *Clubs and Club Life in London* John Timbs listed 42 formed before the nineteenth century, probably a serious under-estimate.[31] A new and different type of club began to appear towards the end of the French Wars, and multiplied especially in the 1820s and 1830s, larger in membership, generally more serious in purpose, and occupying premises designed by leading architects. These included the Travellers (1812), the United Service (1816), the Athenaeum (1824), the Oriental (1824), the University (1824), Crockford's (1827), the Garrick (1831) and the Reform (1832), besides others totalling around 30 by 1850. George Dodd in 1856 suggested that some, like the Guards and the United Service, were originated by returning army officers who, accustomed to mess life, required accommodation in London at an affordable price,[32] but the reasons for the growth of the non-military clubs are different. By the early nineteenth century many of the wealthy were moving out of central London to the fashionable new western suburbs but still needed a base in the West End. The club provided this semi-private environment by admitting only approved applicants for membership and restricting non-member guests to 'strangers' rooms'.[33] With the expansion of travel there were now also more country members who had no town house but needed to visit London occasionally and stay in a setting less public than an inn or most hotels: some clubs, like the Reform, provided lodging-rooms, and most had facilities such as libraries, smoking-rooms, billiard-rooms and suites for private parties as well, of course, as dining-rooms (usually styled 'coffee-rooms'). Clubs were especially useful for single, upper middle-class men who, by convention and economic necessity, often delayed marriage until around the age of 30: here, a bachelor could operate in the right social sphere without the upkeep of an expensive establishment.

Initially, members were drawn mainly from the nobility, the Houses of Parliament, senior professionals such as lawyers and clergy, and colonial and overseas government officials, but not men of business or industry until towards the end of this period. The ambience of the club was that of a great country house or town mansion, usually with a grand reception hall and staircase, elegantly furnished rooms with columns, plasterwork, marble and paintings: the Reform, by Sir Charles Barry, was modelled on the Farnese Palace in Rome, the Athenaeum was designed by Decimus Burton and the Carlton by Robert Smirke. For an entrance fee of around six guineas, members could experience a version of life at the highest social level, conveniently situated, available at almost all times, a magnificent home without domestic responsibilities. But clubs also fitted the new habits and tenor of life of the nineteenth century. Thomas Walker wrote in 1835:

> *Clubs, as far as my observation goes, are favourable to economy of time. There is a fixed place to go to; everything is served with comparative expedition, and it is not customary … to remain long at table. They are favourable to temperance. It seems that when people can freely please themselves, and when they have an opportunity of living simply, excess is seldom committed.*[34]

Here, in contrast to former long drinking sessions, gambling and horse-play, were incipient Victorian values of economy, sobriety and respectability, enjoined by an unwritten but well-understood code of behaviour.

To justify his claims, Walker noted that during 1832 the Athenaeum served 17,322 dinners to its 1,200 members at an average cost of 2/9¾d., and the average consumption of wine was only half a pint. At the Junior United Service Club in 1839 29,527 dinners were served at an average of 2/3d. exclusive of wine. The ordinary 'table d'hôte' meals were not extravagant, and little influenced by 'haute cuisine', even during Soyer's time at the Reform: they were essentially English, chop-house style, but with the meat, game and fish usually of excellent quality. Thackeray believed that the best chops in the world were to be had at the Reform, but it seems that standards occasionally slipped even here, for the Coffee Room Complaints Book includes comments such as 'beef tough', 'pota-toes cold', 'omelette bad' and 'the fish very indifferent'.[35] There was a clear distinction between the ordinary, daily meals for members and the huge banquets arranged for visiting celebrities which Soyer produced for special occasions.

The modest meal prices quoted above must also have been regularly exceeded. In 1856 Nathaniel Hawthorne and a friend enjoyed dinner at the Reform consisting of mulligatawny soup, turbot, lambs' feet, cutlets, a ptarmigan and cheese, accompanied by three bottles of wine: he noticed that the waiters still wore plush breeches and white silk stockings.[36] In *Clubland Cooking* Robin McDouall, former Secretary of the Travellers Club, provides a list of what were (and are often still) favourite club dishes. For soups – lobster bisque, hare soup, crab, asparagus, artichoke and Scotch broth; for patés – sardine, kipper, cod's roe, potted grouse, potted shrimps; fish – sole in many versions, salmon, turbot, trout, whitebait, lobster, kedgeree; pies – grouse and steak, steak and kidney, 'Brookes's Pie' (turkey, beef, veal, lamb and chicken); meat – fillet of beef Wellington, beef olives, escalopes de veau, lamb cutlets champillon, *poulet sauté Marengo*; game – snipe, plover, grouse (Scottish and Yorkshire members would send down hampers); puddings – apple, treacle, Queen's, summer, roly-poly, crème brulée (at the Saville); savouries ('By tradition, clubs specialize in savouries ... If one is drinking a good claret, savouries go better with it') – Welsh rarebit, Angels on Horseback (oysters wrapped in bacon), Devils on Horseback (prunes in bacon), Scotch woodcock, *Beignets Soufflés* (eggs and Gruyère), Canapés Windsor (ham and mushroom on toast). McDouall remarks on the preference of club members for grilled dishes, as 'Grilling is thought to be manly'. An old servant at the Travellers remembered that before 1914 the four-course set dinner, which always had to include game when in season, cost 3/6d. with no charge for draught beer. For luncheon a hot joint and vegetables could be had for 1/6d., with another 6d. for a pudding, but one member invariably ate a whole raspberry tart for the same price.[37]

From chop-houses to restaurants

The 30 or so London clubs of 1850 each had a membership of 500–1,500, and, allowing for some men who belonged to two or three, a combined membership of around 15,000–20,000. They therefore made a substantial contribution to the dining habits of the comfortable classes, but for men who were not eligible for membership, and for those who preferred occasionally to eat elsewhere, there was a hierarchy of establishments in which a gentleman could eat respectably – chop-houses, dining-rooms, coffee-houses, and inns and taverns surviving from earlier times. Until the 1860s or 1870s, the characteristics and menus of these places were largely traditional and unchanging, although at a point of transition towards new forms. George R. Sims, who knew the social scene well, observed:

> The 'eighties saw a very different London from the London of the
> 'seventies ... the popular restaurant as we understand it today had not
> arrived, and the separate table in public eating establishments was as
> unusual as today it is general. In the popular, and in the fashionable
> dining-rooms and taverns ... you sat in small compartments called
> 'boxes', and wooden partitions divided one set of lunchers or diners
> from their neighbours, and ladies were rarely of the party.[38]

By 1880 new types of eating-places were appearing, providing a different, more elegant environment attractive to both sexes and, above all, offering a different cuisine, strongly influenced by Continental styles. Eating out by men and women in these new restaurants would soon become a fashionable leisure activity, all the more so because it carried somewhat daring, exotic associations: unlike earlier, male-dominated eating habits, the new restaurants elevated food into glamour and placed its consumers on to a public stage.

Meanwhile, tavern meals continued to find favour among men who liked plentiful servings of good meat, fish and game undisguised by fancy sauces. Dickens's works abound in such places, based on his own favourite haunts like the Cock Tavern, the Trafalgar and the Albion, where the cooking was good enough for Soyer to enjoy after a day in the kitchens of the Reform Club. The Trafalgar was the venue for the annual whitebait dinners at the end of the Parliamentary session in July, and for a dinner given to Dickens in 1844 when guests included Landseer, Cruikshank and other leading artists and authors. Dickens also enjoyed oyster bars, the famous fish taverns at Greenwich, and the celebrated turtle house, Lovegrove's, at Blackwall. The Albion was popular for after-theatre suppers, and was said to be busiest at midnight, but its menu does not sound at all original – oysters, stewed tripe, broiled kidneys, beef bones (? marrow bones), chicken, chops, steak and Welsh rarebit. Soyer suggested extending the offering by 80 dishes.[39] These old-fashioned inns, like the Fleece in Threadneedle Street, where it was not unusual for a thousand chops and steaks to be consumed in a day,[40] continued to thrive on a strong demand, as did some out-of-town inns like the Star and

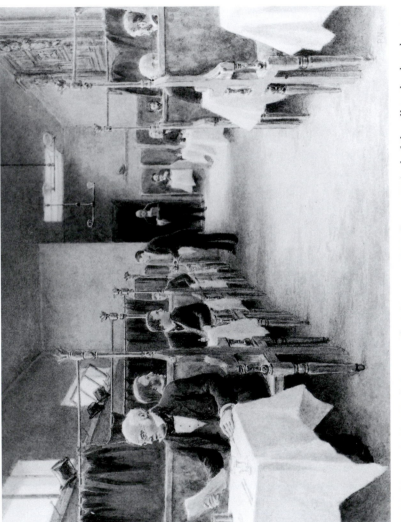

FIGURE 3.2 ◆ *The Cock Tavern, Fleet Street, c. 1880. It was typical of the all-male chop-house, with curtained compartments providing a degree of privacy for City businessmen. The tavern was demolished in 1882.*

Source: © Museum of London.

Garter at Richmond, where Dickens and his wife often went for anniversary celebrations. For him, the romantic traditionalist, good fish, flesh and fowl needed no 'made-up' entrées and little in the way of vegetables, fruit or desserts. This was the sort of dinner Dickens gave to 34 friends in January 1837 at the George and Vulture to celebrate the success of *Pickwick Papers*, where the bill, including wines and cigars, was £11[41] (6/6d. a head). Long after that, critics of the new cuisines remembered, or thought they remembered, the old coaching-inn breakfast where 'William', the grey-headed waiter, took a fatherly pride in offering home-made 'sassingers', new-laid eggs, slices from the mammoth York ham and local heather honey. Edward Spencer echoed the opinions of many nostalgic John Bulls about the 'grease-and-garlic shops', where every dish was 'à la' something and its natural flavour destroyed.

> *It is due to a shameful lack of enterprise on the part of English caterers that a well-cooked English dinner is becoming more difficult to procure, year after year. There are three purely British [sic] dishes which are always 'hoff' [the menu] ... Irish stew, liver and bacon and tripe and onions. Yet hardly a week passes without a new 'diner Parisien' making its appearance, while the cheap-and-nasty 'table d'hôte', with its six or seven courses and its Spanish claret, has simply throttled the Roast Beef of Old England.*[42]

That was written in 1897, and of course it was not true that roast beef had been 'throttled', either then or since. Traditionally cooked meat, usually at large, open grills, was available throughout this period in London's 250 or so chop-houses, some of which, like Dolly's in Paternoster Row, were long established and highly regarded. Stone's, which was begun by a wine and brandy merchant in Panton Street in 1770, reopened as a Coffee House in 1812 and later as Stone's Chop House: close to theatreland, it was patronised almost like a club by actors, authors and sporting men, and according to George Augustus Sala, who was once involved in a fight there, was 'a vicious cesspool'.[43] The description of a 'chop-house' seems to have been loosely used, and could apply to houses which specialised in turtle, both as soup and flesh, and to fish restaurants like Simpson's in Billingsgate, whose 'fish dinners have acquired celebrity on account of the reasonableness of the charge and the unquestioned excellence of the fish'.[44] Selby in 1860 thought that this was, perhaps, the cheapest good

THE
WELLINGTON SET DINNERS,

Served from 3 to 9 o'clock.

Three Shillings each.

Potages.

A l'Indienne, Consommé au Naturel.

Poisson.

White-bait.

Entree.

Côtelettes de Veau, Sauce Tomate.

Rots.

Au Choix.

Entremet.

Pouding à la D'Orsay.

Legumes.

Choux, Pommes de terre.

Served from 4 to 9 o'clock.

Five Shillings each.

WITH DESSERT AND ATTENDANCE.

Potages.

A la Mussarde, Consommé au Tapioka.

Poisson.

Soles à la Maître d'Hôtel.

Entrees.

Timballes de Macaroni à la Milanais, Cannetons aux Petits Pois.

Rots.

Au Choix.

Entremet.

Brioches au Madère.

Legumes.

Flageolets, Pommes de terre, Sautées.

Dessert.

Pommes, Oranges, Noix.

PETITS FOURS ASSORTIS.

Served from 6 to 9 o'clock.

Eight Shillings each.

WITH DESSERT AND ATTENDANCE.

Potages.

A la Crécy, Consommé au Sagou.

Poisson.

Saumon à l'Italienne, White-bait.

Entrees.

Filets de Bœuf, Marinés, Sauce Poivrade, Chaud-froid de Poulets à la Gelée.

Rots.

Oisons.

Hors-d'œuvre.

Mayonnaise de Homard.

Entremets.

Savarins aux Amandes, Gelée aux Fraises nouvelles.

Legumes.

Petits Pois, Pommes de terre à la Reine.

Dessert.

Pommes, Oranges, Noix, &c.

———

PETITS FOUR ASSORTIS.

meal to be had in London, since for 1/6d. one had the choice of three or four kinds of the freshest fish, or three or four joints, together with bread, cheese and celery: there was no requirement to drink, but Bass's Pale Ale, Guinness's Stout, and pineapple punch were available.[45] Better known now was Simpson's in the Strand, which grew out of a Grand Cigar Divan of 1828 and reopened in 1848 using the new title of 'Restoratum'. Though the food was not very different from that of other good chop-houses, the premises were distinguished by their decor and luxury – light and airy rooms, mirrors and reliefs set in gilt frames, silver-plated dishes and cutlery rather than pewter, and separate tables as well as some older box compartments: upstairs was a separate ladies' dining-room (i.e. where ladies might be entertained by men), a transitional stage before mixed dining was fully accepted. At this period Simpson's offered joints (sirloins of beef or saddles of lamb), two vegetables, bread, butter, cheese and celery for 2/-, while another 1/- bought soup and fish (turbot, salmon, etc.). 'This is, par excellence, the Dinner of the Day. The fare is purely

English'.[46] Similar improved establishments appeared in the 1850s, such as Sawyer's in Fleet Street, where compartments were now abandoned: their celebrated 'London Dinner' at 2/6d. gave a choice of two soups, two fish, two entrées, joints, sweets, cheese and salad. The expected crowds of visitors to London in 1851 and subsequently stimulated a considerable expansion in dining facilities, including the Wellington in Piccadilly, described as 'a dining-house for the millions, combining comfort, luxury and elegance with economy'. The Wellington (see menu reproduced above) had the novel feature of two independent kitchens, one English, the other French: as well as 'à la carte' dishes, it offered three set dinners at 3/- (English), 5/- and 8/- (French).[47]

Not all men wanted, or had time for, a substantial meal at midday, and the older pattern of a mere snack at this time, followed by an early dinner at any time from around 4 pm onwards, still survived in some business houses. Oyster bars and shellfish shops provided convenient 'fast' foods, as did sandwich bars for consumption on or off the premises. Garraway's Coffee House, dating back to the mid-seventeenth century, the Jamaica Coffee House, Evett's Ham Shop and others did a large trade in ready-cut sandwiches, but Garraway's seems to have been the favourite. Open from 10 am to 9pm, it was busiest between 11 am and midday, when 'large trays of ham, beef and tongue sandwiches, cut in a most substantial manner, are ranged on the bar': wine, punch, sherry, Pale Ale and stout were the usual drinks.[48] Coffee-houses survived particularly in the City as places for commercial intelligence and business dealings – Lloyd's, the North and South American Coffee-House, the Jerusalem (Near and Far Eastern), the Jamaica, the Baltic and so on. These had separate subscription rooms (three or four guineas a year) for representatives of banks, shippers, agents, newspaper correspondents and stockbrokers, and these became very lively at times of heavy speculation, 'when champagne and anchovy toast are the orders of the day'.

For something more substantial than a snack there were many 'Dining Rooms', superior to cheap 'ordinaries' but moderate in price and perfectly respectable: their prices being 1/3d. or 1/6d. for meat, vegetables and a pudding, their main clients were middle-ranking professionals and clerks rather than senior partners of firms. They were usually open between 12 and 6 pm and depended on a large turnover to keep prices low. As a young journalist George Sims often had lunch at these 'slap-bangs' (from a popular song of the period), his favourites being 'His Lordship's Larder' in Cheapside, Lake and Turners, and Rudkin's 'Salutation' in Newgate.[49] The author of an article on *London Eating Houses* in 1837 believed that there were already around 1,500 such places, divided in quality between a 'democracy' and an 'aristocracy', and that with an average of 60 customers a day (though at the Excise Dining Rooms in Bishopsgate the estimate was 800–900) some 100,000 meals were served daily. What impresses the visitor is the speed and efficiency with which orders are taken and delivered by the male and female waiters, who, in the larger establishments, can earn 30/- to 40/- a week, and have to pay a premium for the privilege of working there and earning tips. There is an atmosphere of order and quietness despite the large numbers, a few friends speaking in whispers in the box compartments, or reading the newspapers which are provided. Some houses have specialities, and a stranger needs an expert guide to discover them, but the usual range covers beef, mutton, pork, veal, duck and turkey, besides soup, fish and puddings. The most expensive dish is mock-turtle soup at 10d.–1/0d. for a pint basin, but a plate of beef is usually 6d., veal or lamb 1d. or 2d. more, potatoes 1d., bread 1d., cheese 2d., fruit pie or pudding 3d.[50]

Traditional fare of this kind long continued to be popular but, as noticed previously, Continental cuisine was becoming available in some first-class hotels in the 1860s and 1870s, and now began to spread to a new group of Franco-Italian restaurants in London. Some writers have tended to exaggerate the extent and speed of this change:

> An important event in the social history of England was the revolution caused by the introduction of Continental cookery, which broke out in the 'sixties of last century.[51]

The 'revolution' was mainly confined to Soho and parts of the West End, nor was it true that there had been no foreign restaurants before this time: La Sablonnière dated from 1700, while Verrey's and Bertollini's already existed. French and Italian communities in Soho had established 'cafés' and 'albergos' serving their own immigrants, mainly refugees from political oppression or young men escaping from compulsory military service. But apart from a few early 'Bohemians' like George Sims and George Sala, who found excitement in penetrating the shadier side of London, these places were not usually frequented by English diners.

What now began in the 1860s was the spread of Continental cuisine into restaurants that would soon become fashionable venues for men and women to enjoy exotic dishes and fine wines in an atmosphere that evoked slightly daring novelty. The taste for new culinary experiences had several causes. As Charles Selby wrote in 1860, 'The men of the present day have travelled, and know a thing or two in the cookery line never dreamed of by their fathers.'[52] The Continent was now easily accessible by steamboats and railways, and foreign holidays were no longer restricted to the very wealthy. The tide of foreign visitors who attended the Great Exhibition in 1851 was now reversed when crowds of British tourists crossed the Channel to witness the spectacular International Paris Exhibition in 1867, many on inexpensive 'package' trips arranged by Thomas Cook and other agents. Britain in the 1860s was enjoying a booming economy and a sense of Palmerstonian confidence after the Crimean War and the Indian Mutiny in the previous decade, and a younger generation of successful businessmen and professionals was eager to adopt new habits of fashion and pleasure seeking. Foreign cuisine was smart and topical, to be read about in books and magazines, discussed, even attempted at home if the 'plain cook' could be persuaded. Travellers who had experienced the restaurants of Paris usually spoke glowingly about the imaginative dishes and modest prices compared with London eating-houses: William Thackeray wrote of good, two-franc (1/-) meals (bifsteack, pommes de terre, galantine of chicken, gruyère cheese, ½ bottle of Mâcon or Chablis) – 'You see many honest English families marching into these two-franc eating-houses at five o'clock, and fancying they dine in great luxury.'[53] For a more elaborate meal Thackeray dined at the Café Foy, where the 7/6d. menu included truffled partridges, and at the famous 'Trois Frères Provençaux' (soup, turbot, truffled chicken, wine, cognac, 5/-), while at the equally celebrated Rocher de Cancale a dinner for six, which included 18 dishes, also worked out at 5/- a head.[54]

Even without crossing the Channel, a good many English people had experienced foreign cuisine in 1851, when Alexis Soyer, who had now left the Reform Club, opened his Gastronomic Symposium of All Nations at Gore House, only a short distance from the Crystal Palace. The

Symposium was more than a series of restaurants, containing works of art, statuary and architecture from many countries: the thousand or so visitors each day could either eat a 2/6d. luncheon in 'The Baronial Hall' or, more expensively, sample dishes from many parts of the world at banquets and evening entertainments. Although Soyer had intended to continue the Symposium indefinitely, he regretfully closed it after a dispute with the licensing authorities who had objected to alleged scenes of dissipation in the gardens at night.[55]

They may have been right. Even in the West End there were areas around Piccadilly, Regent Street and Leicester Square which were not yet fashionable, even respectable, containing many taverns, oyster bars, the Tivoli beer garden, 'night houses', a few 'cafés chantants' and dancing saloons frequented by 'fast' young men and women. Leicester Square was an open space where rubbish was tipped, not laid out in its present form until 1874, and notorious for a basement eating-house, 'The Shades'. 'Night houses' were, in effect, clubs for gaming, drinking and womanising, kept by celebrated mesdames like Kate Hamilton, Sally Sutherland and Rose Young. Open until 4 am or later, they did not usually include food as a major element of the diversions – at 'Raleigh's', much frequented by subalterns, food did not extend beyond bacon on toast 'with a dash of biting sauce', while at the 'Café Roche' oysters and champagne were a favourite snack: night houses were often a prelude to a late visit to Cremorne Gardens, where the 'Fairy Bower' and the 'Hermit's Cave' promised exciting encounters. For a more stylish night out 'Mott's' was an elegantly decorated ballroom where the ladies were refined 'actresses' of note, including the famous 'Skittles' and the beautiful 'Sweet Nelly Fowler', while at Evans's Supper Room guests were entertained by boy choristers and fake 'negro' minstrels.[56]

This was the background – more Regency than Victorian – in which groups of Franco-Italian restaurants appeared in the 1860s and 1870s. At first they were patronised mainly by the 8,000 or so French immigrants lodging around Soho, but their novel cuisines and modest charges soon appealed to 'Bohemian' English artists, actors and authors, though not until somewhat later to the great and not so good of the '*fin de siècle*'. They included the restaurants started by the Gatti brothers in Adelaide and Villiers Streets, the Café Royal in Regent Street (1865), Pinoli's in Wardour Street (1869), Monico's, Pagani's, Romano's in the Strand (1874),

Oddenino's, Frascati's, Kettner's, the Criterion (1873) and perhaps up to a hundred less well-known names. Baedeker's *Guide to London* of 1879 recommended many of them alongside traditional inns and hotels, commenting that 'In the first-class restaurants the cuisine is generally French': in most, the 'table d'hôte' dinner was around 3/6d., sometimes with wine included, though 'à la carte' dishes were considerably dearer – at Romano's hors d'oeuvres 2/-, entrecôte 3/6d., a portion of partridge 6/-, ices 2/-, coffee 1/6d. Several restaurants implied that dining or supping with a lady was encouraged by coyly advertising a 'ladies' room'.[57] It was also a significant sign of changing leisure habits that so many of the new restaurants were located close to the heart of the developing theatre and music-hall world: pleasurable eating was closely associated with pleasurable entertainment for a public that appreciated new tastes in food as well as in music and drama.

Of the many new restaurants, two stand out for the special influence they were to have on future trends. The Café Royal was opened in 1865 by Daniel Nicholas Thévenon, who was born in a small Burgundian village, moved to Paris and opened wine shops there. By 1863 he was bankrupt, and to escape prosecution and probable imprisonment, he and his wife fled to England as Daniel Nicols with a capital of five gold sovereigns. Settling in the French community in Soho, they opened a small café-restaurant in an empty shop in Glasshouse Street but were shortly able to move to better premises at 68 Regent Street: here, the Café Royal was at first far from grand, with the 'Specialités de la Maison' in white letters on the windows. If the cuisine was not exceptional, the wines, and particularly the newly popular champagnes, were ('Champagne Charlie', George Laybourne's hit music-hall song, was also composed in 1865), and by the late 1870s the improved restaurant had a fashionable reputation with, it was said, crowds always waiting for tables. Its 'Bohemian' image was due to the numbers of actors, authors, artists and models who used it almost as a club and described themselves as 'Royalites': their privileged eccentricities and disregard of convention added colour to the place. Nicols became the lessee, and virtual owner, of the Empire Theatre, Leicester Square: he died worth £500,000 at his country estate at Surbiton, large enough to contain a deer park.[58]

Alfonso Nicolino Romano had been a waiter at the Café Royal before setting up his Café Vaudeville in the Strand in 1874 on capital provided by a bookmaker, George Piesse. The premises had formerly been a fried fish shop. In the early days Piesse brought racing journalists, jockeys and trainers to the restaurant, and Romano's retained a sporting as well as a Bohemian clientele. Much of the restaurant's success was due to the ebullient personality of 'the Roman', who joked and gambled with the habitués in (deliberately) broken English: he had learned the art of cookery from Pescarelli, a former sauce-chef of Soyer, but Romano was himself a wine expert and kept one of the best cellars in London. He also had the patronage and advice of some of the leading gastronomes of the day, including Edward Spencer (the journalist 'Nathaniel Gubbins') and Lieut. Colonel Newnham-Davis who, from his travel experiences, introduced Malay curries, Greek moussakas and Nigerian groundnut soup. After an elaborate refurbishment of the restaurant in Moorish style it attracted more famous personalities such as Arthur Sullivan, d'Oyly Carte, the impresario George Edwardes, the Gaiety Girls and leading music-hall artistes. By 1880 some ladies, not of the chorus, were being entertained there.[59]

By this time also, the earlier complaint that the catering trade had not attracted entrepreneurs was beginning to be remedied by men who were not themselves chefs or restaurateurs but who realised the expanding opportunities for commercial enterprise. Felix William Spiers and Christopher Pond had met in Australia in the early 1850s, opening grill-rooms in Melbourne and, later, a more luxurious restaurant attached to the Theatre Royal, which was intended to act as a social and cultural centre with a gallery for art works. On a visit to England in 1861 Pond organised the first England v. Australia cricket match (an 11,000-mile journey by the S.S. *Great Britain* for which 11 English players each received £150), but noticed that there was little organised catering service for railway passengers. They began establishing railway buffets, the first at Farringdon Street for the new Metropolitan and District Railway: ultimately they controlled 200 mainline buffets, owned several bakeries and distribution centres from which fresh food was delivered daily, and in 1866 opened their first full restaurant service, the 'Silver Grill', at Ludgate Hill: here were first- and second-class dining-rooms with waitress service and meals of excellent quality. In 1873 Spiers and Pond moved into the West End, developing the old Wyndham's Theatre into the Criterion Theatre and Restaurant, then refurbishing the Gaiety Theatre and restaurant and establishing others in Drury Lane and at the

London Zoo. After Pond's death in 1882 Spiers moved into the hotel business, acquiring the Holborn Viaduct Hotel, Bailey's in South Kensington and palatial hotels in Brighton, Eastbourne, Worthing and Scarborough.[60] Spiers and Pond therefore became Britain's first great catering chain, based on their recognition of the needs of travellers and tourists for good quality food and service, and often associated with other forms of entertainment. The Criterion perfectly expressed this concept of leisure and pleasure – a music hall to seat 1,000, four dining-rooms with different menus, a ballroom and grand staircase to complement the ladies' dresses.

By 1880 large capital was beginning to be attracted into the catering industry, in response to the perceived demand and encouraged by the ease with which limited liability companies could now be formed: between 1866 and 1874 no fewer than 161 companies involved in the hotel, restaurant and catering trades were registered.[61] Another of the outstanding entrepreneurs of the period was Frederick Gordon, a solicitor, who in 1868 leased Crosby Hall, a fifteenth-century building in Bishopsgate, and without too much injury to the fabric, developed a series of dining-rooms in 'The Great Hall', 'The Council Chamber' and 'The Throne Room' – an early example of historical 'theme' decor. Gordon went on to remodel old inns like the Holborn, where he provided a variety of grill-rooms, dining-rooms and bars, to establish Frascati's restaurant and, later, to manage the chain of 'Gordon Hotels'.

By the end of this period the catering world was, therefore, very different from the male-dominated one of 1830. Grand hotels and exotic restaurants confirmed that a new leisure industry was under way, attracting both sexes of the affluent classes to adopt new tastes and new ways of spending time and money. Interest in, and appreciation of food was now fashionable and legitimate, for as a new publication, *The Epicure's Year Book*, remarked in 1869:

> *Epicurism has been taken up in nearly every popular periodical, and the food question has advanced. The result will be important; the English people will presently learn how to eat.*[62]

Notes and references

1 See generally, F. M. L. Thompson, *English Landed Society in the Nineteenth Century*, London, Routledge & Kegan Paul, 1963.

2 George C. Brodrick, *English Land and English Landlords*, (1st edn, 1881), repub. New York, Augustus M. Kelley, 1968, Table pp. 158ff., pp. 164–5.

3 See Charles Booth, 'Occupations of the People of the United Kingdom, 1801–1881', *Journal of the Statistical Society*, vol. XLIX, 1886, pp. 314–44. Much of the data is analyzed by Guy Routh in *Occupations of the People of Great Britain, 1801–1981*, Macmillan, 1987, pp. 1–17.

4 For details of incomes and domestic budgets in this period see John Burnett, *A History of the Cost of Living* (1st edn 1969), repub. Aldershot, Hants, Gregg Revivals, 1993. See also J. A. Banks, *Prosperity and Parenthood. A Study of Family Planning among the Victorian Middle Classes*, Routledge & Kegan Paul, 1965.

5 Quoted Peter Bailey, *Leisure and Class in Victorian England. Rational Recreation and the Contest for Control, 1830–1885*, Methuen, 1987, p. 68. See the many contemporary quotations in ch. 3, 'The New Leisure World of the mid-Victorians'.

6 Phyllis Hembry, *British Spas from 1815 to the Present. A Social History*, edited and completed by Leonard W. Cowie and Evelyn E. Cowie, Athlone Press, 1997, p. 2.

7 A. B. Granville, *The Spas of England and Principal Sea-Bathing Places*, 2 vols (1st edn, 1841), repub. Bath, Somerset, Adams and Dart, 1971: vol. 1, The North, pp. 28–34.

8 ibid., p. 73.

9 ibid., pp. 152, 186.

10 Gabor Denes, *The Story of the Imperial. The Life and Times of Torquay's Great Hotel*, Newton Abbot, Devon, David & Charles, 1982, p. 30.

11 Granville, op. cit., vol. 1, p. 349.

12 Jane Welsh Carlyle, *Letters and Memorials*, ed. J. A. Froude, 1883, vol. 1, p. 219.

13 For details of hotels before 1840, see Alison Adburgham, *Silver Fork Society*, Constable, 1983, pp. 263–5: for Victorian hotels, Mary Cathcart Borer, *The British Hotel through the Ages*, Guildford and London, Lutterworth Press, 1972, pp. 184–92.

14 Mrs E. M. Ward, *Memories of Ninety Years*, quoted Mrs C. S. Peel, *A Hundred Wonderful Years. Social and Domestic Life of a Century, 1820–1920*, John Lane, The Bodley Head, 1929, p. 18.

15 Walpurga, Lady Paget, *Embassies of Other Days*, quoted Peel, ibid., p. 16.

16 Arthur White, *Palaces of the People. A Social History of Commercial Hospitality*, Rapp and Whiting, 1968, pp. 129–40. On American hotels and restaurants of this period, see Michael and Ariane Batterberry, *On the Town in New York*, New York and London, Routledge, 1999, ch. 3, 1830–1860.

17 *The Times*, 3 Nov. 1855.

18 Albert Smith, *The English Hotel Nuisance*, David Bryce, 1856, p. 15.

19 ibid. p. 26.

20 'Inns, Old and New', *All The Year Round*, 23 June 1866, pp. 559–62.

21 K. Baedeker, *London and its Environs. Handbook for Travellers*, Dulan and Co., 2nd edn, 1879, pp. 6–9.

22 A Hayward, *The Art of Dining, or Gastronomy and Gastronomes* (1st edn, 1852), John Murray, new edn, 1883, p. 1.

23 André L. Simon, 'From Esau to Escoffier, or The History of Gastronomy', in Louis Golding and André Simon (eds), *We Shall Eat and Drink Again. A Wine and Food Anthology*, Hutchinson, n.d., *c.*1948, p. 143.

24 Hayward (1883), op. cit. p. 70.

25 ibid., pp. 37–9.

26 Stephen Mennell, *All Manners of Food. Eating and Taste in England and France from the Middle Ages to the Present*, Oxford, Basil Blackwell, 1985, p. 144. Carême's contribution to 'haute cuisine' is excellently summarised at pp. 144–9.

27 Hayward (1883), op. cit., pp. 73–5.

28 Gregory Houston Bowden, *British Gastronomy. The Rise of Great Restaurants*, Chatto & Windus, 1975, p. 8.

29 Hayward (1883), op. cit., pp. 76–7.

30 Helen Morris, *Portrait of a Chef. The Life of Alexis Soyer*, Oxford, Oxford University Press, 1980, p. 205. See also Andrew Langley, *The Selected Soyer. The Writings of the Legendary Victorian Chef, Alexis Soyer*, Bath, Avon, Absolute Press in conjunction with the Reform Club, 1987.

31 John Timbs, *Clubs and Club Life in London*, John Camden Hotten, 1872.

32 George Dodd, *The Food of London*, Longman, Brown, Green and Longmans, 1856, p. 511.

33 Robert Thorne, 'Places of Refreshment in the Nineteenth-Century City', in Anthony D. King (ed.), *Buildings and Society. Essays on the social development of the built environment*, Routledge & Kegan Paul, 1980, p. 232.

34 Thomas Walker, *The Original* (1835), chapter on London clubs, quoted Dodd, op. cit., pp. 513–14.

35 Moira Johnston (ed.), *London Eats Out. Five Hundred Years of Capital Dining*, Philip Wilson and Museum of London, 1999, p. 73.

36 Sarah Freeman, *Mutton and Oysters. The Victorians and their Food*, Victor Gollancz, 1989, p. 285.

37 Robin McDouall, *Clubland Cooking*, Phaedon Press, 1974, p. 165.

38 George R. Sims, *My Life. Sixty Years' Recollections of Bohemian London*, Eveleigh Nash, 1917, p. 95.

39 Freeman, op. cit., p. 279.

40 Tabitha Tickletooth (Charles Selby), *The Dinner Question, Or How to Dine Well and Economically* (1st edn, 1860), facsimile edn, Totnes, Devon, Prospect Books, 1999, p. 139.

41 Cedric Dickens, *Dining With Dickens. Being a Ramble through Dickensian Foods*, Goring-on-Thames, Elvendon Press, 1984, p. 13. This contains many accounts of meals in Dickens's novels. Also useful is Edward Hewett and W. F. Axton, *Convivial Dickens. The Drinks of Dickens and his Times*, Athens, Ohio, Ohio University Press, 1983.

42 Edward Spencer (pseud. Nathaniel Gubbins), *Cakes and Ale. A Dissertation on Banquets*, (1st edn 1897), Stanley Paul and Co., 1913, pp. 18, 69–71.

43 Virginia Curle, *A History of Stone's Chop House*, Stone's Chop House Ltd., n.d., *c.*1960. Women were first admitted to Stone's in 1921.

44 Dodd, op. cit., pp. 509–10.

45 Selby (Tickletooth), op. cit., p. 144.

46 ibid., p. 146.

47 Anon, *London At Dinner. Where to Dine in 1858*, facsimile of 1858 edn, Newton Abbot, Devon, David & Charles, 1969 (1st edn published 1851 as *London At Table, or How, When and Where to Dine and Order a Dinner, and Where to Avoid Dining*), Advertisements, pp. 5–6.

48 David M. Evans, *City Men and City Manners, with Sketches on 'Change and at the Coffee Houses*, Groombridge and Sons, 1852, pp.145–8.

49 Sims, op. cit., p. 95.

50 'London Eating Houses', *Chambers Edinburgh Journal*, 24 June 1837, pp. 173–4.

51 'Bon Viveur', *Where to Dine in London*, Geoffrey Bles, 1937, p. 11 (This is not the 'Bon Viveur' later adopted by the Cradocks.)

52 Selby (Tickletooth), op. cit., p. 144.

53 M. A. Titmarch (pseud. of William Makepeace Thackeray), 'Memorials of Gourmandizing, in a Letter to Oliver Yorke Esq.', *Fraser's Magazine*, June 1841. In George Saintsbury (ed.), *The Works*, Oxford, Oxford University Press, 1908, vol. III, p. 522.

54 ibid., p. 532, where details are given of 18 dishes.

55 Details of the Gore House Symposium are in Helen Morris, op. cit., pp. 101ff.

56 See D. Shaw ('One of the Old Brigade'), *London in the Sixties*, Everett and Co., 1908, pp. 20–39: George Augustus Sala, *Twice Round the Clock* (1st edn, 1859), repub. Leicester, Leicester University Press, 1971, pp. 338–40.

57 K. Baedeker, *London and its Environs*, 1879, op. cit., pp. 10–15.

58 Guy Deghy and Keith Waterhouse, *Café Royal. Ninety Years of Bohemia*, Hutchinson, 1955, pp. 17–35.

59 Guy Deghy, *Paradise in the Strand. The Story of Romano's*, The Richards Press, 1958, pp. 18ff.

60 Bryan Morgan, *Express Journey, 1864–1964. A Centenary History of the Express Dairy Co. Ltd.*, Newman Neame Ltd., 1964, Appendix A, 'A Short History of Spiers and Pond', pp. 129–35.

61 Thorne, op. cit., p. 239.

62 Anon., *The Epicure's Year Book for 1869* (Second Year), Bradbury, Evans and Co., 1869, Preface, p. VIII.

PART TWO

1880–1914

CHAPTER 4

· · · · · · · · · · · · · · ·

Catering for the masses

The masses

In a powerfully descriptive study of the social structure in 1909 C. F. G. Masterman in *The Condition of England* portrayed the nation as divided into three classes – 'The Conquerors,' 'The Suburbans' and 'The Multitude'. He might have personalised them as 'The Forsytes', 'The Pooters' and 'The Tressells' as representative types of his three categories. It was usual for contemporary observers of the social scene to focus attention on the first group, the affluent, for whom late Victorian and Edwardian England seemed something of a Golden Age, whose extravagant lives were led in the public gaze in the fashion and gossip columns of the newly-emerged popular press, and whose lifestyles evoked a mixture of envy, admiration and condemnation from those outside the privileged circle. 'The Suburbans' were both more numerous and more anonymous, hidden during the day

> in small, crowded offices under artificial light, doing immense sums, adding up other men's accounts, writing other men's letters ... As darkness falls, it finds itself in its own territory, in the miles and miles of little, red houses in little, silent streets, in number defying imagination. Each boasts its high-sounding title – 'Acacia Villa' or 'Camperdown Lodge', attesting unconquerable human aspiration.[1]

Here, houses had names, but for 'The Multitude' only numbers. In cities many lived in one or two rooms in a tenemented house, in a 'back-to-back' cottage or, more favourably, in 'two-up and two-down' terraces in mean, parallel streets. At the lowest level of the poor, now often described as 'the residuum', the priority which the middle classes gave to home and family, to security and respectability, were alien values when set against the constant struggle to survive. These small dwellings had to accommodate many children: in 1877 the birth rate reached its highest recorded level, giving an average family size of 5.8 children, though one in every five families had 10 or more. While living standards for the majority of the population rose between 1880 and 1914, principally due to lower costs of imported foods, there persisted wide strata of society whose poverty contrasted starkly with the gains of others.

Statistics were available to quantify Masterman's impressions. A leading economist, L. Chiozza Money, calculated that the national income in 1911 could be divided into three broadly equal shares, as set out in Table 4.1.[2]

On this estimate, two-thirds of national income went to one-ninth of the population, a degree of inequality scarcely affected by Lloyd George's increase in the income tax two years earlier from 1/- to 1/2d. in the pound. But poverty, long accepted or ignored, was beginning to attract attention from social scientists and from politicians responsive to an electorate that now included many working-class voters. In his vast survey of *The Life and Labour of the People in London* (1886–1902) Charles Booth concluded that 30.7 per cent were existing below a poverty line of 21/- a week for a family of two adults and three children. While his was essentially a formal survey, Booth could not altogether avoid some moralistic judgements: of 'Class A', the lowest, consisting of occasional labourers, streetsellers, loafers and semi-criminals, he wrote that 'their life is the life of savages' and that 'they are, perhaps, incapable of improvement', while 'Class B' were 'inevitably poor', from idleness, shiftlessness and drink:

TABLE 4.1 ◆ *National income distribution, 1911*

Class	Income per annum	No. of recipients, including families
Upper	Over £700	1,400,000
Middle	£160–£700	4,100,000
Working class	Under £160	39,000,000

Source: L. G. Chiozza Money, *Riches and Poverty*. Methuen and Co., 11th edn, 1914.

they find the excitement they crave in the streets or 'in some highly coloured domestic scene'. To the poor of 'Class C', however, Booth attached no blame: these were the deserving poor, the victims of excessive competition and depressions in trade, who were nevertheless 'decent, steady men, paying their way and bringing up their children respectably'. His conclusion that around a third of the inhabitants of London, the wealthy capital of the wealthiest country in the world, were existing in extreme want, was met by many with alarm and incredulity, but was confirmed by Seebohm Rowntree's research in York, *Poverty: A Study of Town Life* (1901), which showed a similar figure of 27.8 per cent in poverty based on the cost of a minimum diet for mere physical efficiency. Here food for a family of five was costed at 12/9d. (63p.) a week, and was less generous than that provided for paupers in the York workhouse.

The worker's lunch

What life was like at this level was well illustrated by interviews conducted by Maud Pember Reeves in 1913. 'Eating out' from anything but necessity was quite irrelevant. There was no evidence of women eating outside the home, but men, when in work, needed to be sustained for their labours, often at great sacrifice to frail family budgets. Thus, 'Mr Y', a builder's labourer earning 25/- a week to support six children under 13, paid 6/6d. a week rent for two rooms and was allowed 3/- a week by his wife for his dinners, ' which', said Mrs Reeves, 'cannot be of a heavy nature'. 'Mr Q', a feather-cleaner also earning 25/- a week, took 6½d. a day for his dinners but also kept 5/- a week for 'clothing and pocket-money' (? including drink) and insisted on another 1/1d. a week for 'relishes' at home, a total of 9/4d. for himself. Another man who worked as a carman for an LCC contractor had to start work at 5 am: he got both breakfast and dinner out, returning home for supper at 7.30 pm.[3] In these and other budgets an amount of between 3/- and 5/- a week for men's dinners was the usual allowance, and feeding the breadwinner was evidently a main priority, sanctioned by wives even to the point of a husband's selfishness. We do not know exactly how the 6d. or so a day was spent. Some men probably bought from street-sellers, still common in London and other cities, though not so numerous as in Mayhew's time as shops took over more of their trade. Cookshops flourished everywhere, selling pies, puddings and savouries of many kinds, while little corner shops cut slices of bread, ham or other meats and made up sandwiches. Six pence would buy a hot meal of roast meat and vegetables at a cheap 'ordinary' or at one of the temperance coffee-houses for working men, though the generally drab surroundings were not enticing, and by now the fish-and-chip shop was all but universal, providing a savoury meal for 2d. or 3d., either indoors or for taking out. In 1910 there were an estimated 25,000 such shops in Britain,[4] making this a major catering industry. Lancashire and Yorkshire industrial towns had phenomenal numbers – 133 in Preston and 317 in Bradford in 1914. An American visitor to England at this time was amazed by the number of these unfamiliar eating-houses:

> It was the luncheon hour [in Oldham] and I was beginning to grow hungry. As I walked along dull streets I noticed several small eating-places labelled 'Fish, Chip and Pea Restaurant' and 'Tripe, Trotters and Cow-heels Restaurant' which astonished me greatly – really astonished me. I had seen only one such before in my life, and that was this same morning in Middleton . . . I pondered over this, thinking that such restaurants must be due to the poverty of the people, and that meat being very dear, these three articles of diet were substituted. Here at Oldham, however, I saw that several of these restaurants stood in very central places where the rents should be reasonably high and the traffic brisk.[5]

Fish and chips had their principal customers among women and children, who could enjoy a 'fast' meal for 1d. or 2d.: working men generally did not regard them as a square meal, any more than the offerings of the tripe, trotter and pea-soup shops. In London eel and mashed potato shops were popular with both sexes and all ages, but a disadvantage of all these types of catering was that they were unlicensed, selling only such drinks as ginger beer, lemonade and local herb brews. At 2d. a pint in most public houses, 6d. would buy two pints of beer and some solid sustenance – bread, cheese and pickles from the bar or a pie from a cookshop. Beer consumption in England and Wales rose to a peak of 40.5 gallons a head a year in 1875–9,[6] and on an estimate of 1899 that there were three million total abstainers, that women drank only half as much beer as men and children under 15 hardly any, this suggests that male drinkers consumed around 103 gallons a year, or an average of 16 pints a week. From the late 1870s consumption began a slow decline as other attractions became more available, but in 1900 average expenditure on alcoholic drinks stood at £4/10/0d. a head a year, or £22/10/0d. for a family of five, around a quarter of working-class earnings and more than enough to keep many families in poverty.[7] That heavy manual labourers needed liquid refreshment, and that beer was itself a food providing around 200 kcals a pint, were justifications offered with some force at a time when water was often unfit to drink. As liquor consumption began to fall and as 'temperance' in the broad sense gained converts, a movement developed to reform pubs by providing light refreshments, tea, coffee and soft drinks and comfortable seating in lounges instead of the 'perpendicular drinking' at the bar. This movement also included the idea of 'disinterested management' by which the publican was paid a fixed salary and did not depend on 'pushing' the sale of alcohol. In 1896 the People's Refreshment Houses Association was formed to acquire existing licensed premises and reform them on these lines, followed in 1903 by the establishment of Trust Houses: its first acquisition was the Wagon and Horses at Ridge Hill, Hertfordshire, where an ex-policeman was appointed as manager. By 1907 various Trusts had bought 233 properties,[8] mostly in small towns and villages, while in the cities the brewery companies, which now owned a high proportion of 'tied' houses, also undertook major building and refurbishment schemes to improve dreary Victorian premises. This was the beginning of a recognition that men and women wanted more from a pub than the opportunity merely to drink as much beer or spirits as they could afford. Some pubs put on a free snack (as many saloons did in America), and in Salford some supplied a potato pie, cheese, pickles, a pint of beer and a piece of twist tobacco, all for 4½d.[9] A forerunner of future trends was at the Mason's Arms at Headington Quarry, north of Oxford, where an enterprising landlady served fish and chips in a shed at the rear of the premises.[10]

For many workers, however, there was no alternative to eating at the workplace if time or means precluded a visit to a catering establishment. Most small factories and workshops had no fixed meal-breaks, and workers ate what they had brought from home or bought outside while at their benches, especially when they were paid on piece-rates and needed to maximise output. Probably the worst of all eating environments was the coal mine, where the dust-laden atmosphere quickly contaminated any exposed food. By 1914 a 20-minute break was usually allowed in an eight-hour shift for the 'snap' that miners brought down in tin cans and boxes, one for food and one for drink, which gave necessary protection against the rats. Of his first day down the pit at 13 James Griffiths wrote that 'there can be no more joyful banquet than the miner's "snap" time', when he had 'bread and butter and cheese – with a tomato for "afters" – all swilled down with pearl barley-water which Shoni [his brother] had found best for slaking a thirst'. [11] At a somewhat superior social level, the elementary schoolmistresses described by D. H. Lawrence brought their cooked dinners from home and warmed them on the little staffroom stove: one had a dish of meat, potatoes and brussels sprouts, another, more advanced, a savoury vegetarian mess of beans and brown gravy. 'I'm not really a vegetarian,' said Maggie, 'I don't like to bring meat to school.'[12] Lunch was an occasion for fine social distinctions, and in some occupations poverty was ashamed to present its public face. Edward Spencer observed of 'the poor, wretched, half-starved [City] clerks whose state nobody ever seems to attempt to ameliorate', that lunch in the office consisted of 'a thick slice of bread and a stale bloater, or possibly a home-made sandwich of bread and Dutch cheese – the whole washed down with a tumbler of milk or, more often, a tumbler of the fluid supplied by the New River Company'; meanwhile, their employers were 'swilling turtle at Birch's [the famous turtle restaurant] or enjoying a substantial meal at a chop-and-steak house'.[13]

Canteens provided by employers had made little progress before the First World War, a government Report on Factories and Workshops in 1918 estimating that there were barely a hundred in existence in 1914.[14] The leading exceptions were a few large firms employing mainly female labour whose philanthropic owners were also pioneers of model housing and community services. These included the chocolate and cocoa firms Cadbury, Rowntree and Fry, the soap manufacturer Lever Bros. and the mustard-maker, Colman of Norwich. These provided large dining-halls serving meals at cost price, facilities for food brought in to be warmed, and usually breaks for tea, coffee or milk at mid-morning and mid-afternoon. In the Girls' Institute at Lever's Port Sunlight, food was available at from 1d. to 4d; at Bournville, where Cadbury's employed 3,600, the long day at the busy season was from 6 am to 5.30 pm and was enlivened by a cup of tea and a biscuit on arrival, half an hour for breakfast, 15 minutes for mid-morning lunch and an hour for 'dinner'. The most

FIGURE 4.1 ◆ *Canteen for girls and women at Cadbury's chocolate factory, Bournville, c. 1900. Among the most philanthropic employers, they devoted 40,000 square feet to three separate dining-rooms for men, women and clerical staff, where meals were served at cost price.*

Source: Courtesy of Cadbury World.

expensive item on the menu was roast beef and two vegetables for 4d., but plates of cold meat could be had for 1d. or 2d., sausages, eggs, pies and puddings also for 1d. and tea or coffee ½d. Employees bought tickets in advance so that demand could be estimated, and presented them at long counters where they were served. At Hartley's jam factory at Aintree a dining-room for 600 supplied potato pie, hot-pot or sausage and 'mash' for 2d., and on Fridays fish from Grimsby at 1d., with chips another 1d. Colman's had the novel idea of a glass showcase by the factory gate displaying specimens of the day's menu: each day there was a different '*plat du jour*' as well as the standard offerings such as salt beef, stew with dumplings and fried fish at 2d., soup, beef patty and puddings 1d.[15]

Such canteens were early examples of mass catering, unique in scale outside military establishments. In 1902 Cadbury's devoted 40,600 square feet to this purpose: they had 'the most extensive dining accommodation in the United Kingdom', requiring vast dining-halls (separated for male, female and clerical staffs), large numbers of buyers, carriers, cooks, servers and cleaners. Factory canteens were responsible for significant innovations in feeding great numbers in a short time while still offering a choice of menu – for example, the display of model dishes, the alternating '*plat du jour*', the advance ordering by ticket and the counter system, an early form of cafeteria service.

Children in need

Factory canteens in this period were justified not so much in terms of increased output – though this was never wholly disregarded – as by humanitarian concern for the welfare of female workers, many of whom were little more than children. Most of the large chocolate firms had a policy of not employing married women, so their labour forces consisted mainly of girls under 21 and often under 16. At the end of the century concern about the welfare of children moved into the public sphere as part of the anxiety about 'National Efficiency' and Britain's ability to compete industrially with rapidly developing economies like Germany and the United States. The tardy provision of elementary education, not compulsory until 1880, revealed large numbers of poor, ragged and hungry children whom, under the 'payment by results' system, teachers had to try to cram through annual examinations. In 1885 Dr Crichton-

Browne published a *Report on the Alleged Over-Pressure of Work in Public Elementary Schools* in which he suggested that there was 'a larger question than dullness – perhaps the largest and most important of all – that of starvation'. Earlier, sporadic efforts to feed hungry schoolchildren by voluntary agencies (see chapter 2) had done little more than scratch a vast surface: in 1889 the London School Board estimated that 44,000 children (12.8 per cent of all those in attendance) were habitually in need of food, but that less than half were receiving school meals.[16] Further voluntary efforts followed by the London Schools Dinner Association, by left-wing organisations such as Socialist Dinners and the Independent Labour Party, and by the Penny Dinner movement by which parents were expected to contribute 1d. towards the cost of hot meals on three or four days a week in winter.

Meanwhile, anxieties about the health of the nation and, especially, about the 'physical degeneration' of urban populations developed from two related directions. Although general mortality rates had improved, falling below 20 deaths per 1,000 for the first time in 1881, child mortality remained stubbornly high and, in particular, the death rate for infants under one year actually increased from 154/1,000 in 1855–9 to 158/1,000 in 1895–9: in one district of Sheffield in 1901 it reached 234/1,000, a quarter of all babies.[17] With the birth rate beginning to decline, children – especially fit and educated children – were now regarded as national assets, necessary for efficient industrial production and for the defence of Britain's vast overseas possessions. In *The Heart of the Empire* (1901) C. F. G. Masterman argued that England's unprecedented urban growth had produced a typical 'City Type', stunted, narrow-chested, easily wearied, yet voluble, excitable ... Seeking stimulus in drink, in betting, in any unaccustomed conflicts'.[18] Such fears seemed to be confirmed by Britain's poor military showing in the South African War (1899–1902), and by the high proportion of young volunteers, supposedly in the prime of life, who were rejected for service as medically unfit. The Inspector-General of Army Recruiting reported that in the period 1801–1002, 04.0 per cent of men had been rejected, but that this seriously under-represented the real extent of ill health since recruiters were instructed not to submit men for medical examination who were obviously unfit or undersized: he believed that the true figure was nearer 60 per cent.[19] In this atmosphere of national anxiety, imperialism became closely linked with social reform and, especially, with plans for improving the health of children – the next generation of workers and soldiers. In 1904 the Inter-Departmental Committee on Physical Deterioration recommended the introduction of games and physical training in schools, the establishment of a school medical service, and that 'definite provisions should be made ... for dealing with the question of underfed children'.[20]

A fierce ideological debate ensued. Many people believed that the provision of food was a fundamental family responsibility, and that to hand this over to public authorities would be a first step towards a socialist state. The Education (Provision of Meals) Act (1906), initiated by one of the new Labour Party MPs, William T. Wilson, and adopted by the Liberal government, was therefore a compromise, though an important development in social policy, even hailed as 'the beginning of the construction of the welfare state'.[21] School meals were to be the responsibility of local education authorities, not of the hated Poor Law: free food might be supplied to 'necessitous children,' identified by teachers and, after 1907, by the new school medical service with its regular examinations. Local authorities were allowed, but not required, to levy a special rate of not more than ½d. in the pound towards the cost of meals, but parents were expected to contribute where possible and voluntary agencies were encouraged to co-operate.

The Act fell far short of the national school meals service for all children which developed during the Second World War. It was not adopted everywhere, and in some areas voluntary provision continued without public funding, but by 1912/13 100,000 children were being fed in London and 258,000 in the rest of the country. It was recognised, however, that these numbers did not include all those in need, since a good many parents declined the offer on account of the stigma attaching to it – to accept free food was practically equivalent to acknowledging pauperism. In London, where five out of every six schools served meals, menus were drawn up under medical advice, costing an average of 1½d. a meal.[22] Some schools provided breakfasts, most only dinners and a few both, depending on needs or the political complexion of the local authority. The results of feeding programmes were generally regarded as very successful in improving height, weight and general health of poor children, and their ability to concentrate on their lessons, a fact often noticed by teachers. In Bradford in 1907 a research project with 40 children showed that after breakfasts and dinners had been provided for three months they made rapid weight gains as well as improvements in table manners and hygiene. A general free school meals service was quickly started, with a central kitchen despatching food to dining-halls by motor vans and tram cars: by 1908/9 3,500 Bradford children were receiving meals. Unusually, both breakfast and dinner were provided throughout the year, not only in winter, menus having been drawn up for the different seasons. For breakfast children had porridge, bread and treacle and milk in winter, in summer bread and jam, milk, currant loaf and cocoa; dinner included potato and onion soup, hashed beef with savoury balls, Yorkshire cheese pudding, shepherd's pie, fish and potato pie with parsley sauce, rice pudding, baked jam roll and so on – the kind of meals that artisan or even lower middle-class families might have had. It was unfamiliar fare to many poor children, who were accustomed to little more than bread, margarine, tea and occasional chips, and was sometimes rejected until new tastes developed.[23]

Concern for the health and welfare of deprived children had mixed motives which went well beyond mere charity: it was also a response to the discovery of the extent and causes of poverty by social investigators, to fears about national inefficiency and to the social discontent which lay behind the growth of radical political formations.[24] These anxieties were expressed in many and varied ways such as housing and sanitary reforms, the Charity Organisation Society, the Settlement Movement and the Salvation Army, but particular attention was focused on children who, whatever the faults of their parents might be, could be regarded as the innocent victims of forces beyond their control. Some, it was believed, could only be adequately protected in total institutions like Shaftesbury and Barnardo Homes, but much could be done for others by clubs which offered healthy activity, fun and games, and annual outings and camps in the fresh air, combined with discipline and training in good citizenship. Some of these, like the Boys' Brigade and the Church Lads' Brigade, also had strong moral objectives and the hope of halting the decline in church attendance, but others such as the Children's Country Holiday Fund aimed simply to enable poor children to spend a week or a fortnight away from city slums. Said to be the earliest boys' club in the modern sense, the Hulme Club of Manchester held its first summer camp in 1887,[25] a precedent for many others. Day outings, organised by churches, chapels and Sunday Schools, had existed long before this, involving mothers in preparing sandwiches and baking cakes, and by the end of the century there were many local charities like the Newcastle-upon-Tyne Poor Children's Holiday Association. In 1891 this organised a steamer trip to South Shields with a substantial tea of pies, buns, cakes, oranges and milk; some children were ragged and without shoes, and quickly demolished the banquet. On a much larger scale, the Fresh Air Fund was founded in 1892 by the publisher C. Arthur Pearson in conjunction with the Ragged School Union. By 1909 it claimed that more than two million children from the slums of London and other cities had been taken for a day's outing to the coast or countryside: one of its patrons, Millicent, Duchess of Sutherland, explained that each 9d. contributed by the public covered all costs for a child, including 'fine feasts on meat-pies, bread and butter and buns and oranges – a day that is as a glimpse of Paradise to the poor little mites who live in the darkness of squalid back courts and the mean streets of our cities'.[26]

The most enduring of the open-air institutions was, of course, the Boy Scouts movement, originated by General Baden-Powell who had used boys as messengers during sieges in the South African war. The movement retained a semi-militaristic image, combined with physical fitness, patriotism and character building, especially developed in the annual summer camps. Here, boys were encouraged to be self-reliant, including making and cooking their own meals:

> Every Scout must, of course, know how to cook his own meat and vegetables, and to make bread [i.e. bannocks] for himself without regular cooking utensils. [Recipes for meat included 'kabobs' on skewers.] Scouts should also know how to kill and cut up their cattle. Cattle are generally poleaxed, or a spike is driven into the forehead with a mallet, or a big, sharp knife is driven into the spine just behind the horns.[27]

The first catering chains

By the later nineteenth century the conditions existed for entrepreneurial enterprise in providing eating-places attractive to a broad band of customers from the lower middle classes and upper working classes – not the rich, and certainly not the poor, but the growing numbers of the respectable sort of people whom Masterman had typified as 'The Suburbans'. Not all had yet made that migration, but they shared the standards of order, cleanliness, speech and dress which distinguished them from many of 'The Multitude'. In London many were commuters by train, tram and Underground: here and in other cities many were girls and single women working in offices as 'female typewriters', telephonists and clerks, or as sales assistants in the huge, new department stores where neatness, politeness and a fair education were required. Many men and women now lived too far from home to return for meals during short lunch-breaks, but needed eating-places close to hand where they could be served quickly in clean, pleasant surroundings. Places like this were also needed for the growing number of lady shoppers coming up to city centres from the suburbs or the country, meeting friends for lunch or tea and requiring the conveniences of 'ladies' rooms'.

Catering chains of a modest scale had first appeared in the reformed coffee-houses previously described (see Chaper 2), temperance institutions aimed at working men and providing basic food: although some described themselves as 'Coffee Palaces', most were dreary places with bench seating and bare, sanded floors. What was significant about them, however, was that they were established on a corporate basis: in 1878 they included the People's Café Company (12 in London), the Coffee Tavern Company (also 12 in London), the Liverpool Coffee Tavern Company (30), the Manchester Coffee Tavern Company (8), the Leeds British Workman Public Houses (17) and Lockhart's Cocoa Rooms (10 in Liverpool and the Newcastle area).[28] Although some continued to grow slowly subsequently, they had little general appeal and many suffered from poor management and financial control. One of the most successful was Robert Lockhart's Cocoa Rooms, which, in true temperance spirit, he generally positioned next door to public houses. From Liverpool he moved to London, where by 1884 he had established 23 premises, their opening time of 5 am suggesting that their chief customers were manual workers. Another, somewhat similar pioneer of mass catering was John Pearce, who began with a coffee-stall 'in the gutter' in the East End of London in 1866. In a later interview for *The Caterer and Hotel Keepers' Gazette* he recalled that his customers were 'a motley lot – printers going to and from work and artizans and mechanics, with a sprinkling of swells returning home after a party or a spree ... with a few women of course,

and I daresay some doubtful characters – we can't pick and choose customers in my trade'. Pearce opened his first coffee-shop in London in
1870, and in 1882 much larger premises in Farringdon Street which
could serve 6,000 meals a day. This was the beginning of the 'Pearce and
Plenty' chain, shortly floated as a company with the encouragement of
Sir Arthur Sullivan. After some years of successful expansion, he began
a chain of superior teashops in 1892 known as 'The British Tea Table
Company' 'serving a better class of customer'. These became the larger
part of his enterprise. By 1905 there were 26 Pearce and Plenty 'depots'
around London, their name suggesting something more like a canteen
than a restaurant, but 56 British Tea Table cafés, 'largely patronized by
young people of both sexes in business, by people shopping, and visitors
to London'. The two companies by then employed 1,500, had their own
bakeries, confectionery and mineral water departments. John Pearce concluded his interview in a philosophical mood:

> A most entertaining volume could be written concerning the rise and
> growth of the middle-class eating establishments [sic]. In the old days, the
> good old days as the unknowing say, everything was left to chance and
> there was scarcely any choice in the way of food – beef and mutton, mutton
> and beef all the year round. And very indifferently served, by slovenly
> attendants in shirt-sleeves and bare arms. Then the places were so stuffy,
> and the table-linen always more or less soiled, and it was always a question
> of take it or leave it . . . Well, thank goodness, we have changed all that.[29]

By the 1880s and 1890s higher standards were certainly beginning to be
set by commercially run chains, now generally describing themselves as
'teashops'. Several of these began as offshoots of other businesses, having
the advantages of commercial experience and financial resources to back
them. For example, the well-known chain of ABC cafés developed from
the baking trade, where in 1859 Dr Dauglish had patented a revolutionary method of bread making whereby instead of being fermented by
yeast, the dough was aerated by carbonic acid gas injection into a closed
cylinder: the process greatly reduced the time needed for bread making,
and produced more loaves to the sack of flour than the traditional
means.[30] By 1862 the Aerated Bread Company had established model
bakeries and retail shops in London and several other cities; precisely
when it began also to sell refreshments in some of these is uncertain, but

AËRATED BREAD COMPANY'S DEPÔT (LUDGATE HILL) : MID-DAY.

FIGURE 4.2 ◆ *The ABC (Aerated Bread Co.) teashop, Ludgate Hill, 1900. An ABC retail bakery began selling refreshments to passengers near London Bridge station in c. 1884, which soon developed into a successful chain. Like Lyons (first opened in Piccadilly, 1894), they provided moderately priced lunches and teas in clean, comfortable surroundings, and were popular with middle-class customers of both sexes.*

Source: Mary Evans Picture Library.

probably around 1884 when the enterprising manageress of the London Bridge shop began serving tea to 'regulars' at the back and persuaded the directors that there was a demand from travellers and commuters.[31] By the late 1880s a successful chain of ABC cafés was operating in London. Similarly, the Express Dairy Company's cafés began as a minor adjunct of the milk retailing business started by Robert Barham who had acquired what was reputed to be 'Nell Gwynne's Dairy' in the Strand in 1849. Like other 'dairies', it sold glasses of milk, soda water, cakes, buns and hard-boiled eggs over the counter. From the 1870s George Titus Barham developed the food side of the rapidly expanding milk business, and in the 1880s opened teashops in prosperous London suburbs like Blackheath and Hampstead where light meals were served to seated customers. Despite the failure of the Express to recruit an old family friend, John Sainsbury, as manager of the provisioning business, the teashops grew to 39 in 1913, not the largest but one of the earliest of the teashop chains.[32]

The tea and coffee trades provided other obvious opportunities for expansion into catering. The Kardomah Cafés evolved from the Liverpool China and India Tea Company founded in 1868 by the Vey brothers, who first served liquid tea to visitors to an Exhibition Café in the 1880s, though it was their coffee which became particularly associated with the chain of Kardomah restaurants at the end of the century. By then tea and coffee had become cheap commodities as a result of reduced tariffs and the development of vast new sources of supply in India, Ceylon, Brazil and Africa. It was now a highly competitive trade which depended on quality assurance, brand names and advertising: teashops were useful for publicising the name and for selling the generally packeted products in the fronts of the premises – in the case of Kardomah the aroma from the large coffee-roasting machines which pervaded neighbouring streets was advertisement in itself. In 1889 Thomas Lipton, the prototype of the new multiple grocers, began offering tea at 1/7d. a pound, 'The Finest the World Can Produce', around 1/- less than family grocers charged. In 1900 he opened the huge Alexandra restaurant in the City Road, which operated as a Trust (trustees Lady Phillips, the Hon. Charles Russell and Lipton) with an anticipated modest dividend of 3 per cent. There were three large floors of dining-rooms, and kitchens at the top with steam chests capable of cooking 1½ tons of potatoes and 1,200 puddings at the same time. The fare was geared to a working-class clientele, offering a three-course meal of soup, roast pork or large steak pudding with two vegetables and tea, coffee or cocoa for 4½d.; other items included Irish stew 2½d., roast or boiled beef or mutton 2½d. and pork chops 4d.

Successful chains depended on a large demand to take advantage of the economies of scale and a limited range of offerings. Another, individual type of catering establishment was the café attached to a large department store where customers were already 'captured' and needing refreshment after their shopping exertions. By the later nineteenth century London and many provincial cities had magnificent, multi-department stores which transformed shopping into a glamorous experience where dreams of luxury and fashionability could be indulged. But after tiring hours round the galleries ladies needed rest and refreshment. A Mrs Fuller, an American, believed that there was a lack of suitable eating-places for 'ladies of the leisured class', and in 1889 opened the first of the somewhat up-market Fuller's Cafés. In fact, by then many department stores had installed tea-rooms, restaurants and 'rest rooms'. In 1863 William Whiteley opened his haberdashery store, 'The Universal Provider', in Westbourne Grove, and in 1872 added a Refreshment Room, though his application to sell alcoholic drinks was refused 'in the interests of morality' – the implication presumably being that ladies might be pestered by drunken men. Around 1887 a Fish Bar was also attached to the fishmonger's department, where 'tempting little fish luncheons, popularly denominated SNACKS, may be had at all hours'. At Holloway William Pearce Jones had started an ironmongery business in 1867, expanding into 'Jones's Gigantic Emporium' by the 1880s: here there was 'an elegant buffet where light refreshments can be obtained at extremely low prices, and supplied with a promptness and politeness which might well be copied by other establishments'.[33] To enhance the pleasurable experience of such places the 'dainty' teas were often accompanied by 'café music' from a pianist or ladies' trio.

This was the state of the light catering trade in which J. Lyons and Co. emerged with remarkable speed to become the largest and most successful of all the chains and the household name always associated with the English teashop. The fact that so much of this catering development occurred in the 1880s – a decade which contemporaries viewed as a downturn, even a 'Great Depression', in the economic prosperity Britain had enjoyed for the last thirty years – is somewhat puzzling. For the first time Britain's almost monopolistic position as the world's leading manu-facturing and trading nation was being challenged by the rise of competi-tors, especially Germany and the United States. Free Trade, which had been erected almost into a religion, was now being questioned as cheap imports flowed into Britain: in 1886 there were unusually high rates of unemployment among skilled workers – 10.2 per cent among engineers and shipbuilders, 13.5 per cent among carpenters and joiners – and unemployed demonstrations in Trafalgar Square and Pall Mall, where the windows of gentlemen's clubs were smashed. In these respects the later 1880s did not appear a very propitious time for investment in catering ventures. On the other hand, the 'Great Depression' directly affected the pockets of relatively small numbers of people: more were benefiting from lower prices of imported foodstuffs, had more disposable income, more leisure and more opportunities for travel and enjoyment than previous generations. It is important to stress that the new catering institutions were largely, though not exclusively, concentrated on London, where a migratory population travelling in and out daily provided a mass market unique in Europe. By 1911 London's population reached 5½ million: here was congregated much of the commerce, the public administration and professional services of the country, these three occupations doubling from 940,000 in 1881 to 2,040,000 in 1911, including 590,000 women.[34] These white-collar and white-blouse workers particularly needed light refreshments served quickly in clean, comfortable surroundings.

Two further factors encouraged the growth of this kind of catering in the late 1880s. In 1887 the nation enthusiastically celebrated Queen Victoria's Golden Jubilee with a sense of pride in achievements at home and in the Empire. Visitors swarmed into London, including many tourists from Europe and America. Associated with the celebrations major exhibitions were organised in provincial cities, which attracted great numbers: two million people attended the Liverpool exhibition in 1886, five million in Manchester in 1887, comparable with those who had visited the Crystal Palace in 1851. With a stand at Manchester dis-playing his firm's tobacco products, Montague Gluckstein (partners Isidore Gluckstein and Barnett Salmon) had been struck by the high prices and poor quality of the refreshments on offer there, and decided to bid for the refreshment contract for the next great event, the Newcastle Jubilee Exhibition, also in 1887. Although successful, the partners did not wish the established tobacco firm's name to be extended to catering, and appointed Joseph Lyons, a relative of Rose, the wife of Isidore, to manage the refreshment contract. Joseph, then 40, was running a market stall in the Liverpool area, probably selling artists' materials as he was a watercolourist and also a composer of verse and songs, with a strong interest in the theatre and music hall.

Lyons' flair for showmanship was demonstrated at the Newcastle Exhibition, where he hired a top Hungarian band to play in 'The Indo-Chinese Pavilion Café'; by contrast, the rather plain fare of tea, scones, shortbread and French pastries won warm praise and were a financial success. In 1888 he supplied the Glasgow Exhibition where, in 'The Bishop's Palace Tea Rooms', the waitresses were dressed in Mary Stuart costumes. After some twenty smaller exhibitions, Lyons secured the refreshment contract for the new, permanent exhibition site at Olympia in 1890, where he also staged some elaborate shows including 'Venice in London' (with 50 gondolas). By then the catering business had grown to a scale which needed a depot and headquarters close to Olympia, and he acquired the premises of a former piano manufacturer, a Mr Cadby – the future Cadby Hall.[35]

It was a natural step to move into permanent teashops, the first in September 1894 at 213 Piccadilly, the former premises of a harness-maker. It was nevertheless a prestigious location, for which the lease cost £30,000, and there was such public interest in the opening that the 200 seats were immediately filled and excited crowds had to be accommodated outside on benches. With financial backing from Salmon and Gluckstein, Lyons made his first teashop a glamorous experience in contrast to its competitors. The double-fronted exterior, distinguished only by the fascia board in gold leaf, hardly prepared customers for the lavish interior decorated in the style of Louis XVI since a café was properly 'French'.

> Red silk covered the walls and gas-lighted chandeliers hung from the ceiling. You sat in a red plush chair, and were served by a very smart waitress in a grey uniform with voluminous skirts down to the floor.[36]

This was, of course, a teashop, not a restaurant. There was almost no cooking except for toasting: all food was supplied centrally from Cadby Hall's kitchens and bakeries and warmed on hot plates. The shop made a point of serving freshly brewed tea for each customer, but the range of offerings was at first quite simple and out of keeping with the glamorous surroundings – mutton pies 7d., scones, toast, tea-cakes, apple pie, prunes and custard, iced Bovril; a few more exotic items included truffled foie gras sausages 3d. and French pastries 2d. upwards. This was evidently the sort of fare people wanted: the early customers were mainly male, but by the end of the century there were large numbers of women, especially on Wednesday and Saturday 'matinée days'.

The immediate, phenomenal success of the first shop, which showed a profit of £11,400 and declared a dividend of 10 per cent at the end of the first year[37] is not easy to explain. It clearly arrived at the right moment and, unlike its rivals which were located mainly in commercial areas round the City, it had the advantage of a situation in the busiest shopping district of central London. This suggests that it derived its custom not so much from clerks and workers in the immediate area as from shoppers, visitors and tourists. While its charges were low, it gained from an expensive ambience, which made a visit to Lyons a memorable experience. No doubt, too, the quality of the food and the standard of service were superior to those of existing cafés. New Lyons teashops followed in rapid succession – 2 more by the end of 1894, 12 in 1895; by 1900 there were 37 in London and footholds had been established in the provinces with 6 in Manchester, 4 in Liverpool and 2 each in Leeds and Sheffield. Growth reached its peak in 1910 when 24 new shops were opened; by 1914 the Lyons' total reached 180, many more than any competing chain.

Long before this Joseph Lyons had decided that there was a market for supplying full meals which the teashops were not equipped to meet. The huge Popular Café was opened in 1904, also in Piccadilly, with accommodation for 2,000 and a four-course luncheon for 1/6d.; afternoon tea from 3 to 6 pm was accompanied by music from the young Victor Sylvester. A full eight-course dinner cost 2/6d. (Kettner's restaurant charged 7/6d. for seven courses at this time), and there was also an after-theatre supper at 1/6d. The designation 'Popular' was justified only by its modest prices. The decor was of a different order from the teashops, evoking grandeur and opulence. There were two marble staircases and galleries to the Grand Hall; the Banquet Room had an ornate painted ceiling, while the Grand Café had marble arches in white and gold and was illuminated by 50 crystal electriliers. Meanwhile, Lyons had already moved further up-market with the Trocadero Restaurant and was soon to launch the Corner Houses, to be described in the next chapter. In an interview for *The Caterer* in 1904, the year the Troc. opened, Joseph Lyons explained what he had set out to change about the catering trade of his early days:

> *I found that not only were the so-called restaurants dirty, but the tablecloths were soiled and greasy and the waiters wore unclean shirts and aprons and their general appearance was slovenly, with a suggestion of prolonged interviews with Bacchus the previous night. There was no quick service, and there were no joints or dishes ready except the eternal 'roast or boiled with veg.' and College Pudding to follow. A steak or chop took half an hour to forty minutes to cook, and the tea and coffee, Oh, the teas and coffees I have suffered from!*[38]

Eating out at leisure

Although Lyons, the ABC and other teashop chains aimed to provide simple, palatable food, they were primarily associated with a brief break from the working day or other activity rather than with recreation for its own sake. It is significant that Lyons concentrated their expansion on the busy hearts of commercial cities; resort towns were almost ignored before 1914, teashops only being established in fashionable places like Southport (1910), Brighton (1910) and Eastbourne (1911)[39] where there were substantial resident populations. There were none in more plebeian resorts like Blackpool, where, in any case, the demand would have been mainly restricted to the summer season.

Nevertheless, by the late nineteenth century increased leisure had become a normal expectation for the working classes. Working hours were now generally reduced to nine a day, with a Saturday half-day: as well as the four Bank Holidays many employers granted manual workers a week's holiday, while those in public services and the professions could expect two to three weeks. Financial resources obviously constrained the type and length of holidays, but by 1900 civil servants, local government employees, teachers, postmen, police and firemen, and most clerks and shop assistants in larger firms were receiving holidays with pay, the length varying from four days upwards according to rank. With a few exceptions like railway employees, most manual workers did not yet enjoy holidays with pay, and among the poorest even the Bank Holidays were resented as involving a compulsory loss of wages.

Charles Booth believed that the growth of holiday making had been one of the most remarkable changes in the habits of the people in recent years. Workers now saved for their holidays, as in the past they had saved for boots and shoes: especially in the North of England there were 'Going Off' savings clubs, while for members of co-operative societies the annual 'dividend' often went for this purpose. Estimates of holiday expenditure vary greatly, but £4 or £5 a year appears to have been quite common, and up to £15 for a highly skilled Lancashire spinner earning £206 a year.[40] Young single men and women were particularly keen to take holidays, often as courting opportunities, and were financially able to do so while living at home: even two holidays a year were not unknown – a girl weaver in Lancashire in 1911 earning £1/8/10d. a week took a week's holiday in June costing £3 and five days in September for £1/10/0d., both at or near the coast.[41]

In the poorer levels of the working class annual holidays were rarely possible unless they could be spent with a relative in the countryside or hop-picking in Kent. At 'round about a pound a week' every penny was needed for necessities, and holidays were limited to occasional day outings or picnics when food was brought from home. 'Day outs' continued to be very popular, facilitated by excursion trains and the new charabancs, and so also did traditional events like fairs (now increasingly mainly fun-fairs) and race meetings where stalls selling ginger-bread and toffee-apples survived alongside the newer ice cream, candy-floss and fizzy drinks. Another older institution which continued throughout the period was the Pleasure Garden, where music, dancing and entertainments accompanied the refreshments served in 'supper boxes' or the picnics brought by visitors. By now, many of the once-fashionable London gardens had disappeared under bricks and mortar (Vauxhall Gardens closed in 1859), but many continued, often attached to inns and taverns where stronger drink than tea was available. These, like Cremorne Gardens, had a more democratic character than their predecessors, and as Warwick Wroth observed in 1907 'were frequented (if invidious distinctions must be made) by the lower middle classes and the "lower orders"'.[42] Probably by then Cremorne had ceased to be the Bohemian resort of the 1870s and 1880s that George Sims had experienced when it was 'quite the thing' to stay until 4 am, and where the habitués included 'the fair and frail, the gallant and the gay, light-hearted youth and wicked old age, frolicking Bohemia and wild-oats-sowing Belgravia'.[43]

Equally traditional was the 'beano', the annual celebration usually organised by workers in smaller firms rather than large companies: it bore some relationship to the still earlier drinking usages intended to demonstrate the fellowship of a trade. A feast of food and drink was the centrepiece of these occasions, often following an excursion to a country inn. The 'beano' described by Robert Tressell was probably quite typical. The thirty or so employees of this firm of builders and decorators each paid 5/-, deducted from their wages over the previous month, 2/6d. for dinner at the Queen Elizabeth Inn, 2/6d. for conveyance there by horse-brakes. On this Saturday in August the men had been paid off at midday instead of the usual 1 pm so they could go home, wash and change. They reassembled at 'The Cricketers' and made their way slowly, with stops for refreshment, arriving at the Queen Elizabeth at 3.40 pm and quickly sitting down to the meal:

> *The dinner was all that could be desired. There was soup, roast beef, boiled mutton, roast turkey, roast goose, ham, cabbage, peas, beans and potatoes, plum pudding, custard, jelly, fruit tarts, bread and cheese, and as much beer or lemonade as they liked to pay for, the drinks being an extra. Everything was cooked to a turn, and although the diners were somewhat bewildered by the multitude of knives and forks, they all, with one or two exceptions, rose to the occasion and enjoyed themselves famously ... Nearly everyone made a point of having at least one helping of everything, and some of them went in for two lots of soup.[44]*

This account from around 1906 might have been written fifty or more years earlier. The food was what men (for there were no women present) enjoyed most, the traditional roasts, nothing fancy or 'French'. Whether the employer contributed is not clear – probably not – but many firm's outings were subsidised in whole or part as a token of gratitude for effort and loyalty. Mr G. Delgado, a stationery manufacturer of Finsbury, took his 80 staff in the 1890s to inns or hotels at Broxbourne, Hastings, Sandgate, Margate and Brighton, where they dined in the Masonic Room at the Pavilion. Here again, the menus were of the traditional, coaching-inn type – at the Royal Oak, Hastings, roast beef (apparently no preliminaries here), roast and boiled mutton, roast chicken and ham, peas, potatoes etc., Royal Oak Pudding, gooseberry and rhubarb tart, stewed fruit and blancmange, cheese and salad. Perhaps some of the lighter dishes like the chicken and blancmange were included for the lady employees present. Some works' outings involved long journeys and major planning. When the large electrical firm, Ferranti Ltd, took their staff to visit the Electrical Exhibition at Olympia, they left Manchester by train soon after midnight, arriving in London at 6 am. Breakfast was laid on at Slater's Restaurant – fried fillet of fish, grilled chop or ham and eggs, rolls, preserves, tea or coffee; lunch was in the Pillar Room at Olympia (a Lyons contract), following the usual pattern of roast meats and Yorkshire pudding, though with two concessions to stylish modernity the meal began with Consommé en Tasse and ended with Charlotte Russe.[45]

A more recent development in the later nineteenth century was a cult of the open air, a wish to escape from overcrowded cities to the peaceful, healthful countryside. Some young men enjoyed a free camping 'holiday' by joining the Volunteer Corps which had been formed at the time of the French invasion scare in 1859 and later developed into the Territorial Army. Independent camping and hiking holidays were also developing, with sites approved by the Camping Club of Great Britain, founded in 1901, while exploration of the countryside was greatly encouraged by the spread of the bicycle, bringing personal mobility to all levels of society except the very poorest. By the 1880s cycling was becoming a boom leisure activity when the 'safety cycle' with two equally sized wheels replaced the dangerous 'penny-farthing', and pneumatic tyres, patented by J. R. Dunlop in 1888, made riding more comfortable for both sexes. By then 230 cycling clubs existed for those who liked organised outings, and a new machine costing around 9 guineas – or, more likely, a second-hand one at much less – was affordable for many urban workers.[46] By the end of the century cycling was often associated with the emancipation of 'the new woman', with new thought and, as with some of H. G. Wells's characters, with socialism; Robert Blatchford's 'Clarion Cycling Clubs' aimed at spreading the gospel among young people, and offered members the opportunity of buying a machine by small monthly instalments. The Cyclists' Touring Club (1878) and the National Cyclists' Union campaigned to improve country roads and signposts and negotiated moderate tariffs for cyclists at hotels and boarding-houses, but for single days out at weekends most cyclists carried their own provisions in saddle-bags, picnicking by the still quiet roadsides or stopping at country inns, many of which had been decaying since the railways passed them by. The cycling boom also helped to create the village teashop where hungry travellers could enjoy home-made scones, new-laid eggs and healthy 'Hovis' bread.

As well as the now well-established commercial travel agencies like Thomas Cook, there were, by later in the century, non-profit-making bodies organising holidays in the countryside, often intended for students or underprivileged groups. The Polytechnic Touring Association, established in 1872, had a holiday home in Brighton, and later one in Switzerland, the Arlington Travel Club was associated with the City Literary Institute, while the Toynbee Travellers' Club provided for members of Toynbee Hall, the first of the 'Settlements' where Oxford undergraduates mixed with London East Enders.[47] Best known of these ventures into popular recreation was the Co-operative Holidays Association, founded in 1891 by the Revd T. A. Leonard, once described as 'the father of the open-air movement'.[48] This established hostels in areas like the Lake District, providing simple food and lodging, and offering 'healthful ways of an out-of-door-life among the hills instead of the tawdry pleasures of popular holiday resorts'. Other declared objectives were 'to help people to find joy in music, literature, nature study and that best of all exercises, walking'.

More working people were attracted to the 'tawdry pleasures' than those who responded to the somewhat earnest pleas for rational recreation. The stereotypical working-class holiday was a family affair, a week at the seaside with all the fun of sea and sand, donkey-rides and roundabouts for the children, pierrot shows, variety theatres and ballrooms or gentle strolls along the proms and piers for the adults. But the week at Blackpool, Skegness or Clacton had to be managed economically, the commonest way being to hire one or two bedrooms in a lodging-house: wives would then shop for food which the landlady cooked for a small fee. The superior alternative was the boarding house, where either all or some meals were provided. Lunch could conveniently be taken at one of the many cafés or fish-and-chip shops which abounded in popular resorts, and which now came in a variety of forms from the little back-street shop which only sold for 'taking out' to restaurant-type fish-and-chip 'palaces' in the main thoroughfares, where a full meal of cod, haddock or plaice with chips, peas, bread and butter and tea was served. Fish and chips had evidently moved somewhat up the social scale: at Fleetwood in 1906 the proprietor of a large shop seating 70 divided his customers into three classes according to their appearance and status.[49] Some landladies were also particular about sexual segregation: at Yarmouth a boarding-house was kept for men only by a formidable Mrs Powell who supplied her clients, known as 'Ma Powell's lambs', with a generous full board for one guinea a week.[50]

Holidays were special occasions, breaks from the ordinary, when people looked forward to eating out not only well but differently, sampling things that were not part of the everyday diet. Seaside resorts naturally sold many sea-foods, some locally caught, such as cockles and mussels, shrimps, oysters and jellied eels, not as basic articles of diet but as snack 'relishes' usually sold at open booths and eaten while standing. Pies of many varieties, savoury and sweet, cakes, pastries, tarts, and fancy breads, often with local names and flavours, were sold by the many bakers and confectioners, while pork butchers purveyed many sorts of tasty pig-meat made into sausages, faggots, saveloys and haslet as well as cow-heels, trotters and brawn. These could be taken for a picnic on the beach, where cups of tea were sold or kettles boiled, and scores of itinerants with lemonade, fruit, nuts and sweets tempted pennies out of unusually open pockets.

Children's tastes, it was felt, might reasonably be indulged on holiday, for if father was entitled to his extra pint or two of beer in the evening, should not children enjoy their own treats? As well as the striped mint 'rock' or the candy-floss two things were especially associated with holidays – soft drinks and ice cream. Locally made herb drinks such as horehound, ginger beer, nettle beer and sarsaparilla were still popular, though now being overtaken by frothy, carbonated drinks, manufactured either by large firms with brand names or, more cheaply, by small, back-street concerns which relied on sugar, tartaric acid and artificial colourings for their penny bottles bearing exotic names. In 1913 the official estimate of total production, almost certainly an under-estimate, reached 80.5 million gallons a year, or around 16 pints a head. Very small shipments of Coca-Cola syrup from America began in 1911 but the name was scarcely known here before the First World War: on the other hand, the long-established Schweppes drinks were now widely advertised and so also were newer products like 'Iron Brew' (1901), 'Vimto' (1908), 'Tizer' ('the Appetizer') and fruit drinks like 'Idris' and 'Kia-Ora' (1911).[51]

The most ephemeral, the fastest of all 'fast' foods to disappear, was, of course, ice cream. As previously mentioned, Henry Mayhew had described it as a new product in the London streets in 1850, but its popularity had then spread rapidly. The trade became dominated in the 1870s by Italian immigrants, many of whom came from Barga and Lucca in Umbria and from Naples and Sicily, their great ambition being to progress from a barrow to a shop in the image of Carlo Gatti. In the 1850s he had run a pastrycook's business in Hungerford Market, also selling ices and soft drinks, but when the market was demolished in 1864 he was generously compensated and began buying ships carrying natural ice from Norway: ultimately he owned a fleet of 24 ships and several large ice stores. He also did much to popularise the highly decorated ice-cream carts in the London streets selling 'hokey-pokey' in ½d., 1d. or 2d. 'licks'[52] ('hokey-pokey' was an English corruption of the seller's cry, 'Gelati. Ecco un poco', an invitation to taste a small free sample). It is estimated that in 1900 there were around 700 barrows in London and large numbers in all cities and resorts. By then, as well as the summer open-air trade, ice cream had moved into fixed all-year shops, usually combined with confectionery and soft drinks, of which there were said to be 336 in Glasgow in 1905. Here, vanilla-flavoured ice was sold in shallow dishes with a spoon, not yet in cones or wafers; in the street it was served in three sizes of tub-shaped glasses, the lower halves of which were solid to suggest a larger content and also to facilitate licking by the customer's tongue: after use the glass was lightly washed or merely wiped. Both 'penny licks' and ice-cream 'parlours' often came in for condemnation, the former by Medical Officers of Health who believed that unclean glasses passed from mouth to mouth in poor districts were a source of infectious diseases such as tuberculosis, the latter because some puritanical town councils objected to the shops' late opening hours and the dangers to the morals of young people who were wasting good money on a useless product. 'Penny licks' were generally outlawed by local authorities in the 1920s, replaced by cones and wafers and by the harder, striped blocks of 'Neapolitan' ice cream of different colours and flavours, wrapped in waxed paper for consumption elsewhere.[53]

FIGURE 4.3 ◆ *An ice-cream seller and his customers, 1877. The street trade in ices began* c. *1850, but one of the sellers told Henry Mayhew, 'I don't think they'll ever take greatly on'. Before the introduction of cones and wafers, ices were usually licked from shallow glasses which were then casually wiped by the seller.*

Source: © Museum of London.

Notes and references

1 C. F. G. Masterman, *The Condition of England*, Methuen and Co., 1909, p. 70.

2 L. G. Chiozza Money, *Riches and Poverty*, Methuen and Co., 11th edn, 1914, p. 48.

3 Mrs Pember Reeves, *Round About a Pound a Week* (1st edn, 1913), republished Virago, 1979, pp. 114, 122, 164. Maud Pember Reeves, a New Zealander, was the wife of the Agent General for the New Zealand Government.

4 John K. Walton, *Fish and Chips and the British Working Class 1870–1940*, Leicester, Leicester University Press, 1992, p. 5.

5 Theodore Dreiser, *A Traveller at Forty*, Grant Richards Ltd, 1914, pp. 181–2.

6 T. R. Gourvish and R. G. Wilson, *The British Brewing Industry 1830–1980*, Cambridge, Cambridge University Press, 1994, Table 2.3, p. 30.

7 For details of consumption and expenditure on alcohol, see John Burnett, *Liquid Pleasures. A Social History of Drinks in Modern Britain*, Routledge, 1999, pp. 126ff.

8 Robert Thorne, 'The Movement for Public House Reform, 1882–1914', in Derek J. Oddy and Derek S. Miller (eds), *Diet and Health in Modern Britain*, Croom Helm, 1985, p. 244.

9 Robert Roberts, *The Classic Slum, Salford Life in the First Quarter of the Century*, Manchester, Manchester University Press, 1971, p. 87.

10 Raphael Samuel (ed.), *Village Life and Labour*, Routledge & Kegan Paul, History Workshop Series, 1975, p. 156.

11 James Griffiths, *Pages from Memory*, J. M. Dent, 1969, p. 9. Griffiths first went down the mine in 1903: he ultimately became Minister of National Insurance in the Labour government, 1945–50, and Deputy Leader of the Parliamentary Labour Party, 1956–9.

12 D. H. Lawrence, *The Rainbow* (1915), quoted Brigid Allen (ed.), *Food. An Oxford Anthology*, Oxford, Oxford University Press, 1994, pp. 185–7.

13 Edward Spencer ('Nathaniel Gubbins'), *Cakes and Ale. A Dissertation on Banquets, etc.*, (1st edn, 1897), Stanley Paul and Co., 1913, pp. 36–7.

14 Sir Noel Curtis-Bennett, *The Food of the People, being the History of Industrial Feeding*, Faber and Faber, 1949, p. 201.

15 ibid., pp. 189–95. Curtis-Bennett drew heavily on J. E. Budgett Meakin, *Model Factories and Villages*, T. Fisher Unwin, 1905.

16 M. E. Buckley, *The Feeding of School Children*, G. Bell and Sons, 1914, p. 16.

17 Gilbert Slater, *Poverty and the State*, Constable and Co., 1930, pp. 173, 176.

18 C. F. G. Masterman, *The Heart of the Empire* (1st edn, 1901), Brighton, Sussex, Harvester Press, 1973, p. 8.

19 Report of the Inter-Departmental Committee on Physical Deterioration, vol. 1, Report and Appendix, Cd. 2175, 1904, p. 96. On concerns about national health, the Empire and army recruitment, see Bentley B. Gilbert, *The Evolution of National Insurance in Great Britain*, Michael Joseph, 1966, pp. 83ff.

20 Report, ibid., Summary of Recommendations, p. 91.

21 Gilbert, op. cit., p. 102.

22 Sir Charles Elliott, 'State Feeding of School Children in London', *The Nineteenth Century and After*, vol. LXV, Jan.–June, 1909, pp. 864–5.

23 Laura Mason, 'Learning How to Eat in Public: School Dinners', in Harlan Walker (ed.), *Public Eating. Oxford Symposium on Food and Cookery, 1991*, Prospect Books, 1991, pp. 207–8.

24 See generally on this Gareth Stedman Jones, *Outcast London. A Study of the Relationships between Classes in Victorian Society*, Harmondsworth, Middlesex, Penguin, 1976.

25 J. A. R. Pimlott, *The Englishman's Holiday*, Faber and Faber, 1947, p. 157.

26 Quoted Alan Delgado, *The Annual Outing and Other Excursions*, George Allen & Unwin, 1977, pp. 80–1.

27 Lieut.-General R. S. S. Baden-Powell, *Scouting for Boys. A Handbook for Instruction in Good Citizenship*, C. Arthur Pearson, revised edn, 1909, pp. 112, 115.

28 E. Hepple Hall, *Coffee Taverns, Cocoa Houses and Coffee Palaces. Their Rise, Progress and Prospects*, S. W. Partridge, 1878, Directory.

29 John Pearce, interviewed by S. J. Adair Fitz-Gerald in *The Caterer and Hotel-Keepers' Gazette*, 16 Jan. 1905, 'Chats With Caterers', pp. 14–15.

30 Report relative to the Grievances Complained of by the Journeyman Bakers, PP (3027), vol. xlvii, 1862, pp. lxi–lxiii.

31 Denys Forrest, *Tea for the British. The Social and Economic History of a Famous Trade*, Chatto & Windus, 1973, p. 182.

32 Bryan Morgan, *Express Journey, 1864–1964. A Centenary History of the Express Dairy Company Ltd.*, Newman Neame Ltd, 1964, pp. 21–40.

33 Alison Adburgham, *Shops and Shopping, 1800–1914*, Barrie and Jenkins, 2nd edn, 1989, pp. 154, 156–7.

34 B. R. Mitchell and Phyllis Deane, *Abstract of British Historical Statistics*, Cambridge, Cambridge University Press, 1962, Table: Labour Force 1, p. 58.

35 For this section I acknowledge my debt to the recent and overdue history of Lyons by Peter Bird, *The First Food Empire. A History of J. Lyons and Co.*, Chichester, West Sussex, Phillimore, 2000, pp. 13–20.

36 Julian Salmon speaking at a London School of Economics seminar in March 1963, quoted Forrest, op. cit., p. 184.

37 Bird, op.cit., p. 41.

38 Joseph Lyons, interviewed by S. J. Adair Fitz-Gerald, in *The Caterer and Hotel-Keepers' Gazette*, 15 June 1904, 'Chats with Caterers', p. 239.

39 Bird, op. cit., Appendix 4, Teashops and Other Restaurants of J. Lyons and Co. Ltd., pp. 348ff.

40 Pimlott, *The Englishman's Holiday*, op. cit., pp. 151–2.

41 W. Hamish Fraser, *The Coming of the Mass Market, 1850–1914*, Hamden, Conn., Archon Books, 1981, p. 80.

42 Warwick Wroth, *Cremorne and the Later London Gardens*, Elliot Stock, 1907, Preface, p. V.

43 George R. Sims, *My Life. Sixty Years' Recollections of Bohemian London*, Eveleigh Nash, 1917, p. 39.

44 Robert Tressall (Noonan), *The Ragged Trousered Philanthropists* (1914), quoted Brigid Allen (ed.), *Food. An Oxford Anthology*, Oxford, Oxford University Press, 1996, pp. 294–6.

45 Delgado, op. cit., pp. 17, 21, 126–7.

46 Fraser, op. cit., p. 81.

47 Pimlott, op. cit., pp. 169–70.

48 Oliver Coburn, *Youth Hostel Story. The First Twenty Years*, The National Council of Social Service, 1950, p. 6.

49 John K. Walton, *Fish and Chips and the British Working Class, 1870–1940*, Leicester, Leicester University Press, 1992, p. 34.

50 Robert Cecil, *Life in Edwardian England*, B. T. Batsford, 1969, p. 107.

51 For details see John Burnett, *Liquid Pleasures. A Social History of Drinks in Modern Britain*, London, Routledge, 1999, esp. pp. 100–4.

52 Elizabeth David, *Harvest of the Cold Months. The Social History of Ice and Ices* (ed. Jill Norman), Harmondsworth, Middlesex, Penguin Books, 1996, pp. 347–8. The famous Gatti's Restaurant in the Strand was opened in 1862 not by Carlo but by two of his nephews.

53 I acknowledge my thanks and debt to two chapters in Harlan Walker (ed.),

Public Eating. Oxford Symposium on Food and Cookery, 1991, Prospect Books, 1991: Francis McKee, 'Ice Cream and Immorality', pp. 199–204; Robin Weir, 'Penny Licks and Hokey-Pokey. Ice cream before the Cone', pp. 295–9.

CHAPTER 5

Catering for the classes

The classes

*Seldom in human history can such rich food have been prepared so
regularly by so many for so few. If the arts, in general, did not flourish,
at least the culinary art reached new heights.*[1]

Late Victorian and Edwardian England was a Golden Age for the gourmet, an age of grand hotels and luxurious restaurants where famous
chefs drew on the finest foods from all parts of the world and served
meals literally 'fit for a king'. If Edward VII himself chose to eat out, the
ranks of 'Society' found it fashionable to do so, to see and be seen in
lavish surroundings which only those at the summit of the scale could
achieve at home. Euphoric recollections of the time before the Great
Deluge of the war changed so much, typified by W. Macqueen Pope's
Twenty Shillings to the Pound. A Lost Age of Plenty, 1890–1914 (1948),
evoked nostalgia for a time when income tax stood at 8d. in the pound in
1885 and only reached 12d. in 1909, when a house in St James's could be
rented for £200 a year and the necessary staff of cook, parlourmaid and
housemaid cost £64. 'There can be little doubt that for the well-to-do and
for no inconsiderable part of the middle class, the acme of material comfort and well-being was achieved during the reign of King Edward VII.'[2]

Such verdicts need qualification. Comfort and well-being certainly
did not characterise the lives of the poor, or even of many of the

respectable working class. And although Britain remained the wealthiest society in the world, her shares of industrial output and foreign trade were now falling in face of the rise of more efficient competitors like Germany and the United States. Complaints were heard that British industrialists lacked the drive, enterprise and ambition of their forefathers and that their energies now went into grouse shooting, yachting and other diversions. But although there was a minor war in South Africa, and rumours of a greater one to come, the future seemed secure enough: more was to be feared from Lloyd George's 'People's Budget' of 1909 which aimed to redistribute wealth by raising income tax to 14d. in the pound on incomes over £3,000 a year, with a further 5d. 'super-tax' on those over £5,000. The House of Lords indignantly rejected it, but was forced to give way a year later.

Capitalists had grown ostentatious in their wealth, epitomised in Veblen's famous phrase (1899), 'conspicuous consumption'. In his chapter on 'The Conquerors' C. F. G. Masterman noted

> *the private competition for supremacy in social standard. Where one house sufficed, two are now demanded; where dinner of a certain quality, now a dinner of a superior quality; where clothes, or dresses, or flowers, now more clothes, more dresses, more flowers.*[3]

That, of course, was nothing new, but in Edwardian England social competition was encouraged by the changing structure of the rich, where the incomes of the landed aristocracy were now often exceeded by those of successful financiers, merchants and industrialists. For parvenus the rules of Society could be learned from handbooks of etiquette and the pages of ladies' journals, and could be demonstrated in the theatrical settings of grand hotels and restaurants.

In 1900 the wealthy were defined by a leading economist as those having incomes of more than £700 a year. Even at this relatively modest level, their numbers were tiny – 280,000 income tax payers who, with their families, represented around 1,400,000 people. They took one-third of national income. Below them, and taking a second third, was the broader band of the middle class with incomes of £160–£700 a year: here were 820,000 income tax payers or 4,100,000 people.[4] This left 39,000,000 people with less than £160 a year, discussed in Chapter 4. Here we are concerned with the two other classes, the 'comfortable' and the 'rich', the potential diners-out, though those near the base of the 'comfort' class were unlikely to be seen at the Savoy or the Café Royal. In the late nineteenth century there was much discussion in journals about how incomes should be allocated, in itself an indication of anxiety about status and the demands of a competitive society. As early as 1875 an article entitled 'Life At High Pressure' suggested that the problem for the middle classes was not so much the cost of living, but that the *style* of living had risen so much. 'We need many things that our fathers did not, and for each of these things we must pay more.'[5] In 1901 *The Cornhill Magazine* carried a series of model budgets for different income levels, starting with the lower middle class earning £150 a year. The example taken was that of a solicitor's clerk living in a London suburb. 'Plain living will be a matter of course on £150 a year'; nothing is allowed for his meals at work (he presumably took something from home), still less for any social eating-out: the only recreation is a modest annual holiday for the family of four, costing £5. But at £250 a year things looked rather different. There was now a maid-of-all-work at a wage of £12 a year and board, the husband was allowed £30 for his lunches and, often, teas in town (12/- a week or 2/- a day), and more generous family holidays at £12. This was the genteel sort of man who would take his meals at a dining-room, a Lyons or ABC teashop rather than at a tavern or cook-shop.[6] With an income of £800 a year a young professional couple were just within the 'rich' bracket, but G. Colmore's budget warned that here they have to keep up appearances and that they belonged to a society many members of which were much wealthier. Rent, rates and taxes take £130, and there is now a cook and a housemaid – more will be needed when there are children. 'If she [the wife] and her husband want to dine out at all, they must live within what I would call the dinner-party radius', that is, within the range of reasonable cab fares. This would apply whether their dining was with friends or at a restaurant, but the couple would do well to confine themselves to 'a limited amount of dining-out'. It was assumed that they would occasionally attend theatres and concerts, that the husband should have an allowance of £70 a year for his clothes and subscription to his club, where he might take lunch or tea and an occasional drink. 'Entertaining' is set at £35 a year, and £50 for holidays, quite sufficient for more than one stay at first-class hotels in England, Switzerland or the Côte d'Azur.[7]

English society was becoming increasingly secular. Formal religious observance had been in decline since at least 1851, when the first Religious Census had revealed that rather fewer than half the population regularly attended any place of worship. Subsequently, the discoveries of geologists, Darwinians and anthropologists had further eroded Christian faith in puritanical aversions to enjoyment: a Gospel of Pleasure was replacing the mid-Victorian Gospel of Work. Between 1850 and 1900 the number of theatres in London doubled, and in the provinces quadrupled: there were booms in lawn tennis and croquet, in golf and cycling, in bridge and a host of indoor games which no longer had to be justified as 'improving'. Above all, a great increase in holiday making characterised the Edwardian age, exemplified by a king who took annual vacations in Biarritz or Baden-Baden, who loved yachting, shooting and horse-racing as well as more private sports. An article in *The Times* in 1876 had already defended a growing trend towards 'a mingled mass of *perfectly legitimate pleasures* [my italics] ever thrusting themselves forward in a variety of shapes'.[8] Second and third generations of the founders of successful businesses were not prepared to devote such time and energy to their offices: profits were still sufficient to support a pleasant lifestyle, while education at public school and university had often developed cultural and sporting interests. True leisure, of course, should not merely be amusement, 'passing the time', but recreation which revived body, mind and spirits. In mid-Victorian times privacy and home-centredness had characterised middle-class life, distinguishing it from the more open social relations of the classes both above and below it. Now lives were lived more in public, in travel and holidaying, in visits to theatres, concerts and exhibitions, in clubs, institutions and societies of every conceivable kind. '"Home, Sweet Home" does not form the centre of attraction it once did... We do almost everything in public. Every idea nowadays assumes the form of a society – and these, of course, must be supplemented by their music, their eating and drinking.'[9] These trends presented major opportunities for commercial exploitation: as Peter Bailey writes, 'The contest for the hearts, minds and pockets of the new leisure class had only just begun.'[10]

Dining out versus dining in

In explaining the growth of eating out at this time two sets of reasons, one negative and one positive, are important. Eating in public was an alternative to eating and entertaining at home, and despite the prosperity of the middle and upper classes there were increasing constraints on domestic budgets. The maintenance of the paraphernalia of gentility was becoming more expensive as fashions in furnishing and decor and in the content and service of meals constantly changed, and although the numbers of domestic servants continued to rise to a peak of 1,600,000 in 1914 their wage levels also increased as more attractive employments for women opened in shops, offices and factories.[11] Further strains on resources, such as the higher costs of private education for both boys and girls, and the longer period of dependency of the former, were contributory factors in the decline of the birth rate which began in the 1870s.[12] In particular, the costs of giving domestic dinner parties rose sharply as higher standards of cooking, presentation and service were now expected. In a letter to *The Englishwoman's Magazine*, 'Mrs S.', with three servants and an allowance of £26 a month for food, complained that she could only rarely give 'little dinners', which she estimated cost 16/- per person, including wine. Her housekeeping allowance did not run to this, and 'Mr S.' had to make an extra contribution.[13] This amount would have been quite sufficient to dine her guests at a top hotel or restaurant. In similar vein, Mary Hooper wrote of

> The difficulty of getting up little dinners for five or six persons without incurring too great an expense or too severely taxing the powers of the cook. Such dishes as the honoured cod and oyster sauce and the haunch or saddle of mutton, always costly, are now quite beyond the reach of persons with small incomes.[14]

But there was also another difficulty:

> It would, of course, be ridiculous to expect a cook to send up a dinner of many different dishes in a totally different style to that to which she had been accustomed[15] [that is, the French style].

Here was the problem. Only in the very wealthiest households was a chef employed who could accomplish 'haute cuisine', but this, or some approximation to it, was well beyond the abilities of a 'plain' or even a 'professed' cook. But by the end of the century guests at a fashionable dinner would not be satisfied with cod and saddle of mutton: if an English roast of some sort still survived on the menu, diners would also expect a variety of French entrées, relèves and *entremets*, served by waiters in the now accepted '*à la Russe*' style. This would almost certainly mean buying in such dishes from professional caterers at considerable expense, and hiring extra staff to help in the kitchen and the dining-room.

In domestic dining the usual pattern since the later eighteenth century had been service '*à la Française*' in which the meal consisted essentially of two large courses, each containing several dishes. As guests entered the dining-room soup and fish were already on the table: the hostess helped to the soup, the host to the fish. These were then 'removed' and replaced by at least two entrées such as 'made' dishes of veal, duck, chicken and sweetbreads; dishes of vegetables and sauces were uncovered, and gentlemen helped the ladies to these, and then themselves. After the remains were cleared, a second course was brought in, usually comprising the principal roast meats together with game, pies, cold meats and salads; the tablecloth removed, the dinner concluded with puddings, tarts, compôtes of fruit, jellies, ices and cheeses.[16] This was the form of service favoured by Mrs Beeton in the 1860s and later, but it had some serious inconveniences: there were difficulties in keeping dishes warm through two long courses, the passing around of dishes and the helping to them by the guests themselves was troublesome, while the time spent by the host in carving several joints often made for a very extended meal.

Service '*à la Française*' had suited Georgian country house parties, which began in the late afternoon and lasted into the early evening, but it was inappropriate for the faster pace of life and the later hour of dining towards the end of the century. The alternative, service '*à la Russe*', had spread from the Russian court to France and England, where it was in use at large public banquets as early as 1814. In the new style, each of the eight or ten courses was brought round by waiters and offered from serving dishes: a particular course might be declined without giving offence to the host since relations were more impersonal, mediated by servants. Meats were already carved or jointed in the kitchen or at the sideboard by staff: appropriate vegetables and sauces for each dish were brought round, so the table was left free for glasses, candelabra, an epergne and the floral decorations which were now considered essential. Dining of this sort was quicker, more controlled by rules of etiquette, but more expensive of labour, serving dishes, cutlery, plates and glasses – often five for the different wines. Mrs Beeton in 1861 advised against it for households without sufficient resources, suggesting only two specimen menus of this kind compared with 81 for service '*à la Française*' or for a transitional type which ran to five courses, but by the 1880s '*à la Russe*' was usual for fashionable dinner-parties given by the upper classes, despite the costs. A trend towards somewhat greater simplicity is noticeable towards the end of the century, when a leading society hostess, Lady Jeune, wrote that 'No dinner should last more than an hour and a quarter if properly served [and] should consist of no more than eight dishes: soup, fish, entrée, joint, game, hors d'oeuvre [a strange placing, meaning a savoury?], and perhaps an ice, but each dish should be perfect of its kind'.[17]

The relevance of this discussion to the history of eating out is that in dining in public at top hotels and restaurants service '*à la Russe*' was invariably used and guests were already accustomed to it. It seems not to have been noticed in the literature on the subject that this must long have been the norm in such places. Tables for two, four or six people would have been too small for a multiplicity of dishes served together, and in well-run establishments chefs and their staffs were ready to cook dishes to order, and waiters to serve them without delay. Service '*à la Russe*' gave greater scope for chefs to prepare original entrées and, especially, 'flying dishes' which had to be served immediately, and it also gave greater choice to diners, who could select from a long à la carte menu. By the 1890s fashionable London hostesses were inviting guests to dine in leading hotels and restaurants: it was no more expensive than a dinner party at home, it offered foods and a cuisine that could not be provided there and a setting of luxury that could not be matched. For hosts its great virtue was convenience and release from anxiety, for guests the opportunity to experience unfamiliar dishes and to participate in an entertainment provided by observation of other diners. Freed from the presence of domestic servants, diners felt less restrained in conversation and gossip. Talk, believed Masterman, was the great characteristic of the age, especially of the London 'Season' when most entertaining took place:

All quick and novel sensations are pressed into the service of an ever
more insistent demand for new things... For the most part it is talk-talk-
talk, talk at luncheon, tea and dinner... It is talk usually commonplace,
sometimes clever, occasionally sincere, of a society desirous of being
interested, more often finding itself bored... What does it all mean? No
one knows. What does it all come to? Again, no one knows.[18]

The growth of eating out was closely associated with other forms of entertainment. London was recognised as the centre for leisure activities by
residents and visitors: it offered concerts, art galleries, museums and
public lectures for the serious-minded, theatres and music-halls for the
more light-hearted. Many of the leading restaurants were located close to
these attractions in the West End: some, like the Criterion Theatre and
Restaurant and the Gaiety Theatre and Restaurant directly linked food
and entertainment, but many restaurants provided early, pre-theatre dinners and also late after-theatre suppers. As *The Caterer* argued in 1901,
restaurants were themselves one of the major attractions of the capital:

> *London is becoming a more popular pleasure resort because of the*
> *substitution of dingy old chop-houses for the glittering comfort of the*
> *palatial restaurant.*[19]

There were, then, practical and economic reasons favouring eating out,
but these were outweighed by the social and psychological pleasures of
dining in the public sphere, and not in an all-male environment.

> *The Club Dinner is not what it was. Men don't dine at their clubs*
> *nowadays; they go with their wives, or with the wives of others, to*
> *partake of the Restaurant Dinner. These Restaurant Dinners are*
> *comparatively recent institutions [1902] so to speak, having come into*
> *vogue in the last few years, but they have become almost, if not*
> *altogether, the greatest feature of the Night Side of London high life.*

The author, Robert Mackray, went on to notice that fashions shifted
between hotels like Claridge's, the Carlton, the Savoy and the Cecil, and
between such restaurants as the Trocadero, the Criterion, Prince's and
Frascati's. You got the best dinner in London at such places, 'and see the
most interesting company in them as well'.[20] After the theatre one should
go to the Carlton for supper and observe the clientèle:

*There a well-known man of fashion, here a celebrated actress in a
ravishing gown. There a gallant soldier back from the Front, here an
authoress, a lady playwrite of great renown; there a great lady, a
princess, here a man of genius whose fame is worldwide... You
read stories into the smiling faces; you make guesses, you build up
little romances. In a word, you are looking on at another phase of the
show.*[21]

Not specified here, though almost certainly present, were visitors from
overseas, especially from America now that Atlantic liners were themselves luxurious, floating hotels. Similarly, there was much reverse traffic from Britain at this time, and it seems likely that American dining
habits influenced Britain and that the more open, democratic society
there loosened the traditional reserve of the English in public. In some
respects the new trends in eating out had developed earlier on the other
side of the Atlantic: America had many more ethnic restaurants, French,
Italian, German, Chinese and other, reflecting the diverse origins of its
people, and hotels like the Waldorf Astoria (1893) and the Ritz Carlton
(1902), built to the highest standards of magnificence: here were ballrooms, Palm Gardens and 'Peacock Alleys', ideally suited to display
ladies' dresses, jewellery and fine feathers. Some American men, however, tended to disapprove of the convention of full evening dress at
dinner, and the development of Grill Rooms in English hotels and restaurants, where informal dress was acceptable, was partly in response to
American male preferences. Dancing between courses at dinner also
began in America in the 1890s at places like the Café de Beaux Arts and
cabarets were introduced at the Columbus Circle around 1905, soon to be
followed by Dixieland jazz bands.[22]

The traffic was two way. Leading actors and actresses, opera and
music-hall stars, literary lions and sporting personalities were regular
diners on both sides of the Atlantic, lending an air of exoticism and
reflected significance to the occasion. Their presence contributed to the
performative aspects of dining out by which a host could display his
'savoir-faire' in a structured association with the great. While the restaurant was democratic in the sense that it was open to those who could pay
and behave properly, it was also a 'territory of snobbery' and a 'passageway to a world of excitement, luxury and desires'.[23] This was enhanced

by the theatricality of the decor – the lavish use of marble, mosaics, grand staircases, mirrors, chandeliers and silk wall-coverings – which provided for the bourgeoisie an escape from reality, a sense of belonging to another world of power and prestige, both remote from everyday life yet, if only briefly, attainable.

Women diners

Essential to the full enjoyment of this style of dining was the presence of women. Ladies had, of course, eaten in select hotels, but usually in their own suites or in small, private dining-rooms. They had taken tea, cakes and ices at confectioners' shops, had lunched in an upstairs room at Simpson's and at vegetarian restaurants, but what was new towards the end of the century was their presence in the evening in public restaurants. They were not required to be especially clever or witty – to be too much so could detract from a male-dominated occasion: their principal function was to be decorative and compliant, beautiful if possible or at least attractive, dressed, coiffured and adorned fashionably to reflect the good taste of their host. When Lieut. Col. Newnham-Davis, the restaurant critic of the *Pall Mall Gazette*, took a lady to dine, he invariably chose the menu, often pre-arranged by discussion with the maître d'hôtel in the morning. There was no question of the lady choosing for herself: it was assumed, and accepted, that he knew best where and what to eat, and that the 'little lady', as he often described her, would enjoy and admire his choice.

Nevertheless, the mere presence of ladies in public restaurants was a new phenomenon, which André Simon described as nothing less than a 'revolution':

> There were restaurants where gentlemen could and did entertain their fair friends, but ladies did not bare their shoulders and show off their fine feathers in public dining-rooms to be stared at by all and sundry and, perhaps, sit in the same room as a demi-mondaine... Escoffier's exquisite cooking tempted the fairest and noblest to dine in public for the first time, whilst Ritz's exquisite taste and tact provided for them the perfect setting and warded off undesirable company. Both men were responsible for this revolution, for so great a change may rightly be called a revolution.[24]

If the soft, pink shades of the lamps at the Savoy flattered complexions, Escoffier's naming of his creations after great ladies did even more for their reputations – the Soufflé Sarah Bernhardt, the Pêches and Toast Melba, the Poulard Adelina Patti and the Oeufs à la Chimay (after the Princesse de Chimay). The deliberate exploitation of a new market of diners was certainly part, but only part, of the explanation for the revolution. By the end of the century women of the middle and upper-middle classes whose lives had been bounded by domesticity were beginning to participate in many public spheres formerly closed to them – in higher education and universities, in the arts, the professions and local politics. Married women were beneficiaries of the spread of birth control, emancipating them from constant child bearing which had confined them to home; now, with an average family size falling to only three or four children, often completed by the age of thirty, they could be seen in public without embarrassment, free to enjoy legitimate pleasures. Those who dined at the Savoy or the Café Royal were not likely to be among Mr Wells's 'new women', still less strident suffragettes, but they were proclaiming a degree of emancipation, a right to share in the pleasures of a new kind of social experience, a passageway to modernity. Locality and environment were, however, necessary for ensuring respectability and protection: restaurants in areas like Soho, frequented by Bohemians, or in the Haymarket haunts of prostitutes were out of bounds. An important attribute of the fashionable restaurant was its openness and permeability, at once revealing but reassuring.

While all-male eating-places of the older, tavern type survived strongly up to 1914, it was unusual for unaccompanied women to dine together in the better restaurants. At the Berkeley in Piccadilly Lieut. Col. Newnham-Davis noticed that two ladies were dining together before going to the opera – 'the Berkeley is a place where ladies can dine and lunch without an escort'.[25] For him, the pleasure of dining out was to entertain a lady, preferably one of wealth or importance. Unusually and by the request of an old friend, he took a governess in a girls' boarding-school to dine out at Willis's Rooms: she was endeavouring to write a novel and wanted some local colour about London society. When he met her at 8.30 pm he was prepared for a primness of attire, but found the little governess looking very nice in a low-necked black silk dress with a tiny diamond heart hung round her neck by a little gold chain. By prior arrangement with M. Fayat they had plovers' eggs, Soupe Henri IV, brill with mushrooms in a Burgundy sauce, noisettes of lamb with dressed *haricots verts* and new potatoes, *poulet polonnaise* with savoury rice and chicken liver, asparagus in *sauce mousseline*, and strawberries served in a silver dish over a bed of ice. The meal for two cost £1/5/0d., plus 6/- for a bottle of hock and 3/- for coffee and liqueurs. The would-be authoress, however, was more interested in the ambience and the other guests. The Colonel explained that Willis's was as near a Parisian restaurant as could be found in London, with its crimson couches by the walls, scarlet-seated chairs and great ormolu clock, while from the room upstairs were heard the strains of Horvath's orchestra. This evening two 'grandes dames' were dining, Sir George Lewis, a group of Guards officers, and a leading financier, but the host picked out other names from the table reservations book – several peers, minor Cabinet ministers, composers, poets and editors. 'Miss Morgan wrote them all down, and was happy'.[26]

Towards the other end of the gastronomic scale, Newnham-Davis wished to sample a vegetarian restaurant, evidently a new experience for him. In 1889 there were 34 of these in London and 18 in provincial cities like Manchester where the first annual meeting of the Vegetarian Society had been held in 1848 at Hayward's Hotel. On that occasion the menu had included savoury omelette, macaroni omelette, rice fritters, savoury pie, plum pudding and flummery, a diet which *Punch* described as 'humbug' and 'greens to the green'.[27] Nevertheless, vegetarian restaurants had become quite popular as cheap, respectable eating-places used mainly by the lower middle classes, by women, Fabian socialists and food reformers. Bernard Shaw had been converted in 1881 when 'I fled to the purer air of the vegetarian restaurant', and Gandhi, studying law in London, used them with approval. Newnham-Davis inspected two, the Ideal Café in Tottenham Court Road, which also operated as a social centre and ladies' chess club, and the better-known St George's Café in St Martin's Lane. This was a red-brick building of Elizabethan style with leaded windows and 'little black-dressed waitresses flitting about'. The Colonel asked for the best dinner of the house, and the menu he was given is shown below.

GRAND SHOW OF PRIZE VEGETARIANS.

FIGURE 5.1 ◆ *Grand Show of Prize Vegetarians* (Punch's *Almanack for 1852*). *The first annual meeting of the Vegetarian Society was held in Manchester in 1848, and despite* Punch's *sarcasm the number of vegetarian restaurants grew to 34 in London and 18 in the provinces by 1890. Respectable and usually non-alcoholic, they were popular with women.*

Source: © Punch, Ltd.

HORS D'OEUVRE

Flageolets with cream and spinach

Fried duck's egg and green peas

Lent pie or stewed fruit

Mixed salad

Cheese

Dessert

He drank a bottle of ginger beer in preference to the natural fruit wines on offer. The bill was 1/6d. for dinner, plus 2d. for the ginger beer and 2d. for very good coffee. His only comment was that he 'went forth feeling rather empty'.[28] The sanitised atmosphere of such places even allowed a reverse of normal roles, enabling women to entertain men there. In E. M. Forster's *Howards End* (1910) Margaret Schlegel has been taken by Mr Wilcox to lunch at Simpson's for the first time. Attempting to order fish pie, she was reprimanded: 'Fancy coming for fish pie to Simpson's. It's not a bit the thing to go for here'; and was persuaded to have saddle of mutton, carved at the table, followed by Stilton cheese. To return the hospitality, and as a new experience for him, Margaret took Mr Wilcox to Eustace Miles's vegetarian restaurant in Chandos Street. 'It's all proteids and body building, and people coming up to you and, beg pardon, but you have such a beautiful aura'. Gourmets of the traditional school like Edward Spencer thought vegetarian food monotonous and unsatisfying, and believed that 'the prejudice against animal food is, happily, dying out, and if ridicule could kill we should not hear much more of the cranks'. At the one and only vegetarian restaurant he visited he began to 'swell wisibly' and so did his (male) companion: 'I feel for all the world like a captive balloon.'[29]

Ladies did not, of course, eat in exclusively male territories like gentlemen's clubs, and even in the ornate splendour of the Café Royal they were slightly daring adventuresses who fitted its Bohemian reputation. The male habitués were an odd mixture of artists and authors like James McNeill Whistler, Augustus John, Oscar Wilde and his clique of Max Beerbohm, Aubrey Beardsley, Frank Harris and Sir William Rothenstein, rubbing shoulders with George Sims of *The Referee*, the cartoonist Phil May, the racing fraternity and ex-public school and army 'Boy-Ohs'. Bernard Shaw attended as the dramatic critic of the *Saturday Review* as the editor, Frank Harris, held his weekly meetings there, but decided that it was a waste of money to pay Café Royal prices for his plate of macaroni and bottle of Apollinaris. After the Wilde scandal in 1894 and the death of the Café's founder, Daniel Nicols, in 1897, its prestige suffered until Auguste Oddenino, former manager of the Criterion, took over and refurbished the premises with shaded lamps, Minton china and crystal glassware. This was a deliberate attempt to attract more respectable women than the models, actresses and dancers who had formerly frequented, a policy furthered when the 'salons privés' were closed in 1909. By 1914 more women, often with literary associations, were regularly at the Café – Katherine Mansfield and Nancy Cunard, members of the Bloomsbury Set like Virginia and Leonard Woolf and Clive and Vanessa Bell, together with Lytton Strachey, E. M. Forster and the colourful Nina Hamnett, friend of Sickert and Epstein, who wore her hair cut short and her legs in trousers.[30]

The age of Escoffier

Closely related to the presence of women two other things were essential for the success of the new style of dining – the quality of the food itself and the environment in which it was served. André Simon believed that

> *During the forty years from 1871 to 1910, which might be called the Escoffier era, the Grande Cuisine or Cuisine Classique gained for fine food as a fine art the recognition and patronage of the leaders of Society both in England and in the United States. It was during that period that hotels were first built in London and New York where, thanks to César Ritz, luxury and good taste reached in perfect harmony heights never before attained.*[31]

What is interesting here, apart from the precision of the dating, is the identification of the 'revolution' with the names of two individuals. The period marks the rise in public status of great chefs and 'maîtres d'hotel', no longer household servants concealed in noble establishments, but, as Carême had once hoped, figures of international renown. As Edward, Prince of Wales, remarked when Ritz left the Savoy, 'Where Ritz goes, I go', while in the great restaurants chefs were now familiarly known by their nicknames – 'the Roman' (at Romano's) and 'Oddy' (at Oddenino's). In Victorian times the appreciation of fine food had often been considered too sensual for public discourse, at least in mixed company; now, knowledge of cuisine was acceptable, even requisite, for fashionable discussion, debated in restaurant guides, the columns of society journals, women's magazines and, not least, at the dinner table itself. In a devoutly monarchical age, others followed where Edward dined out, if usually in private rooms entered by a separate door. Although a 'bon viveur', he was not perhaps a true gourmet: his preferences ran to game such as snipe and woodcock stuffed with truffles or foie gras in Madeira sauce, eggs in aspic and richly flavoured dishes of lamb and chicken, but for Sunday lunch he often returned to plain roast beef and Yorkshire pudding: favourite drinks were champagne, white Burgundy and hock, accompanied by sparkling Apollinaris water ('Polly').[32]

   The name of Georges Auguste Escoffier (1847–1935) dominated 'haute cuisine' at this period. The son of a blacksmith, he was apprenticed to his uncle, a chef, at 13, and on completion worked in fashionable restaurants in Nice and Paris. Called up for military service during the Franco-Prussian War in 1870, he was taken prisoner at Metz, later returning to a leading Parisian restaurant, Le Petit Moulin Rouge, where he prepared dinners for Garibaldi, the Prince of Wales, Sarah Bernhardt and other celebrities. From 1878 he was *chef de cuisine* at hotels and restaurants in Cannes, Nice and Monte Carlo, where at the Grand Hotel he worked closely with the general manager, César Ritz. Meanwhile, in London the impresario D'Oyly Carte opened the magnificent new Savoy Hotel in 1889 and persuaded Ritz to take on the management: he in turn coaxed Escoffier to come as *chef de cuisine* and another friend, Échenard, as maître d'hôtel.

These three established the immense reputation of the Savoy and the popularity of French cuisine. After a disagreement with Carte in 1897 Ritz and Escoffier moved to the newly built Carlton Hotel, which also quickly became a temple of gastronomy patronised by the great European royalty, the wealthiest commoners, famous actresses and singers.[33]

At these places Escoffier responded to the opportunity to present magnificent, novel dishes, though at much cost to his own great energy and creativity. He complained that 'Novelty is the universal cry', and that night after night he lay awake trying to create new dishes: catering was now a highly competitive business where restaurants vied with each other over originality of dishes and decor. Ultimately they had to make a profit, and one reason for Escoffier's departure from the Savoy was a disappointing level of returns from the restaurant due to his insistence on the highest quality of ingredients and staffing.[34] Other of his innovations were commercially successful, however, particularly the pre-theatre dinner where a shortened four-course menu was served in half an hour, and the after-theatre supper available from 11 pm to 12.30 am, which greatly increased the fashion for late dining. At the Savoy the link between food and entertainment was particularly strong since D'Oyly Carte was the impresario of the hugely popular Gilbert and Sullivan operas staged in the neighbouring theatre. The hotel had been opened to the strains of the specially imported Johann Strauss's orchestra, and music continued to be played in the dining room, even, after some difficulty with the licensing authorities, at Sunday concerts. Sunday lunching or dining, sometimes justified as allowing domestic servants to attend church, began to change Victorian sabbatarianism towards a more Continental pattern in which rational recreation on the Lord's day came to be acceptable.

In his restaurants Escoffier perfected the à la carte menu with a long list of offerings. Previously most restaurants provided a table d'hôte with restricted choice or, for serious gourmets, arranged special menus after prior consultation with the customer. Though both these forms continued, the à la carte system went between these two extremes, giving a wide choice without prior ordering. But Escoffier noticed that not a few English diners were confused by its length, language and uncertain cost, and therefore introduced a shorter 'prix fixe' menu containing many dishes from the carte.[35] He also originated a major reorganisation of kitchen functions known as the 'partie system'. In the past one chef had usually been responsible for a whole dish: now, sous-chefs concentrated on particular parts for which they were specialists, the dish then being assembled by the originator: for example, Sole Mornay would be prepared by a fish chef but with ingredients delegated to a vegetable chef and a *saucier*. This was 'Taylorism' – specialisation and the division of labour along the lines of industrial production applied to catering: it made for a better product, but also saved time and put the dish on the customer's table more quickly, in line with the demands of a brisker age.[36] Although he could produce highly elaborate dishes for banquets and grand occasions, the general trend of Escoffier's menus was towards rather shorter, lighter meals with milder flavours, more acceptable to women and to guests who did not wish to spend a whole evening at table. 'The complicated and sometimes heavy menus [of the past] would be unwelcome to the hypercritical appetites so common nowadays.'[37] For ordinary diners the sequence of courses followed a fairly standard pattern. Most began with an hors d'oeuvre, a cold appetiser quickly assembled to amuse diners while the main dishes were being prepared: caviar or oysters remained popular, or a varié of smoked meats, fish and dressed salads. This was followed by soups – a choice of thick or clear – and a fish course, commonly sole in a variety of sauces, or salmon, lobster or whitebait: then entrées of jointed, sauced meats which gave most scope for the chef's ingenuity. Roast meats requiring carving by the host, usual at domestic dinner parties, were not appropriate in top-class restaurants: here, sometimes after a sorbet, there would be game or poultry, often truffled, then sweets such as an ice bombe, roulade or Charlotte Russe, dessert and perhaps a savoury. Rather than producing conventional dishes Escoffier invented many original ones which often became established in chefs' repertoires, for example Soufflé d'Ecrevisses à la Florentine, Brochettes d'Ortolan, Pêches à l'Orientale and Canard en Chemise, as well as those dedicated to famous ladies – Soufflé Tetrazzini, Mousseline de Volaille Patti and, of course, Pêche Melba.

French cuisine naturally predominated at the Savoy, though English, American, Russian and Indian dishes were available in the Grill Room. But Escoffier's fame was spread by the grand occasions, like one for visiting royalty in July 1895 (see menu).[38]

Cantaloup

Consommé à la Française

Velouté à l'Italienne

Truite Saumonée Royale

Paupiettes de Sole aux Fines Herbes

Selle de Pré-salé aux Laitues

Petits Pois Bonne Femme

Suprêmes de Volaille Montpensier

Mousseline à l'Anglaise

Sorbet au Clicquot Rosé

Cailles aux Feuilles de Vigne

Brochettes d'Ortolans

Salade Alexandra

Soufflé d'Ecrevisses à la Florentine

Fonds d'Artichauts à la Moëlle

Pêches Princesse

Biscuit Glacé Savoy

Mignardises

Raisins. Nectarines

Especially spectacular were parties arranged for visiting millionaires like that for Krupp when the fountain gushed champagne, and that for Kessler, the champagne magnate, when the courtyard was flooded and the dinner served to guests on Venetian gondolas. To celebrate an expedition to the North Pole the Pilgrims Club gave a dinner for which the Winter Garden was transformed into an illusion of snow and ice with waiters dressed in Eskimo furs.[39] But ultimately, Escoffier said, the greatest talent of a chef was to use simple ingredients presented in the most elegant way. After almost twenty years at the Carlton, he retired at the outbreak of the First World War to his villa in Monte Carlo, living until 1935 when he died aged 88. An obituary described him as 'a genius of the kitchen, king of chefs and chef of kings, a man who wrought great changes in the cuisine of hotels and restaurants throughout the world, and especially in this country'.[40]

The environment

Dining in a great hotel or restaurant was a 'fête spéciale', transforming the meal into an occasion to be admired and remembered. It was necessary that the decor should reflect style, luxury and grandeur, that it should be 'other-worldly', a departure from the conventional or commonplace. French styles of the Louis XIV–XVI periods were natural choices to match the cuisine, and baroque and rococo decoration was also common. At the Savoy one entered by the Genoese Hall with a coffered ceiling, figured panels and rouge-royal marble pillars, then ascended to the Restaurant by a double marble staircase to a room panelled in mahogany with a gold and silver frieze; there were also individually styled private dining-rooms named and decorated after the Gilbert and Sullivan operas, and a magnificent Mirror Ballroom. Electric lighting throughout was an innovation, as were the hydraulic lifts and the 70 bathrooms to the bedrooms. Another French ambience was evoked at the Café Royal, described in 1890 by the anonymous author of *Nocturnal London*:

> *Once in the coffee-room [i.e. restaurant] you may consider yourself fully*
> *in Paris, you actually feel that by simply entering you have left London*
> *far behind. The gorgeous gilded Palace! Why, you would think that a*
> *piece of Versaille's famous palace had been cut off and brought over to*

England. In vain you may search here for the so much abused English style of decoration, whether Queen Anne or anything you like. The Café Royal is purely French, regular Louis XIV....[41]

In such places reality was also transformed by Palm Courts, conservatories and Winter Gardens, where tea could be taken to the accompaniment of a small orchestra. Music was an important adjunct to the interest and atmosphere. At Gatti's, the Queen's and elsewhere orchestras were lodged in galleries above the dining-room as in medieval times: at the Queen's Restaurant in Leicester Square a fine orchestra conducted by John Barbirolli's father played each night and also gave Sunday concerts.[42] At Romano's the gallery, known as the 'Pigeon Hole', had a different function, containing tables where one was unseen from below, much in demand by those who wished to dine discreetly. Mario Gallati, who was a head waiter at Romano's around 1910, remembered that

The atmosphere at Romano's was like champagne. The place was always full of royalty and members of the nobility, of famous sportsmen, political figures, European potentates, Eastern maharajahs and other people in the news. At Romano's, not once, but many times, belted earls really did drink champagne out of chorus girls' slippers ... I remember when lovely, red-haired Ruby Miller, then the toast of the town, had to be carried out to a cab because both her slippers were wet through.[43]

The decor here was themed in Oriental style, with much use of warm reds and gilding, exotic and erotic; more soberly, the Grill Room was converted from the old kitchen to resemble a Russian farmhouse. Although famed for its cuisine, one wonders whether the attractions of Romano's were not more sexual than alimentary. As one habitué later wrote:

I dined more often at Romano's than anywhere... It was the favourite rendezvous when the Gaiety and Daly's [music halls] drew all the bucks and bloods, grandees and lordlings, and the musical comedy chorus supplied wives for half the susceptible peerage.[44]

Although no one style of decor predominated in restaurants, it often followed the current trends in interior design. In the 1880s 'Baroque' and 'Gothic' styles were common, usually with much faking by stucco, mock-Classical friezes and imitation marble. Subsequently, the influence of the

Pre-Raphaelite movement was evident in coloured mosaics, tiles and stained glass – the Criterion Restaurant marked this departure, and was followed at the Holborn Restaurant, the Metropole and Avenue Hotels. These were, perhaps, too 'aesthetic' for popular tastes, and French and rococo styles continued to prevail.[45] At the Trocadero (1896) rich golds contrasted with the soft colours of walls and ceilings, while for the Hall Professor Moira designed an elaborate frieze of Arthurian legends. As Joseph Lyons proudly explained in 1904:

> *A few years ago it occurred to us to start a restaurant on a larger scale, to appeal to another section of the British public who desire a different class and, perhaps, higher form of eating [than the teashops]... Our banqueting and private dining-rooms [are] the most charming and luxurious extant.*

By then, extensions had provided nine main dining-rooms, seating 1,200 guests (the Empire Hall, the Louis Sixteenth Room, the Blue Saloon, etc.), besides smaller rooms for parties of from 4 to 20.[46] The 'Troc.' was at that time Lyons' flagship, but its scale was soon exceeded by the first Corner House in Coventry Street, opened in 1909. A multi-storeyed building, partly of Carrara marble, it accommodated 2,000 diners in separate rooms, each with its own menu and price, intended to cater for a variety of patrons. An American visitor, who had compared some of the best English hotels unfavourably with those in the United States, was evidently impressed, though not with the clientele:

> *I recall ... being struck with the size and importance of it, even though it was intensely middle-class. It was a great chamber, decorated after the fashion of a palace ballroom, with immense chandeliers of prismed glass hanging from the ceiling, and a balcony furnished in cream and gold ... where a large stringed orchestra played continuously during lunch and dinner. An enormous crowd of very common-place people were there – clerks, minor officials, clergymen, small shopkeepers – and the bill of fare was composed of many homely dishes such as beef-and-kidney pie, suet pudding and the like, combined with others bearing high-sounding French names... It catered to an element not reached in quite the same way in America... The food was excellent, and the service, while a little slow for a place of popular patronage, was good.[47]*

Where to dine

It was generally accepted that for the best and most fashionable dining out the dining-rooms of the great hotels were superior to all but a handful of top restaurants. Almost all hotels now opened their dining-rooms to the public – even the formerly very private Brown's Hotel did so in 1880. From this time until 1914 there was a rush of new hotel-building as well as extensions and refurbishments of the existing, financed now by hotel companies rather than private owners. As a consequence of international travel and tourism, guests expected ever higher standards of elegance, comfort and service: English hotels had to compete with the best in Europe and America, where the Waldorf Astoria (1893), Sherry's Hotel (1898), the Ritz Carlton (1902) and others were equipped to the height of luxury.[48]

In England London remained the magnet for new catering investment. A string of great hotels included the Grand (1880), the Metropole (1885), the Victoria (1887), the Savoy (1889), the First Avenue (1893), the Russell (1897), the rebuilt Carlton and Claridge's (1897), the Ritz (1905), the Waldorf (1906), the Strand Palace (1907) and the Regent Palace (opened 1915). Outside London there was much less activity. In provincial towns passing travellers stayed in railway hotels or modernised former coaching inns, and some of the larger 'county' hotels were still venues for the older pattern of public dinners, concerts and supper balls, but the habit of couples dining out at night merely for the pleasure of it had scarcely penetrated to the more conservative provinces. Two exceptions to this, however, may be noted. One was a consequence of the spread of the motor car, of which by 1909 there were 40,000, mainly wealthy, licence holders, while for those who did not own or drive a car, a Daimler with chauffeur could be hired for three guineas a day.[49] The car, with greater convenience and mobility than the railway, did much to encourage the cult of the countryside and escape from the increasingly crowded cities. For some people it meant the purchase of a country cottage or architect-designed bungalow at the coast as an accessible weekend or summer retreat, often associated with sports such as golf, for others a touring holiday to the still relatively unfrequented Cotswolds or Lake District, or merely an evening's drive to a riverside restaurant at Richmond or Maidenhead. Routes and choices were facilitated by the Royal

Automobile Handbooks which first appeared in 1904, and by the Automobile Association's star listing of hotels from 1912. This renaissance of the countryside suggests that some people were reacting against the grand metropolitan hotels, which a critic described as:

> the monster eating-houses and mammoth hotels of today 'run' by companies and syndicates ... the elaborate and wholly unnecessary furniture and decorations ... marble pillars, Etruscan vases, nude figures, which only serve to distract attention from the banquet.[50]

The other, more important, occasion for dining outside London was at resort hotels while on holiday. By this time the great days of the inland spas were passing or passed, though some still clung to their former glory and even extended existing accommodation. At Harrogate the Grand and the Majestic were both built in 1903, at Bath the Christopher (1880) and the grandiose Empire (1890), while at Woodhall Spa in Lincolnshire, 'the last aristocratic spa', three new hotels were added by 1914.[51] A handbook still listed 29 Inland Watering Places in 1891, but these were greatly outnumbered by nearly 200 Seaside Watering Places,[52] the old designation still surviving. In the late nineteenth century seaside resorts were among the fastest-growing parts of the country, and many now had large resident populations (in 1901 Brighton 123,000, Hastings 65,000, Southport 48,000, Blackpool and Bournemouth each 47,000)[53] besides the annual influx of visitors, well able to support large hotels. Some change in the pattern of hotel residence is noticeable at this time, however, again partly a result of the greater ease of travel by car. Whereas at the Imperial, Torquay, some guests had stayed for several months during the winter season, there was now more trade in shorter holidays and weekends throughout the year.

Successful hotels and restaurants, wherever located, depended not only on the quality of the food and the environment but, equally important, on the skill of the management, and this period sees the rise in public recognition of the general manager as it does that of the chef. Two very contrasting types may be noticed here, though both illustrate what entrepreneurial flair and talent could achieve from obscure origins. César Ritz, born in 1850, was the son of a Swiss smallholder in the village of Niedewald. After a series of jobs as a waiter, he rose to become maître d'hôtel at hotels in Nice and then, at 27, at the Hotel Grand National at

Lucerne, regarded as one of the premier hotels in Europe. Within another ten years he had scraped up capital to buy leading restaurants and hotels in Cannes and Baden-Baden, where he met D'Oyly Carte and was persuaded to take over the management of the new Savoy in 1889, which the trio of Ritz, Escoffier and Échenard turned into one of the world's most renowned hotels. In 1896 the Ritz Hotel Syndicate was formed with capital from the oil magnate, Gulbenkian, to establish the Ritz Hotel in Paris, and later to open another Ritz in London in 1905, which he never saw. In 1902 he suffered a complete breakdown and spent the next 16 years in nursing homes in Lucerne, dying in 1918.[54] Meanwhile, the cuisine of the London Ritz under M. Malley acquired a reputation for original creations comparable with that of the Savoy.[55]

Equally famous, though of a very different character, was the Cavendish Hotel, kept by Rosa Lewis for 34 years. Rosa Ovendon was born in 1867, one of nine children of an East London watchmaker/repairer; she ended a Board School education at 12 and went to work as a domestic servant to a middle-class family. At 16 she moved to become an under-kitchenmaid in the household of the exiled Comte de Paris, heir to the French throne, at Sheen House, Mortlake, absorbing French cuisine and vocabulary. At 20 she became cook to Lady Randolph Churchill, catering for visits by the Prince of Wales and leading politicians, but after her marriage to a waiter in 1892 the couple acted as concierges for 'premises of convenience' for the Prince in Eaton Terrace while Rosa developed a successful business as outside caterer for fashionable dinner parties, such as those of the Astors in Curzon Street. In 1902 she bought the lease of the Cavendish Hotel, extending and furnishing it as an English country house, more like a club than a hotel, and with private suites, one permanently reserved for Edward VII. Rosa traded on her personality as a cheeky, rather raucous, 'Cockney sparrow' but also on her own reputation for an excellent cuisine: her cooking was particularly noted for game and, especially, quail which she made into pies and puddings. Her menus were elaborate and costly, a typical one from 1908 being reproduced below.

CAVENDISH HOTEL

Dîner du 26 Juin, 1908

Consommé aux Ailerons

Truite foide à la Cavendish

Blanchailles

Soufflé de Cailles à la Valencienne

Pièce de Boeuf à la gelée en Bellevue

Jambon de Prague aux fèves

Poularde froide à la Parisienne

Salade

Asperges en branches

Pêches à la Marron

Bombe glacée Dame Blanche

Friandises

Laitances à la diable

She often complained at the trend towards shorter menus, blaming this on society hostesses who had formerly paid three guineas a head for her catering services but would now give only one.[56] In 1908 Rosa began writing a cookery column for the *Daily Mail*, which included her famous quail pudding.

From Baedeker's Guide to London of 1908 it appears that prices for meals at the top hotels and restaurants did not vary greatly, probably due to the effects of competition. Luncheon was normally a table d'hôte, the most expensive at the Ritz (6/-); the Savoy, Claridge's and the Carlton charged 5/-; the Hotel Cecil and the Hyde Park only 3/6d. There was more variation in the price of dinners, since some like the Ritz only served à la carte meals from 10/6d. upwards: where table d'hôte dinners were available they usually ranged between 5/- and 8/-, while for the shorter menus of grill-rooms and supper-rooms 3/6d. was common. Prices were lower in restaurants pure and simple than in hotels – at the Trocadero luncheon was 3/6d. and dinner from 5/-, but at the Criterion lunch was only 2/6d. and dinner from 3/6d. to 5/0d., and at the Popular Café lunch or supper could be had for 1/6d.[57] Still cheaper meals were available in the many French and Italian restaurants in Soho, where Robert Mackray considered the 2/- dinner at the Boulogne and the 1/6d. one at Guermani's 'amazing value' for their five or six courses.[58] At the Comedy Restaurant,

COMEDY RESTAURANT

Hors d'œuvre variés

Consommé Caroline   Crème à la Reine

Sole Colbert

Filet Mignon Chasseur

Lasagne al Sugo

Bécassine Rôtie

Salade de Saison

Glace au Chocolat

Dessert

Panton Street, Newnham-Davis enjoyed an excellent meal, which included snipe, for 2/6d (see menu).

This was not, of course, a place at which the Colonel would entertain a lady, still less at the Restaurant Lyonnais, where he had an eatable dinner for 8d. – 'Soupe, 1 viande, 2 légumes, dessert, café, pain à discretion'.[59] But there were at least a dozen foreign Grand Restaurants where cuisine and service were impeccable, such as the Café Royal, Romano's, Verrey's, Kettner's, the Coburg, Gatti's, Frascati's and the Monico as well as the 'English' menus at Simpson's, Rule's and Scott's. He warned that for a really 'artistic' menu the diner must be prepared to pay a high price: his most expensive menu for two was at the Savoy – 'Two couverts 1/-; bortch 3/-; soles Savoy 6/-; mousse jambon 6/-; poulet polonaise 8/-; salade 2/-; foie gras 6/-; asperges verts 7/6d.; pêches glacées vanilla 7/-; one bottle champagne 133 15/-; café 2/-; liqueurs 2/-; Total £3/5/6d.'[60]

Eating out by the wealthy was not, of course, confined to hotels and restaurants. Long rail journeys required provisioning, since scheduled stops at stations with buffets were usually very brief and the quality of the food a constant complaint. Wise passengers brought a picnic in a cleverly designed wicker basket supplied by Fortnum and Mason or other caterers, and the railway companies themselves sold luncheon boxes at various prices. The first full meal to be served at table in a railway carriage was in 1874 by the Midland Railway, followed in 1879 by the Great Northern Railway which cooked meals en route and served them in a version of the American Pullman car, furnished with satinwood panelling and velvet seats.[61] Eating in the open air was also popular, either for tea in the garden, for picnic excursions or for attendance at sporting events.

These were in a sense extensions of a domestic party in the controlled setting of people of one's own class, for example in the separate enclosures at race meetings or at shooting parties where the 'guns' and their ladies were served at a distance from the beaters. Eating in the street was unthinkable, but, extraordinarily, when the snobbish American, Theodore Dreiser, visited Oxford for a day with an English friend, they decided that to save time they would not take luncheon in a hotel but rather self-consciously, it must be said, munched sandwiches of meat and marmalade (? Cooper's 'Oxford') as they walked.[62] A 'picnic' of a very different kind occurred when Edward VII attended Covent Garden, where supper was taken in a room behind the royal box in an interval between 8.30 and 9.30 pm. Six footmen were sent down in the afternoon with gold and silver plate, napery and tablecloths, and a dozen hampers of food followed later: nine or ten courses included consommé, lobster mayonnaise, plovers' eggs, trout, duck, lamb cutlets, chicken, ham and tongue jelly, desserts of strawberries and other fruits, and French patisserie. Strangely, when Edward stayed at Biarritz with Mrs Keppel and her children, 'Kingy' would have a picnic set up by the roadside, where numbers of passing carriages and motor cars would then congregate.[63]

The picnic remained a very popular institution in Edwardian England, visits to more distant beauty spots facilitated by easier travel. Menus were becoming somewhat lighter than the gargantuan spreads suggested by Mrs Beeton in 1861, but still substantial: her revised edition of 1906 proposed for 10 people: 5 lb of cold salmon (8/9d.), two cucumbers, mayonnaise, a quarter of lamb with mint sauce, 8 lb of pickled brisket, a tongue, a galantine of veal, a chicken pie, salad, 2 fruit tarts and cream, 2 dozen cheesecakes, 2 jellies, 1½ lb of cheese, 6 lb of strawberries and bread, butter and biscuits, at a cost of £3/11/1d. not including drinks. *The Girls' Own Paper* in 1880 believed that 'fitted baskets are only suitable for a small party of three or four persons' and that 'cabbage leaves pack well around cool dishes and contrast well with the pure white of the table-napkins'.[64]

More luxury foods were necessary for Henley Regatta or for a race meeting at Ascot or Goodwood – foie gras, chaudfroid of quails, plovers' eggs, curried prawns and various galantines; champagne was always the preferred drink, with something stronger for the men. Professional catering was now usual for such events. 'The catering arrangements are generally entrusted to a well-known catering firm who make a speciality of these affairs. In this way, the whole service gives satisfaction to the participants without trouble to the givers, and materially enhances their reputation as a successful host or hostess.'[65] For autumn or winter shooting parties hot dishes were needed, and were brought from the house punctually at midday when the ladies joined the 'guns' in a marquee set out with tables, chairs and silverware. Edward Spencer recommended Lancashire Hot-Pot, plover pudding, jugged duck with oysters, woodcock pie, rabbit pie and lark paté: 'a heavy luncheon is a mistake if you want to "shoot clean" afterwards'.[66]

Notes and references

1 Robert Cecil, *Life in Edwardian England*, B. T. Batsford, 1969, p. 101.

2 Sir Charles Petrie, *Scenes of Edwardian Life*, Eyre and Spottiswoode, 1965, p. 30.

3 C. F. G. Masterman, *The Condition of England*, Methuen and Co., 2nd edn, 1909, p. 21.

4 L. G. Chiozza Money, *Riches and Poverty*, Methuen and Co., 11th edn, 1914, pp. 44–5.

5 W. R. Greg, 'Life at High Pressure', *The Contemporary Review*, March 1875, p. 633.

6 G. S. Layard, 'A Lower-Middle Class Budget', *Cornhill Magazine*, New Series, Vol. X, Jan.–June 1901, pp. 657–66.

7 G. Colmore, 'Eight Hundred a Year', *Cornhill Magazine*, ibid., pp. 790–8.

8 *The Times*, 20 June 1876, quoted Peter Bailey, *Leisure and Class in Victorian England*, Methuen, 1987, p. 68.

9 Bailey, ibid., p. 90.

10 ibid., p. 188.

11 John Burnett, 'Domestic Servants, Introduction', pp. 127–72, in *Useful Toil. Autobiographies of Working People from the 1820s to the 1920s* (1st edn, 1974), Routledge, 1994.

12 See generally, J. A. Banks, *Prosperity and Parenthood. A Study of Family Planning among the Victorian Middle Classes*, Routledge & Kegan Paul, 1965.

13 *The Englishwoman's Domestic Magazine*, vol. XI, Nov. 1871, pp. 318–19.

14 Mary Hooper, *Little Dinners. How to Serve them with Elegance and Economy*, C. Kegan Paul, 1878, Preface, p. V.

15 ibid., p. VII.

16 For the history and details of service *à la Française* see Peter Brears, 'The Waning of a Long Tradition', ch. 5 in C. Anne Wilson (ed.), *Luncheon, Nuncheon and Other Meals. Eating with the Victorians*, Stroud, Gloucester-shire, Alan Sutton Publishing, 1994, pp. 91–116.

17 See generally, John Burnett, *Plenty and Want. A Social History of Food in England from 1815 to the Present Day*, Routledge, 3rd edn, 1989, ch. 9, 'High Living', esp. pp. 198ff.; Valerie Mars, 'Service à la Russe. The New Way of Dining', ch. 6 in C. Anne Wilson (ed.), *Luncheon, Nuncheon and Other Meals*, ibid., pp. 117–44.

18 Masterman, op. cit., pp. 44–5.

19 *The Caterer and Hotel Keeper's Gazette*, August 1902, p. 345.

20 Robert Mackray, *The Night Side of London* (1st edn, 1902), reprinted Bibliophile Books, 1984, pp. 69–70, 90, 93.

21 ibid., pp. 89ff.

22 Michael and Ariane Batterberry, *On the Town in New York*, New York and London, Routledge, 1999, p. 71 passim.

23 Joanne Finkelstein, *Dining Out. A Sociology of Modern Manners*, Cambridge, Polity Press, 1989, p. 14.

24 André L. Simon, 'From Esau to Escoffier, or the History of Gastronomy', in Louis Golding and André L. Simon (eds), *We Shall Eat and Drink Again. A Wine and Food Anthology*, London, Hutchinson, n.d., *c.*1948, p. 144.

25 Lieut. Col. Newnham-Davis, *Dinners and Diners. Where and How to Dine in London*, Grant Richards, 1901 (1st edn, 1899), p. 208.

26 ibid., Ch. XIX, 'Willis's Rooms (King Street)', pp. 133–9.

27 Colin Spencer, *The Heretic's Feast. A History of Vegetarianism*, Fourth Estate, 1993, pp. 263–4, 274 (the definitive history).

28 Newnham-Davis, op. cit., pp. 51–6.

29 Edward Spencer ('Nathaniel Gubbins'), *Cakes and Ale. A Dissertation on Banquets, etc.*, Stanley Paul and Co., 1913 (1st edn, 1897), pp. 131–2.

30 Guy Deghy and Keith Waterhouse, *Café Royal. Ninety Years of Bohemia*, Hutchinson, 1955, p. 59 passim.

31 Simon, op. cit., p. 143.

32 Leslie Frewin (ed.), *Parnassus near Piccadilly. The Café Royal Centenary Book, An Anthology*, Leslie Frewin, *c.*1965, p. 47; Gregory Houston Bowden,

British Gastronomy. The Rise of Great Restaurants, Chatto & Windus, 1975, pp. 13–14.

33 A detailed account of his career is in Escoffier's autobiography, *Memories of My Life*, translated by Laurence Escoffier, New York, Van Nostrand, Reinhold, 1997.

34 Derek Taylor, *Fortune, Fame and Folly. British Hotels and Catering from 1878 to 1978*, IPC Business Press, 1977, p. 89.

35 Escoffier, *Memories*, op. cit., pp. 89–90.

36 Stephen Mennell, *All Manners of Food. Eating and Taste in England and France from the Middle Ages to the Present*, Oxford, Basil Blackwell, 1985, p. 159.

37 Georges Auguste Escoffier, *A Guide to Modern Cookery* (1st edn, 1903), Hutchinson, 1957, p. xii.

38 Alison Leach (ed.), *The Savoy Food and Drink Book*, Pyramid Books, 1988, p. 17.

39 Compton Mackenzie, *The Savoy of London*, George G. Harrap, 1953, p. 73.

40 *The Caterer and Hotel-Keeper*, 15 Feb. 1935.

41 *Nocturnal London* (1890), quoted Deghy and Waterhouse, op. cit., p. 48.

42 Mario Gallati, *Mario of the Caprice. The Autobiography of a Restaurateur*, Hutchinson, 1960, p. 38. Gallati was then, 1905, a waiter at the Queen's.

43 ibid., pp. 46–7.

44 Sir Harry Preston, *Leaves From My Unwritten Diary*, Hutchinson, 1936, p. 59.

45 Arthur Finch, 'Principal Changes in the Interior Decoration of Hotels and Restaurants, 1878–1928', *The Caterer and Hotel-Keeper's Gazette*, reproduced in Taylor, op. cit., pp. 119–23.

46 Joseph Lyons, interviewed by S. J. Adair Fitz-Gerald, 'Chats with Caterers', *The Caterer and Hotel-Keeper's Gazette*, 15 June 1904, p. 239.

47 Theodore Dreiser, *A Traveller at Forty* (1st edn USA, 1913), Grant Richards, 1914, pp. 80–1.

48 Michael and Ariane Batterberry, *On the Town in New York*, pp. 161, 180.

49 W. Hamish Fraser, *The Coming of the Mass Market, 1850–1914*, Hamden, Conn., Archon Books, 1981, p. 82.

50 Edward Spencer, *Cakes and Ale,* op. cit, pp. xiii–xiv.

51 Phyllis Hembry, *British Spas from 1815 to the Present Day. A Social History*, ed. and completed by Leonard W. Cowie and Evelyn E. Cowie, Athlone Press, 1997, pp. 155–6. 168–9, 232.

52 J. A. R. Pimlott, *The Englishman's Holiday. A Social History*, Faber and Faber, 1947, Appendix 1, pp. 270--2, 'Seaside Watering Places (1896–7 edn)'.

53 ibid., p. 174.

54 Arthur White, *Palaces of the People. A Social History of Commercial Hospitality*, Rapp and Whiting, 1968, pp. 147–61.

55 Bowden, *British Gastronomy*, op. cit., p. 28.

56 For full details, see Daphne Fielding, *Duchess of Jermyn Street*, Eyre and Spottiswoode, 1964; Anthony Masters, *Rosa Lewis. An Exceptional Edwardian*, London, Weidenfeld & Nicolson, 1977.

57 Karl Baedeker, *London and its Environs. Handbook for Travellers*, Leipzig and London, 1908, pp. 3–13.

58 Mackray, *The Night Side of London*, op. cit., p. 96.

59 Newnham-Davis, op. cit., pp. 16, 96.

60 ibid., pp. 31–2.

61 Jan Read and Maite Manjón, *The Great British Breakfast*, Michael Joseph, 1981, p. 71.

62 Dreiser, op. cit., p. 144.

63 Masters, *Rosa Lewis*, op. cit., p. 85, from an account by Mrs Keppel's children's nanny.

64 Quoted Dorothy Hartley, *Food in England* (1st edn 1954), Little, Brown and Co., 1999, p. 603.

65 J. Rey, *The Whole Art of Dining, with Notes on the Subject of Service and Table Decorations*, London, Carmona and Baker (n.d.), *c.*1914, p. 112.

66 Edward Spencer, op. cit., pp. 44–8, 54.

PART THREE

1914–1945

CHAPTER 6

• • • • • • • • • • • • • •

The First World War, 1914–1918

Life in wartime

The First World War brought great and lasting changes to English society, stark contrasts between the horrors of casualties on one hand and, on the other, improved material conditions of many civilians, a growing recognition of women's rights and a commitment of government to major social reforms in health, education and housing for the families of the 'heroes'. Our concern is with what came to be called 'The Home Front' and, more particularly, with the vital problem of feeding a population during Britain's first experience of a total war which, directly or indirectly, affected the whole nation.

The impact of the war on food began to be felt immediately after the outbreak on 4 August 1914, with panic buying of expected scarcities such as flour and sugar. Despite this, *The Caterer* reported on 15 August that 'We are able... thanks to the self-control of the public, to find our food supply certain under any circumstances for at least half a year',[1] quite sufficient, it was believed, for a war which would be over by Christmas. In fact, as Robert Roberts remembered of his mother's little shop in Salford, the children were despatched to buy up supplies from the multiple grocers like Lipton's and the Maypole Dairy to be resold at a profit: one forage yielded 28 lb of margarine and 20 lb of sugar which

Mrs Roberts sold off in small lots to her 'regulars': middle-class women were also flocking in from the suburbs with horses and traps and bassinets to buy half-sacks of flour and sugar. The President of the Board of Trade, Runciman, complained to Parliament about greedy, better-off people who formed long queues of motor cars at stores and bought up as much as they could persuade the assistants to allow, causing 'great hardship, especially among the poorer classes'.[2] Retail food prices rose sharply throughout the war, from 100 points in July 1914 to 233 points in November 1918,[3] despite price controls on some essential items. Such inflation would have been disastrous for working-class budgets had not earnings generally kept pace and, in some cases, exceeded the rise. With a strong demand for labour, unemployment was virtually ended, and the wages of labourers, barely at subsistence level before the war, now showed the largest increases, narrowing the former wide gap between the earnings of skilled and unskilled workers. Some families where all the members were employed, often on war work, enjoyed combined incomes unthinkable in peacetime – in one instance, as much as £18/12/4d. a week.[4] Women and girls were also beneficiaries, moving from low-paid domestic service and sweatshops to munitions factories: in July 1914 3.2 million women were employed in industry and commerce, by July 1918 5 million. Roberts noticed that by 1916 abject poverty had disappeared from Salford, and mothers with several sons in the forces were receiving three times as much in government allowances as their husbands had given them before the war.[5] On the other hand, the earnings of middle-class salaried employees, less protected by trade unions, tended to lag behind inflation – in 1920, by which time the cost of living index peaked at 266 points, the salaries of civil servants had risen on average by only 67 per cent.[6] Moreover, they were now paying much more in taxation, income tax having increased from 1/2d. in the pound to 5/- by 1917, and the exemption limit lowered from £160 to £130 a year: there were also sharp increases in indirect taxes, especially on beer, spirits, tobacco and petrol, as well as on surtax and estate duties.

The fortunes of the rich, who had enjoyed the fruits of Edwardian prosperity, varied considerably. Those on fixed incomes naturally suffered from price rises and shortages, not least of the domestic servants on which their lifestyles had depended. Many nobility surrendered their country estates and town mansions for hospitals and convalescent homes, moving to London flats, which were now at a premium. Titled women gave their names and time to good causes, helping to organise Red Cross and Women's Voluntary Service activities. Industrialists engaged on war work often did very well, and there was much complaint in the press about 'profiteering' which the government did something to control by an Excess Profits Tax. Extravagance was condemned and simpler lives approved as patriotic: most public dinners, balls and presentations were given up, and there was a public outcry about a lavish Lord Mayor's Banquet in November 1917, at the height of food shortages. Restaurants, unless part of hotels, were required to close at 10 pm: 'treating' to drinks became an offence (to protect servicemen from over-generous well-wishers) and late suppers went out of favour in darkened streets and fear of air-raids. But there was no evidence of widespread decline in the restaurant habit: on the contrary, many people ate out to conserve domestic supplies, and there was much dining by and for soldiers on leave from the Front, a psychological compensation for the horrors of the trenches.

> *Such days were times of gaiety, of eating and drinking at restaurants, of frequenting shows and theatres, of hurried courting and quick marriages... The great hotels and restaurants were thronged for feasting and dancing... It became a convention that if soldiers were not fighting they must be enjoying themselves. How else could it be? Eat, drink and be merry, for tomorrow –.*[7]

Extravagant meals with cocktails, champagne and liqueurs, costing up to £2/10/0d. for two, were often criticised for corrupting young officers who had no experience of spending money sensibly, and particular concern was directed at nightclubs which, according to Lord Curzon, were 'haunts of temptations and dens of iniquity': some had been open until 4 am before the Clubs (Temporary Provision) Act required closure at 12.30 am. Hotel teas, however, where misconduct was unlikely to occur, were also very popular at 2/6d., and 'Tango Dances' became a new craze.

London was the hub of this social activity and experienced further population growth as the centre of the expanded government administration and a main staging-post for military personnel. But fears about a collapse of holiday-making did not materialise, partly because many people had more money to spend and needed release from wartime anxieties, and partly because the better-off could not now take holidays abroad and turned back to English resorts. When Lyons proudly opened their magnificent Regent Palace Hotel in 1915 it was fully booked from the first, mainly with tourists,[8] and although many hotels were requisitioned, in both London and resort towns, those that remained generally thrived despite shortages of supplies and skilled staff.[9] Now that 'cures' at Baden-Baden were out of bounds, some English spas experienced a considerable revival, one advertisement suggesting that 'the German Navy cannot navigate the Buxton waters',[10] while Blackpool still took its usual 'Wakes' holiday-makers from Lancashire and Yorkshire towns. Indeed, Blackpool's economy, like that of some other resorts, benefited from large numbers of soldiers billeted there during the winter off-season – 10,000 of these as well as 2,000 Belgian refugees, for whom the government paid landladies not ungenerous allowances.[11]

The food front

Britain entered the war on a wave of patriotic enthusiasm and confidence in the might of her Navy, her Empire and her allies to quickly defeat the enemy. A 'War Book' prepared in advance contained detailed plans for the defence of the realm but made only indirect reference to the question of food,[12] though it was well known that agriculture had long been in a state of decline and that under the policy of Free Trade Britain now relied for her basic foods on cheap imports from overseas. In 1914 we imported four-fifths of our wheat, mainly from North America, almost all sugar (mainly beet sugar from Austria-Hungary, now closed), three-quarters of our cheese, two-thirds of ham and bacon and three-fifths of butter, besides all tea, coffee, cocoa, tropical and sub-tropical fruits. Yet for the first two years of war little was done to interfere with the workings of a free market, and although prices were rising rapidly and food queues forming, the Liberal government under Asquith was unwilling to impose firm controls, fearing a spread of public discontent which was already erupting on 'Red Clydeside'. As late as October 1916 the President of the Board of Trade assured Parliament that there was no need to appoint a Food Controller, and that 'We want to avoid any rationing of our people in food'.

Within one month there was a major change of direction. A Food Department was established, which became the nucleus of the later

Ministry, a Food Controller (Lord Devonport) was appointed, and in December Asquith resigned as Prime Minister and was replaced by Lloyd George.[13] Our main concern here is with the development of policies affecting eating out rather than those which applied to the civilian population generally, though the two were not unconnected. The new Controller moved cautiously, hoping that much could be achieved by voluntary restraint. Bread, the staple diet in poorer homes, was the first to receive attention when the price of the 4 lb loaf rose to 10d., twice the pre-war level. In October 1916, the King's Proclamation was issued and read in churches on four successive Sundays, urging people to reduce their consumption of bread and pastry by a quarter – a sacrifice which would not have borne too hardly on the royal households: more importantly, bread prices were fixed and flour mills taken under government control. As the war dragged on and casualties mounted, a sense of common purpose and need for fair shares developed in which it was felt that privilege and wealth should not be allowed to escape the sufferings of ordinary people – in particular, that they should not be able to avoid the growing food scarcities by eating luxury meals in restaurants. In December 1916, a Public Meals Order applying to all hotels, restaurants and other eating-places limited the number of courses in daytime meals to two, and at evening dinners to three (though it did not attempt to limit quantities). In April 1917, the amounts of meat, sugar and fats allowed in public restaurants were controlled, and a 'meatless day' introduced, which required that no meat was to be served on one day each week. After a trial of only a month, the Order was revoked, mainly as a result of strong criticism by experts in the Food Committee of the Royal Society that to restrict home-grown meat would only increase the consumption of imported cereals, now in very short supply. 'It naturally made the public and the press ask if the Food Controller knew what he was about.'[14]

The food situation was at its most critical in the spring of 1917 when Germany launched a major U-boat campaign on merchant shipping: more than two million tons of shipping were sunk, and at one point Britain had only 3–4 weeks' supply of food in stock. Attention was again focused on wheat, which had to run the gauntlet of attacks in the Atlantic, but on this occasion government policy was more sensible. Instead of attempting to ration bread, which would have hit the poor especially, flour was made to go further by raising the extraction rate. The first 'war bread' had appeared in November 1916, with a hardly noticeable increase in the extraction rate from the normal 70–72 per cent to 76 per cent: subsequently it was gradually increased to reach 92 per cent in April 1918; at the same time there was a compulsory addition of 5 per cent of flour from barley, oats or rye.[15] The effect was to produce a darker, heavier loaf with more bran, almost indistinguishable from wholemeal: it was not popular with people who were accustomed to very white, roller-milled flour, though it had support from most nutritionists and the Vegetarian Society.[16] At the Café Royal, where white bread was still being served, there were public accusations until an official investigation discovered that the whiteness was produced by the addition of potatoes.[17]

Hesitantly, the government accepted the need for greater controls, especially after the resignation of Devonport in May 1917, and his replacement by the more energetic Lord Rhondda. Despite streams of exhortations from 1,200 local Food Economy Committees, and calls to 'Eat Less Bread and Victory is Secured' and 'The Kitchen is the Key to Victory', voluntary restraints had not achieved very much: compulsion had to come. Minor measures included the prohibition of the manufacture of ice cream, an Order limiting teashops to serving no more than 2 oz. of bread or cakes between 3 pm and 6 pm (after this time they could sell any amount up to the value of 1/3 d.),[18] and a Cake and Pastry Order which outlawed crumpets and sugar icing and specified the permitted ingredients of cakes, buns, scones and biscuits. William Beveridge, the Permanent Secretary of the Ministry of Food, described how 'the chiefs of the Ministry sat in solemn inquisition round the library table, passing from hand to hand for judgement a selection of sugared cakes bought as specimens that morning: the exhibits later furnished a sumptuous tea for the typists of the sugar department'.[19] By the end of 1917 meat was increasingly scarce, and despite the earlier failure of the 'meatless day,' in January 1918 two such days a week were prescribed for all eating-places between 5 am and 10.30 am: the breakfast rasher of bacon now disappeared.

Meanwhile, there had been much government concern about the extent of drinking and the harmful effects of alcohol on war production, especially in munitions factories and shipyards. The small pre-war prohibition movement now gained support as a patriotic campaign which would save valuable grain supplies, a publication by Arthur Mee entitled

PLATE 1 ◆ *A London coffee stall, 1881. Henry Mayhew estimated that there were around 300 in London in the mid-nineteenth century. Some appeared as early as 3 or 4am for men on their way to work; others only began around midnight for the accommodation of "night walkers", "fast gentlemen" and "loose girls".*

Source: © Museum of London.

GENTLEMEN'S DINING ROOM.

PLATE 2 ◆ *The Gentlemen's Dining Room at Simpson's restaurant in the Strand, c. 1905. Simpson's began as the 'Grand Restauratum' in 1848 when the nomenclature was still uncertain. It became famous for its roast meats, wheeled to the tables and carved to the customer's order. There was also a first-floor dining-room where ladies could be entertained.*

Source: Mary Evans Picture Library.

PLATE 3 ◆ *Lunch at Claridge's Hotel, c. 1910. In the 1850s Mr and Mrs Claridge bought a small hotel in Brook Street which had been established by a French chef, Jacques Mivart, in 1815. The Claridges developed it into the most exclusive hotel in London, patronised by visiting royalty and the nobility.*

Source: Mary Evans Picture Library.

PLATE 4 ◆ *An after-theatre supper at the Savoy restaurant, with professional dancers giving a 'refined exhibition' of the tango, c. 1912. Guests needed instruction in the new dance craze which was sweeping London just before World War One.*

Source: Mary Evans Picture Library.

PLATE 5 ◆ *A VE Day street party, 1945: painting by Kevin Walsh. The shared privations of six years of war had stimulated community feelings, and despite the continuation of food rationing there were many public celebrations of the end of the war in Europe.*

Source: © Kevin Walsh, The Oakwood Grange Collection.

PLATE 6 ◆ *Variety in a bun. The first 'Wimpy Bar' opened in 1953 at the Coventry Street Corner House when Lyons acquired the UK rights from its American inventor, Eddie Gold. McDonald's first burger bar in Britain did not appear until 1974, at Woolwich.*

Source: The Advertising Archive.

PLATE 7 ◆ *Britain's favourite food? The Café Spice, Prescott Street, London, proudly displaying some of its dishes and ingredients. In 1998 there were 8,500 Indian restaurants, and it was claimed that chicken tikka, with a sale of 23 million portions a year, was Britain's most popular restaurant dish.*

Source: The Travelsite/Neil Setchfield.

PLATE 8 ◆ *The way some eat now. A nouvelle cuisine sorbet in the form of an artist's palette, from Le Manoir aux Quat' Saisons.*

Source: Courtesy of Le Manoir aux Quat' Saisons.

'Defeat or Victory' selling 100,000 copies in 20 days: it argued that prohibition of alcohol could feed the nation for three months and save £1,000 million – alcohol was, in effect, 'a pro-German poison'.[20] The government wisely declined to go so far, but when it was reported that in some munitions areas not only was 'Saint Monday' being observed but even 'Saint Tuesday' and 'Saint Wednesday,' Lloyd George declared that 'Alcohol is doing more damage in the war than all the German submarines put together'. Acquisition of the whole liquor trade was considered, but rejected in favour of ever-tightening controls over its sale, ultimately reducing the opening hours of licensed premises from 19½ hours to only 5½ hours a day. Beer output was cut to save grain and sugar, from 33 million 'standard' barrels a year to 13.8 million by 1918, though since its strength was also diluted the resultant barrelage was 19 million. While beer in moderation was tolerated as an aid to effort by manual workers, heavy consumption of spirits was regarded as an unnecessary evil: whisky, brandy and rum were compulsorily diluted, the duty on spirits was doubled (to 30/- a gallon), and the sale by off-licences of small quantities for use in pocket-flasks was forbidden: consumption of spirits fell from 35 million gallons a year in 1915 to 15 million in 1918.

Control of the liquor trade went furthest in a few, highly sensitive, munitions areas where the Central Control Board had powers to take over all production and distribution of alcohol on the grounds of national efficiency. This was done in the Carlisle and Gretna area, the Cromarty Firth and Enfield Lock, where heavy drinking was causing serious delays in war production and threatening public order. In the Carlisle and Maryport areas 250 licensed premises were taken over, half of them closed as 'redundant', and salaried managers put in the remainder: there was complete Sunday closing, no sale of spirits on Saturdays ('the spiritless Saturday'), and no sale of any alcoholic drink to people under 18.[21] From the government's point of view, at least, liquor control was highly successful – in Beveridge's opinion 'one of the outstanding social facts of the war': one result was a huge reduction in the number of convictions for drunkenness, from 3,390 a week in 1914 to 543 by 1918.[22]

During 1917 public discontent over food shortages and lengthening queues reached a peak, with a reported 3,000 people waiting at a multiple grocer's store in the Walworth Road. There was also strong resentment about the better-off who could still eat substantial meals in

FIGURE 6.1 ◆ *The first Cost Price Restaurant, Old Ford Row, Bow, 1914. These were established by local charities for the poor and when hoarding at the outbreak of war drove food prices up steeply. Sylvia Pankhurst and members of the Women's Social and Political Union were leaders of the movement for these 'restaurants', which provided a simple lunch of two courses for 2d. (1d. for children) but only soup in the evening.*

Source: Photo by A.J. Bartram. Reproduced by permission of Tower Hamlets Local History Library and Archives.

restaurants, where 5 oz. of meat, or twice this amount of game or poultry, were allowed for lunch or dinner: there were many complaints about evasions of the regulations and about a 'black market' for scarce supplies, for which there were 20,000 convictions during the war.[23] In November 1917, the *Herald* published an article, 'How they Starve at the Ritz', by a reporter who claimed that he had been served a six-course dinner including hors d'oeuvres, smoked salmon, soup, fish, meat entrées, cheese and other savouries;[24] (it is possible that, allowing for half-courses except the meat, this just met the regulation). By then, public opinion had generally come round to accepting some degree of compulsory rationing. Some local schemes began operating in November, and on 1 January 1918 sugar was rationed nationally: in February meat and some other foods were rationed in London and the Home Counties, and the rationing was extended to the whole country in April. The scheme provided 8 oz. sugar per head per week, 5 oz. butter and margarine combined, 4 oz. jam, 2 oz. tea and 8 oz. bacon: fresh meat was rationed by price rather than weight to allow for variations in quality and cuts, customers having four coupons a week, each valued at 5d.[25] The scheme applied to all hotels, restaurants and public eating-places as well as the home. Although it was generally acknowledged as necessary and fair, it put heavy burdens on catering establishments which had to detach customers' coupons for any meat meal (though not for fish, eggs or vegetables), count them, check against their records of meals served, and return them weekly to Food Offices, which would then allocate supplies on the basis of past demands. The other foods used in catering continued to be rationed by bulk, again based on the number of users, and the two morning 'meatless days' also continued. Not surprisingly, there were many complaints from hoteliers and restaurateurs about the costs and inconvenience of detailed regulations and some gave up the struggle, but as will be shown, most survived by various strategies. Some customers were also dissatisfied with what was put before them. One lady complained that for 5/- she was given 'a minute whiting, all head and tail, one egg in a pipkin, and a small spoonful of unsweetened macaroni pudding', while at a Torquay hotel another was served a tiny amount of meat, no potatoes and a scrap of cabbage: on asking whether she might have some rice or maize to accompany it, she was informed that the 'vegetable chef' did not know how to cook them.[26] Not all people fared so well as those at the Ritz.

Communal feeding

Food shortages and a growing sense of community stimulated a variety of public feeding initiatives for groups who, it was felt, had special need. As in many developments in social policy, these initiatives came first from voluntary sources and were later adopted and extended by the state. They began almost immediately on the outbreak of war when, in the autumn of 1914 the disruption of the local economy in the East End of London resulted in increased unemployment and poverty in what was already a distressed area. A charitable Fund for National Relief was quickly opened, to be administered by local committees to one of which, that for Poplar, Sylvia Pankhurst was appointed. Together with colleagues from the Women's Social and Political Union, she set up 'Cost Price Restaurants', the first opened on 31 August, serving two simple courses at midday for 2d. (1d. for children), and soup and bread in the evening for 1d. Others followed in Bethnal Green and other poor areas. They were aimed particularly at mothers and children since the school meals programmes had been stopped in some districts, and what one newspaper described as 'Penny Carltons' took over the provision. Some of the 'restaurants' also included Mothers' Clinics for food and treatment of babies, and depots providing subsidised milk.[27] Concern for the welfare of children was an important effect of the war: the number of Infant Welfare Centres, now receiving government grants, increased greatly, and in February 1918, a Milk (Mothers and Children) Order allowed local authorities to supply milk and other foods to expectant and nursing mothers and to children under 5, where necessary at the expense of the rates.[28] Although most metropolitan boroughs and many county boroughs offered these services, it appears that the take-up of free foods was quite small: the old working-class prejudice against 'hand-outs' still survived, and most mothers merely requested priority tickets for milk for which they paid the full price.[29] This was, perhaps, further evidence of their improving material standards as the war progressed, the official Report on the Cost of Living (1918) noting that free school meals for 'necessitous children' had declined by around four-fifths in England and Wales since 1914; in Liverpool and Birmingham 'it is hardly necessary to provide any meals at all'.[30]

Despite the optimism, the same report had to acknowledge that although the number of children entering school in a poorly nourished condition had fallen, it was still around half of that of 1913. At the height of the food shortages in 1917 the government itself ventured into the provision of cheap catering establishments, at first called Communal Kitchens, later National Kitchens and even National Restaurants. Lord Rhondda favoured them on the grounds that cooking for large numbers would have considerable food economy, and that they would free more women from domestic duties for war work. The first was opened in May 1917 in Westminster Bridge Road by the Queen herself, who proceeded to serve customers with meat and vegetables, rice pudding and cornflour and rhubarb jelly.[31] The Ministry set up a National Kitchens Department, which worked through municipalities and voluntary bodies, serving meals at cost or subsidised price, sometimes only as 'takeaways' but usually on a cafeteria basis in local halls and even public bath-houses. They were not hugely successful. Mrs Peel thought that 'In those days people had not learned the art of buying their dinners at public kitchens,' though they might have been more popular if located in more attractive surroundings without the atmosphere of soup kitchens. Not surprisingly, they were opposed by the catering trade, which considered them unnecessary and unfair competitors to existing cheap eating-places, especially when the Kitchens Department actually took over a Spiers and Pond restaurant in Ludgate Hill with the aim of bringing down prices in the area. The National Kitchens were an interesting experiment, a symbol of the new democracy which the war was encouraging, though if it was hoped that all social classes would dine together in egalitarian comradeship, this did not happen. In a strangely worded report on them, the *New Statesman* commented that 'Communal suggested communism, Socialism, fair dealing for all, consideration for the poor, abolition of distinctions of rank and money'[32] – it is not quite clear whether this meant approval. At least one kitchen survived the war in a revised form as 'The VC Restaurant' run by the Veterans' Commerce Ltd. for demobilised servicemen.[33]

Many more people experienced eating out during the war in factory canteens, the number of which greatly increased under government encouragement from around 100 in 1914 to 1,000 by 1918, supplying about a million meals every day. Their motives were not now mainly philanthropic, as in the past, but as part of the campaign for National Efficiency, designed to increase output and reduce absenteeism in war industries. As an official publication, *Feeding the Munition Worker*, argued:

> *There is now an overpowering body of evidence and experience which proves that productive output... is largely dependent upon the physical efficiency and health of the worker... You cannot get health, work and a reasonable output apart from good, nourishing food.*[34]

Plentiful, appetising meals provided during the long working hours, often extended to overtime, were also believed to reduce the heavy drinking to which some workers turned as an escape from fatigue. In 1915 the social reformer, Seebohm Rowntree, was appointed Director of the Welfare Department of the Ministry of Munitions, and a Canteen Committee was set up under the Central Control (Liquor Traffic) Board – the link between food and temperance was now explicit. It was made compulsory for all factories engaged in munitions to establish a canteen the costs of which could be set off against the Excess Profits Tax. It was recommended that the midday meal should provide around 1,000 calories for women and 1,250 for men, about one-third of daily requirements, and specimen menus for three-course meals were drawn up which would not have disgraced a pre-war middle-class home. A weekly dinner menu as suggested by the Canteen Committee of the Central Control Board appears below.

SUGGESTED DINNER MENU

Monday	*Tuesday*	*Wednesday*
Scotch broth	Pea Soup	Mutton broth
Roast beef	Boiled mutton	Roast pork
Sausage and mashed potatoes	Curried beef and rice	Irish stew
Stewed fruit	Stewed fruit	Stewed fruit
Ginger pudding	Jam roll	Rice or sago pudding
Thursday	*Friday*	*Saturday*
Lentil soup	Vegetable soup	Tomato soup
Boiled beef and carrots	Roast mutton	Liver and bacon
Tripe and onions	Steak and kidney	Potatoe pie
Stewed fruit	pie or pudding	Stewed fruit
Apple tart	Stewed fruit	Raisin pudding
	Bread and butter pudding	

Despite efforts, the Central Control Board was unable to bring about any significant increase in the provision of food in licensed premises, where it was usually met with the response that 'Liquor Pays Best'. In 840 canteens for munitions, transport and dock workers, and in 500 residential hostels for war workers, however, it was able to insist that more than 95 per cent were 'dry'.[35] In the State Purchase areas of Carlisle and Gretna, where existing public houses had been either closed or taken over, the Control Board set up some of its own 'Taverns' where food, beer and soft drinks were supplied, but no spirits: in other surviving pubs licensees were given substantial commission on the sale of food. It was hoped that these reformed premises would operate as popular social centres, some being comfortably furnished and having pianos, billiards tables and other games, and in one case, even a small cinema,[36] though their somewhat earnest air lacked the conviviality of the traditional pub.

Dinners and diners

The habit of eating out did not end during the war: in some respects it continued to grow, though it was much changed. If there were now more people who wished, and could afford, to eat out, there were fewer places to go, scantier menus, earlier closing hours, poorer service and higher prices. In February 1917, a noted gourmet, Thomas Burke, wandered around his old London haunts:

> They were either empty or filled with new faces. Rule's was deserted.
> The Bodega had been besieged by, and had capitulated to, the Colonial
> army, and Yates's Wine Lodge was filled with women war-workers. Truly,
> London was no more herself. She was not even an English city, like
> Leeds or Sheffield or Birmingham . . . Even the old chop-houses, under
> prevailing conditions, were offering manufactured food like spaghetti
> and disguised offal.[37]

War had to some extent democratised society. There were now few grand evening occasions, but more people at lunch and more men and women in uniform than in formal dress. At the Trocadero:

> The rooms looked like a Service mess-room. Every guest looked like
> every other guest. Men and women alike had fallen victim to the

devastating plague of uniforms, and all charm, all significance, had
been obliterated by khaki and blue serge.[38]

Before the war, wrote Burke, 'People went to Covent Garden not to listen
to music but to be seen, just as they went to the Savoy or to the Carlton
to be seen, not to procure nourishment'.[39] Now it was more a question of
the latter. While 14 large hotels in London were requisitioned, including
the Hotel Cecil and the Great Central, Marylebone, the survivors benefited from the hotel famine and struggled with the shortages of food and
staff. In a wave of rumours about foreign spies, almost all chefs and waiters of German or Austrian origin were dismissed and interned, and anti-
German feeling even extended to regarding Hock as unpatriotic. Many
British staff also volunteered, and at the Café Royal it is said that half the
kitchen staff of a hundred joined the French forces on the first day,[40]
while at the Savoy the manager, Reeves-Smith, was left with a 'skeleton
staff of clumsy boys and tired old men'.[41] At the Cavendish most meals
were prepared by Rosa Lewis herself with the help of only two assistants
and some of the wives of resident Guards officers.[42]

Although the great restaurants were unable to keep up pre-war standards of cuisine, most were able to serve acceptable meals by the use of
various strategies. The limitation of courses to two at midday and three
in the evening allowed for some creative accounting, since soup, fish,
poultry and game were only rated as half-courses and cheese not at all: a
dinner of a vegetable hors d'oeuvre, soup, fish or chicken, meat, dessert
and a savoury was therefore legal. At the Savoy kidneys, bacon and
mushrooms disappeared at breakfast and rissoles were often substituted
for meat, but the fact that the hotel served as the headquarters of Hoover's
Relief Committee and the American Luncheon Club perhaps ensured
some extra supplies.[43] At the height of the shortages in the spring of 1917
notices were placed on the tables inviting guests to take polenta or a rice
cake instead of bread,[44] but the Savoy's cellars evidently did not run dry,
for at the Victory Ball in November 1918, when Royal Flying Corps pilots
swung from the chandeliers, 2,700 wine glasses were smashed.[45] Thomas
Burke thought that the Café Royal had changed less than other places:

Ideas were still being discussed as though they mattered. Epstein and
Augustus John, both in uniform, were there, and Austin Harrison had
his usual group of poets. It was reassuring to see the old domino-playing

*Frenchmen, who seem part of the fixtures of the place, in their
accustomed corner.*[46]

Fish was not rationed, but good qualities were very difficult to obtain. At
the Carlton, Escoffier who had used 30 salmon a week could now
scarcely find two, but discovered that venison was not included in the
food restrictions (perhaps in deference to hunting on royal and noble
estates). Much of it was from old, tough animals, but minced and mixed
with eggs it became a 'gastronomic delight' : some was made into moussaka and some stewed, served with chestnut sauce and noodles. For an
Armistice Day Dinner, hurriedly announced on 11 November 1918, every
table was reserved by regular customers by 1 pm, and Escoffier had to
prepare for 712 covers. He had then in stock only two haunches of veal,
6 legs of lamb, 10 chickens and 15 kg. of pork: he put all this through the
mixer, added some truffles and pre-war tins of pâté de foie gras, and converted the mixture into noisettes 'Mignonnettes d'Agneau Saint-
Alliance'. 'Never lose your head, even when faced with great difficulty.
That must be the motto of every chef de cuisine.' The full menu for the
occasion is reproduced below.[47]

There must have been some additional supplies here, as there were at
the Cavendish, where Rosa Lewis cajoled food from market stall-holders
and from Fortnum and Mason, regarding this as legitimate comfort for
her 'boys' returning to the Front. Lloyd George, Kitchener, Mrs Patrick
Campbell, Ellen Terry, Isadora Duncan, J. M. Barrie and other celebrities
were often there, but her favourites were the young airmen, Americans
and subalterns who were given free meals if they could not afford to pay
and loaded with food parcels on departure: the Cavendish has been
described as 'a social first-aid post'.[48]

The lesser restaurants like those of Soho were not so well placed to
procure private supplies. The old Schweitzerhof, 'where four wonderful
dishes were placed before you at a cost of tenpence by some dastard spy'
was gone, as were Italian 'tables d'hôte' at a shilling: the lowest price was
now 1/9d., and 4/- for something more elaborate.[49] Even so, such prices
were now affordable by many who had not been pre-war diners-out:

*Soho blossomed. Owing to its nearness to Government and other offices,
the vast army of girl clerks and their soldier friends and admirers met
there for luncheon, where, in its many little restaurants, in spite of the*

THE CONSECRATION

Diner au Champagne

Consommé du Père la Victoire

Velouté Renaissance

• • •

Mousseline de Homard à l'Américaine

Riz à l'Indienne

• • •

Petits Pâtés de Volaille à la Bruxelloise

• • •

Mignonnettes d'Agneau Sainte-Alliance

Petits Pois à l'Anglaise

Pommes de Terre Canadiennes

• • •

Faisan en Cocotte Périgourdine

Salade des Capucins

• • •

Coeurs de Céleri à l'Italienne

• • •

Les Bombes de Réjouissance

Symbole de la Paix

• • •

Les Douces Dragées de Verdun Libératrices

Friandises

• • •

Liqueurs de France Café Mode Orientale

Fine Champagne, 1865

Vieille Chartreuse du Couvent

---

* * *

*food regulations, the foreigners who kept them managed to make more
or less palatable, though not very substantial, meals out of what
material was procurable.*[50]

Small cafés, teashops and the like, charging less than 1/3d., were
exempt from the meal and coupon regulations, though they too suffered
from the general shortages. Fish and chip shops were especially vulner-
able as many North Sea and Icelandic trawlers were requisitioned, and
because they were heavy users of frying oils and dripping, estimated to be
up to 1,000 tons a week. Fryers were forced to use unpopular substitutes
for the usual cod or haddock – ling, catfish (sold as 'Scotch hake') and coal-
fish ('blackjack') – and in many towns a quarter or more of shops closed.
On the other hand, fish and chips, usually costing 3d., were valuable as a
cheap, convenient meal for war workers and more popular than the food
at National Restaurants. Fish Fryers' Associations regularly petitioned the
government for recognition of their national importance, claiming that
they contributed to both nutrition and morale, and even that they stood
between the poor and social discontent. It appears that their arguments
were accepted, for in January 1918, the Ministry of Food took control of all
oils and fats and guaranteed supplies to the trade at fixed prices.[51]

Overall, the catering trades did not do well out of the war, almost all
showing substantial falls in profits. The reasons are fairly obvious – the
restrictions on food and staff, the cessation of most large public functions, fewer wealthy visitors from overseas and the licensing regulations
which reduced drinking and late suppers. Partly due to Rosa Lewis's generosity, the Cavendish faced bankruptcy at the end of the war:[52] in 1915
the Savoy, Claridge's and the Berkeley declared no dividends for the pre-
ceding year, while even Lyons showed a fall of £79,900,[53] and the 'JP'
(John Pearce) chain of cheap restaurants suffered a 50 per cent fall in
gross profits.[54] But in the later years of the war profitability generally
revived, especially in London with strong demand from the large numbers of civilian staff and military personnel. In the year ended 31 March
1919, which admittedly included four months of post-war boom, Lyons
announced a record profit and a dividend of 35 per cent.

Notes and references

1 *The Caterer and Hotelkeepers' Gazette*, 15 Aug. 1914, p. 462.

2 Robert Roberts, *The Classic Slum. Salford Life in the First Quarter of the Century*, Manchester, Manchester University Press, 1971, pp. 149–50.

3 John Burnett, *Plenty and Want. A Social History of Food in England from 1815 to the Present Day*, 3rd edn, Routledge, 1989, p. 250, citing A. L. Bowley, *Prices and Wages in the United Kingdom*, 1914–1920, 1921, p. 35.

4 Mrs C. S. Peel, *The Way We Lived Then, 1914–1918*, Bodley Head, 1929, p. 76.

5 Roberts, op. cit., p. 164.

6 John Burnett, *A History of the Cost of Living* (1st edn, 1969), Aldershot, Hampshire, Gregg Revivals, 1993, p. 309.

7 Caroline E. Playne, *Society At War, 1914–1916*, George Allen & Unwin, 1931, p. 232.

8 Peter Bird, *The First Food Empire. A History of J. Lyons and Co.*, Chichester, West Sussex, Phillimore, 2000, p. 79.

9 Derek Taylor, *Fortune, Fame and Folly. British Hotels and Catering from 1878 to 1978*, IPC Business Press, 1977, p. 5. At the outbreak of war many German and Austrian chefs and waiters were interned, though some later reappeared as 'Swiss'.

10 Playne, op. cit., p. 226.

11 John K. Walton, *The Blackpool Landlady. A Social History*, Manchester, Manchester University Press, 1978, pp. 168–70. Not all resorts fared so well: Scarborough's trade suffered badly after a German naval bombardment in December 1914, and the Isle of Man was much affected by the closure of the Manx steamers: some 600 hotel and boarding-house keepers went out of business.

12 Sir William H. Beveridge, *British Food Control*, Humphrey Milford, 1928, p. 5. Beveridge was Permanent Secretary at the Ministry of Food during the First World War.

13 For full details, see Beveridge, op. cit., and L. Margaret Barnett, *British Food Policy During the First World War*, George Allen & Unwin, 1985, who offers a somewhat more favourable interpretation of events than Beveridge.

14 Beveridge, op. cit., p. 36.

15 Burnett, *Plenty and Want*, op. cit., p. 253, n.10.

16 Colin Spencer, *The Heretic's Feast. A History of Vegetarianism*, Fourth Estate, 1993, p. 29.

17 Gregory Houston Bowden, *British Gastronomy. The Rise of Great Restaurants*, Chatto & Windus, 1975, p. 35.

18 Caroline E. Playne, *Britain Holds On, 1917–1918*, George Allen & Unwin, 1933, p. 68.

19 Beveridge, op. cit., p. 36.

20 Playne, *Society at War*, op. cit., p. 235.

21 Further details are in Henry Carter, *The Control of the Liquor Trade in Britain: A Contribution to National Efficiency during the Great War, 1915–1918*, Longmans, Green and Co., 2nd edn, 1919, ch. VIII. (Carter was a member of the Central Control Board); T. R. Gourvish and R. G. Wilson, *The British Brewing Industry, 1830–1980*, Cambridge, Cambridge University Press, 1994, pp. 317–36.

22 Beveridge, op. cit., p. 104.

23 Taylor, op. cit., p. 6.

24 Barnett, op. cit., p. 142.

25 Beveridge, op. cit., p. 211.

26 Peel, op. cit., p. 102.

27 E. Sylvia Pankhurst, *The Home Front. A Mirror to Life in England during the World War*, Hutchinson, 1932, pp. 40–4, 212.

28 Beveridge, op. cit., p. 263 n.

29 Barnett, op. cit., p. 150.

30 Report of the Sumner Committee on *The Working Classes' Cost of Living (1918)*, Cd. 8980, para. 51.

31 Peel, op. cit., pp. 83–4.

32 *New Statesman*, 27 April 1918, cited Barnett, p.151.

33 *The Caterer and Hotelkeepers' Gazette*, 14 May 1921. The restaurant was in New Street, Blackfriars. It opened on a self-service basis.

34 Sir Noel Curtis-Bennett, *The Food of the People. Being the History of Industrial Feeding*, Faber and Faber, 1949, p. 211.

35 Carter, *The Control of the Liquor Trade*, op. cit., pp. 91–2.

36 ibid., pp. 214–18.

37 Thomas Burke, *Out and About. A Note-Book of London in War-Time*, George Allen & Unwin, 1919, pp. 11–12.

38 ibid., pp. 16, 79, 108.

39 ibid., p. 69.

40 Captain D. Nicols Pigache, *Café Royal Days*, Hutchinson, 1934, pp. 66–7. Pigache was the grandson of the founder of the Café Royal, Daniel Nicols, and acted as manager, 1921–9.

41 Stanley Jackson, *The Savoy. The Romance of a Great Hotel*, Frederick Muller, 1964, p. 61.

42 Anthony Masters, *Rosa Lewis. An Exceptional Edwardian*, Weidenfeld & Nicolson, 1977, p. 108.

43 Compton Mackenzie, *The Savoy of London*, George G. Harrap, 1953, p. 76.

44 Bowden, op. cit., p. 34.

45 Jackson, op. cit., p. 62.

46 Burke, op. cit., p. 22.

47 Auguste Escoffier, *Memories of my Life*, trans. Laurence Escoffier, New York, Van Nostrand Reinhold, 1997, pp. 167–70.

48 Masters, op. cit., pp. 105–7.

49 Burke, op. cit., pp. 50–2.

50 Peel, op. cit., p. 67.

51 John K. Walton, *Fish and Chips and the British Working Class, 1870–1940*, Leicester, Leicester University Press, 1992, p. 19.

52 Masters, op. cit., p. 111.

53 *The Caterer and Hotelkeepers' Gazette*, 15 June 1915, p. 237.

54 ibid., p. 420.

CHAPTER 7

◆ ◆ ◆ ◆ ◆ ◆ ◆ ◆ ◆ ◆ ◆ ◆ ◆ ◆ ◆ ◆

After the deluge, 1918–1939

'Happy days are here again'?

The abrupt ending of the war in November 1918 was not followed by an equally rapid return to the 'normalcy' which many people desired. Others, however, had no wish to return to pre-war inequalities in wealth and social standing: the war had demanded enormous sacrifices which now required compensation from a state which had learned the value of collective action and the need for greater intervention in daily lives. Many believed that the sacrifices of the millions should now herald a new age of prosperity and opportunities for all, of better homes and health, improved education for the young, welfare for the old, and protection for the worker against the scourge of unemployment.

The civilian population had survived food shortages, not without inconvenience and complaint, but without the serious malnutrition which afflicted enemy countries. The Prime Minister, Lloyd George, went so far as to say that 'the food question ultimately decided the issue of this war', referring to the collapse of the Central Powers as due, in part, to the sheer hunger and fatigue of German workers and soldiers. If the British diet had changed in ways unpalatable to many people, it had done so in directions which modern nutritionists would approve – less red meat, butter, fats and sugar, more vegetables, potatoes and near-wholemeal bread. Price fixing of essential foods, rationing and public control of catering establishments had resulted in some social levelling of con-

TABLE 7.1 ◆ *Weekly per capita consumption of essential foodstuffs in the average working-class family (lb), 1914 and 1918*

	1914	1918	Change %
Bread and flour	7.33	7.55	+3
Meat	1.49	0.96	−36
Bacon	0.26	0.56	+115
Lard	0.22	0.17	−23
Butter	0.37	0.17	−54
Margarine	0.09	0.20	+122
Potatoes	3.41	4.38	+28
Cheese	0.18	0.09	−50
Sugar	1.29	0.62	−52

Source: *Report of the Sumner Committee on the Working Classes' Cost of Living*, Board of Trade, PP, Cd. 8980, 1918.

sumption, of which the working classes were the main beneficiaries, their daily calorie intake having fallen by a mere 3 per cent, as shown in Table 7.1.

Decontrol of food began with understandable, but unjustified, haste. The government was anxious to respond to public pressure for the ending of rationing, and to allay fears of social unrest from expectant civilians and demobilised soldiers. By the end of 1918 bread, cakes and pastries were returned to pre-war standards, tea and some meats were derationed, followed by other foods in early 1919. But the government had not predicted such a rush of demand, sharp rises in prices and a return to queuing. Price controls and coupons for meat, butter and sugar were hastily reintroduced in September 1919, though only briefly except for sugar, which remained officially on ration until November 1920. In the spring of 1921 the Ministry of Food and all remaining controls ended.[1]

Images of the state of English society in 'The Long Weekend' which followed are confusing and contradictory – on one hand of 'the roaring twenties' and the 'bright young things' of the jazz age, of a rapid growth of mass entertainments such as the cinema, dance halls and the wireless, of holidays and shorter working hours; on the other, dismal pictures of hollow-cheeked men in long dole queues, of hunger marches and disconsolate women and children in the slums of depressed areas. Both are true, neither is representative. A brief post-war boom raised retail prices to a peak of 266 points in 1920 (cf. 1906–10 = 100): thereafter, as the economy moved into depression, they fell to 148 points in 1933, around 50 per cent higher than before the war.[2] What mattered was how incomes and wages fared in relation to these unaccustomed price movements. The salaried classes, people on fixed incomes and workers in 'safe' industries little affected by unemployment tended to benefit, as their earnings held up better than the price falls: the main sufferers were unskilled workers whose wages were less protected by trade unions and whose jobs were uncertain. But now that food supplies had returned to free-market conditions, Britain again imported her basic needs from overseas, and gained from major falls in world food prices. The result was that for those who managed to stay in work, real wages (i.e. what money wages would buy in terms of goods and services) rose by an average of around 35 per cent between the wars: standards of living and amounts of disposable income grew correspondingly.

Averages, of course, conceal groups and individuals. The rich were never quite so rich again as in Edwardian times, hit by continued high levels of income tax, surtax and estate duties, and by the agricultural depression which reduced rent-rolls. 'England is changing hands', it was said in 1920, when many great estates and houses were on the market. The Duke of Rutland complained that although he might be able to keep up Welbeck Abbey on a reduced scale of expenditure, it seemed impossible that his heir would be able to live there: many country mansions were turned into public schools, hospitals or hotels or remained derelict, and whereas in 1918 305 peers had owned 10 million acres of land, by 1929 210 occupied 'only' 5½ million.[3] There was now less of a royal model for extravagant, luxurious dining: although the Prince of Wales and his set often ate out, George V kept a more modest court than his father had done, and was himself no gourmet. Industrialists and businessmen, many of whom had done well in the war, fared variously according to the nature of their enterprises – owners of collieries, shipyards, cotton mills and some engineering firms lost much due to the collapse of overseas trade, while those in the new light and consumer industries survived much better. J. Lyons and Co. declared their largest-ever profit of £968,950 in 1929, the same year as the Great Crash on the stock exchange. This reflected a buoyant demand from middle-class customers as the numbers of professional, managerial and clerical employees grew from 2.4 million in 1911 to 3.4 million in 1931, an increase of 41 per cent. This included a marked expansion of 'business girls' which most struck Mrs C. S. Peel:

> *Now London and other large towns teem with restaurants, tea shops, fruit shops and sweet shops. These cities must be prepared to feed the huge day population which returns to its dormitory suburbs at night...* *The coming of girls into business, and their consequent possession of personal incomes accounts to some extent for the kind of food offered and the premises in which it is served, and possibly the fact that young women drink less alcohol... Business girls needed cheap, decent accommodation, which the ABC and similar places afforded.*[4]

Solid breakfasts, where porridge was followed by eggs and bacon, were beginning to give way to American-style cereals and toast; longer journeys from home and later evening meals created more demand for a midday meal, for men as well as women. Yet the extent of eating lunch in any sort of restaurant was still directly related to income and class. When the first-ever enquiry into national eating habits was carried out in 1936/7 it discovered that in every social group, even including the wealthiest, the majority of husbands or chief earners went home for their midday meal. The survey divided the population into five income groups, as set out in Table 7.2.

TABLE 7.2 ◆ *Where the midday meal was eaten, 1936 (by income group)*

	Annual income	Approximate % of GB population
AA	£1,000 or over	1
A	£500–£999	4
B	£250–£499	20
C	£125–£249	60
D	Under £125	15

Midday meal %				
	AA	A	B	C	D
In restaurant	39.3	35.8	25.7	10.8	4.7
At home	52.9	53.9	61.1	50.6	59.5
Takes lunch with him	0.7	–	7.3	34.8	26.2
No information	7.1	10.3	5.9	3.8	9.6

Source: Sir William Crawford and H. Broadley, *The People's Food*, London, William Heinemann, 1938, Tables, pp. 28 and 55.

Lunching in any public eating-place was only at all common in the two wealthiest groups, and very rare in the two poorest: over all the five groups 23 per cent took a restaurant meal, but if the sample is 'weighted' to allow for the different numbers in the groups, the proportion falls to only 8 per cent. Even in London, where lunching out was most common, between a third and a half of husbands returned home at midday. The investigators concluded that:

> Restaurant meals are not typical of the English public. Those who spend their days in the heart of London are apt to forget this, and assume that the whole population follows their own midday habit.

Apart from cost, they believed that the other most limiting reason was time:

> So far as the businessman or the workman is concerned, his midday meal is much hampered by the time available. The two-hour break from noon till two o'clock which prevails in many Continental countries is unknown here ... The Englishman's lunch is reputed to be his most scamped meal ... Junior members of the world of business often 'make do' with sandwiches and a drink.[5]

Regrettably, the survey did not extend to evening meals eaten out. Had it done so, it would have found the proportions even lower and even more dictated by economic gradations. The attention of most social investigators between the wars understandably focused on the conditions of the poor and on the new problem of mass unemployment. Between 1920 and 1939 an average of 14.4 per cent of the workforce were unemployed and in the worst years of the depression, 1931–2, 22 per cent. On unemployment insurance benefit and the even less generous scales of public assistance (the 'dole') there was no question of eating out for pleasure beyond an occasional treat of fish and chips, only of survival. If the proportion of people in poverty was somewhat lower than at the beginning of the century, as most investigators believed, it still left a quarter of all children in that condition and, as the nutritionist John Boyd Orr estimated, around a third of the nation which did not achieve a standard of diet required for good health.[6]

Good living

In 1929 André Simon, the founder of the Wine and Food Society, was propagating the revival of English gastronomy:

We are happily approaching the greatly to be desired stage when the art of good living is again receiving proper attention. Today, only ten years after the Great War, we are not yet back to the pre-war level, but on our way there.[7]

In fact, England never returned to the extravagant heights of Edwardian 'haute cuisine', and, on the other hand, Simon regretted that here, unlike in France, the more homely 'Cuisine Bourgeoise' of the provinces had not developed. Hotels and restaurants for the middle classes too often relied on

gaudy trappings, blinding illumination, noisome bands, everything, in fact ... likely to distract the attention of diners from the poor quality of the food.[8]

Although social life in London was much less touched than that in industrial cities in the North and Midlands, no part of the catering trade was totally immune from the economic depression and the instability of prices. A noticeable change in restaurants was a reduction in the size and complexity of menus, partly to keep them within the reach of cost-conscious customers. But the author of *Where to Dine in London* also believed that appetites were smaller than formerly, and that the increased number of women diners preferred lighter meals, less heavily meat based and less strongly flavoured. In his opinion there were now (1937) too many restaurants in London – witness the number of failures and empty tables –– and that many over-spent on attractions such as dance bands and cabarets to the detriment of the food. In such places late supper with a floor show had almost taken the place of dinner, and fancy names were given to dishes which could not be legitimately produced at the price.[9] Following the Wall Street crash in 1929, *The Caterer and Hotelkeeper* reported an 'anxious time' in the industry, and a feature of the trade press became advice on economy, making the best use of all materials, including scraps. Every issue of the *Hotel Review* in the 1930s included recipes made from leftovers which might be offered for a 2/- lunch. Outside London and a few luxury resort hotels, 'haute cuisine' was evidently not what most people expected or could afford: 'plain English fare' with 'a cut off the joint' was still the favourite, a 2/6d. menu for a Sunday dinner in the *Hotel Review* of January 1930, suggesting: Cream of Veal and Barley Soup, Roast Loin of Lamb with Mint Sauce, Mashed Parsnips and Baked Potatoes, Orange Marmalade Pudding with Lemon Sauce, or Cheese and Biscuits,[10] dishes which would scarcely have taxed the culinary ingenuity of most provincial cooks.

London remained the centre of fashionable cooking, but looking back in 1934 Thomas Burke recorded some significant changes since before the war. There was now much greater mobility of the population as a result of the motor car: the Victorian Sunday was being replaced by 'a day of pagan refreshment', more like a Continental holiday, when people travelled out of London to places of interest and amusement. Others journeyed into the capital, where public places were now usually open on Sundays and where restaurants provided 'refreshment of nerves and spirit . . . A show of splendour which these places have democratised'. They have 'discarded their old Gothic heaviness of menu and decoration'; dinners are becoming more 'a race against time', where people do not linger before rushing on to something else. Eating was often directly associated with other pleasures, especially with dancing, which became a craze in the 1920s. The 'thé dansant' had been first introduced in hotels just before the war, but the 'diner dansant' with dancing between courses in the dining-room and late-night cabarets were now standard attractions in leading restaurants.[11]

In the early years after 1918 the climate had seemed set fair for a major expansion of catering to provide for a new generation of pleasure-seekers who, if they had not actually experienced the horrors of war, had at least suffered its privations. In 1921 a new Licensing Act extended drinking hours to 11 pm and, provided some food was served (which could be merely a sandwich), to 12.30 am. A 'Brighter London Society', formed in 1922, attracted support from public figures like Lord Curzon, the Foreign Secretary, and Gordon Selfridge, the department store owner. Some top restaurants spent up to £50,000 on redecoration, £12,000 a year on dance bands and £1,000 a week for cabaret stars, some brought over from America: introduced at the Metropole Hotel as 'The Midnight Follies' by Sir Francis Towle, they were at first banned by the London County Council, but later allowed.[12]

Little now seemed permanent in the catering world, as tastes and fashions changed rapidly. In the uncertain economic climate after 1921 renowned restaurants disappeared as former customers deserted and visitors from overseas dwindled. Hotel closures included the Cecil, the Midland Grand, De Keyser's, the Tavistock, the Salisbury and Morley's, while once-famous restaurants like the Gaiety, The Pall Mall, the Globe, St James's and Les Gobelins also closed their doors. Yet in more confident times around 1927 a cluster of great new hotels was built – the Mayfair, the Park Lane, Green Park, the Dorchester and Grosvenor House. Successful new restaurants which depended on the skills of their managers and chefs to attract a fashionable clientele included Quaglino's, Sovrani's, the Ivy, the Hungaria, Quo Vadis (1926), the Restaurant Boulestin (also 1926), Isola Bella, L'Escargo Bienvenu and Prunier's (1935), while in 1928 Lyons had added the Oxford Street Corner House to their two existing multi-restaurants. In Soho small Italian restaurants proliferated, and a growth of other ethnic restaurants made dishes available from Spain, Germany, Austria, Hungary, Turkey, America, Russia and even Japan, as well as from India and China. The catering characteristics at this time were variety, novelty and diversity, no longer so dominated by the French style as in the days of Escoffier.

Shorter menus, slimmer waistlines and thinner pockets gave less scope for extravagant creations, but 'haute cuisine' survived at the Savoy under the *chef de cuisine* Latry, Herbedeau at the Ritz and the Carlton, and the chef who approached a household name, Marcel Boulestin, who opened the Restaurant Française in 1925, designed by Clough Williams-Ellis, and the Restaurant Boulestin the following year. He became widely known through his book, *Simple French Cooking for English Homes*, his columns in *Vogue* and his series of demonstrations in 1937–9 on the new medium of television, making him the first 'TV chef'. At a time when there was little formal training for the trade, Boulestin's influence was also spread by establishing his own cookery school. He was the culinary icon of the age, while other formerly famous restaurateurs never fully recovered from the trauma of the war, let standards slip or gave up the increasingly competitive struggle. Though Rosa Lewis continued at the Cavendish throughout the period, it was never the same again. 'Since 1914, now that they are all gone, I do not consider anything that I do of any value.' Debutantes whose mothers remembered the Clarendon in its glory days still came to dance to the pianist, 'Hutch', in the dusty, Edwardian lounge, but little cooking was now done there and Rosa abandoned her once-profitable outside catering. After a visit in 1932 Aldous Huxley wrote that 'It was like staying in a run-down country house – large, comfortable rooms, but everything shabby and a bit dirty'.[13]

Where to dine?

In the inter-war years choices of where to dine were greatly facilitated by guidebooks intended mainly for visitors and tourists, giving locations, prices and special characteristics of hotels and restaurants. One of the earliest, published in 1924, unusually, by a woman, Elizabeth Montizambert, categorised four types of London restaurants by the prices of their tables d'hôte – 'the luxurious', 8/- to 10/-, the moderate (good food in pleasant surroundings), 3/6d. to 5/-, 'the amazing' (an excellent lunch for 2/6d. to 3/-), and the very cheap, a simple meal for 1/6d. to 2/- suitable for less affluent businessmen and women and for students.[14] In the first group were the restaurants and grill-rooms of the leading hotels like Claridge's, the Carlton, the Savoy, the Ritz, the Metropole, the Cecil, the Berkeley and Princes: these were comparable in standard with the best restaurants such as the Café Royal, Oddenino's, Pagani's, the Ivy, the Tour Eiffel and Verrey's. In the moderately priced group she placed Frascati's (with Winter Garden and music), the Criterion, Gatti's, the Cavour, Kettner's, the Villa Villa, the Trocadero and Hatchett's, while Group 3, 'the amazing, . . . have discovered the secret of how to provide a meal of four or five courses for half a crown' (2/6d.): these included the Samovar, the Chantecleer (hors d'oeuvre, omelette, cutlet, vegetables, sweet or cheese), Reggioni's and several 'artists' restaurants' in Chelsea such as the Good Intent and the Winona in Wigmore Street. For the very cheap, but eatable, she suggested the Venture, behind Regent Street, 'where the wife of a Major-General has opened a gay little yellow and black restaurant where she supplies food at this perilous price – a good lunch for 1/6d', the Borthwick Restaurant and the Singing Kettle in Regent Street – a four-course dinner for 2/6d.[15]

Also in the early 1920s, 'Diner-Out', who contributed articles on food and wine to the *Daily Mail*, published his own guide to London restaurants, which included many examples of menus. In the earlier tradition, when taking guests out to dine he insists on discussing the menu in advance with the maître d'hôtel: 'He is on his mettle, the reputation of his house is at stake ... I get the best.'[16] In these cases the menu is not a table d'hôte or even à la carte, and the bill is correspondingly higher. Entertaining a Bishop and his lady at Claridge's ('There is a dignity about the hotel that suggests the serenity of episcopal palaces') 'Diner-Out' arranged 'a chaste little dinner for four' with the courtly manager, Mr Charles. This is reproduced below.

CLARIDGE'S

Huitres Musgrave

(fried oysters with strips of bacon)

....

Tortue Vraie

(turtle soup)

....

Filets de Sole Savile

(soles flavoured and sauced)

....

Perdreau Piermartini

(partridge)

....

Salade . Pommes Byron

(potatoes with a sauce of red wine, butter and sliced truffles)

....

Soufflé glace

....

Even so, this was a considerably more modest menu than those described by Newnham-Davis a quarter of a century earlier. The bill for four, including two excellent bottles of Barsac, coffee and champagne liqueurs, was £4/17/6d., the basic cost of the food being 15/6d. per person. Lunch in the Ritz Grill-Room was also strongly recommended. 'It is quiet ... the music of the orchestra lends itself to the reposeful atmosphere of the place. It is soft enough and far away enough not to interfere with talk ... Quiet, pleasant, well-groomed, well-bred people frequent it – not the flashy kind nor the new rich who drink champagne for breakfast.' He and 'Mabel' chose from the 6/6d. table d'hôte, reproduced below.

RITZ GRILL-ROOM

Hors d'oeuvre

(9 or 10 varieties)

....

Oeuf Bourguignonne

ou

Filet de sole Américaine

(sauce of tomato and lobster roe)

....

Poitrine de Veau Farcie

Pommes à la crème

ou

Emincé de Volaille à la Reine

(minced chicken with mushrooms)

ou

Baron d'Agneau à la Broche

(spit-roasted lamb)

Haricots Panachés   Pommes Fondants

....

Saint Honoré

(gateau with whipped cream)

....

A bottle of Barsac '69 cost 8/6d.; coffee and liqueurs added another 8/0d. For a 'somewhat thrilling and unusual' meal one might go to the Chinese Café in Oxford Street, opened in 1919, with a huge, numbered menu of 271 dishes, all authentically cooked: ordering a large variety of half-portions, the bill for three was 12/0d. But of all the restaurants described, 'Diner-Out' considered that the Louis XIV dining-room at the Piccadilly Hotel took the crown (menu below). 'Not since pre-war days, we all agreed, had we eaten such an imposing dinner ... Used to the shorter and simpler menus of post-war conditions, we thought it impossible to go through it' (but they did).

PICCADILLY HOTEL
Les Hors d'oeuvres Moscovite
(with caviar)
....
La petite Marmite Henri IV
(clear, strong soup)
ou
La crème Dame Blanche
(cream soup)
....
Le Saumon poché
La Sauce Mousseline
Les concombres
(poached salmon in an Hollandaise sauce with
whipped cream and cucumbers)
....
La selle d'Agneau Orloff
(saddle of lamb, sliced with alternate layers of
puréed mushrooms and topped with sliced truffles)
Petits Pois Pommes Noisette
....
La Chasse Royale
(pheasant, quail or larks stuffed with foie gras)
....
La neige des Alpes
(iced sorbet)
....
La poularde du Mans en Casserole
La salade Lorette
....
Les Asperges de Paris
La Sauce Divine
(asparagus in sauce)
....
L'Ananas glacé à la Piccadilly
(pineapple)
....
La corbeille de Friandises
(basket of sweetmeats)
....
Moka
(coffee)
....

This was a dinner of Edwardian proportions, richness and quality; the cost is not disclosed.[17]

'Bon Viveur's' guide of 1937 shows little change in the restaurant scene just before the outbreak of the Second World War.[18] Prices were somewhat higher than the low levels of the mid-1920s – in the 'Restaurants de Luxe' category luncheon was now around 8/6d. and dinner nearer 15/- – and music, dancing and cabarets were more general now except at Claridge's, where a Hungarian Orchestra played only in the Foyer. In the Mayfair Ambrose's famous band performed, at the Café de Paris Lou Stone, while at the Grosvenor House special Gala Night dinner-dances cost £3/3/0d. Such places were the nurseries for celebrity dance-band leaders, many of whom broadcast regularly on the BBC. Greater importance was also placed on decor. At Romano's, designed in Moorish style, dance hostesses were available to instruct and partner gentlemen; the San Marco represented the Doge's Palace in Venice; Frascati's boasted a Palladian Winter Garden and Balcony; and Quo Vadis had a picture gallery established by Edward Craig, grandson of Ellen Terry. In these Italian restaurants prices were considerably lower at around 5/0d.–7/6d. for a five-course dinner. Another notable feature in 1937 was a section in the guide on 'Restaurants of the Nations', indicating that it was now poss-ible to sample the cuisines of virtually the whole world in London. Curries had long been available in leading hotels for the tastes of ex-Army and colonial officers, but Indian restaurants only now received serious attention: recommended were Veeraswamy's in Regent Street (real Indian punkahs with fans, excellent Madras curry, Birianis and Kebabs), the Delhi in Tottenham Court Road (where the Rajah of Sarawak was an enthusiastic customer) and the Mysore in South Kensington – set lunch or dinner only 1/9d. Though remarkably cheap, these served gen-uine Indian dishes, correctly spiced and cooked, but 'Good curry, unfor-tunately, is the exception rather than the rule in London, and travesties of this noble dish are all too often met with in the menus of inferior restaurants. It is not sufficient to do up a little mutton and rice with curry powder.'[19]

Between the wars the best-known hotel in England and, probably also in the United States, was the Savoy of London, its name nationally adver-tised by the wireless broadcasts of its dance bands, Debroy Somers and the Savoy Orpheans and, after 1924, Carroll Gibbons, under whose

FIGURE 7.1 ◆ *The Savoy Orpheans Dance Band, directed by Debroy Somers (standing, with baton), October 1923. Music and dancing were important aspects of the dining experience between the wars. The Orpheans became nationally famous as a result of their regular late-night broadcasts on the BBC and their huge sales of records. Debroy Somers was succeeded by Carroll Gibbons as leader, and Geraldo and his Gauchos played Latin-American music on the hotel's roof terrace.*

Source: Hulton Archive.

direction three million records were sold in ten months.[20] The Savoy was especially favoured by American visitors, partly for François Latry's classic French cuisine (he was *chef de cuisine* from 1919 to 1942), partly because of the attractions of the American Bar during the period of Prohibition. The Savoy had brought over Harry Craddock from the States, reputedly the highest-paid barman in the world (though himself a teetotaller), the inventor of hundreds of cocktails including the famous White Lady. Cabarets, introduced in 1927 between courses, beginning with 'The Two Black Crows', were also very popular.[21] Latry continued the tradition of providing spectacular banquets for special occasions, like 'The Millionaire's Dinner' hosted by Lionel de Rothschild when it was estimated that a combined capital of £200 million was represented (plump quails imported from Egypt and stuffed with truffles, foie gras served on solid silver dishes), a Twelfth Night dinner which included a huge cygnet pie based on a 500-year old recipe, and a Centenary Luncheon in honour of Brillat-Savarin when crayfish were prepared with foie gras brought from his native village of Belley.[22] Such events received much publicity and contributed greatly to the Savoy's reputation, but were probably not costed adequately: during the depression of the early 1930s the Savoy made a loss for the first time in its history.

Two new restaurants which quickly acquired high reputations deserve mention. In 1919 Mario Gallati, formerly head waiter at Romano's, started as manager of the Ivy, then a small room off Cambridge Circus, with a cook and two waitresses. It rapidly acquired a reputation for excellent French cuisine at moderate prices: situated at the heart of theatreland, it was patronised by C. B. Cochran, who brought stars from his West End shows, but frequent guests also included authors (Wells, Chesterton, Pirandello, Somerset Maugham), politicians (Lloyd George and Churchill), the stage (Gielgud, Edith Evans, Noel Coward), the Prince of Wales and Mrs Simpson, the Aga Khan and Sir Thomas Lipton (who always ordered 'Lipton's Tea' whatever the meal).The premises were rebuilt and greatly extended in 1929, but Gallati refused many offers to establish his own restaurant.[23] It is difficult to say why the Ivy was such an outstanding success. Gallati's personality and meticulous attention to detail were important, but the food, though always excellent, was not intrinsically different from that of other first-class places. A pre-theatre dinner for three which 'Diner-Out' considered worthy of record is reproduced below.

THE IVY
Grapes Fruits au Maraschino
....
Suprêmes de Soles Bonne Femme
....
Tournedos Grillé Sauce Bearnaise
Pommes Sautées
Haricots Verts à l'Anglaise
....
Soufflé en Surprise Hélène
(vanilla ice, whipped cream, meringue
and hot chocolate sauce)
....
Friandises
....

The price was 10/6d. each.[24]

Pruniers, established by Madame Simone Prunier in 1935, had very different origins. The Paris restaurant of the same name founded by her grandfather, Alfred Prunier, in 1872, was already famous, attracting European royalty and celebrities: after her father's early death she managed the Paris house at the age of 22, and was well experienced when she took London premises in St James's Street, the former teashop of Rumpelmeyer.[25] For a restaurant specialising in seafood, the decor was influenced by Captain Nemo's cabin in *Twenty Thousand Leagues under the Sea*, a book which had captured her imagination as a child. Opened to great publicity in January 1935, when a thousand guests were invited to a buffet of champagne, oysters and caviar, it was an immediate success among London's glitterati – on the first full day of business the Prince of Wales's equerry booked a table for eight, including Mrs Simpson.[26] Prunier's was quieter, more restrained than many restaurants had become, one of her innovations being 'soupers intimes' with special dishes and no loud music or dancing. The restaurant specialised in oysters (10 varieties of plain and 7 of cooked), almost all species of fish, also saddle of lamb with truffles and Stilton cheese treated with port and brandy. Simpler menus included a daily 'Poissons du Chef' at 3/0d., and a light early-evening 'Dégustation Hour' from 5.30 to 6.30 pm at 3/6d.

The success of Prunier's depended on the established reputation of the Paris restaurant and on the skill of the *chef de cuisine*, Michel Bouzy, who had been brought to London from Paris: he was well known in France through his cookery book, *Les Poissons* (Paris, 1929) with a Preface by Escoffier.

Guidebooks were intended to advise readers where and how to dine rather than where not to dine: as yet there was no 'Bad Food Guide', but several authors in this period recorded their experiences of disastrous meals. One was E. M. Forster, breakfasting on a boat train from Tilbury to London in the 1930s:

> *'Porridge or prunes, Sir?' That cry still rings in my memory. It is an epitome – not, indeed, of English food, but of the forces that drag it into the dirt. It voices the true spirit of gastronomic joylessness. Porridge fills the Englishman up, prunes clear him out, so their functions are opposed. But their spirit is the same: they eschew pleasure and consider delicacy immoral . . . Everything was grey. The porridge was in pallid, grey lumps, the prunes swam in grey juice . . . Then I had a haddock. It was covered in a sort of hard, yellow oilskin, as if it had been out in a lifeboat, and its inside gushed salt water when pricked. Sausages and bacon followed this disgusting fish. They, too, had been up all night. Toast like steel: marmalade a scented jelly. I paid the bill dumbly, wondering again why some things have to be. They have to be because this is England, and we are English.*[27]

An equally memorable bad lunch was experienced by B. A. Young in 1939 at a place the naming of which 'the laws of libel forbid'.

> *A piquant and somewhat daring innovation to which we were introduced was the serving of the soup before the hors d'oeuvre . . . The soup was a mild-mannered consommé with a strong flavour of Brussels sprouts. It was served piping hot on the sideboard and there left to cool until the waiter was able to immerse his thumb in it without discomfort. With the soup one drank 'Here's How' cocktail if one had had the foresight to conserve any of it until then. This is a bland beverage, somewhat lacking in character, with a faint but quite distinct flavour of something or other. After the soup, the hors d'oeuvre was dished up apologetically, still lacking the sardines [the tin-opener had been*

mislaid]. We were promised that if it turned up in time, we should have the sardines as a savoury, on toast . . . A square of wet mackintosh was served afterwards under the name of boiled turbot. With the fish a bottle of orange-squash was opened and served in tumblers at room temperature with water or soda-water. The fish was followed by a long interval, which was followed by roast mutton cut in flat, brown slices and accompanied by pommes rôties and choux-fleurs bouillés. Salt and pepper were served with this course . . . The fruit salad calls for little remark unless one singles out for mention the powerful flavour of the dried apricots which were used as its foundation. Custard, emollient but lumpy, was served with the fruit salad. The cheese, a transatlantic Cheddar, was just cheese. To conclude the meal finger-bowls and tooth-picks were served to all the guests, and afterwards, those who could afford it had a glass of the eightpenny port, a vintage which lacks the smoothness of the ninepenny, but which is superior in every way to the sixpenny.[28]

For contrast and recovery, two memorably excellent meals enjoyed by epicures may be quoted. One, 'the best dinner I ever ate anywhere', was by Victor MacClure at the Royal Automobile Club in the 1930s: a clear soup with a sprinkling of chervil; Soles belle meunière; Chartreuse of partridge with a creamed bouillon dressing; Soufflé of Cheshire cheese. Evidently, a memorable meal did not need to be long or elaborate, though the enjoyment of the occasion may have owed something to three vintage wines and to the guests who included A. P. Herbert and Vernon Bartlett.[29]

André Simon, prolific author on all aspects of gastronomy and founder of the Wine and Food Society in 1933, experienced a good many 'Memorable Meals' including one at Boulestin's Restaurant where he tasted and enjoyed lampreys for the first time. Probably the crown went to a dinner in the Mikado Room at the Savoy – 'a rare feast and perfect gastronomic symphony'.[30] The menu is reproduced below.

THE SAVOY

The date: 2nd May, 1934.

The place: The Savoy, Mikado room.

The host: Louis E. Harfeld.

The guests: Col. the Hon. Osbert Vesey, Sir Walter
     Schroder, A. W. Folks, E. Price Hallowes,
     Frank Ratto and A.L.S.

The menu: Les Perles du Volga.

          La Bisque d'Écrevisses.

          La Truite Saumonée au Court Bouillon accompagnée d'un beurre blanc.

          Le Baron d'Agnelet à la broche parfumé aux Morillons de forêt.

          La Caille dodue dans sa Gelée tremblante.

          Le Cœur de Palmier Riviera.

          Le Fenouil Braisé Flamande.

          La Coupe de Fraises des Bois rafraîchies.

          La Crème d'Ananas Voilée. Les Gourmandises.*

The wines: Macharnudo La Riva Fino.

          Vin Nature de Rilly-la-Montagne 1929.

          Berncasteler Doctor 1925.

          Domaine de Chevalier 1923.

          Le Grand Musigny 1923.

          Oestricher Eiserberg 1920. Feinste.

          Trockenbeeren Auslese.

          Quinta da Paz 1845. Madeira.

* Caviar; Fish soup with freshwater crayfish; Salmon trout in a savoury stock; Baron
of lamb with wild mushrooms; Quail in aspic; Heart of palm; Braised fennel; Wild
strawberries; Pineapple in cream.

New ways to eat out

Eating out had long been associated with other leisure activities, but in
the inter-war years the combination of food with other pleasures strongly
increased. Dancing and cabarets at dinner were now parts of a total entertainment experience, often timed after a theatre visit: meals of many
courses did not go well with exertions on the dance floor or with the fashionable slim outlines of ladies' dresses. From a commercial point of view,

the sale of drinks showed more profit than that of food, and a natural response to the restriction of licensing hours was to establish 'private' clubs whose members could continue to drink well after 12.30 am when otherwise glasses were supposed to be cleared. Nightclubs became very popular in London in the 1920s, ranging from the respectable like the Night Light which had two princesses and four peers on its committee, to shady covers for crime and drug-peddling where new members could be enrolled merely by a handout to the doorman. Nightclubs were frequently raided by the police and their proprietors fined or even imprisoned – the fashionable Kit-Kat Club was raided the night after a visit by the Prince of Wales and Kate Meyrick, owner of the 43 Club, was sentenced to six months in Holloway in 1924, winning much sympathy from distinguished clients who included the Crown Prince of Sweden and Prince Nicholas of Rumania. Undeterred, she later established the Manhattan (where Paul Whiteman's band sometimes played) and the Silver Slipper with a dance floor of glass.[31] Their heyday was relatively brief. 'Bon Viveur' in 1937 believed that they had all but disappeared and were being replaced by 'Private Parties' where the guests were carefully controlled by invitation only and drinks had to be ordered with 12 hours' notice to comply with the law; several were run by ex-military men, suggestive of their good order.

> The more respectable 'Parties' require evening dress and are open from 11 p.m. until 5 or 6 a.m.: as well as dancing and cabarets they have restaurants, some of which have excellent cuisines. 'The Old Florida' is the resort of the gilded youth of Mayfair. There is no place quite like it. It is neither furtive nor depraved, yet there is an air of gaiety and abandonment... The cuisine is really first-class and the prices are those of any luxury restaurant. Especially to be recommended are the Suprême de Volaille sous Cloche and the Brochette à la Florida, which is chicken liver, bacon, mushroom and chipolata, served with a hot sherry and foie gras sauce.

The Four Hundred in Leicester Square was run by Mr Hector, formerly of the Savoy:

> Dancing is to a dim, religious light in a large room intersected by vaulted pillars... The supper menu is something quite out of the ordinary, as there is a French, an Italian and a Chinese chef.

Very popular also was the Cocoanut Grove in Regent Street, hosted by Captain Gordon:

Southern landscapes lit from below adorn the walls, the pillars sprout green fronds and the band plays in a log cabin.

Specialities here were American and Chinese dishes.[32]

Such activities were essentially London based, though larger provincial cities also had versions of nightclubs and private parties. But the most widespread of inter-war entertainments was the cinema, popular with all classes and ages. From around 3,000 in 1914, many of them small, back-street premises, their number grew to 5,000 in 1939, now including many 'super-cinemas' in Egyptian, Roman, Art Deco and 'other-worldly' styles, some seating up to 4,000 patrons. The cinema was the great escape from the depression to a dream-world of excitement, glamour and romance obtainable for a few pence. By 1939 around 20 million tickets were being sold weekly, and in many towns 40 per cent of the population were weekly attenders.[33] A seat in one of the grand new cinemas of the 1930s bought several hours of entertainment – two feature films, newsreels, cartoons, even an interval stage-show or a Wurlitzer organ, beginning at midday and lasting until late afternoon. People brought sandwiches and a Thermos flask or bought ice cream and chocolates from the attendants. But a natural development for the larger cinemas was to add restaurants serving afternoon tea and evening meals: some also had dance floors, thus providing a total entertainment experience where couples might imagine themselves as the Astaires and Rogers of the movies. In 1929 the luxurious Regal Cinema overlooking Hyde Park opened, offering a Thé Dansant at 3/6d. and a Dansant Soirée Parisienne from 8 to 10.30 pm at 5/6d. There were light meals – coffee, tea, soft drinks, Fruit Cocktails, Sandwiches (foie gras, chicken, ham, tongue, etc.), French and Viennese pastries, and ices – which were quite expensive compared with Soho restaurant prices. *The Caterer* expressed concern in an article on 'The Future of Cinema Catering' that such developments might become 'a menace' to the established trade,[34] but the trend was unstoppable. In 1931 the film corporation, Gaumont-British, opened a 700-seat Kit-Kat Restaurant where moving clouds, sunrise and sunset were projected and the new sound films were shown in part of the restaurant: here was a direct link between dining and viewing. More modestly, the Trocadero Café at the Elephant and Castle incorporated a sound relay system and an HMV wireless and gramophone: a 1/9d. lunch here included Gravy Soup or Whiting with Anchovy Sauce; Minced Veal and Spaghetti or Roast Beef and Yorkshire Pudding or Chop Toad-in-the-Hole; Rice Pudding or Apple Pudding or Blancmange and Jam, and was warmly approved by a party of 18 local schoolmistresses.[35]

An even more important influence on eating-out was the rapid growth of the motor car, with major effects on mobility in and out of the cities where three-quarters of English people now lived and worked. In 1914 there had been only 140,000 motor vehicles of all kinds, but by 1939 there were three million, of which two million were private cars. From the first mass-produced English car, the Austin Seven, in 1921 the industry boomed to a peak in 1935–9, when 300,000 cars were built each year, mainly by huge plants like Morris and Ford, but also by scores of small firms predominantly in the Midlands.[36] In 1923 Citroen advertised their cheapest car at £230, about the annual wage of a skilled engineer, but by the 1930s small cars were available at just over £100, well within the reach of lower middle-class purchasers and, at second-hand, more widely still. Given that in most towns public transport by trams, trolley-buses and motor buses and, in London, by Underground, was cheap and generally reliable, most motoring at this time was a hobby, for pleasure rather than work. As an advertisement for the Standard Light Car put it:

> *Every weekend a holiday. Where shall it be this week? Through*
> *highways and old world towns and villages, or byways to the woods and*
> *fields: a quick straight run to the silvery sea or a dawdle amid hills and*
> *dales. Each weekend a new scene – a new delight.*[37]

Expeditions required provisions – the simplest, the well-tried picnic. For the affluent, picnic-baskets could be elaborate affairs with compartments for bottles, a spirit stove, cutlery, unbreakable Betelware plates, cups and saucers and a folding table strapped to the outside, while the Thermos flask, invented in 1907, provided hot drinks and soup. Food ranged from the simple to the elaborate, Mrs C. S. Leyel's *Picnics for Motorists* (1936) suggesting 60 menus including iced claret cup, mousse of haddock, casseroled grouse, cold rack of Welsh mutton and macedoine of vegetables.[38]

As the advertisement for the Standard suggested, the car, even more than the bicycle, contributed to a rediscovery of the English countryside at weekends and in touring holidays, which became very popular in the 1930s. Small hotels and inns in country towns and villages responded to a new demand for the refreshment of travellers as they had in former coaching days, refurbishing dusty premises, offering table d'hôte meals and accommodation to meet the graded standards of AA and RAC guides. Writing in 1934, Thomas Burke also approvingly noted the new types of public houses being built along arterial roads:

> A recent development has been the family house, which is public house, restaurant and teashop all in one, with gardens and public rooms available to children as well as adults.[39]

The 'reformed' public house had received official support during the First World War when the Central Control Board (Liquor Traffic) had encouraged licensees to provide wider facilities for refreshments, social and recreational amenities and this was also an aim of the Public House Trust companies formed at the beginning of the century: they continued to acquire country inns under professional management, totalling 222 by 1938. These trends were encouraged by the Royal Commission on Licensing (1932), which recommended that the public house should be 'a place where the public can obtain general refreshments of whatever variety they choose in decent, pleasant and comfortable surroundings'.[40] This was sometimes only possible in new, architect-designed premises which could include dining-rooms, tea lounges, loggias, even tennis courts and swimming-pools, but Burke also commended the Trust Houses for 'the happy idea of modernising [old inns] while retaining whatever in the original is beautiful and notable', citing good examples in Shrewsbury, Colchester, Withyam and Long Melford.[41]

The car also spawned another new institution peculiar to the 1930s, the Road House – a kind of country club with restaurants, cocktail lounges and sporting facilities, aimed mainly at the younger motoring set. Built in the bright, contemporary concrete idiom, they did well in summer with midnight swimming-parties and in winter with dancing and cabarets. They represented an extension of the city nightclub into a rural environment, providing sports and fitness for those who wished or a secluded retreat for other activities: most provided a night's accommodation and an absence of awkward questions. Every few miles along the Great West Road notices invited customers to 'Swim, Dine and Dance', but few survived the restrictions and scarcities of the Second World War.

More significant for future trends in eating out was the emergence of a few country town or village restaurants kept by proprietors with a love and understanding of fine food. They were mainly amateurs in the true sense rather than professionals who had risen through the ranks of kitchen or waiting staff in famous restaurants: their success depended on their flair and enthusiasm, a willingness to work all hours and a location accessible by car. Some were in established touring areas like the Cotswolds and the Lake District, others in market towns and riverside villages. In the opinion of epicures like André Simon these places were beginning to revive the reputation of English provincial catering, for long neglected, dreary and monotonous. In 1937 Simon and a party of friends enjoyed a simple, but superbly cooked meal at the Hind's Head, Bray-on-Thames, kept by Barry Neame: Giblet soup; Tay salmon; Saddle of Newbury lamb with creamed mushrooms, Worthing beans and new potatoes; Asparagus; Cheese soufflé; there were eight vintage wines from the magnificent cellar.

> It was a noble evening . . . and it was grand to hear that nice lad,
> Aneurin Bevan, shouting with laughter like a schoolboy, and showing as
> firm an allegiance to Red Wine as to the Red Flag.[42]

At the White Horse, Ipswich, a Trust House, a pleasant lunch included chops and kidneys cooked on a sixteenth-century grill ('Apparently some individuality is still left in such old inns')[43] and at the Miller of Mansfield, Goring-on-Thames, Burke had superb lobster and salmon mayonnaise, cold duck and tipsy cake. These examples were reminiscent of the best eighteenth-century fare, as was the Bell at Clare where in 1929 the landlord still presided at table, carving 'the largest sirloin of beef I have ever seen', and serving vegetables, fresh fruit salad and a huge Cheshire cheese: 'The price of the lunch was half-a-crown (2/6d.). Its quality was level with Simpson's.'[44]

Another inn which was briefly famous was the Spreadeagle at Thame, Oxfordshire, kept by John Fothergill between 1922 and 1931. He had studied at St John's College, Oxford and at the Slade School of Art; he was a friend of leading artists and writers, an aesthete and dilettante who became a connoisseur of food and wine, describing himself in *Who's Who* as a 'Pioneer Amateur Innkeeper'. He was eccentric, snobbish and opinionated, often rude to customers of whom he disapproved for not appreciating the finer points of his cooking.

Three kinds of cooking.
I define three kinds of kitchen:
1.   The French, where the food doesn't taste of what it is, or ought to be, but tastes good;
2.   English hotel, where the food, even when it is food, doesn't taste of anything or tastes badly;
3.   Our kitchen, and the true American, where the food is food, tastes of it, and tastes good.[45]

Until its reputation was established, the Spreadeagle mainly depended on local farmers, up to 60 of whom lunched there on weekly market days and expected a huge 2/6d. meal with three roasts, which they carved themselves – Fothergill weighed one slice of leg of mutton at one pound three ounces. Many of his meals showed little or no profit as he insisted on the finest ingredients: foods were bought from France, Italy, Greece, Norway and elsewhere, and from England cheese from East Harptree, salt from Maldon, mustard from Leighton Buzzard, bacon 'found by accident from the International Stores'. His insistence on Real Food eventually attracted gourmets from London, chauffeur driven in their Daimlers and Rolls Royces, Fellows and wealthy undergraduates from Oxford. His prices were moderate except for special occasions, a typically simple lunch consisting of roast lamb or steak pie, choice of two sweets and cheese, about which two brash young men from Beaconsfield (20 miles) complained:

Wasn't it good? (Fothergill enquired).
Well, the meal's not worth travelling a hundred miles for.
What did you expect? Fireworks?
No. But it isn't like the Berkeley exactly.
But it isn't the Berkeley.
Well, you have such a tremendous reputation, so we've come specially to lunch here.

Most of his customers, who included glitterati like H. G. Wells, the Sitwells, Chesterton, Evelyn Waugh and many others, were more than satisfied with the simple excellence and the ambience of antique furniture, silver and china, but for special occasions like a visit by the Sultan of Muscat he could produce an elaborate banquet of eleven courses, or when the Provost and Fellows of Oriel College chose to celebrate their Annual Dinner there, the first time ever out of College: G. N. Clark pronounced it 'the pleasantest event in their joint lives'. But for all its fame, the Spreadeagle, which depended on an irregular trade and was too exacting in its standards for its moderate charges, was a financial failure, and in 1931 Fothergill was forced to sell up.[46] The time had not yet come when a high reputation could ensure a sufficiently wide and constant public demand in a location which had few other attractions.

Outside London, successful restaurants were mainly in established touring areas and in elegant hotels in spas or resorts, like the Imperial at Torquay, where guests from Scotland and the North of England brought their chauffeurs and stayed for the season.[47] Some large provincial city hotels also had restaurants of repute – in Manchester the Midland Hotel, in Liverpool the Adelphi (opened in 1914) and in Leeds the Queen's Hotel with its Harewood Restaurant – where there were sufficiently large and sophisticated clienteles to support them, but in most smaller towns the old 'County' hotel restaurants did not offer much beyond substantial meals of brown Windsor soup, roast meat, overcooked vegetables and solid puddings, the unchanging fare of the English provinces. Boulestin had not penetrated to these kitchens, his television demonstrations unavailable outside Greater London.

Food and popular culture

Between the wars a variety of new opportunities for eating out opened up for the lower middle classes and for those manual workers who were able to avoid the miseries of unemployment. These opportunities were directly related to the strong growth of leisure and holiday-making which resulted from the rise in real incomes, shorter working hours, holidays with pay, and the development of new kinds of entertainment, both indoor and outdoor, commercial and non-commercial. Attention here is focused on these, though at the same time existing forms of catering in cafés and teashops, pubs and fish-and-chip shops continued, their fortunes fluctuating with changes in the state of the economy. The large catering chains with reserves of capital survived better than small, independent concerns, though the teashop trade generally was adversely affected by the shorter working day, the development of in-house office tea-breaks, and competition from catering by department stores, often now on a quick-service cafeteria basis. Express Dairies did not expand beyond their pre-war chain of 50 teashops and four superior 'Tavistock' restaurants;[48] the ABC teashops amalgamated with Buzzard's in 1918, but the Lyons empire, by far the largest of the chains, continued to grow strongly until customer numbers and spending fell during the worst years of the depression, 1929–1933. Between 1918 and 1939 Lyons opened 132 new teashops, more in the 1920s than in the 1930s, but between 1934 and 1938 23 shops were closed and only 19 new ones opened: teashop losses over the period totalled £374,000. Lyons survived because of their reputation for good value, quality and service, and through effective advertising which included the new image of the waitress, the 'Nippy', launched in 1925 with a modern, stylish uniform to replace the long-skirted Edwardian 'Gladys'. 'Nippy' became an icon of the period, celebrated in a 1930 musical of that name which starred a leading actress, Binnie Hale.[49]

In 1929 Lyons served a record 17½ million customers in their three Corner Houses. An occasional celebratory meal in one of these magnificent buildings represented the height of eating out for people of modest means: in a variety of restaurants, brasseries and grill-rooms within each, with different prices and cuisines, customers could choose between English, French and other Continental menus with what were then exotic dishes like kebabs and moussakas. In 1929 the most expensive item on the tariff was lobster mayonnaise at 2/6d., but hors d'oeuvres ranged from 4d. to 9d., soups were 5d., whitebait 9d., roast beef 11d., ices from 3d. upwards and Meringue Chantilly 5d. In their 'Popular Café' a four-course meal cost 2/6d., but 1/6d. bought an unlimited 'tea' of items on toast, sandwiches, cakes, French pastries and ices. An interesting comment on the times was that Lyons' London shops now sold picnic boxes from 1/0d. upwards, delivered to the customer's door at three times daily and once on Sundays, an early example of the home-delivery meal for a day's outing or a summer evening's picnic in the suburban garden.

Developments which associated food with indoor amusements included the cinema restaurants, previously described, and the dance-hall buffets which offered light refreshments in the afternoon and evening. Immediately popular with the younger generation, who could learn the new quicksteps and foxtrots from schools of dance or, later, from Victor Sylvester's wireless lessons, an estimated 11,000 dance halls were open by 1925.[50] In larger towns these were glamorous places run by the Mecca, Locarno and Palais chains, but there were also thousands of smaller venues in the suburbs and Saturday night 'hops' at village halls. Most provided only snacks, tea, coffee and soft drinks and were not licensed for the sale of alcohol, partly for reasons of public order but also because most women dancers objected to strong fumes from close encounters with their partners.

There was no such problem in the new Milk Bars which flourished briefly in the 1930s. Milk for consumption on the premises had been sold in 'dairies' like the Express and in teashops, and the Black and White Milk Bars in London sold it as well as soups in 25 varieties – a large bowl with 'oyster' crackers for 4d. But the specialist Milk Bars concentrated on 'shakes' with fruit essences, frothy drinks sometimes with an ice-cream topping; the 'bars' were designed in modern, hygienic style with much use of chromium-plate and glass, and customers, mainly young, perched on high stools at the counter. Their success owed much to their trendy novelty, but also to the interest in physical fitness and the advice of nutritionists like John Boyd Orr and Corry Mann that milk was a primary ingredient for good health. The Milk Marketing Board, established in 1933, ran an advertisement campaign to 'Drink More Milk', and the following year introduced the Milk in Schools scheme by which elementary schoolchildren could buy one-third of a pint daily for ½d., half the normal price; by 1936 82 per cent of these schools were operating the scheme, and 2½ million children were learning to enjoy what had been an unfamiliar drink in poorer households.[51] Milk Bars increased strongly in the later 1930s, from around 530 in 1936 to 1,475 in 1938; one, the Meadow Milk Bar in Upper Regent Street, was managed by an enterprising Charles Forte. Together with cinemas, dance halls, sporting and outdoor activities, they represented the emergence of an essentially new youth culture, dependent on the higher earnings and greater leisure of juvenile workers, both male and female, in prospering sectors of the economy such as light industries, retailing and clerical occupations.

Much eating out was also connected with the growth of holiday-making in this period. It is estimated that in 1937 15 million people took at least a week away from home, the important change being the rapid growth of holidays with pay. Although paid holidays were not statutory until after the Second World War, employers in many industries had gradually been persuaded to grant them under collective agreements, while workers in public service occupations already normally had two weeks' paid holidays a year. By 1939 an estimated 11 million people earning less than £250 a year, around two-thirds of the workforce, were enjoying holidays with pay,[52] though in lower income groups with less than £4 a week only one in three were able to take a week away from home.

The cheapest kind of holiday for the reasonably active was hiking or cycling with a rucksack or saddle-bag for provisions and a tent. Rambling became very popular in the 1930s, associated with a discovery of the countryside by townspeople and influenced by the 'Keep Fit' movement of the period. Many young people had previous experience of camping with the Boy Scouts, Girl Guides and other youth associations, knew how to pitch a tent and do simple cooking. The Camping Club of Great Britain, founded in 1901, estimated that half a million members took such holidays in 1938, using their list of recommended sites which charged 8d. a night or 3/0d. a week, prices which even some of the unemployed could afford. Walking merely for pleasure had not been a traditional English amusement: the term 'hiking' was apparently imported from the United States in 1927, but it was particularly well established in Central Europe and especially in Germany, where 'wanderlust' among the forests and mountains was characteristic of young people and students, a romantic, idealistic movement, partly a reaction against authority and militarism. Before 1914 there was already a chain of hostels for walkers in Germany, greatly expanded after 1918 with the support of trade unions, churches, employers and local authorities, providing a network of over 2,000 by 1928. The movement became a target for Nazi takeover after 1933, inculcating quite different values of nationalism and militarism.[53]

As yet, there was no comparable development in England, though there were several non-commercial organisations such as the Co-operative Holidays Association, the Holiday Fellowship and the Workers' Travel Association. The important development for hikers and cyclists was the formation of the Youth Hostel Association in 1930, which provided simple dormitory accommodation for 1/- a night, a cheap breakfast and evening meal and a packed lunch for those who wished: hostellers were required to do some domestic tasks (cleaning, peeling potatoes, etc.) before leaving each morning. The YHA was a rapid success with 80,000 members by 1939 and 275 hostels, mainly in areas of natural beauty or historical interest. The Association had government approval and some financial support through the National Fitness Council at a time of renewed anxiety about the state of national health, though hikers also faced some complaints from farmers about fires, litter and open gates and from moralists about provocative shorts and the sexual opportunities offered by tents. A major issue about access to the countryside for walkers arose in 1932 when a mass 'trespass' was organised to open Kinder Scout in the Derbyshire hills: the arrest of 40 of the demonstrators led to the formation of the Ramblers Association in 1935 and the establishment of the first National Forest Park in 1939.

A superior kind of camping – touring with a caravan – also became popular with the spread of car ownership, one estimate suggesting as many as 150,000 caravans in the mid-1930s,[54] besides those on permanent sites. In *Caravan and Camp Cooking Recipes* J. Harris Stone extolled the culinary delights of the open air:

> *I like my milk without water, my cream with no boracic acid in it, my meat with no anti-putrefying powder peppered over it – and I can get these articles pure in most out-of-the-way districts of England, but hardly ever in towns.*[55]

He suggested that good meals could be made from nature – omelettes from the eggs of wild birds such as starlings and even sparrows, mushrooms gathered from fields near the roadside, and salads from local herbs. These could be supplemented with dry provisions to make curry and Rice à la Mexicaine, and with canned foods for Corned Beef Hash or Salmon Puffs. For caravan cooking, as well as Primus stoves, there were solid fuel ovens such as the Hostess and the Valor.

The most popular holiday, of course, was still a week or fortnight at the seaside with all the amusements that these provided. In 1938 it was estimated that a week at the coast for a husband, wife and two children in a boarding-house cost around £10, more than twice the average weekly wage even when this included holidays with pay. Blackpool in the 1930s had 4,000 boarding-houses, Brighton 2,100 plus 205 'hotels'; resorts also had hundreds of cheaper lodging-houses for holiday-makers who bought their own food to be cooked by the landlady for a small charge, but for the better-off the trend was now towards 'full board' at around 7/6d. a day for adults – part of the pleasure of a holiday was release from shopping and cooking and the expected enjoyment of another's cuisine. But in the 1930s an innovative alternative to the boarding-house appeared with the 'luxury' holiday camps of Butlin, Pontin, Warner and other entertainment entrepreneurs. They grew out of the early twentieth century open-air movements – camping and cycling holidays, summer camps organised by schools and youth associations. Probably the first holiday camp in anything like the modern form was established in 1894 on the Isle of Man by Cunningham, well situated for Liverpool and the Lancashire towns. Several hundred young men slept in tents, but had meals provided in a huge dining-hall, and enjoyed an organised programme of sports and entertainments: by the early 1930s almost all were accommodated in bungalows or dormitories, and 'camping' had become merely a name. By then, 'family camps' had also appeared, like that on Hayling Island founded by Harry Warner in 1931,[56] but the breakthrough into the mass market was principally due to Billy Butlin. Born in South Africa in 1899, he had emigrated to Canada with his mother, served in the Canadian Army during the war, and, subsequently unemployed, was rejected by Toronto Town Council as a lavatory attendant on grounds of lack of education. He arrived in England on a cattle-boat with £5, set up a hoop-la stall at a fair in Axminster and managed to get the sole concession to run the new 'Dodg'em' cars at fairgrounds. Greatly successful, he then established a large amusement park at the small seaside resort of Skegness in Lincolnshire. As a boy, he had enjoyed holiday camps on the Canadian lakes, and believed that permanent, hutted camps with entertainments would be popular here.[57] When he opened his first at Skegness at Easter 1936, initially for 1,000 guests, he chose precisely the right moment: the economy was picking up from the depression, holidays with pay were spreading rapidly, and he could confidently advertise 'Holidays with Pay, Holidays with Play. A Week's Holiday for a Week's Pay': 'all-in' charges were £1/15/0d.–£3 a week according to season, with reductions for children. He hit a segment of the market between the expensive hotel and the cheap boarding-house which provided nothing more than food and a bed, of which he said:

> We had to leave the premises at breakfast and were not encouraged to return until lunch-time. After lunch we were again made not welcome until dinner in the evening ... When it rained, life became a misery ... I felt even sorrier for the families with young children as they trudged around, wet and bedraggled.[58]

At Skegness, opened by the flying heroine Amy Johnson, there was a full daily programme of events and entertainments, indoor and outdoor – the beach, a heated swimming-pool, playing-fields for sports, a concert hall with a fine orchestra, dancing and variety shows with leading stars (Gracie Fields was an early one), a gymnasium, medical centre, chapel, bars and a huge dining-hall serving three cooked meals a day – all included in the price and organised by an army of 'Redcoats' to make sure that everyone enjoyed themselves. Butlin claimed that he had created 'An Eden-on-Sea ... Almost an Earthly Paradise'. By 1938 accommodation had been increased to 5,000, and a second 'camp' opened at Clacton until the outbreak of war temporarily halted further progress. Many smaller holiday camps had emerged by then, making a total of around 200 by 1939, both commercial and non-commercial: several trade unions and political parties had camps (including the British Union of Fascists), and there were special interest camps for music, art, drama and physical fitness, for the more serious minded, but Butlins led the mass market with their cleverly designed programmes of popular culture. A visiting observer reported on the midday meal:

> Lunch was an impressive demonstration of efficiency. I ate at the Kent House second sitting [at Clacton] in a huge, well-lit restaurant with separate tables. The service was speedy and the food was good – soup, meat pie and vegetables, steamed pudding – it was a mass-produced meal, but substantial and well enough prepared. Tea to drink afterwards, and I was told that tea is served at every meal. There were no 'Hi-de-Hi's' or 'Ho-de-Ho's.'[59]

Here was the revolutionary – to some, awesome – concept of a totally packaged holiday, food and fun, amusement outdoor or indoor, rain or shine, a brave new world of leisure for the masses.

Notes and references

1 L. Margaret Barnett, *British Food Policy during the First World War*, George Allen & Unwin, 1985, p. 212.

2 John Burnett, *A History of the Cost of Living*, Aldershot, Hampshire, Gregg Revivals, 1993, Table, p. 307, citing Guy Routh, *Occupation and Pay in Great Britain, 1906–1960*, 1965.

3 Noreen Branson, *Britain in the Nineteen Twenties*, Weidenfeld & Nicolson, 1975, pp. 92–3.

4 Mrs C. S. Peel, *A Hundred Wonderful Years: Social and Domestic Life of a Century, 1820–1920*, John Lane, The Bodley Head (1926), Cheap Edition, 1929, pp. 18-19.

5 Sir William Crawford and H. Broadley, *The People's Food*, William Heinemann, 1938, pp. 56–7.

6 Sir John Boyd Orr and David Lubbock, *Feeding the People in Wartime*, London, Macmillan, 1940, p. 61.

7 André L. Simon, *The Art of Good Living*, Constable and Co., 1929, p. 4.

8 André L. Simon, 'From Esau to Escoffier, or The History of Gastronomy', in Louis Golding and André Simon (eds), *We Shall Eat and Drink Again. A Wine and Food Anthology*, Hutchinson, n.d., *c*.1948, p. 145.

9 'Bon Viveur', *Where to Dine in London*, Geoffrey Bles, 1937, pp. 17–24. (This is not the 'Bon Viveur' adopted later by the Cradocks.)

10 Stephen Mennell, *All Manners of Food. Eating and Taste in England and France from the Middle Ages to the Present*, Oxford, Basil Blackwell, 1985, pp. 189–92.

11 Thomas Burke, *London In My Time*, Rich and Cowan, 1934, p. 150 passim.

12 Robert Graves and Alan Hodge, *The Long Weekend. A Social History of Great Britain, 1918–1939*, Faber and Faber, 1940, pp. 119, 225.

13 Quoted Anthony Masters, *Rosa Lewis. An Exceptional Edwardian*, Weidenfeld & Nicolson, 1977, pp. 103, 152.

14 Elizabeth Montizambert, *London Discoveries. Shops and Restaurants*, Women Publishers Ltd, 1924.

15 ibid., pp. 93–100.

16 'Diner-Out', *London Restaurants*, Geoffrey Bles, n.d., *c*.1924, p. 5.

17 ibid., p. 37 passim.

18 'Bon Viveur', *Where to Dine in London*, Geoffrey Bles, 1937.

19 ibid., pp. 96–7.

20 Alison Leach (ed.), *The Savoy Food and Drink Book*, Pyramid Books, 1988, p. 22.

21 Compton Mackenzie, *The Savoy of London*, George G. Harrap, 1953, p. 91.

22 Stanley Jackson, *The Savoy: The Romance of a Great Hotel*, Frederick Muller, 1964, pp. 66–8.

23 Mario Gallati, *Mario of the Caprice. The Autobiography of a Restaurateur*, Hutchinson, 1960, pp. 57ff.

24 'Diner-Out', op. cit., pp. 73–5.

25 Madame Prunier, *La Maison. The History of Prunier's*, Longmans, Green and Co., 1957, p. 212.

26 ibid., p. 228.

27 E. M. Forster, 'Porridge or Prunes, Sir?', in Louis Golding and André L. Simon (eds), *We Shall Eat and Drink Again. A Wine and Food Anthology*, Hutchinson, n.d., *c.*1948, pp. 56–7.

28 B. A. Young, 'Lamentable Luncheon', in Golding and Simon (eds), op. cit. pp. 103–4. A 'spoof', probably based more or less on experience.

29 Victor MacClure, *Good Appetite My Companion. A Gourmand At Large*, Odhams Press, 1955, p. 220.

30 André Simon, *Food*, Burke Publishing Co., 1949, p. 71.

31 Graves and Hodge, op. cit., pp. 120–2.

32 'Bon Viveur', op. cit., pp. 115–9.

33 John Stevenson, *British Society, 1914–1945*, Allen Lane, 1984, pp. 395–7.

34 *The Caterer and Hotel-Keeper*, 20 May, 1929, p. 635.

35 Stephen Price, 'Eating Out in London. A Social History, 1900–1950', Brunel University B.Sc. Dissertation, 1986, pp. 46–52, which I gratefully acknowledge for details of cinema restaurants.

36 Stevenson, op. cit., pp. 110, 130.

37 Branson, op. cit., p. 223.

38 Ivan Day (ed.), *Eat, Drink and Be Merry. The British at Table, 1600–2000*, Philip Wilson Publishers, 2000, p. 145.

39 Burke, *London In My Time*, op. cit., p. 194.

40 Quoted Basil Oliver, *The Renaissance of the English Public House*, Faber and Faber, 1947, p. 23.

41 Thomas Burke, *The English Inn*, Longmans, Green and Co., 1931, pp. 172–3.

42 Simon, *Food*, op. cit., pp. 80ff.

43 H. B. and G. Hoskins, 'A Week's Tour', in Golding and Simon, *We Shall Eat and Drink Again*, op. cit., p. 203. (The tour was in 1937.)

44 Burke, *The English Inn*, op. cit., p. 69.

45 John Fothergill, *An Innkeeper's Diary* (1st edn, 1931), Faber & Faber, 1987, p. 186. Part of Fothergill's celebrity status came from his book, which was an instant success and often reprinted.

46 Fothergill moved briefly to the Royalty at Ascot, then from 1934 to 1952 to the Three Swans at Market Harborough: it provided him with a living, but he was unable to recreate the style or clientele of the Spreadeagle.

47 Gabor Denes, *The Story of the Imperial. The Life and Times of Torquay's Great Hotel*, Newton Abbot, David & Charles, 1982, pp. 55–6.

48 Bryan Morgan, *Express Journey, 1864–1964. A Centenary History of the Express Dairy Company Ltd.*, Newman Neame, 1964, p. 136.

49 Peter Bird, *The First Food Empire. A History of J. Lyons and Co.*, Chichester, Phillimore, 2000, pp. 108ff. and Appendix 4, pp. 351–2.

50 Stephen G. Jones, *Workers at Play. A Social and Economic History of Leisure, 1918–1939*, Routledge & Kegan Paul, 1986, p. 44.

51 John Burnett, *Liquid Pleasures. A Social History of Drinks in Modern Britain*, Routledge, 1999, pp. 43–4.

52 J.A.R. Pimlott, *The Englishman's Holiday. A Social History*, Faber and Faber, 1947, pp. 212–21, 232.

53 Oliver Coburn, *Youth Hostel Story. The First Twenty Years*, The National Council of Social Service, 1950, pp. 6–14.

54 John K. Walton, *The British Seaside. Holidays and Resorts in the Twentieth Century*, Manchester, Manchester University Press, 2000, p. 67.

55 J. Harris Stone, *Caravan and Camp Cooking Recipes*, The Caravan Club of Great Britain and Ireland, n.d., *c.*1925, p. 4.

56 Colin Ward and Dennis Hardy, *Goodnight Campers. The History of the British Holiday Camp*, Mansell Publishing, 1986, pp. 18–22.

57 Arthur White, *Palaces of the People. A Social History of Commercial Hospitality*, Rapp and Whiting, 1968, pp. 169–70.

58 Butlin, quoted Ward and Hardy, op. cit., p. 60.

59 Pimlott, op. cit., Appendix III, 'Notes of a visit to Butlin's Holiday Camp at Clacton-on-Sea, August 1946', pp. 280–1. This was still under post-war food restrictions, but was probably not very different from 1939.

CHAPTER 8

The worst of times? The Second World War, 1939–1945

The nation rationed

One of the strange ironies of the Second World War, a conflict total in its global scope and human involvement, is that more people ate out than ever before and, probably, never again until the most recent years. In May 1941, an estimated 79 million meals a week were eaten by civilians outside their homes, rising to 170 million by December 1944,[1] equivalent to an average of around four meals a week for every man, woman and child. This was not mainly luxury eating for pleasure – though this did not wholly disappear – but public eating in a large variety of communal establishments which the government either encouraged or provided as a means of sustaining dietary standards and public morale at a critical period of food scarcity. Due partly to these programmes and, more generally, to the rationing schemes which this time were quickly introduced, a second surprising consequence of the war was that despite the shortages of many accustomed foods, the nation as a whole was never better fed and, in particular, the standards of the poorer part of the population were substantially improved. By contrast with the privations of the poor and unemployed during the depression, the war years represent a turning point in material standards as well as in expectations of what a new world could and should bring.

In some respects at least Britain was better prepared for war in 1939 than it had been in 1914. Though heavily dependent on imported foods to the extent of 60 per cent of normal needs, Britain's agriculture had been reviving in the later 1930s under government encouragement and was now capable of a large expansion. Food imports which had averaged 22 million tons a year in 1934–8 were reduced to 10½ million tons by 1942–4,[2] saving shipping space for the materials of war. A Food (Defence Plans) Department had been established in 1936, which became the nucleus of the Ministry of Food on the outbreak in September 1939: rationing schemes had been devised, ration books printed, and an elaborate organisation of 1,200 local food offices set up. The government had evidently learned lessons from the last war, when it had long resisted taking what it had wrongly assumed to be the unpopular step of rationing. This time it was not only expected but even desired. Before it began officially, a grocer in the East End of London complained that the war was bringing 'all the rich people from the West End to take the poor people's food': in his temporary absence, his assistant was allowing a couple in a chauffeur-driven car to carry off 112 lb of sugar, which he made them return for an allowance of 3 lb each.[3] Rationing of sugar, butter, bacon and ham began on 8 January 1940, followed by meat (by price, not weight) in March, tea in July, then cheese, margarine, cooking fats, preserves and sweets. The customers' coupons guaranteed that they could buy these items at controlled prices, the amounts varying with the state of supplies: later, customers also had 'Points' coupons which could be spent on mainly imported foods such as canned meat (including the new American 'Spam' and 'Mor' pork meats), breakfast cereals, rice, dried fruits, peas and beans, which could not be guaranteed as always available but gave the purchaser a choice of what was in stock. The essence of the British system was that it was not total rationing as in Germany: bread, potatoes and other vegetables were unrationed, so that people could always fill up on these if hungry, nor were fish, chickens and other poultry, rabbits and game, though these were often scarce, and caused criticism of those who could afford to pay high prices. But other important features of the rationing system which benefited all classes were the special distribution schemes which provided additional proteins, vitamins and minerals to pregnant and nursing mothers and to children. Children under one year were entitled to two pints of milk a day, those under five and their mothers to one pint at a subsidised price or free in cases of need: they also had access to orange and rose-hip juices, cod-liver oil and vitamin supplements as part of a coherent welfare policy designed by nutritionists headed by the Chief Scientific Advisor, Professor J. C. Drummond. Less popular, though also important, was the margarine fortified with vitamins A and D, which often had to replace butter, and the raising of the extraction rate of flour from 70 per cent to 85 per cent, which saved carrying space and added iron and B vitamins but produced a heavier, grey-brown National Wheatmeal loaf which some people found unpalatable.[4]

Most people accepted rationing without too many grumbles, believing it to be generally fair and, as they were constantly told by Ministry posters and wireless broadcasts, an important contribution to the war effort in which housewives could play an essential part. Men missed their beef and their bacon and eggs, restricted to one a week, women craved for sugar, cream and icing for cakes, children for ice cream and sweets. Dissatisfaction mounted as the war dragged on, and weekly rations were at their lowest in January 1943, after three years of privation – meat 1/2d. (equivalent to about 1 lb including bone), bacon and ham 4 oz, sugar 8 oz, cheese 3 oz, fats 8 oz (2 oz butter, 2 oz cooking fats, the rest margarine), sweets and chocolate 3 oz. Housewives were encouraged – often driven – to economise on these, to increase their use of vegetables, especially the home-grown products of the 'Dig For Victory' campaign, and to adopt recipes which used as little of rationed foods as possible, like the famous 'Woolton Pie' invented by Latry, *chef de cuisines* at the Savoy (potatoes, leeks, carrots and parsnips). Scores of books and pamphlets of advice on recipes and substitutes were published, perhaps more useful to middle-class women deserted by their domestic servants and now obliged to learn cookery skills. The author, Sheila Kaye-Smith, thought that to give a dinner party in wartime had to be a 'swindle' – rabbit instead of chicken, evaporated milk in place of cream, etc.;[5] she had not cooked before, but now wished to have 'some personal experience' of it after the war, even if good cooks again became available. André Simon's *Wine and Food Quarterly*, which managed to continue publication throughout, suggested Carottes de Gaulle (a patriotic variant of *à la Vichy*) as an entrée, and roast potatoes as a main dish 'which are so delicious and satisfying that one hardly misses the beef or lamb of better days',[6] while in *They Can't Ration These* a Free Frenchman, the Vicomte de Mauduit, offered recipes for hedgehog, squirrel-tail soup, roast sparrows and consommé of snails.

Availability of unrationed foods varied considerably, resorts and tourist centres generally much better supplied than industrial towns, especially those where heavy bombing disrupted normal distribution. On a visit to Blackpool in April 1942, Nella Last was astonished at the 'lavish luxury' of the shops:

> *There was everything as in peacetime, and the only restrictions I saw were of '7 Coupons' etc. or the 'points' value on tinned goods. Tinned fruit, first-grade salmon and every possible kind of lovely foods on 'points'. Whole roast chickens, potted herrings, cooked sausages ready for carrying away, plates of attractive salads, fried chicken – all coupon-free. And the cakes! Stacks of lovely cakes, pies, biscuits, tarts, gateaux ... fancy cakes of every kind.*

And in March 1943:

> *The shops in Windermere and Ambleside were a sight to see, with lavish displays of cakes and pastries ... windows with a large variety of toffee, sweets and chocolates.*[7]

There were complaints about the high prices sometimes charged for uncontrolled foods. At Leamington in January 1942, Mrs Milburn found:

> *No fish today, but most other things – at a price. A tiny bundle of two sticks of rhubarb was 9d., a tiny lettuce 9d. ... and a small cake which would ordinarily have been 9d. was 1/2d.*

And in July that year :

> *I bought my weekly groceries ... and they came to 2/7½d!!! Many things were not available, and so one just had the weekly ration of butter, lard, margarine, cheese, bacon and sugar – 2/7½d.*

Like others, she got occasional 'presents' of scarce things a packet of suet, three oranges 'surreptitiously placed quickly in my basket', and once a duck:

> *About sixpence a mouthful I reckoned. Not worth the bother and the money – a hen is much better – but if one will go black marketing – well!*[8]

In fact, prices were held in check much better than in the previous war, when rapid inflation had threatened social stability. Between 1939 and the end of 1944 official food prices rose only by 20 per cent compared with 130 per cent in the First World War, a remarkable success achieved by price controls and food subsidies which ultimately totalled £152 million a year. Spending power, however, was restricted by heavily increased taxation: income tax at 5/- in the £ in 1939 rose to 7/- in 1940 and 10/- after 1941, while surtax on incomes over £5,000 a year and an Excess Profits Tax which could reach 100 per cent, reduced the living standards of the wealthy. But now that labour was in short supply, the wages of manual workers rose by 64 per cent during the war, well ahead of the cost of food.[9]

A major difference between the two wars was, of course, the far greater extent of bombing and air-raid damage in the second, which had important effects on eating patterns both at home and in public places. Many of the communal feeding arrangements (to be discussed later) were intended to alleviate the effects of bombing as well as the disruption of family life due to the evacuation of children, the military conscription of men and the employment of married women in war work. Many commercial catering establishments suffered destruction or serious damage. By 1945 the Aerated Bread Company was only able to operate two-thirds of its teashops, while J. Lyons and Co. had 70 fewer working and only one London shop which remained unscathed: some of their staff nobly continued 'blitz feeding' from tents pitched on the pavement or from 'Temporary Teashops' in mobile canteens.[10] The Regent Palace Hotel was twice bombed, the Savoy – conveniently situated for German bombers on the Thames – three times, necessitating major structural reinforcement of the River Room and the provision of all-night shelters with curtained cubicles for late diners, while after damage to gas mains, the Ritz kitchens for several days cooked on upturned electric radiators.[11] Other casualties included the Langham and Cavendish hotels, Madame Tussaud's Restaurant and the Café de Paris, crowded with people dining and dancing to 'Snakehips' Johnson and his band: a direct hit killed 80 people, but one of the most macabre features was the looting of rings and jewellery from the dead and dying. Many other hotels in London, and elsewhere, totalling 300, were requisitioned by the government for offices, training establishments, hospitals and convalescent homes,

FIGURE 8.1 ◆ *London carries on. Despite the bombing, catering restrictions and staff shortages, most restaurants managed to stay open during the Second World War: they were greatly valued as aids to morale as well as supplements to the domestic rations.*

Source: Hulton Archive.

though around a third of these were later handed back. The confusion at the outbreak of war is illustrated by the Imperial Hotel, Torquay, which was taken over by the Air Ministry in 1939: long-staying and other guests were given seven days to leave and all staff, including the manager, were dismissed: next month, with a change of plan, the hotel was handed back, devoid of furniture and staff.[12] All the larger holiday camps, including those of Butlin, were acquired as ready-made accommodation for servicemen, and Butlin built others in Wales and Scotland on the advantageous terms that he could buy them back after the war at three-fifths of their original cost.[13]

It was considered important for morale to continue as much public entertainment as circumstances allowed. Some cinemas ran all-night shows for which patrons settled down with food and blankets: at the height of bombing theatres transferred their last performances to 5.30–8.00 pm, and the blackout tended to curtail late-night amusements generally. Yet many of the great London hotels managed to continue their dinner-dances with reduced menus and smaller bands (Carroll Gibbons at the Savoy now had only five players) and even to provide midnight cabarets. At the top levels of society public life seemed least changed. The diaries of Sir Henry ('Chips') Channon record that in late September 1939, lunch at the Ritz had become 'fantastically fashionable': 'Ritzes always thrive in wartime, as we are all cookless. Also in wartime the herd instinct rises'. A year later, despite the bombing, dining at the Dorchester he found 'half London [society] there', and in the lobby 'people settled down for the night with rugs'. On 5 November 1940, also at the Dorchester: 'London lives well. I've never seen more lavishness, more money spent or more food consumed than tonight; and the dance floor was packed. There must have been a thousand people.'[14]

Hotels and restaurants struggled with shortages of food and staff, especially those which had employed large numbers of Italian, German and Austrian chefs and waiters, who were now interned as enemy aliens; waitresses replaced men in top restaurants, and in 1941 Lyons began to adopt a self-service, cafeteria system: by 1945 all their teashops had been converted and the 'Nippy' had disappeared for ever.[15] But boredom was one of the great enemies of the war effort, and people took whatever breaks from the monotony they could. Nella Last fondly remembered a trip from her home in bombed Barrow-in-Furness for a picnic at Coniston

Lake in May 1942 – 'I packed such a nice tea – a tin of fruit, shortbread, sponge cake and wholemeal bread and butter.'[16] Holidays, in moderation, were not discouraged, and the government even promoted 'Holidays at Home' for which local authorities organised concerts, sports, open-air dancing and other activities. For most people, however, a holiday still meant a few days away from home. Hiking and camping were still popular for a cheap holiday, and after an initial fall the Youth Hostel Association doubled its membership to 100,000 by 1943.[17] Seaside resorts fared variously, since from 1940 the east and south coasts from the Wash to Bexhill were closed to holiday-makers, later extended to Dorset: only Brighton remained open. 'Safe' resorts in the south-west and north-west benefited, and Blackpool was described as enjoying 'spectacular prosperity'. This was partly due to the fact that around a million troops were billeted in the town's many boarding-houses during the war years, as well as many evacuees and civil servants from London.[18]

The five-shilling meal

Commercial catering posed a problem for the Ministry of Food. On one hand, the government was keen that people should be able to supplement their limited rations by eating out, and recognised that there were useful economies of scale by feeding large numbers: 'To cater for a million is to save the nation's wealth, and to "do more with the less".'[19] On the other hand, it was unacceptable to the new spirit of egalitarianism if the better-off were able to avoid the privations of the majority by luxury eating in public places. Inequality of sacrifice seemed to be demonstrated during the Blitz when the East End of London suffered disproportionately more than the wealthier West End, and in September 1940 an angry demonstration of East End women forced their way into the Savoy Restaurant demanding food and the use of the hotel's deep shelters.[20] Shortly afterwards, the bombing of Buckingham Palace did much to restore social unity, though the opinion persisted, and with some justice, that the rich could buy their way out of hardship. As a Bradford woman complained:

> People who eat at home . . . have only the food for which they have coupons. People who feed in restaurants and canteens have their rationed food at home and what they eat in restaurants and canteens is extra. This is absolutely unfair.

And on 10 May 1945, two days after VE Day, when a schoolmistress went to York for a celebratory lunch at 'Terry's' restaurant (cold pork pie or spiced ham, salad, and what passed as ice cream – 'interesting but dear') she was moved to comment: 'I say there are many people whom this war hasn't even touched.'[21]

Initially, the Ministry devised plans for rationing catering establishments by requiring customers to surrender coupons from their domestic ration books – for example, a quarter of their weekly meat ration for a meal containing meat. This was rejected after serious consideration, partly because of the administrative complexities involved, partly because if it were to apply to all caterers it would run contrary to the government's encouragement of factory and school canteens and other communal feeding arrangements. Moreover, it was discovered that commercial restaurants were taking only around 3 per cent of total rationed foods anyway.[22] The alternative, which was adopted, was to require people staying in hotels or boarding-houses for five or more nights to surrender their ration books, but otherwise caterers would be allocated supplies on the basis of the number of meals served, of which they would have to make regular returns. There would be no 'meatless days' as in the First World War, but, as the war progressed, an ever-tightening framework of controls and regulations which Harry Salmon, Chairman of J. Lyons, estimated to reach 6,000. Table 8.1 includes only a few of the more important.

The most irksome results of these regulations were the very limited quantities of meat and fish and the disappearance of butter and cream for cooking. The 5/- limit on price little affected the cheaper eating-places like those of Soho, but hit hard the menus of luxury hotels and restaurants which before the war had often charged at least twice as much as this. They complained strongly that because of the high overheads needed to maintain their standards of comfort and service 5/- would not cover the costs of an acceptable meal, and that it was nationally important that prestigious catering should be available for statesmen, politicians and military leaders, many of them from overseas. The Ministry relented by allowing house charges on a graded scale of from 1/- to 6/-, and a dancing or entertainment charge of 2/6d.; additionally, it permitted a supplement to the menu of up to 3/6d. for caviare or oysters, where these were available. This meant that at the Savoy, for example, a dinner-dance could cost up to 17/- without wine, provided diners and waiters could negotiate the complexities of the regu-

TABLE 8.1 ◆ *Regulations affecting commercial catering, 1940–1942*

July 1940	Meat allocation restricted to 60% of January 1940.
July 1940	Caterers encouraged to voluntarily restrict meals to one main course.
July 1940	Prohibition of use of sugar in cakes and biscuits: no sugar icing permitted.
Sept. 1940	Not more than $\frac{1}{12}$th oz of butter to be served with a meal.
Oct. 1940	Manufacture of cream prohibited.
Dec. 1940/Jan. 1941	Meat allocation reduced to $\frac{1}{3}$rd that of Jan. 1940, now including pork and offal.
March 1941	Food (Restriction on Meals in Establishments) Order. Meals restricted to one main dish of meat, fish, poultry, game, eggs or cheese: these to carry two stars**. Customers might also have one 'subsidiary' dish (one star*) containing less than $\frac{1}{3}$rd in weight of fish, eggs or cheese, or might choose two 'subsidiary' dishes. Soup was not counted as a dish.
March 1941	Meat allocation further reduced to 25% of Jan. 1940.
April 1941	Use of milk in bread, biscuits, bakery goods, ice cream, chocolate and confectionery prohibited.
Dec. 1941	Introduction of 'Points' rationing.
March 1942	Caterers allowed 4 'Points' for every 10 main dishes served and 2 for every 10 'subsidiary' dishes (these could be used for tinned meats such as 'Spam', tinned fish, tinned and dried fruit, breakfast cereals, rice, tapioca, etc.).
May 1942	White flour and white bread prohibited: loaves to be National Wheatmeal of 85% extraction rate.
June 1942	Meals in Establishments Order. Revoked the Order of March 1941. Maximum of 3 courses allowed – 1 'main' dish containing 25% or more of meat, offal, fish, game, poultry or eggs, plus 1 'subsidiary' dish containing less than 25% of meat, fish or eggs. Customers might choose 2 'subsidiaries' instead of 1 'main' and 1 'subsidiary', and all might add a third dish provided it was neither 'main' nor 'subsidiary' (e.g. soup, hors d'oeuvres). The maximum charge for food was to be 5/-, not including drinks or house and entertainment charges.
Sept. 1942	Manufacture of ice cream prohibited.
Dec. 1942	Allocation of fish restricted to 2 lb for every 100 meals served.

lations – some diners learned how to bend them – for example, though Crêpes Suzette were not permitted, one could order a pancake together with a brandy and a liqueur and concoct one's own at table.[23] Top-class restaurants often managed to maintain acceptable standards as they had better stocks of non-perishable goods and better access to things like chickens, game and venison. The claim that ordinary citizens who had never before dined at an exclusive restaurant could now do so for 5/- was, therefore, something of a myth. As the menu from the Savoy in 1944 shows (reproduced below), the minimum charge without entertainment was 11/-.

SAVOY RESTAURANT LUNDI 24 AVRIL 1944
THE MEALS IN ESTABLISHMENTS ORDER, 1942.
By the terms of this Order, it is not permissible (1) to serve or consume more than three courses at a meal; (2) to serve or consume more than one dish marked ★ and one marked ¶, or two dishes marked ¶ (but dishes unmarked may be ordered instead of those marked or in addition to them, provided that the limit of three courses is not exceeded): (3) to serve or consume food after midnight (4) to exceed the authorised charges shewn

AUTHORISED CHARGES: HOUSE CHARGE 6/-
MAXIMUM FOR FOOD 5/-   with Oysters – 8/6
DANCING – 2/6
VIN ROUGE PREMIER CHOIX – per Bottle 12/6

DINER DU JOUR AU CHOIX

LES HORS D'ŒUVRES
¶ Hors d'Œuvre Choisis   ★ Saumon Fumé

SPECIALITES

¶ Le Hors d'Œuvre chaud Savoy (Flan de Crustacés)
¶ La Fine Compote Algérienne au Fromage de la Région
¶ Le Risotto aux Fruits de Mer
¶ Le Caviar du Gourmet de la Riviéra

LES POTAGES

Consommé Froid   Minestrone Casalinga
Consommé aux Baguettes Dorées
La Petite Marmite Chez-Soi   Crème Monselet à l'Orge

LES ŒUFS

¶ L'Omelette Fourrée dorée Bordelaise

LES PLATS DU JOUR →

LE BUFFET FROID

★ Pressed Pork   ★ Galantine

LES LEGUMES

Mousseline Parmentier   Pommes Sautées   Pommes Nature ou Persillées
Choux-fleurs   Endives
Carottes au Beurre

LES ENTREMETS

Bavarois Framboise   Gâteau Délysia
Feuilleté aux Fruits   Coupe Royale

Fromage

LES PLATS DU JOUR

¶ La Rillette en Terrine au Vin Tourangeau

¶ Le Pâté comme dans le Centre du Continent

¶ Le Cocktail Succès de Montreal

¶ La Citronnette de Poisson comme Chez-Nous

★ Le Homard Rafraîchi Garni à la Russe
Cold Lobster garnished with Vegetable Salad.

★ La Couronne de Perles aux Fruits de l'Océan
Pilaw Rice garnished with Shell Fish

★ Le Suprême de Halibut Restaurant Drouant
Fillet of Halibut.   White Wine Sauce, Mushrooms and Mussels.

★ Le Médaillon de Bœuf Gourmande
Chopped Beef (as Tournedos) with White Wine Sauce and Mushrooms

★ Le Quartier de Chevreau rôti, Gratin Brillat-Savarin

Roast Kid.   Gratin of Jerusalem Artichokes.

★ La Bécasse des Marais rôtie de Côte d'Or
Roast Woodcock in Red Wine Sauce

★ La Côtelette de Gibier du Garde Champêtre
Minced Game (Cutlet shape) with White Wine Sauce and Mushrooms

★ Le Coq du Surrey Farci Derby
Chicken with Rice and Mushrooms

★ Le Suprême d'Oie sauté au Vin de Joigny
Escalope of Goose Saute with Mushrooms.   Red Wine Sauce

★ Le Ramier des Forêts du Châtelain
Wood Pigeon with Mixed Vegetables.   Chasseur Sauce

★ Le Game Pie du Devonshire
Hot Game Pie

★ Le Rable de Lièvre à la Crème et Champignons
Saddle of Hare.   White Wine Sauce with Mushrooms.

★ La Galantine de Poulet Charcutière au Vin des Iles
Chicken Galantine with Mixed Salad and Samos Wine Jelly.

★ La Mousse de Jambon au Vieux Madère
Mousse of Ham in Madeira Wine Jelly

★ Le Pie en Gelée.   Salade de Saison
Game Pie in Jelly with Season Salad.

At a somewhat more modest level, lunch at the Bristol Grill (English menu) cost 6/- and dinner (French menu) 7/6d. or 10/- with entertainment (menu reproduced below).

BRISTOL GRILL

BY ORDER OF THE MINISTRY OF FOOD NOT MORE THAN THREE COURSES MAY BE
SERVED AT A MEAL INCLUDING ONE DISH OF EITHER EGG OR FISH OR MEAT OR
POULTRY OR GAME.

SATURDAY, 30th JUNE, 1945

Luncheon	Dinner
SET LUNCH … … 5/-	MAXIMUM FOOD CHARGE 5/-
MAXIMUM FOOD CHARGE 5/-	ENTERTAINMENT CHARGE 2/6
HOUSE CHARGE… … 1/-	HOUSE CHARGE… … 2/6

Luncheon

Potage Minerva

Grilled Cod, Parsley Sauce
or
Savoury Omelette or Braised Venison
or
Roast Pork
or
Cold Meat and Salad
Spring Greens
New Potatoes

Fresh Cherries
or
Jellies

Dinner

Hors-d'Œuvre Variés
or
Consommé Double
or
Crème Sultane

Suprême d'Aiglefin Bercy
or
Langue de Bœuf Jardinière
or
Caneton d'Aylesbury Rôti
or
Viande Froide et Salade
Petits Pois Frais
Pommes Nouvelles

Mignardises
or
Blancmange Vanois

The greatest problem for chefs was the small amount of meat allowed, which worked out at around one pennyworth per meal. Much ingenuity went into inventing substitute or ersatz dishes using large amounts of vegetables, especially potatoes, and unfamiliar kinds of flesh and fowl such as kid, offal like hearts and tripe, pigeons and even rooks. At the House of Commons restaurant, 'Canapé Cheval' was offered in 1943 and (tongue in cheek?) 'Chicken Ancienne' in 1945.[24] Vegetarians naturally adapted well to wartime restrictions, and were allowed to exchange their meat coupons for additional dairy products – 83,000 people so registered. Vegetarian restaurants prospered, while the growth of interest in the movement is also evidenced by the foundation of the Vegan Society in 1944.[25]

Examples of dishes provided by leading chefs were collected by Irene Veal in 1944, a few of which are listed in Table 8.2.

Hotels which survived bombing, requisitioning and the closed coastlines were generally well filled. In September 1940, *The Times* carried an

TABLE 8.2 ◆ *Sample dishes offered by leading London chefs, 1944*

The Savoy	Onion Soup, Bread Soup, Herrings L'Indienne.
The Dorchester	Calf's Head, Loin of Hare, Haddock Monte Carlo.
Grosvenor House	Vegetable Cutlet, Rabbit Campagnarde ('with mushrooms if available'), Leeks on Toast, Bengal Potatoes (fried with chutney).
The Mayfair Hotel	Many dishes with dehydrated mutton, e.g. Moussaka, Cornish Pasties, Mutton Croquettes.
Royal Court Hotel	Flan Fribourgée (cheese and potato), Saumon Florentin (tinned salmon and spinach).
Madame Prunier's	Moules Chowder (mussels replacing American Clam Chowder), Sardine Otero (potato, 1 sardine in oil), Croquettes de Pommes Land Girl (mashed potato and dried egg powder).
Simpson's-in-the-Strand	Simpson's Creamed Spam Casserole (potatoes, tomatoes and Spam), Simpson's Spam Pancakes.
The Albert Restaurant	Mock Duck (mashed potato, onion, haricot beans, parsley) – 'Serve with brown gravy or other sauce which may be preferred.'
Selfridge's	Tripe Hotpot.
The House of Lords	Creamed Salmon (tinned salmon 'or, indeed, any small pieces of fish that you may have'), Risotto (rice and mixed vegetables).[26]

Source: Irene Veal, *Recipes of the 1940s*, John Gifford, 1944, pp. 90–151.

advertisement for 'Sanctuary Hotels' recommended by Ashley Courtenay which included the Grand Hotel, Torquay and the Queen's Hotel, Penzance, where 'a sense of security cannot be beaten', but by 1941 an editorial was complaining that 'hotels are filled with well-to-do refugees who too often have fled from nothing. They sit and read and knit and eat and drink, and get no nearer the war than the news they read in the news-papers.'[26] In provincial hotels the type of food offered was simple and consistent with the 1942 Order – at the Midland Hotel, Derby, hors d'oeu-vres, chicken, spinach and potatoes and 'an ice-cream sweet with a fancy name',[27] or at the Queen's Hotel, Birmingham, hors d'oeuvres ('mostly the same old potato, cabbage, carrot, parsnip and beetroot with a nice fat sardine'), soup, fish and a chocolate mould ('it soon palled as it needed more sugar').[28] Such places did not have the same pressure to maintain standards as the top London restaurants. At the Savoy Latry decided to retire in 1942, was succeeded for only a year by Marious Dutrey (who managed to obtain supplies of venison and smoked herrings from Scotland), then by Camille Payard until 1946. Latry, whose son had fought at Dunkirk and with the Maquis until captured and imprisoned in Belsen, had little sympathy for complaining meat-eaters – 'Tell them it's steak or ships', he ordered the waiters,[29] who now brought vegetables to table served on the plate to restrict portions and save staff time. The Ivy, with its reputation for the finest French cuisine, found the scarcities and the 5/- limit particularly difficult. 'How we did it at the Ivy still remains a minor miracle', wrote Gallati, but mainly, he confessed, by the profits on wines and other drinks. He devised a dozen ways of serving Spam with spicy sauces, but often stood at the door of his restaurant to warn customers that there was only this, tripe and onions and dried egg omelette on the menu: his 'mayonnaise', made from flour and water, vinegar, mustard and egg powder, 'made me shudder to serve it'.[30] At Prunier's famous fish restaurant three-quarters of the staff were French and were called up, including the *chef de cuisines* and the manager. In 1941 it still advertised a 'Blackout Dinner', including oysters, at 10/6d., but the 5/- maximum and the severe rationing of fish hit the restaurant hard. Prunier's were at first granted only a 6d. house charge, raised after strong protests to 2/6d. for lunch and 4/- for dinner: frozen cod was served as unidentified 'Poissons', while 'Pigeon Paté' was the product of rooks.[31] At the Cavendish Hotel, badly damaged by a landmine and incendiaries, Rosa Lewis took on a new lease of life at 72, repeating the generosity she had shown to the forces in the First World War, and still trying to procure girl assistants from Fortnum and Mason's for her 'boys'. Salmon and game birds came from her country clients, and there was 'nursery food' like scrambled eggs and bread-and-butter pudding, served with copious quantities of champagne and whisky.[32] Not all famous restaurants survived, quite apart from bombing. Kettner's was forced to close for several months for black market offences, and the Quo Vadis was shut for the duration when its Italian proprietor, Peppino Leoni, was interned in an Aliens Camp on the Isle of Man, and later was sent to cook in a working-class café in South Wales. While on the island he and other leading Italian chefs produced good dishes from the vegetables collected by the working parties, an occasional chicken and, once, a 20-stone pig which came their way. Quo Vadis was bomb damaged, and did not reopen until New Year's Eve 1946.[33]

Eating-places of a less exclusive kind remained well supported, among the most popular being Lyons' Corner House Brasseries, where a generous hors d'oeuvre, a tasty 'made' dish and a sweet cost only 1/9d.: a tall glass of iced coffee for 5d. added a touch of luxury.[34] In the early years of the war several London pubs continued in the old chop-house style, serving roast beef or mutton with two vegetables for 2/0d., pudding another 6d,[35] while sandwich bars like those of Fortnums and Forte's thrived ('thin slices of Spam and beetroot go wonderfully together, especially if Marmite is used instead of mustard').[36] Eating out in the provinces was something of a gamble. At Blackpool, previously noticed for the large quantities of food on sale, Nella Last and friends in April 1942 went to 'where we always go, Jenkinson's, which is about the highest class of place, and serves the best meal. We had clear soup, roast beef and baked potatoes, carrots and cabbage, and then apple tart and custard with coffee made with milk – all perfectly cooked and served – for 3/- per head.'[37] But at the Little Kitchen in Leamington Mrs Milburn was not so well pleased: 'M'yes, it was called meat in the pie, but... However, we were fed'. And in 1943 at her usual, preferred restaurant:

All tables were reserved, so I tried the cafeteria, my first experience of this kind of meal. Even wartime difficulties did not make me enjoy this method of serving oneself... A slop of meat (not too bad, but a bit

gristly), far too much potato and gravy and masses of cabbage. Next,
three prunes and a half, and not too bad custard ... Walked off to a
table, to find I had forgotten my knife, fork etc. The coffee was vile, so I
left it.[38]

She might have done better at a fish-and-chip shop, of which in 1939
22,370 were registered. The importance of fish and chips to the nation's
diet was better recognised in this war than in the first, and it was
accepted that cheap, tasty 'fast' food was a useful supplement to rations,
especially for people who had little opportunity for cooking. Although
potatoes were generally abundant, the fryers faced difficulties with fish
supplies and with cooking fats, not least because different parts of the
country had distinct preferences for different kinds – dripping, lard or
edible oils. The Ministry granted fryers privileged allocations which
were not less than 75 per cent of the pre-war level,[39] but even so, demand
often exceeded supply. Shops could not usually open every day and
closed early, while the display of a notice 'Frying Tonight' was the signal
for an early queue to form. The survival of the neighbourhood fish-and-
chip shop in working-class districts was an important boost to morale at
a time when so much else was changing, and as the *Northern Daily
Telegraph* reported in 1941 without too much exaggeration: 'Your fish
and chips will help to win the war.'[40]

Communal feeding

In 1943 the Wartime Social Survey investigated where a large sample of
working men and women had eaten on the previous day. While the
numbers eating breakfast or their evening meal away from home were
quite small (8 per cent in the latter case), a majority of people now ate
their main midday meal 'out' – 22 per cent in a canteen, 11 per cent in
a café and 2 per cent in a British Restaurant; 15 per cent brought food
from home and another 4 per cent supplemented this in a canteen – a
total of 54 per cent who ate away from home, and a major change since
pre-war times. Furthermore, a quarter of those surveyed also had mid-
morning and mid-afternoon tea-breaks with snacks, as it had been found
that productivity fell significantly after about two hours' work unless
revived.[41]

Even these statistics did not cover the full extent of eating outside the home, since many emergency feeding centres had been established during the Blitz in 1940, initiated mainly by the Women's Voluntary Service and similar bodies. These ran canteens, both permanent and mobile, bringing hot drinks and food to bombed-out civilians, evacuated mothers and children, the fire service, police and air-raid wardens and the tens of thousands who nightly took refuge in public shelters or the London Underground. All these depended on large numbers of women volunteers to organise, cook and serve simple meals, often in difficult or even dangerous conditions. Marguerite Patten worked in an all-night canteen in Bradford;[42] a woman employed at Shell Mex House spent every Sunday night from 10 pm till 8 am at a YMCA canteen at Waterloo Station, where she came to 'hate the sight of sausages, 36 across and 36 down, on huge trays in the oven';[43] while in Coventry after the blitz, WVS workers cooked stew in the open air in a main street. Unlike commercial caterers, feeding centres received privileged allocations of supplies. Nella Last worked in a WVS canteen in heavily bombed Barrow-in-Furness in 1941, initially for the men working on demolition sites: they were provided with soup, pies and sandwiches and in the evening sausages and mash, beans on toast, egg and chips, potato cakes and waffles, all at low charges (plate of tomato sandwiches, 2 large cakes and a large cup of tea, 8d.).

> It will be a grand place when we get going, for there is a nice room for reading and writing, a billiard table and dart board, and servicemen are encouraged to bring their wives. I will try and cook oddments at home, and think up fresh recipes to keep the menu list attractive.[44]

Some helpers were rather offended by the quantities of food available in these places. Mrs Trowbridge, a middle-class lady of Bradford who also helped in a WVS canteen for Air Raid Precaution (ARP) workers and police, was 'astounded and disgusted' at the food available, and 'for which they paid ridiculously low prices'.

> After a jolly good dinner at midday, there were cups of tea again at 3 p.m., and from about 4.45 to 6.45 p.m. we were harried to death cooking and serving egg and chips, sausage and chips, fish and chips and scones and biscuits or jam tarts. They turned up their noses at salad or

sandwiches – they must have a cooked tea... Our husbands, on the other hand, didn't see an egg for months at a time, nor a tomato... The [women] ARP workers spend their time playing cards, table-tennis, skylarking with the police and male staff, painting their faces and finger-nails – to say nothing of an afternoon at the 'Lido', bathing and sunbathing.[45]

Factory canteens were strongly encouraged by the government as aids to productivity, and had been installed in all the 'shadow' munitions plants in 1938: from 1940 they became compulsory in all factories employing more than 250, and received greater food allowances than commercial caterers. Unlike pre-war canteens, they now had to provide for shift-workers and night-workers, with breakfasts, midday meals, teas and suppers, as well as tea-trolleys and snacks at frequent intervals. By April 1942, 7,528 factory canteens were operating, by the end of the year, 11,635, while by 1945, 50 million meals were being served weekly.[46] Lord Woolton, the Minister of Food, described the expansion as 'One of the greatest social revolutions that has taken place in the industry of our country', for he rightly believed that good, cheap meals, as well as lunchtime concerts ('Workers' Playtime'), tea-breaks and music relayed to work benches were doing much to improve the quality of life in the factory. But although a woman visitor to a factory canteen expressed delight at getting a three-course meal, including the traditional meat and two vegetables, for 1/2d.,[47] canteens were not universally popular, the Wartime Social Survey finding that although cooked meals were available for 61 per cent of workers interviewed, only 22 per cent had eaten them on the previous day. Apart from nearness to home, main reasons for not using canteens included dislike of the food (32 per cent of men, 25 per cent of women), and preference for a packed meal from home (14 per cent of men, 8 per cent of women), but some respondents said that they had never eaten in public and were too shy to do so, preferring to eat their packed food in solitude beside their machines.[48] Unfamiliar dishes were an important reason for non-use of canteens. A former hotel chef who now managed a canteen was reported as saying that he 'despaired of Birmingham's taste in food... The workers only wanted fish and chips, cream cakes, bread and butter, and brown gravy over everything. They would not eat salads, and did not like savouries'.[49]

One experiment in communal feeding which was tried in 1941 but quietly abandoned was to provide coalminers underground with a full, hot meal in the middle of their shift in the hope of increasing output. Cooked meals were brought down in bulk Thermos containers and served to men on the spot during their 20-minute break, apparently ignoring the cramped conditions, the hot, dusty atmosphere and the short time for digestion. The report on the experiment concluded that 'The miner is a conservative individual, and innovations in his habits are hard to establish'.[50] The men much preferred their traditional 'snap' of sandwiches, pies and cold tea, and to enjoy a cooked meal later at the pit-head canteen or at home. One successful feeding experiment, however, was for agricultural workers, a key group in the campaign to grow more food. From 1942 the Ministry of Food in collaboration with the WVS organised a 'Rural Pie Scheme', providing meat and fruit pies and sandwiches in village halls and mobile canteens for workers in the fields. At its peak, 1¼ million snacks a week were supplied to 5,000 villages.[51]

In towns, an even more important innovation was the British Restaurant, the nearest thing to a nationalised catering service ever seen in England. The idea grew out of the need for emergency feeding during the Blitz when a Londoner's Meal Service was formed by volunteers to feed air-raid victims, but from 1940 Lord Woolton began to plan a nationwide scheme for up to 10,000 publicly run, non-profit-making eating-places, open to all – in effect, state cafés. By the Local Authorities (Community Kitchens and Sale of Food in Public Air Raid Shelters) Order of January 1941, local authorities were reimbursed by the Treasury for the capital cost of such restaurants, which otherwise were to be self-supporting, though the London County Council managed to negotiate a separate agreement by which any trading losses would also be met.[52] Their original description as 'Community Kitchens' or 'Communal Feeding Centres' was strongly opposed by Churchill in a minute to Lord Woolton:

> It is an odious expression, suggestive of Communism and the workhouse ... I suggest you call them 'British Restaurants'. Everybody associates the word 'restaurant' with a good meal.[53]

The name stuck, and judged by their popularity his expectation was justified. By May 1941, there were 800 in 176 towns: at their height in 1943 they totalled 2,160, serving 650,000 midday meals a day at under 1/0d., and also breakfasts and evening meals. They were located mainly in areas not already served by factory canteens; they were used not only by manual workers, but by professionals, women and students (there were five in Bournemouth, and the former exclusive Pitt Club in Cambridge became one), and many had a 'takeaway' service. Despite the institutional ambience of local halls, most people enjoyed the traditional dishes which reflected the 'home cooking' of the volunteers who worked under paid supervisors. A typical menu from the Byrom Restaurant, Liverpool, offered Meat or Fish and Two Vegetables 6d., Soup 1d., Pudding 3d., Tea, Coffee or Cocoa 1d.: 'Today's Menu' was Fish Pie or Beef and Dumpling, Currant Pudding or Milk Pudding. In the Wartime Social Survey investigation 60 per cent of those using a British Restaurant considered it 'Very Good', another 21 per cent thought it 'Good, considering the circumstances, price and locality' and only 15 per cent voted it 'Bad'.[54] The skills of the cooks evidently varied, but one should not take as representative the opinion of an upper-class epicure who was more accustomed to dining at the Ivy:

> An enormous all-beige meal, starting with beige soup thickened to the consistency of paste, followed by beige mince full of lumps and garnished with beige beans and a few beige potatoes, thin beige apple stew and a sort of skilly... Very satisfying and crushing, and calling up a vision of our future Planned World – all beige also.[55]

Apart from such opinions, the main criticism of British Restaurants came from the commercial catering trade towards the end of the war, which objected that the restaurants were departing from their original purpose of feeding hungry war workers and now, according to *The Caterer*, were being used for private parties, teas and even wedding receptions, with the unfair advantages of generous allocations of rationed foods, subsidised prices and some volunteer labour: 'British Restaurants are serving people who can afford to go to ordinary catering establishments... They are able to charge prices which threaten to drive private caterers out of business.'[56] But by then, British Restaurants had become firmly established in the fabric of British society, and the new Labour government in 1945 decided to continue them under the new name of 'Civic Restaurants': in February 1949, with rationing continuing, there were still 678, serving three million meals a week.[57]

FIGURE 8.2 ◆ *A simple wartime canteen, with cafeteria service, c. 1943. All war factories employing more than 250 were required to provide a canteen: by 1943 there were also 2,160 'British Restaurants' run by local authorities and open to all. A typical menu offered soup, 2d., mince, potatoes and beans, 9d., sultana roll, 3d. and tea 1½ d.*

Source: © Associated Newspapers.

Social policy during the war was particularly concerned with the nutritional welfare of children who, it was feared, might be suffering from the effects of evacuation, family disruption and working mothers. The special allocation schemes for those under 5 have previously been noticed: for those over this age there were major expansions in the schools meals and milk programmes. In 1941 Lord Woolton was reported as saying:

> I want to see elementary school children as well fed as children going to Eton and Harrow. I am determined that we shall organise our food front that at the end of the war ... we shall have preserved, and even improved, the health and physique of the nation.[58]

The comparison may not have been appropriate, but his hope of generally improved nutritional standards was justified. In 1938 only 160,000 children in elementary schools received school dinners, two-thirds of them free and aimed particularly at undernourished children in the depressed areas of high unemployment. During the war the whole concept of school meals radically changed from a mainly free service for 'necessitous' children towards a universal provision for children of all classes, providing a balanced, main meal of around 1,000 kcals, one-third of their daily energy needs. By 1942 one million children were eating school meals, by 1945 1¾ millions, 36 per cent of the school population:[59] only one in seven of these were free, the rest, heavily subsidised, costing 4d. or 5d. a day. Though well short of 'universal', they were a major supplement to children's diets, sometimes the one cooked meal they received during the day. Some school canteens also provided breakfasts and substantial teas for those staying on for evening activities.[60] Also, the Milk in Schools scheme, begun in 1934, was greatly expanded from 22 million gallons a year to 43 million gallons, providing a third of a pint a day either free or heavily subsidised: by 1945 around three-quarters of all children in elementary schools were 'drinking out' at the mid-morning break.

All these various institutions – factory canteens and emergency feeding centres, British Restaurants and Rural Pies, school meals and milk – amounted to a huge increase in consumption outside the home. Sometimes enforced, but more often, it seems, chosen and enjoyed, they represented a major change in English eating and social habits. Men and women, adults and children, who had always eaten in the intimacy of their own homes, now mingled with crowds of strangers in unfamiliar surroundings, eating food prepared by others and, often, sampling dishes of a new kind. The question would be whether this was a purely temporary excursion into public eating necessitated by the extraordinary conditions of war, or whether it would continue, perhaps even grow, when peace and normal life returned.

Notes and references

1 Angus Calder, *The People's War, Britain 1939–1945* (1st edn, 1969), Pimlico, 1992, p. 386.

2 *How Britain Was Fed In War Time. Food Control, 1939–1945*, HMSO, 1946, p. 5.

3 E. R. Chamberlin, *Life in Wartime Britain*, Batsford, 1972, p. 75.

4 For full details of rationing and food policy see R. J. Hammond's volumes in the Official History of the Second World War, Vol. I, *Food: The Growth of Policy*, 1951; Vols II and III, *Studies in Administration and Control*, 1956, 1962, HMSO and Longmans, Green and Co.

5 Sheila Kaye-Smith, *Kitchen Fugue*, Cassell, 1945, p. 106.

6 André Simon (ed.), *Wine and Food: A Gastronomic Quarterly*, No. 33, Spring 1942, p. 29: No. 34, Summer 1942, p. 90.

7 Richard Broad and Suzie Fleming (eds), *Nella Last's War. A Mother's Diary, 1939–1945*, Bristol, Falling Wall Press, 1981, pp. 200, 241. Nella Last was a Mass Observation respondent.

8 Peter Donnelly (ed.), *Mrs. Milburn's Diaries. An Englishwoman's Day-to-Day Reflections, 1939–1945*, Abacus, 1995, pp. 146, 220, 250.

9 John Burnett, *A History of the Cost of Living*, (1st edn, 1969), Aldershot, Hampshire, Gregg Revivals, 1993, pp. 303, 312–13.

10 Peter Bird, *The First Food Empire. A History of J. Lyons and Co.*, Chichester, West Sussex, Phillimore, 2000, pp. 119–20.

11 Calder, op. cit., p. 176.

12 Gabor Denes, *The Story of the Imperial. The Life and Times of Torquay's Great Hotel*, Newton Abbot, Devon, David & Charles, 1982, pp. 68 0.

13 Colin Ward and Dennis Hardy, *Goodnight Campers. The History of the British Holiday Camp*, Mansell Publishing, 1986, p. 68.

14 Robert Rhodes James (ed.), *Chips. The Diaries of Sir Henry Channon*, Weidenfeld & Nicolson, 1967, pp. 221, 265, 272.

15 Bird, op. cit., p. 120.

16 Broad and Fleming (eds), op. cit., p. 206.

17 Oliver Coburn, *Youth Hostel Story. The First Twenty Years*, The National Council of Social Service, 1950, p. 87.

18 John K. Walton, *The Blackpool Landlady. A Social History*, Manchester, Manchester University Press, 1978, pp. 187–8.

19 L. H. Lampitt, 'The Function of the Food Industry', Lecture delivered at the Royal Institution, 1940 and published in Royal Institution, *The Nation's Larder, and the Housewife's Part Therein*, G. Bell and Sons, 1940, p. 79. Dr Lampitt was Research Director of J. Lyons and Co.

20 Chamberlin, op. cit., pp. 54–5.

21 Dorothy Sheridan (ed.), *Wartime Women. An Anthology of Women's Wartime Writing for Mass Observation, 1937–1945*, Mandarin, 1991, pp. 148, 239.

22 Hammond, op. cit., Vol. I, pp. 288–90.

23 Alison Leach (ed.), *The Savoy Food and Drink Book*, Pyramid Books, 1988, p. 24.

24 Calder, op. cit., p. 406.

25 Colin Spencer, *The Heretic's Feast. A History of Vegetarianism*, Fourth Estate, 1993, pp. 309, 317.

26 Norman Longmate, *The Way We Lived Then. A History of Everyday Life During the Second World War*, Hutchinson, 1977, p. 72.

27 Sheridan (ed.), op. cit., p. 188.

28 Donnelly (ed.), op. cit., p. 116.

29 Stanley Jackson, *The Savoy. The Romance of a Great Hotel*, Frederic Muller, 1964, p. 176.

30 Mario Gallati, *Mario of the Caprice. The Autobiography of a Restaurateur*, Hutchinson, 1960, pp. 95–7.

31 Madame Prunier, *La Maison. The History of Prunier's*, Longman and Co., 1957, pp. 254–64, 285.

32 Anthony Masters, *Rosa Lewis. An Exceptional Edwardian*, Weidenfeld & Nicolson, 1977, pp. 173–85. Casualties in the bombing of the Cavendish included Lord Kimberley, a private secretary of Churchill, cousin of P. G. Wodehouse and reputedly the model for Bertie Wooster.

33 Peppino Leoni, *I Shall Die on the Carpet*, Leslie Frewin, 1966, pp. 172–4.

34 Author's recollection from 1943.

35 T. A. Layton, *Dining Round London*, Noel Carrington, 2nd edn, 1947, p. 25.

(Layton was a caterer and wine merchant and contributed articles to *Time and Tide*: the first edition of his book was in 1945.)

36 ibid., p. 58.

37 Broad and Fleming (eds), op. cit., pp. 199–200.

38 Donnelly (ed.), op. cit., pp. 116, 176.

39 Hammond, op. cit., Vol. III, p. 741.

40 John K. Walton, *Fish and Chips and the British Working Class, 1870–1940*, Leicester, Leicester University Press, 1992, pp. 19, 53.

41 Gertrude Wagner, 'Wartime Social Survey. Food During the War. A Summary of Studies', TS (undated), Central Office of Information, 1943, p. 12.

42 Marguerite Patten, *Century of British Cooking*, Grub Street, 1999, p. 128.

43 Longmate, op. cit., p. 86.

44 Broad and Fleming (eds), op. cit., p. 173.

45 Sheridan (ed.), op. cit., p. 86.

46 Sir Noel Curtis-Bennett, *The Food of the People, Being the History of Industrial Feeding*, London, Faber and Faber, 1949, pp. 237ff.

47 Chamberlin, op. cit., p. 81.

48 Wagner, 'Wartime Social Survey', op. cit., p. 13.

49 Calder, op. cit., p. 387.

50 Curtis-Bennett, op.cit., pp. 260ff.

51 Hammond, op. cit., Vol. II, p. 414; Calder, op. cit., p. 385.

52 Hammond, op. cit., Vol. II, p. 385.

53 Quoted Christopher Driver, *The British at Table, 1940–1980*, Chatto & Windus, 1983, p. 33.

54 Wagner, 'Wartime Social Survey', op. cit., p. 15.

55 Frances Partridge, *A Pacifist's War* (1978), quoted Driver, op. cit., p. 35.

56 *The Caterer*, 21 Sept. 1945, p. 5; Hammond, op. cit., Vol. II, p. 395.

57 Hammond, ibid., Vol. II, p. 411.

58 Lord Woolton in *The Times*, 3 October 1941.

59 Many children still returned home for lunch, either because they lived nearby, their mothers were cooking anyway, or because they did not like school dinners. In a Wartime Social Survey, *School Meals in Scotland*, Report No. 33A, August 1943, 44% of the children surveyed said that they did not like them, pp. 2–7.

60 Personal note: As a sixth-former in a Nottingham Grammar School I sometimes ate away from home for almost two days – school lunch, school tea for Air Cadet training, school fire-watching overnight, breakfast in a local canteen, school lunch again, tea at home. At Christmas I worked as a Post Office sorter and ate at a British Restaurant: in the summer holidays we worked at a school-organised Harvest Camp, where our teachers cooked meals and made sandwiches for our lunch in the fields.

PART FOUR

1945–2000

CHAPTER 9

From austerity to affluence, 1945–1970

Hopes deferred: control and decontrol, 1945–1954

*When all this is over, and I can order with old-time carelessness 'a nice
Dover sole', 'a pound and a half of Scotch salmon', 'a couple of
lobsters', or what about 'a bit of smoked haddock for breakfast'? ... And
when I do not feel inclined to cook I want to be able to drive without
care for petrol or the police, to some well-appointed grill-room and eat a
chop or a steak with 'pommes allumettes' for half a crown [2/6d.]
instead of having to stodge through a typical schoolroom dinner for five
shillings and a two-shilling cover charge.*

Sheila Kaye-Smith, Kitchen Fugue (1945), pp. 208–9.

Such expectations, understandable after six years of privation, would
not be fulfilled until rationing finally ended in 1954. Any hopes of a
rapid return to pre-war plenty were quickly dispelled by a world food
shortage compounded by a dollar crisis and the ending of American
Lend-Lease supplies. Moreover, the new Labour government elected in
1945 concentrated resources on its priorities of reviving output, nation-
alising basic industries and constructing the promised Welfare State,
policies in which private consumption had to take second place to public

good. For the immediate future the slogans of 'austerity' and 'pro-ductivity' offered little consolation to a war-weary nation which had hoped for a rapid ending of rationing and a solution of the acute housing shortage which the demobilisation of millions of servicemen exacer-bated.

In fact, food rationing not only continued, but fell to its most stringent levels in 1947–8 when allowances were even lower than in wartime and bread itself was rationed for the first time. A restricted diet, which had been accepted as an essential requirement of winning the war, now became increasingly unpopular,[1] not allayed by government assurances that the nation was not only adequately nourished, but actually better fed than in peacetime. From the summer of 1945 housewives' complaints about continued shortages and rising prices began to develop into a protest campaign, the British Housewives League. Organised by Irene Lovelock, a vicar's wife from South London, it sprang into headline news in February 1946 over cuts in rations and the ending of American imports of dried eggs which had been a valued substitute for the ration of one shell-egg a week. In the face of a national outcry, Ben Smith, the Minister of Food, relented, allowed their importation,[2] and shortly afterwards resigned. The League also campaigned against what it considered dis-courteous, high-handed treatment by some shopkeepers and exorbitant prices charged for imported fruits in short supply, some of its predomi-nantly middle-class members taking a self-denying stand not to buy pineapples at 7/6d. each, grapes at 6/- a pound and tangerines at 2/0d. each. The government responded by prohibiting the import of 'luxury fruit'.[3] But the greatest public anger arose in July 1946, when the new Minister, John Strachey, announced that in view of poor world harvests bread would be rationed on the basis of two large loaves per person per week (one for children under 6) after its size had already been surrepti-tiously reduced from 32 oz to 28 oz. Until then, bread, though never very popular because of its dark colour, had always been available in any quantity, and held symbolic importance as the nation's staple. Now, con-sumers had to present 'Bread Units' to bakers, while in restaurants bread served with soup counted as a course and the diner had to forgo a pud-ding (illogically, the toast on which a sardine or Welsh rarebit was served was exempt). The Housewives League presented a petition with 600,000 signatures,[4] but to no avail: bread rationing continued until 1948, though it caused more resentment than actual hardship, and most people got as much as they wanted. Shopkeepers were incensed about collecting coupons and form-filling, and one baker declared that he would go to prison rather than do so, voicing a growing opinion that 'This country is getting worse than Germany under the Nazis'.[5]

Support for the Labour government's food policies fell to its lowest point in the early months of 1947 when a freak winter was followed by floods and cuts in basic rations – meat fell to 13 oz a week, butter and margarine combined 6 oz, cheese 1½ oz, cooking fat 1 oz, sugar 8 oz and milk 2 pints. The Ministry desperately sought supplements to the dwindling diet by importing whalemeat, which had a modest success judged by the sale of 600 whalesteaks a day in a Lyons Corner House, though by 1950 4,000 tons remained unsold. In 1948 10 million tins of the even less popular fish, snoek, began arriving from South Africa, which it was hoped might substitute for Portuguese sardines. Snoek was a large, ferocious fish similar to barracouta, which when displeased was said to hiss like a snake and bark like a dog. A poster campaign for 'Snoek Piquante' suggested recipes to enliven this tasteless dish, but the public continued to regard it as a bad joke and millions of tins eventually ended as cat food.

Frustrated housewives were bombarded with advice from government leaflets and, from 1946, 'Woman's Hour' programmes on the radio, on which Marguerite Patten and others offered economical recipes, as did Philip Harben on the newly revived but very restricted television service: in 1947 Patten herself appeared for the first time with recipes for 'Eight-Minute Doughnuts', 'Hamburgers' and 'Hungarian Goulash', the two latter using whalemeat.[6] The government regularly monitored public opinion through its Social Surveys, cautiously releasing one food after another as supplies improved: in 1948 preserves came off the ration, in 1950 dried fruits, ice cream, fish, poultry and rabbits became more available, but decontrol of many foods waited until after the Conservative victory at the General Election in 1951. In 1952 tea was derationed, in 1953 sugar, eggs, cream and sweets, and in 1954 fats and the long-desired meat. Meanwhile, by 1950 co-operative societies and Sainsbury's had opened the first self-service stores, and in 1951 Birds Eye first put frozen peas on the market. By the early 1950s Marguerite Patten's recipes for home cooking now included pasta and ravioli, Quiche Lorraine, fried scampi, steak Diane and Tournedos Rossini,[7] indicating that some new fashionable tastes were developing as eating out and Continental holi-days increased. However, it would be wrong to exaggerate the extent of such changes on the general public or the influence of one particular book, Elizabeth David's *Mediterranean Food* (1950), which was greatly admired in sophisticated circles. Most consumers simply wanted to return to a free choice of the foods they had enjoyed before the war, and for many years to come remained faithful to firmly traditional tastes. This was clearly demonstrated in 1947 when a Gallup Poll survey invited a cross-section of the population to select their 'Perfect Meal, if expense were no object and you could have absolutely anything you wanted'. It was not specified whether this would be eaten at home or in a restaurant, but the clear inference is that it would be in the latter. The 'Perfect Meal' is reproduced below.

Though these were the most popular choices, there were some inter-esting variations: 69 per cent of people did not want anything before their soup (only 6 per cent named a sherry); tomato soup was the most popu-lar, followed by oxtail and Scotch broth; for the fish course only 4 per cent chose salmon and the same number prawn cocktail; for the main course chicken was closely followed by roast beef and a mixed grill (duck a mere 3 per cent); a green salad instead of vegetables was favoured by only 2 per cent, while for the sweet trifle at 12 per cent was closely fol-lowed by apple pie (11 per cent) and rice pudding (8 per cent). Such con-ventional choices were perhaps unsurprising in the austerity year 1947, but more remarkable were the results of a second 'Perfect Meal' survey in 1962, by which time a free market in food and rising standards of living were well established. Now the choices of most popular dishes followed exactly the same order as before with only one small change – fruit salad

THE PERFECT MEAL, 1947
Sherry
Tomato soup
Sole
Roast chicken
Roast potatoes, peas and sprouts
Trifle and cream
Cheese and biscuits
Drinks. Wine and coffee

and cream took the place of trifle. Below the surface, however, a few new trends were noticeable: 29 per cent of people now wanted wine with the meal compared with 10 per cent in 1947; fewer people asked for any kind of soup and prawn cocktail had become the favourite 'starter', while roast meats had declined by 11 per cent for the main course and chicken, turkey and duck all increased.[8] The ideal of 1962 was somewhat lighter, less carnivorous and rather more alcoholic, but not basically different: tastes were still plain and English, there was no Continental 'haute cuisine', no mention of luxury foods like game, lobster, caviar or foie gras, and no support yet for Indian or Chinese dishes.

This discussion has taken us forward in time. In the immediate postwar years the owners of hotels and restaurants shared the public's impatience to end rationing and controls. Anxious to recondition bomb-damaged premises with government support, the trade stressed its value to the national economy, especially to dollar earnings from the American tourists who were beginning to return: in 1947 earnings from overseas visitors brought £30 million, a figure which the trade argued could be greatly expanded if restrictions were removed and, as Harry Salmon, the Chairman of Lyons, said, 'we are allowed to put our own houses in order'.[9] But luxury eating was not acceptable to an egalitarian government, and the three-course, 5/- limits on meals were not removed until 1950 when Labour was seeking re-election in the face of declining popularity. Rationed allocations to caterers continued until 1954, though on a rather more generous scale as visitors poured into London for the Festival of Britain in 1951 and Queen Elizabeth II's Coronation in 1953: it also seems that 'black market' supplies were now more available and less publicly condemned than in wartime.[10]

Subsidised public eating, which had been greatly expanded during the war, continued in the years of austerity. Factory canteens were seen as a vital element in the drive for productivity, while British Restaurants – renamed 'Civic Restaurants' in 1947 – continued to be mocked by some but valued by many. The 1,800 British Restaurants operating at the end of the war fell rapidly, however, as the Ministry's financial support ended and local authorities were left to maintain them, but in 1949 there were still 678 Civic Restaurants serving around three million meals a week,[11] more than any single commercial catering chain. On the other hand, school meals expanded well beyond their previous level under the impetus of R. A. Butler's Education Act of 1944 which made it a statutory duty of local education authorities to provide a school meals service: together with school milk, which was now made free, these were to be integral parts of the emerging Welfare State which placed particular importance on improving the health of children. School dinners were either free for the children of parents on a means-tested basis or, for the great majority, at a subsidised price which covered approximately half the cost. It was required that the meal should be 'suitable in all respects as the main meal of the day', usually consisting of meat and vegetables followed by a pudding, while later regulations provided that it should contribute 42 per cent of daily protein and 33 per cent of energy needs. The take-up was never universal, as some children preferred to go home or to bring a packed lunch, but at its peak in 1975 70 per cent of all children were eating school dinners: by then, inflation had raised the charges considerably, and the proportion of free meals had risen from only 4 per cent in 1954 to 12 per cent.[12]

Commercial caterers struggled against food and labour shortages to satisfy a pent-up demand. London's largest firm, Lyons, had ended the war with 70 fewer teashops, and between 1938 and 1951 it opened only one new one, sensing that tastes were changing since the time when these had been the cornerstone of their food empire. Self-service had been introduced from 1941 onwards to save labour, and was applied to all Lyons teashops after 1945: customers who had expected a return of the 'Nippy' waitresses were disappointed by the cafeteria system which they associated with queueing and the factory canteen. The post-war teashop became less popular as younger people wanted something more exciting than traditional fare of meat pies, sausages and steamed puddings for lunch, while 'tea' of toast and cakes was declining as a late-afternoon meal. The three huge Corner Houses underwent change from the late 1940s, incorporating smaller, specialised restaurants with limited choices, again economising on staff and waste. The first of these 'themed' restaurants was the 'Haversnack' in 1952, followed by the 'Bacon and Egg' and the 'Grill and Cheese' in 1954, but easily the most successful was the 'Wimpy Bar' opened at the Coventry Street Corner House in 1953 when Lyons acquired the UK rights from its American inventor, Eddie Gold. Together with the 'Whippsy Milk Shake' the hamburger was a sensation at the Ideal Home Exhibition in 1954, echoing Lyons' first incursion into exhibition catering in the 1880s, and was quickly taken up in other Corner Houses and some teashops. At Coventry Street the average time spent by a 'Wimpy' customer was 20 minutes, and there was a 77 per cent occupancy rate of seats between 10.30 am and midnight.[13] It was the beginning, as yet unrealised, of the fast food revolution which was to transform catering in future years.

Already in 1945 food writers and journalists were beginning to revive the pre-war practice of recommending good places to eat, especially for the benefit of expected tourists and visitors. T. A. Layton contributed regular articles to *Time and Tide*, later published in book form as *Dining Round London*, in 1945 and 1947. Even at this early date, many pre-war restaurants were operating, like Simpsons-in-the-Strand and Scott's ('Homes of the Trenchermen'), Shirreff's Wine Parlour (a grilled lemon sole 2/9d.) and the Bolivar, part of the Langham Hotel and much frequented by BBC staff (three-course luncheon 3/6d.). Publicly at least, restaurants were keeping within the 5/0d. limit and at Pinoli's the three courses including excellent hors d'oeuvres cost 4/0d., the Ivy also 4/0d. plus a house charge, while in 1947 dinner-dances were described as 'suddenly very popular' in top-class places like the Savoy, the Normandie and Quaglino's: together with house and music charges, these cost 11/6d. Around Soho, Isola Bella, Quo Vadis and Romano Santi were recommended: somehow L'Écu de France managed to offer *fricassé de veau*, Boulestin's *coq au vin rouge* and Antoine's braised pigeon. Four Chinese restaurants were suggested, especially Ley-On's in Wardour Street, also several Greek, Spanish, Hungarian and Scandinavian places, while for a snack a sandwich bar was suggested – Fortnum and Mason's, Forte's Milk Bar or the Moo Cow Milk Bar in Baker Street with 'a vast range of every conceivable food'.[14]

Rising gastronomic standards, and rising prices, are noticeable after the ending of the 5/-. meal limit in 1950. Madame Prunier dated 1952 as the return to normality in her famous fish restaurant, while hotels in London and fashionable resorts were busy rebuilding, refurbishing and redecorating for Coronation celebrations: even at the distant Imperial Hotel at Torquay a new restaurant was opened with the unusual proviso that in future all menus would be in English as appropriate for 'The English Hotel in the Mediterranean Manner'. The special carte for the opening[15] was firmly traditional, but still lacking red meat, as the menu reproduced below indicates.

HOTEL IMPERIAL, TORQUAY, CARTE FOR OPENING OF NEW
RESTAURANT

Melon Cocktail in Port Wine

***

West Indian Turtle Broth
with Golden Cheese Straws

***

Filet of Sole 'St Christopher'

***

Breast of Chicken 'Imperial Torquay'
Salad of the English Riviera

***

Strawberry Ice Cake 'Elizabeth'
Devonshire Dainty Delights

***

Empire Coffee

Even at Prunier's, a leading London centre of 'haute cuisine', soup, fish, chicken and a fruit-based dessert was offered for a special Coronation Lunch on 2 June 1953. As the restaurant in St James's Street commanded a view of the procession Madame Prunier had erected tiers of balconies for her guests, tickets for which had been sold a year ahead. As the police closed the streets in Central London at 7.00 am, guests arrived at 5.30 for breakfast, and after the procession viewed the ceremony on a specially installed television set. Lunch was served shortly after midday, a surprisingly modest meal though no doubt superbly cooked. 'I kept my clients till five in the evening, yet all I charged them was fifteen guineas [£15/15/0d.] a head, and champagne was the only extra.'[16]

Whether as a result of necessity or of choice – probably something of both – restaurant menus were now shorter and simpler than before the war. Peppino Leoni, who had successfully reopened Quo Vadis, believed that

War and rationing had considerably shrunk the English stomach. Five-and six-course dinners were a thing of the past, and nobody wanted them any more, even if they had been legal. I soon realised that what people wanted was well-cooked food, attractively presented, in relatively small portions. They were satisfied with three courses.[17]

Mario Gallati at the Caprice thought the same:

> *When rationing was eventually lifted, it was said that the rich would*
> *proceed to gorge themselves on mountainous meals to make up for*
> *those lost years. This didn't prove to be so. Our stomachs must have*
> *shrunk...and people today [1960] don't have anything like the*
> *appetites they had before the war... When I was at Romano's in the early*
> *1900s most of our patrons were colossal eaters... It was quite usual for*
> *us to serve six- or seven-course meals. Between the two wars, even at*
> *The Ivy, four- and five-course meals were not unusual. Today, however,*
> *three-course meals are the vogue, and many people even forgo the*
> *dessert or cheese course.*[18]

The three-course wartime limit evidently had some lasting effect on meal habits. But Gallati's account of Edwardian diners identified them as 'the rich' and 'the aristocracy'. Now, diners-out comprised a broader, less affluent clientele who had more calls on their incomes, more other amusements and less inclination to spend a whole evening at table, even if they had the appetites for it. Eating in public, before the war mainly restricted to a privileged minority, had been familiarised and democratised by British Restaurants, factory canteens and, not least, by the communal feeding of millions of servicemen and women. Now, first under austerity and then under free choice, it was coming to be enjoyed as a recreation of the many – not of all and not in the old form of luxury eating, but in new styles and new places which catered for an emerging mass market.

Social trends

The modern growth in eating out for pleasure dates from the end of rationing in the mid-1950s and was part of wider social changes which would ultimately transform the lives of English people. New tastes in food, drink and dress, in furnishing and decor and in leisure and entertainment, many of which were popularised by the now mass medium of television, depended on a sustained rise in the standard of living between 1945 and 1970, greater than in any previous quarter-century. Despite inflation as controls and subsidies were gradually removed after 1951, earnings generally kept well ahead of prices under a strong demand for labour, powerful trade unions and low rates of unemployment. Harold Macmillan, the Conservative Prime Minister, could claim with some justification that the people had 'never had it so good'. Among the chief beneficiaries were manual workers, juveniles and women, groups who were historically among the lowest paid. But as the economy began to move towards a post-industrial stage, more people now worked in professional, managerial, technical and clerical occupations, enjoying comfortable standards and rising expectations of fuller, more varied lifestyles than their parents had done. By 1964 43 per cent of people had bought, or were buying, their own homes and 42 per cent owned a motor car: the first motorway, the M1, opened in 1958 and commercial television, begun in 1955, was busily advertising convenience foods, new kitchen equipment, package holidays and other paraphernalia of a consumer boom. It was often said that Britain was becoming a 'middle-class society' with around a third of the population in that contentious category, twice the proportion as at the beginning of the century. In 1961 Mark Abrams of Research Services Ltd divided the population into six socio-economic groups on the basis of occupation and income, as set out in Table 9.1.[19]

The figures in Table 9.1 suggest a middle class of around 32 per cent – the most likely group of eaters-out – but now joined by the equally large, well-paid skilled workers (35 per cent). The landed aristocracy were apparently too small for separate mention, while the pensioners in

TABLE 9.1 ◆ *The social structure, 1961*

Grade	Description	Per cent
A	Upper middle class – higher managerial, professional or administrative, incomes over £1,750 p.a.	4
B	Middle class – intermediate managerial, professional and administrative, incomes £950–£1,750 p.a.	8
C1	Lower middle class – supervisors, clerical, junior managerial, professional and administrative, income under £950 p.a.	20
C2	Skilled working class, incomes £650–£1,000 p.a.	35
D	Working class – semi-skilled and unskilled workers, incomes £350–£625 p.a.	25
E	Lowest-grade workers, casuals, State pensioners, incomes under £340 p.a.	8

Grade E had not yet swollen to their later large proportion. The English people of the 1960s were workers, earners and spenders, with an ever-widening range of wants to spur their energies.

Food had always been the largest item in any budget: the lower the income the greater the proportion that had to go to this basic need. At the end of rationing in 1954 it took an average 33 per cent of consumers' expenditure, in 1963 23.3 per cent and by 1970 only 20.2 per cent,[20] indicating not any reduction in food consumption, but rising real incomes of which housing, consumer goods, vehicles, transport and leisure now took greater proportions. In 1956, the amount spent on meals in hotels, restaurants and boarding-houses had been tiny, averaging only 5/0d. a week: men spent considerably more than women (8/2d. compared with 2/3d.), office staff more than manual workers, and Londoners most of all (see Table 9.2).

Further light on eating out at this period was shed by a nationwide survey of *The Foods We Eat* in 1958. Surprisingly, 6 out of every 10 men lived close enough to their work to go home for the midday meal: 22 per cent took it at their workplace, either in a canteen or as a packed meal brought from home and 12 per cent went to a café or restaurant (or pub). These statistics referred to meals during the working week, Monday–Friday; on Saturdays, now either a whole- or half-day holiday, 8 per cent of all adults lunched in a café or restaurant, suggesting that this was part of a recreational outing, but on Sundays a mere 2 per cent did so – Sunday lunch, which was the traditional family meal of a roast, vegetables and a pudding, was still firmly at home.[21] The main evening meal

TABLE 9.2 ◆ *Average expenditure per meal, 1956*

		Restaurants	**Canteens**
Breakfast	Men	2/5d.	1/4d.
	Women	–	10d.
Midday Lunch	Men	4/1d.	1/11d.
	Women	3/2d.	1/8d.
Tea	Men	3/0d.	1/5d.
	Women	2/10d.	1/1d.
Evening Dinner	Men	18/9d.	–
(London only)	Women	6/4d.	–

Source: *Consumers' Expenditure on Meals and other Food Eaten Outside the Home*, The Social Survey, Central Statistical Office, June 1956 (PRO Ref. RG 33/224).

FIGURE 9.1 ◆ *A group of teenagers in a coffee bar, early 1960s. The new coffee bars, using the espresso machine invented by Gaggia of Milan in 1946, replaced the pre-war Milk Bars with a trendy, contemporary image which went with new fashions in dress, music and decor. In 1960 there were an estimated 2,000 in Britain, 200 in the West End alone.*

Source: Hulton Archive.

– 'tea', 'high tea' or 'dinner', depending on income and local usage – was also overwhelmingly at home. Eating out in a restaurant in the evening was rare: only 5 per cent of adults did so on Saturdays in summer and 2 per cent in winter.[22] The English were a home-loving people, and outside the wealthiest group in London the habit of evening dining out for pleasure was not yet established.

By the 1960s demographic changes were beginning to affect this pattern. Household size was shrinking as families had fewer children: in 1961 households contained an average of 3.1 people, a figure which would fall to only 2.56 by 1985, when the once 'typical' family of two adults and two children then accounted for only 11.9 per cent of households: on the other hand, one- and two-person households had risen to 54 per cent of all. Family eating patterns, which in the past were geared to the large number of mouths to be fed, were adapting to catering for small groups of individuals for which the cooking of large joints of meat, vegetables and puddings was not appropriate. One response to this change was the increased use of convenience foods and ready-made meals: another was to eat out more often, allowing more choice and variety as well as less domestic labour. This was especially important as more and more women entered employment and 'housewife' became almost a pejorative term. Before the war domesticity had been the norm for most wives: men provided, wives dispensed, kept house and cared for husbands and children. The war had already begun to change this, when many married women had taken on unaccustomed jobs; some subsequently returned to domesticity, but in 1951 22 per cent of married women were employed outside the home. A survey that year estimated that wives at home spent an average of 75 hours a week on housework,[23] an amount increasingly unacceptable to younger women. By 1959 one in three married women were in employment, by 1985 52 per cent. More wives worked, not only to escape domestic drudgery, but for job satisfaction, the companionship of others and, not least, for the material benefits which a double income could bring. Eating out, like family limitation, was part of the wider movement for women's independence and freedom from traditional constraints: it was labour saving, pleasurable and now financially possible.

Others who also enjoyed greater freedom and disposable income at this time were juveniles. In the past, many had entered low-paid manual work at 14 and had to wait years to reach adult wages, even if there were jobs for them. The 1944 Education Act raised the school-leaving age to 15, and later to 16: secondary education was now universal, and growing numbers were staying on for further studies and university entrance. All this meant that young workers were at a premium and that the better-educated ones could achieve much higher earnings. The late 1950s and 1960s saw what was described as a 'teenage revolution': young people were spending more on new fashions in dress, popular music, leisure and entertainment, creating a distinctive youth culture. As yet, they were not frequent eaters-out, but they congregated in the evenings in the trendy coffee-bars which followed in the wake of Milk Bars with a more adult, sophisticated image. Their attractions were the hissing espresso machines invented by Achille Gaggia in 1946, and the bright, contemporary decor of the bars; some served light snacks, but for the price of a cup of coffee young people could spend an hour or two in a non-alcoholic environment which represented independence and modernity. The first, the Moka Bar in Frith Street, was an instant success, selling 1,000 cups a day, and was quickly copied: in 1960 there were an estimated 2,000 in Britain, 200 in the West End of London alone.[24] The boom began to fade in the 1960s as proprietors discovered that there was little profit in coffee alone, and many turned into cafés or trattorias with Continental dishes and confectionery: by then teenagers could eat cheaply in a Wimpy Bar (460 by 1969) or in a Spaghetti House, the first of which opened in 1955 with a notice in the window, 'Spaghetti, But Not On Toast'.[25]

Another social change influenced eating out at this time. Holidays were always occasions for eating outside home, and now with statutory holidays with pay they greatly increased (see Table 9.3). After 1945 4½ million servicemen were gradually demobilised, collecting their gratuities but with little to spend them on in austerity Britain: because of the housing shortage many young married couples were having to live with parents, and were only too keen to enjoy a holiday. Even a working holiday on a farm, promoted by the Ministry of Agriculture's campaign to 'Lend a Hand on the Land' at harvest-time, attracted around 200,000 a year into the early 1950s,[26] while tens of thousands of East Enders continued to flood into the hop-fields of Kent. But more people wanted the organised amusements of a holiday camp, for which there was a peak demand in 1948 when 200,000 people failed to get a booking in a Butlin camp. Otherwise, a seaside holiday in a boarding-house or 'private hotel' remained the most popular vacation and generally offered good value at around 15/0d. a day. The winner of 'The Ideal Landlady' competition at Blackpool in 1951, still under rationing, fed her guests with porridge and a cooked breakfast, soup, a roast and a hot pudding for lunch, for tea ham, tongue or chicken salad with cakes, and a late supper of sandwiches and more cakes.[27] By the 1960s such traditional resorts were beginning to face competition from package holidays abroad, and in 1970 the British Travel Association estimated that £465 million was now spent on foreign holidays compared with £782 million at home.[28] Tourists were preferring a change of scene, reliable weather and, not least, different food and drink: in 1961 a coach party of Welsh miners touring in Spain sent home the English chef they had thoughtfully brought with them because they had come to prefer Spanish cuisine.

Overseas travel eventually had a major influence on British food tastes, though as Table 9.3 indicates, this was hardly significant before

TABLE 9.3 ◆ *Numbers of holidays in Britain and abroad, 1951–1975* (millions)*

	In Britain	**Abroad**
1951	25	2
1961	30	4
1971	34	7
1975	40	8

* Four or more nights away from home.

TABLE 9.4 ◆ *Destinations of holidays abroad, 1966 and 1975 (per cent)**

	1966	**1975**
Spain	22	34
Italy	17	7
France	14	14
Irish Republic	9	4
Austria	7	3
Switzerland	7	3
Greece	1	4
All Europe	94	87

* Adults only.

Source: Social Trends 9, 1979 edn, HMSO, 1978, Table 12.20, p. 187.

the later 1960s. Meanwhile, a growing interest in the pleasures of eating out in Britain was indicated by the foundation in 1950 of the Good Food Club by Raymond Postgate, a social historian, political journalist and gastronome who believed that the standards of restaurant cooking and service could be improved by the personal recommendations of correspondents published in regular editions of *The Good Food Guide*. The 'Club' – membership of which was conferred merely by purchase of the Guide – was conceived as a campaigning organisation based on a broader consuming public than its more elite predecessor, André Simon's Wine and Food Society.[29] The first edition in 1951 carried over 500 recommendations of hotels, restaurants, inns and pubs where satisfactory food could be obtained: later, greatly expanded Guides were selling 50,000 copies a year by 1980. In 1961, ten years after the first edition, Postgate, 'the self-elected Chairman of British gastronomy', reported to members that 'moderate congratulation on our progress is permissible' and went on to reflect on the state of things in 1951:

> *Food in Britain is nothing like as bad as it was ten or so years ago. But then, it was intolerable in those days. There is still a lot of dreadful food served in this island, but at that time there was practically nothing else at all but dreadful food. One had to single out for praise places where a joint and two veg. were merely edible, and the staff was neither obviously incompetent nor unbearably rude, they were so rare. Rarer still were the pubs and hotels where you got enough to eat; we were still under the influence of rationing and helpings were tiny. In fact, meek though we were, if we hadn't all been pretty hungry we probably would have refused to eat what we were offered ... Nothing, however repellent, was what it should be.*[30]

Postgate was, perhaps, over-anxious to claim credit for the good effects of the Guides, and the mainly well-educated, professional people who took the trouble to report their experiences probably enjoyed his complaints, but they were not universally shared. At the same time in the early 1950s Fanny and John Cradock were contributing restaurant reviews to the *Daily Telegraph*, 'not for the privileged visitor, but for Browns, Joneses, Smiths and Robinsons in whom we are primarily interested'. Their gastronomic visits were published in two books in 1952 and 1953, the first a touring guide (which assumed that the Smiths and the Browns now had a car), the second, timed for the Coronation, restricted to London restaurants. In contrast to Postgate's criticisms, they encountered much good cooking, honest ingredients and willing service. In *Around Britain With Bon Viveur* (1952), they explored inns and hotels in small towns and villages, sometimes in quite remote places which seemed almost untouched by modernity: here some of the meals they described with approval might have been served in a coaching inn a hundred or more years earlier. At the Royal Hotel, Symonds Yat in the Wye Valley they enjoyed superb salmon, tender roast beef and garden peas, at Brockhampton Court Hotel poached turbot, roast shoulder of lamb and golden sponge pudding. The White Hart, Nettlebed, Oxfordshire, provided excellent kidney soup, a large grilled sole and trifle, while at the Cottage Hotel, Hope Cove, Devon, there was dressed-crab salad, lamb and new potatoes, strawberries and cream and a savoury of asparagus tips. In the Lake District there were many good places – the Royal Oak, Keswick (table d'hôte lunch with lobster, 5/6d.), the Scafell Hotel, Rothswaite (excellent braised pheasant). In such places the fare was simple and unadorned, but well cooked and from local sources: only rarely were Continental dishes on offer where a hotel employed a foreign chef – at the Bear, Woodstock, (filet de sole Walewska, soufflé Grand Marnier) or the Lakeside Hotel, Newby Bridge (*boeuf à la mode* with *epinards à la crème, beignets soufflé à la vanille,* 'all at very moderate prices').[31] Good cooking was evidently to be found in 1951 if one knew where to look and, probably, where to avoid.

Writing about food was becoming a minor industry, and reading about it a popular recreation. As well as books, newspaper and magazine articles, there were now television programmes in which TV 'personalities' performed culinary feats on a theatre-like stage – several had, in fact, earlier attempted stage careers. They aimed to introduce new recipes and techniques to a nation just emerging from rationing, but it is difficult to assess their impact. Cookery articles and demonstrations may well have been read or viewed mainly for interest and amusement – a survey in 1963 showed that although 91 per cent of purchasers of women's magazines read the cookery recipes, only 9 per cent had actually tried one in the previous fortnight.[32] But in the opinion of food writers one author, Elizabeth David, did make a ground-breaking contribution to changing the ingredients and flavours of food in Britain: as Christina Hardyment puts it, 'If interest in food now amounts to a new kind of religion, then David was its Messiah'.[33] From an upper middle-class family (her father was Rupert Gwynne, Conservative MP for Eastbourne), she studied in France and Germany in the 1930s, travelled in Italy and Greece, and during the war worked for the Ministry of Information in Egypt. The first edition of *A Book of Mediterranean Food* published in 1950 was an instant success, revised as a Penguin in 1955 and republished many times since; six more books followed, with details of the cuisines of other European and Middle Eastern countries. Her recipes were drawn from bourgeois, even peasant, provincial cooking:

> *It is honest cooking ... none of the sham Grande Cuisine of the International Palace Hotel. 'It is not really an exaggeration', wrote Marcel Boulestin, 'to say that peace and happiness begin geographically where garlic is used in cooking'.*[34]

Garlic was only one of 'the ever-recurring elements' of Mediterranean food which she advocated and which included olive oil, saffron, rosemary, basil, marjoram, pimentos, aubergines, olives, melons and limes, besides the wine required in most of her recipes. She admitted that in 1950 'almost every essential of good cooking was either rationed or unobtainable', but by the 1955 edition, 'I think there is scarcely a single ingredient, however exotic, mentioned in this book which cannot be obtained somewhere in the country, even if it is only in one or two shops' (she mentioned some in Soho and Tottenham Court Road).[35]

Not all her recipes were exotic – there were quite simple ones for soups, omelettes, risotto and spaghetti – but she was mainly addressing sophisticated readers who were enjoying foreign travel and cuisines, and outside London and larger provincial cities her immediate influence was limited: Christina Hardyment's judgement is that 'For the majority of Britons her books were fantasies and inspirations rather than guides to be taken literally'.[36]

Apart from holidays abroad, most people's experience of foreign food in the 1950s would have been in a French or Italian restaurant, rare outside London. 'Bon Viveur's' guide to London eating-places in 1953 recommended restaurants ranging in price from a few shillings to a few pounds, one in the moderate category, the Celebrité, New Bond Street, offering a four-course table d'hôte for 17/6d. (for example, Hors d'oeuvre,

Whitebait, Chicken casserole, Mille Feuilles). More expensive places included the Five Hundred Club, Albemarle Street, where an à la carte dinner (goujons of sole, faisan Souvaroff, poached pear farced with almond purée, Brie and celery) cost 30/- without wines, while at the Ivy, still under the direction of M. Abel, the Cradocks and a guest enjoyed a three-course luncheon with a vintage Burgundy for £3/14/3d. At the Brief Encounter, opposite Harrod's, the 'Debutante's Bar' served 30 hot and cold hors d'oeuvres for 6/0d., and Leoni's Quo Vadis was flourishing again (ravioli, suprême de volaille alla Yolanda, zabaglione, 10/0d.). At Isola Bella, sole bonne femme cost 4/6d., ossi bucchi alla Romano 5/6d. For contrast, at the Chelsea Pensioner Restaurant, Lincoln Street, excellent chicken and mushroom soup cost only 8d., escalope of veal 4/6d. and lemon pancakes 1/0d.[37]

These were revived and revised versions of pre-war dishes, not Elizabeth David's petit bourgeois provincial cuisine. Her immediate influence was on a few restaurants outside London, where there was less established tradition, and in the opinion of Christopher Driver pride of place goes to George Perry-Smith who opened the Hole in the Wall at Bath in 1952. In reply to an editor who asked him for his recipes, he said that he could not supply any since almost everything he did was derived from David. He served 'the modish, continental dishes of those gastronomically innocent times' – risotto, ravioli, bouillabaisse, Hungarian goulash, chili con carne, quiche Lorraine – but all carefully and authentically prepared. His reputation spread, rather as John Fothergill's had done in the 1920s, through personal recommendation, but unlike Fothergill he had a number of disciples who spread his influence wider. Driver has traced at least a dozen, several of whom worked at the Hole before opening their own restaurants in Salisbury, Bristol, Lincoln, Durham, Shepton Mallet, Marlow and elsewhere.[38]

The challenge of the new

By the 1960s interest in food, cooking and eating out was becoming something of a national preoccupation, no longer restricted to wealthier gourmets, but shared across gender, regions, ages and social classes. This was due partly to its popularisation by the mass media, especially television, which discovered that food was a topic for which there was an audience eager for imitation and fantasy, partly to the emergence of new kinds of restaurants offering 'fast' food and ethnic cuisines which appealed particularly to young, first-time eaters-out. In *Cooking People* (1967) Michael Bateman paraded a dozen authors, cooks and restaurateurs who, he believed, were having a major influence on British eating habits: they included, besides Philip Harben, André Simon, Elizabeth David and Marguerite Patten, household names like Robert Carrier, Len Deighton, Ambrose Heath and Clement Freud. Few of these had had conventional training as chefs: they had learned by experience, as gifted amateurs with a flair for communication and demonstration. Only two of his 'cooking people' had come through the traditional catering channels – Silvino Trompetto, who worked his way through restaurants and clubs to 'the pinnacle', *chef de cuisine* at the Savoy, and Mario Gallati of the Caprice. Bateman's comments about him might apply to many of the others:

> *Watching Mario at work puts one in mind of a film director, a theatre*
> *manager, an impresario. Running a restaurant is putting on a show...*
> *On the menu is a fabulous variety of English and Continental delicacies,*
> *caviar, oysters, lobster, pressed duck and so on. He doesn't eat the stuff.*
> *All this food is the material of the show he puts on.*[39]

While the cookery writers were mainly addressing the housewife, the columnists of the daily press and Sunday Supplements were recommending where and, sometimes, where not to eat out. In effect, this was a two-way relationship in which new dishes or styles were first experienced in a restaurant and later attempted at home, or, alternatively, one in which domestic recipes were interpreted by commercial caterers. Marguerite Patten's list of trendy dishes of the 1960s would now pass as very conventional – prawn cocktail, sole Veronique, spaghetti Bolognese, Shish Kebab, coq au vin, cheese fondue, Black Forest Gateau[40] – but it would be interesting to know where these were first experienced, whether in a restaurant, on holiday at home or abroad, or at a friend's dinner party, some of the items perhaps imported from the local supermarket.

Hotels generally stuck to well-tried menus, either English or French, but with some concession to American tastes as the numbers of overseas tourists grew to seven million in 1970. Tourism was now the fourth largest earner of foreign currency, and most tourists spent most of their time and money in London. The hotel industry did not begin to revive seriously until the mid-1950s, but from then there was much refurbishment and expansion. The first new hotel, the Westbury, was built in 1956,[41] shortly followed by huge constructions such as the Hilton, Park Lane (1963, 509 bedrooms), the Royal Garden (14 storeys) and the new Cavendish (1966, 15 storeys).[42] By then, the upper end of the hotel business was becoming dominated by large, highly capitalised companies which could finance the great outlays on buildings, staff and running costs. In London the Savoy Group and Grand Metropolitan led the field, but Trust House Hotels made spectacular growth in the 1960s, acquiring Brown's Hotel, the Hotel Russell, Grosvenor House, the Waldorf and the Hyde Park Hotel, while elsewhere they took over existing hotels in resorts and spas, cathedral and university towns (the Randolph, Oxford and the Blue Boar, Cambridge): by 1970 they owned 181 hotels. Their rival, Forte Holdings, had been established by Charles Forte in 1935 as a catering service at airports, as Spiers and Pond had done for railway catering in the previous century: in 1958 Forte entered the hotel business, and in 1970 merged his 43 acquisitions with Trust Houses as Trust House Forte Ltd, the largest hotel group in the United Kingdom.

Hotel catering, adapted to feeding large numbers, did not generally produce originality: on the contrary, the presence of so many tourists in London tended to encourage the development of a standardised 'International' style, an amalgam of mainly American, English and French cuisines. At the Savoy Trompetto still provided the established classics of 'haute cuisine' but was bold enough to include some very English dishes like steak-and-kidney pie and bread-and-butter pudding.[43] Prices had now risen sharply in the period of inflation: in 1970 the table d'hôte luncheon at the Savoy cost from 37/6d. and dinner from 63/0d. comparable with the Connaught Hotel, described in the *Good Food Guide* as 'the discreetest, least glossy and, in many ways, the most comfortable of the London grand hotels': here, table d'hôte lunches and dinners were both from 38/6d. upwards.[44] A growing interest in foreign cuisines was, however, illustrated at the formerly traditional Imperial Hotel, Torquay, which in 1959 hosted an International Gastronomic Festival in which André Simon and the Wine and Food Society participated. This became a regular event organised as weekends at which visiting chefs prepared national menus from different countries and regions, the first from the

Auvergne. The 'Gastronomic Weekends' (at 16–21 guineas) became so popular that by the late 1960s six were held each year.[45]

By 1961 Postgate declared that there had been considerable improvement in restaurant catering over the past ten years, but there was still plenty to complain about:

> The new grills still all announce themselves as supplying Angus beef... But the meat does not taste the same. Nor could it, indeed, unless Angus were as large as Texas; there isn't that amount of Angus beef in the world. The chickens turning on the spits in their millions are real birds – they must be – but their nature has been transmuted. They are battery birds, monstrously multiplied broilers, and they taste of dry wood... Canned music bellows at us. Curries are still commonly served with chip potatoes and wet, boiled vegetables. Mass-produced 'ice-cream', not made of cream, is an almost inevitable dessert.[46]

Another ten years on, in 1970, Postgate claimed 'enormous improvement' in British catering:

> It is difficult now even to remember, let alone to describe, that great grey plain of desolation in 1949, the unending and never-varying sequel of sullen and ill-managed hotels and unfriendly restaurants serving overcooked meats and sodden vegetables.

However, he went on to cite some of the criticisms made by the Club's members – the growing use of frozen vegetables and convenience foods. The 'mark-up' on wines of up to 200 per cent, lighting so dim that one cannot see what one is eating, and, again, the increased use of canned music, for which the manufacturer of the '"Symphonette" claimed that "Each tune is carefully chosen, not for entertainment, but for sales effect."' In what was to be his valedictory editorial, Postgate chided the British people for being too reticent either to commend good food or to condemn the bad:

> There is still a decayed Puritan atmosphere in parts of Britain. It is considered no longer actually wrong, but certainly ignoble, to concern oneself passionately with the quality of food or wine. The editor has been, usually kindlily, reproached for declining from a historian into a 'public stomach'.[47]

He need not have been despondent about the growth of interest in eating out. The 1970 edition of the *Guide* sold 100,000 copies: more than 40,000 reports had been received, and the weighty volume now included 1,600 recommended eating places. In the highest category of restaurants with cuisines of genuine originality, imagination and professional skill, there were 20 listed in London and 50 in the provinces, places of national and international fame. The Hole in the Wall at Bath was 'approved by too many members to list'; the Sharrow Bay Hotel, Ullswater, charged 40/0d. upwards for dinner, while at Thornbury Castle, Gloucestershire, the three-course menu, 'eclectically Mediterranean', was 35/0d. plus a 41/0d. cover charge. In London, the renowned Caprice Restaurant 'stays nostalgically the same' (dinner 47/6d.), at Carrier's lunch was 50/0d., dinner 70/0d., at L'Étoile venison cost 22/6d., jugged hare 19/6d. This was luxury eating for well-heeled tourists and expense-account businessmen rather than ordinary Londoners, but a selection of menus of the 1960s from less fashionable places (see Table 9.5) shows that it was quite possible to eat well for £1 or less.

TABLE 9.5 ♦ *Moderately priced London restaurants, 1960s*

Cresta Restaurant	Tripe à la Polonaise 3/6d., Cromesquies 4/0d., Hungarian Goulash 6/6d., Escargots aux Fines Herbes 8/0d., Zabaglioni 5/0d.
Chez Auguste	Pâté de foie 4/6d., Spaghetti Bolognese 6/6d., Moules Marinière 7/6d., Six Whitstable Oysters 8/6d., Suprême de Volaille Sous Cloche 12/6d., Crêpe Suzette 6/6d., Baklava 2/6d.
Schmidt's Continental Restaurant	Mixed hors d'oeuvres 1/9d., Omelettes 2/6d., Wiener Schnitzel Garnie 4/6d., Roulade of Beef Bourgeoise 4/9d., Dover Sole Meunière 5/6d.
Khyber Restaurant	Bindi Bhajee 3/6d., Sheek Kabab 4/0d., Rougan Jose 5/6d., Madras Chicken 6/0d., Lobster Biriani 8/9d., Stuffed Porota 1/6d.
Kettner's	Smoked Scotch Salmon 7/6d., Sole Waleska 8/6d., Lobster Thermidor 10/6d., Steak Chateaubriand (for 2 persons 30/0d.), Aubergines Frites 2/0d., Soufflé Grand Marnier 5/0d.
The Ox On The Roof	Pimentos, Sauce Vinaigrette 2/6d., Aioli with Shrimp Salad 4/6d., Pâté of liver with truffles 4/6d., Scampi Fritti 6/6d., Filet Goulash Stroganoff 7/6d., Marron Glacé 2/0d., Figs in Syrup 2/0d.

Source: Menus in the author's collection.

Jack Straw's Castle
The menu for this restaurant is reproduced below.
Source: Collection of menus in the author's possession. That of the Ox on the Roof is handwritten on a paper measuring 20 × 15 inches.

Jack Straw's Castle
BILL OF FARE

Cover charge 2/-   **May 1964**

Hors d'Oeuvres

Smoked Salmon 10/6   Smoked Trout 6/6   Prawn Cocktail 7/6   Melon 3/6

Caribbean Cocktail 3/6   Potted Shrimps 4/6   Grapefruit 3/6   Chefs Paté 4/6

Soups

Lobster 5/-   Turtle 4/6   Vichysoisse 3/6   Soup of the day (clear or thick) 2/6

Fish

Scampi, Meunière, Fried or Provençale 10/6

Dover Sole, Meunière, Fried, Grilled or Colbert 12/6

Lobster Thermidor or Newburg

Scotch Salmon

Blue Trout

Grills

Mixed Grill 14/6   Fillet Steak 15/6

Double Lamb Cutlets 12/6   Entrecôte Steak 15/-

Pork Chop 10/6   Rump Steak 14/6

Kidneys and Bacon 10/6

Roasts

Duckling 14/-   Chicken 12/6   Whole Spring Chicken 13/6

Vegetables

Selection of Fresh Vegetables 2/6   Potatoes 2/-

Cold Table (including choice of Salads)

York Ham 12/6   Roast Beef 12/6   Chicken and Ham 14/-   Ox Tongue 12/6

Roast Lamb 12/6   Roast Pork 12/6   Veal and Ham Pie 9/6

Sweets

Choice from the trolley or Sweet of the day 4/6

Cheese

Selection of Cheeses 4/-

Savouries

Mushrooms on Toast 3/6   Welsh Rarebit 3/6   Scotch Woodcock 4/-   Roes on Toast 3/-

Fresh Fruit

Coffee 2/6

The selected menus given in Table 9.5 indicate the variety of cuisines available in London at this time – the traditional English and French in older-established places, the ethnic, and the new wave of informal, 'amusing' restaurants represented by the Ox, strongly influenced by Mediterranean cooking. There were also growing numbers of French bistros and Italian trattorias with innovative dishes aimed at a new market of young adults who were enjoying foreign holidays and disposable incomes. Prices were usually well below those of the West End in places like Chelsea which was only just beginning to be fashionable: decor and service were simple and informal, reminiscent of bourgeois cafés in the French or Italian provinces. Gregory Bowden traces the origins of the new styles to the 1950s and a group of amateur bon-vivants – Alfred and Ruby at the Ox, Bill Stoughton at the Watergate Theatre Restaurant, Dr Hilary James, a psycho-therapist, who opened the Matelot in 1952 and, later, La Bicyclette, Walter Baxter at the Chanterelle, and the ex-Etonian Nick Clarke, who bought a transport café in 1959 and transformed it into the successful 'Nick's Diner'. Dishes were then unfamiliar and exciting – ratatouille, tortillas, cassoulet, arroz alla Valenciana, scampi Provençal, noisettes de porc Touraine, Boeuf en Croute, Taramasalata, as well as garlic bread and chicken in the basket with sweetcorn pancakes.[48]

Trattorias also had the small-scale intimacy of bistros, but a different origin from within the resident Italian community which was swollen by numbers of ex-prisoners of war. Some developed out of the espresso bars of the 1950s, serving snacks and, later, full meals, but some of the first authentic trattorias were the Toscana (1954) and La Dolce Vita, named after the popular film. Trattorias sold pasta in many shapes and sauces, minestrone soup, veal and chicken dishes and Italian wines, especially Chianti and Asti Spumante. Spaghetti became so popular with the younger set that the specialist Spaghetti House opened in 1955 in Goodge Street, appropriately in the London University area where there was a strong demand from hungry, impecunious students. Also increasingly popular were pizzas, which developed from individual caterers into large chains – Pizza Express, with its first restaurant in 1969, and Pizza Hut, an American import, first opened in 1973.[49] Pizzerias aimed at a young, less affluent market than trattorias, serving a tasty, satisfying food based on a cheap ingredient, dough, which could be eaten quickly on the premises, in the street or as a takeaway: it was true 'fast food', the new, trendy equivalent of fish and chips. Another American import, Kentucky Fried Chicken, unusually opened first outside London, in Preston, Lancashire in 1965, in the heartland of the fish-and-chip trade with its long tradition of eating out: as in other fast food chains, the almost invariable accompaniment of the now cheap, mass-produced chicken was 'French Fries'.

These innovations had characteristics in common with the specialised, themed restaurants like the Wimpy Bars, the Bacon and Egg, Grill and Cheese, Chicken Fayre and Seven Stars opened by Lyons in the 1950s: they relied on cutting costs by concentrating on a limited range of cheap, easily cooked products. The same concept was applied to meat, for those who could afford to pay more, by the London Steak Houses, lineal descendants of the Victorian chop-houses. The first opened in Baker Street in 1962, but parking difficulties in central London resulted in a migration to the suburbs: ultimately there were 47, including several in provincial cities.[50] In the Midlands and North a similar development was the 'Berni Inns', created by Frank Berni. These also specialised in steaks but extended to chicken and fish dishes cooked on open grills in the view of customers: they were populist, pub-like in atmosphere with box benches, and usually 'themed' with rural, sporting or other decor; there were ultimately 100 'Bernis', offering a half-pound Argentinian rump steak with chips, peas, roll and butter and a pudding or cheese for 7/6d.[51] Pubs themselves now also joined in the boom in eating out as the great breweries which controlled most licensed houses at last realised that there was profit in selling food as well as drink – one sold the other. The microwave oven made it possible to put on a range of pre-prepared dishes, usually bought in from commercial catering firms, even when described as 'home-made'. Other brewery chains introduced 'Carveries' where customers chose from three or four roast joints with vegetables and sweets included in an 'all-in' moderate price: a Sunday lunch for families and friends in such places was an attractive alternative to home cooking while retaining the traditional meat ritual. Carveries were again usually 'themed' with images of 'Olde England' and rural plenty (for example, the 'Harvester' chain): the pub was often becoming indistinguishable from the restaurant and, in the views of some, returning to what the English inn had once been, before the Victorians turned it into either a beerhouse or a gin palace.

FIGURE 9.2 ◆ *Chinese restaurant, Wardour Street, London, 1945–6. There was not more than a handful of Chinese restaurants in central London at this time: these slightly daring middle-class diners look rather bemused by the unfamiliar food.*

Source: © 2002 Topham Picturepoint.

Even more significant for future trends in eating out was the rapid growth of Indian and Chinese restaurants after the end of rationing in the mid-1950s. In the words of Christopher Driver, they represented 'a collision of food cultures . . . Nothing like it had happened since the medieval world had discovered the spice routes'.[52] The difference was that while in the past spices had been rare, expensive commodities mainly restricted to the wealthier classes, modern transport and marketing systems had now democratised their use to the public at large. Indian cuisine already had a lengthy history in Britain derived from the presence of imperial military and civil officials in that country, and versions of curries had been available in English hotels and clubs since the eighteenth century for their acquired tastes. Queen Victoria had curry prepared by Indian chefs every day in the royal kitchens in case it was requested, though it was usually untouched. Probably the first authentic Indian restaurant was Veeraswamy's in Regent Street, founded in 1925 after a popular Indian café had catered for visitors to the British Empire Exhibition at Wembley. Veeraswamy's was the creation of Major Parmers, ex-Indian army, who had become so addicted that he brought over his former cook. Before and during the Second World War there was still only a handful of Indian restaurants in London and in one or two other towns (there was one in Cambridge, patronised mainly by Indian students), but after Independence in 1947 numbers of Punjabis migrated to work in Britain's undermanned industries like Bradford's woollen mills and Woolf's Rubber Factory at Southall, Middlesex. Restaurants quickly sprang up, at first catering for the young, male immigrants who had few facilities for cooking in their lodgings, but which soon appealed also to the local populations. In the 1955 *Good Food Guide* the Bombay Restaurant in Manchester was noted, where a couple who tasted Indian food for the first time were so excited that they missed their last bus home. The 1961 *Guide* noted four in London – Veeraswamy's the most distinguished (15 curries, 6/6d.–10/6d., tandoori chicken 12/6d.), the Shah (chicken vindaloo 5/0d., prawn patia 4/6d.), the Karachi Restaurant and the Star of India. Numbers increased rapidly in the 1960s with Bangladeshi immigrants, who became the main restaurant entrepreneurs, establishing small chains like the Taj Mahals and the Kohinoors. In 1966 a Report on *The British Eating Out* by the National Catering Inquiry described as a 'fallacy' the view that 'Britons are sometimes said to be rather conservative in our food choice'. Of a random sample of people in seven cities, 51 per cent said that they had visited foreign restaurants – 31 per cent a Chinese one, 8 per cent an Indian and 5 per cent each a French or Italian: the highest Indian proportion, 11 per cent, was in London and Cardiff, while in Liverpool 48 per cent had been to a Chinese restaurant.[53] By

1970 there were an estimated 2,000 Indian restaurants in Britain, having penetrated every city, most small towns, suburbs and even some villages to become a national institution.

It is not diffcult to explain why Indian restaurants sprang into popularity. They offered tasty dishes with a touch of exoticism affordable for the general public for an evening out or a Sunday buffet lunch with half-prices for children. Service was usually quick and courteous: together with its decor, the restaurant evoked images of British hegemony in the days of the Raj, memories for those who had served there during the war and fantasies for those who had never been further east than Skegness. There were dishes for most tastes – Madras curries for the 'machos', mild tandooris, birianis, khorma and tikka sauces: much of the food served was, in fact, adapted to British tastes – masala sauce was not Indian at all, but a British invention – and the tandoor clay oven was commercialised by Gaylord in London in 1964. Dress was as informal as one liked, and the new, popular drink, lager, went better with the food than expensive wine. Indian restaurants were therefore of almost universal appeal, cutting across age, gender and, with the exception of a few upmarket establishments, social class.

Chinese cuisine lacked the familiarity and nostalgic appeal of Indian but its rise to popularity was even more dramatic: by 1970 there were 4,000 Chinese restaurants in Britain, twice as many as Indian. Before 1914 there had been only one in the West End, the Cathay in Piccadilly Circus established in 1908, besides a handful in Limehouse and the Liverpool docklands catering mainly for Chinese sailors, though an article in the *Illustrated London News* in 1920 about one in 'The Chinese Quarter of the East End' stressed that it was clean and welcomed non-Chinese customers.[54] A few more appeared in Central London in the 1930s, including one very successful restaurant owned by Mr Ley-On who drove a Rolls-Royce and had a string of race-horses, one of which, Kai Ming, won the Derby.[55] During the Second World War several more appeared with the patronage of American and Commonwealth forces, but 'the rice bowl revolution' really began from the mid-1950s when many Chinese migrated to Hong Kong, and thence to Britain, after Mao Tse Tung came to power. For many of these, semi-literate and unskilled in British trades, opening a restaurant was an instinctive ambition, and by the late 1950s they could be found in most English towns, soon developing into small chains like the Asiatic, the Rice Bowl and the Good Earth. The cuisine in the earlier restaurants was Hong Kong Cantonese, with typical items such as sweet and sour dishes, sliced beef with oyster sauce, pork dumplings, stir-fried vegetables and chop suey (in fact, invented in San Francisco). But China had many regionally distinct cuisines, of which Pekinese was generally regarded as the superior – roast and barbecued meats and chicken, shark's fin soup, giant prawns, Peking duck, etc. These began to open with the Tung Tsing Restaurant in Golders Green in 1961 and the Richmond Rendezvous in 1963, but both, and other, Chinese cuisines soon became available elsewhere – especially in the China Towns of Soho and Manchester.

English diners had to learn to enjoy Chinese food, but it was a quickly acquired taste. It was tasty and exotic, but not so strongly flavoured as Indian and had a wider appeal for women and children: the ambience was Oriental, if only made of plastic panels, and it was fun to experiment with chopsticks before resuming easier, Western cutlery. Service was usually swift and polite, and the uninformed diner was helped by set menus and 'banquets' which avoided embarrassing choices: on the other hand, a party of the more knowledgeable could compose their own feast from the huge range of dishes on offer. A meal in a Chinese restaurant represented an 'occasion', yet it was cheap enough for a 'businessmen's lunch', a student's alternative to the college canteen, or a more elaborate, celebratory evening out. Restaurants were usually inexpensive, partly because basic ingredients like rice and vegetables were cheap and dearer meats and fish were used only sparingly, partly because most were independently owned and their proprietors, families and kin were prepared to work long hours and to stay open after other eating places were closed. Before the McDonald's revolution it almost seemed that Chinese restaurants and takeaways were taking over British catering.

Notes and references

1 See generally on public opinion about rationing, Ina Zweiniger-Bargielowska, *Austerity in Britain. Rationing, Controls and Consumption, 1939–1955,* Oxford, Oxford University Press, 2000, esp. ch. 2i.

2 ibid., p. 214.

3 Michael Sissons and Philip French (eds), *Age of Austerity*, Hodder and Stoughton, 1963, p. 137.

4 Christina Hardyment, *Slice of Life. The British Way of Eating Since 1945*, BBC Books, 1995, p. 25.

5 Sissons and French (eds), op. cit., p. 40.

6 Marguerite Patten, *Post-War Kitchen*, Oxford, Past Times, 2001, pp. 33–4.

7 Marguerite Patten, *Century of British Cooking*, Grub Street, 1999, p. 161.

8 The Perfect Meal. Gallup Poll surveys conducted on behalf of the *Daily Telegraph*, 1947 and 1962. Quoted by permission of Social Surveys (Gallup Poll) Ltd.

9 Reported in *The Caterer and Hotelkeeper*, 24 Aug. 1946, p. 13.

10 Zweiniger-Bargielowska, op. cit., pp. 168–9.

11 R. J. Hammond, *Food: Studies in Administration and Control (Vol. II)*, HMSO and Longmans, Green and Co., 1956, p. 411.

12 John Burnett, 'The Rise and Decline of School Meals in Britain, 1860–1990', in John Burnett and Derek J. Oddy (eds), *The Origins and Development of Food Policies in Europe*, Leicester, Leicester University Press, 1994, pp. 65–6. In 1945 1,650,000 children, 40% of the school population, had been eating school dinners.

13 Peter Bird, *The First Food Empire. A History of J. Lyons and Co.*, Chichester, West Sussex, Phillimore, 2000, pp. 191–5.

14 T. A. Layton, *Dining Round London*, Noel Carrington, 2nd edn, 1947.

15 Gabor Denes, *The Story of the Imperial. The Life and Times of Torquay's Great Hotel*, Newton Abbot, Devon, David & Charles, 1982, p. 81.

16 Madame Prunier, *La Maison. The History of Prunier's*, Longmans, Green and Co., 1957, pp. 287–9.

17 Peppino Leoni, *I Shall Die On The Carpet*, Leslie Frewin, 1966, p. 182.

18 Mario Gallati, *Mario of the Caprice. The Autobiography of a Restaurateur*, Hutchinson and Co., 1960, p. 97.

19 On changes in social structure, occupations and earnings from 1945, see John Burnett, *A History of the Cost of Living* (1st edn, 1969), Aldershot, Hampshire, Gregg Revivals, 1993 edn, pp. 290ff.

20 *Social Trends* 9, 1979 edn, HMSO, 1978, p. 124.

21 Geoffrey C. Warren (ed.), *The Foods We Eat. A Survey of Meals*, Cassell, 1958, Table, p. 64.

22 ibid., Table, p. 118.

23 Patten, *Post-War Kitchen*, op. cit., p. 73.

24 Edward Bramah, *Tea and Coffee. A Modern View of Three Hundred Years of Tradition*, Hutchinson, 1972, ch. 5, 'The Boom in Coffee Bars', pp. 67ff.

25 Hardyment, op. cit., p. 90. The first of the Spaghetti House chain was opened by Lorenzo Fraquelli in Goodge Street in 1955.

26 Colin Ward and Dennis Hardy, *Goodnight Campers. The History of the British Holiday Camp*, Mansell Publishing Ltd, 1986, p. 75.

27 John K. Walton, *The Blackpool Landlady. A Social History*, Manchester, Manchester University Press, 1978, p. 195.

28 John K. Walton, *The British Seaside. Holidays and Resorts in the Twentieth Century*, Manchester, Manchester University Press, 2000, pp. 64–6.

29 Alan Warde, 'Continuity and Change in British Restaurants, 1951–2001. Evidence from the Good Food Guides', Paper delivered at the Seventh Symposium of the International Commission for Research into European Food History, Alden Biesen, Belgium, October 2001. For an account of Postgate and the early Guides, see Christopher Driver, *The British At Table, 1940–1980*, Chatto &Windus, 1983, pp. 48–53. Driver was Editor of the Guides from 1969 to 1982.

30 Raymond Postgate, *The Good Food Guide, 1961–1962*, Cassell, 1961, pp. 11–12.

31 Frances Dale and John Cradock, *Around Britain with Bon Viveur*, John Lehmann, 1952. (Their tour was in 1951.)

32 J. C. McKenzie, 'Recipes and the Housewife', *Home Economics*, March 1963, pp. 16ff.

33 Hardyment, op. cit., p. 91. Hardyment provides an excellent account of David's life and contribution, pp. 91–6.

34 Elizabeth David, *A Book of Mediterranean Food*, Harmondsworth, Middlesex, Penguin Books, revised edn, 1955, Introduction, p. 9.

35 ibid., pp. 12–13.

36 Hardyment, op. cit., p. 92.

37 *Bon Viveur in London* (Fanny and John Cradock), H. A. and W. L. Pitkin, for the *Daily Telegraph*, n.d. (1953).

38 Driver, op. cit., pp. 55, 163–4, 190.

39 Michael Bateman, *Cooking People*, London, Leslie Frewin for the Cookery Book Club, 1967, p. 231.

40 Patten, *Century of British Cooking*, op. cit., p. 197.

41 Derek Taylor, *Fortune, Fame and Folly. British Hotels and Catering from 1878 to 1978*, IPC Business Press, 1977, p. 11.

42 Mary Cathcart Borer, *The British Hotel through the Ages*, Guildford and London, Lutterworth Press, 1972, pp. 232–3, 250. Rosa Lewis, who owned the Cavendish through two world wars, died in 1952: the old hotel was demolished in 1963.

43 Alison Leach (ed.), *The Savoy Food and Drink Book*, Pyramid Books, 1988, p. 26.

44 Raymond Postgate, *The Good Food Guide, 1969–1970*, Revised edn, by Christopher Driver, Consumers' Association and Hodder & Stoughton, 1970, London section, p. 28.

45 Gabor Denes, op. cit., pp. 90–8. This book includes many of the gastronomic menus of the 1960s.

46 *The Good Food Guide, 1961–1962*, op. cit., pp. 11–15.

47 *The Good Food Guide, 1969–1970*, op. cit., pp. viii–xi.

48 Gregory Houston Bowden, *British Gastronomy. The Rise of Great Restaurants*, Chatto & Windus, 1975, pp. 83ff.

49 Hardyment, op. cit., pp. 87ff.

50 Bird, op. cit., pp. 196–7.

51 Taylor, op. cit., p. 12. Frank Berni died in 2000. In 1990 the chain was sold to Whitbreads, who renamed it 'Beefeater Inns'.

52 Driver, op. cit., p. 73.

53 *The British Eating Out*. A Report from Britain's National Catering Inquiry, sponsored by Smethursts Foods Ltd, 1966, Table, p. 8.

54 Moira Johnston (ed.), *London Eats Out. 500 Years of Capital Dining*, Philip Wilson and Museum of London, 1999, p. 99.

55 Bowden, op. cit., p. 148.

CHAPTER 10

· · · · · · · · · · · · · · · ·

A revolution at table, 1970–2000

The way we eat out now

One of the most striking changes in recent times has been an explosion of interest in all matters to do with food, especially in cookery both in and outside the home. To turn the pages of weekend newspapers, glance at the lists of best-sellers in bookshops or switch on the television to see cookery programmes competing for top viewing-time with soap operas one might conclude that eating is a principal obsession of our consumer society. Food has become part of a huge entertainments industry in which superstar chefs perform feats of dexterity, critics vie with each other in admiration or vituperation about memorably good or awful meals, while lavishly illustrated books and magazines evoke fantasies in a dream-world of gastronomic delights. In response to a seemingly insatiable appetite, a record 1,170 food and drink-related books were published in the United Kingdom in 2001.[1]

This escalation of interest in food, now widely diffused across classes, regions, ages and genders, grew steadily after the end of rationing in the mid-1950s, but much more strongly from the 1970s. To acknowledge that one took pleasure in food, was acquainted with notable restaurants, exotic dishes and the varieties of wines became fashionable requirements as the relics of Victorian reticence about matters gustatory were replaced by a vocabulary of appreciation, part of the wider change in modern society in which pleasure is no longer viewed as faintly immoral indulgence. In the past, consumption of food and drink outside the confines of the home had been mainly associated with men, either at work or at leisure in their pubs and clubs: now, social eating became more important, a shared experience between men and women and, often, between adults and children. While an interpenetration of commercial and domestic catering brought a great variety of new, ready-made meals into the home, restaurants differentiated themselves by upgrading quality and service and inventing original combinations of ingredients and flavours not available in the supermarket. Consequently, to invite guests out for a meal became widely acceptable: as Reay Tannahill remarks, until quite recently it would have been regarded either as a reflection on the hostess's cooking or her unwillingness to exert herself.[2]

The choice of venue ranges from the luxury hotel or restaurant which confers status and savoir-faire on the diner (Tell me *where* you eat and I will tell you what you are), down to the Sunday lunch in a pub carvery or Indian buffet or the family outing to a burger bar or pizza house: all provide convenience, sociability and a sense of occasion. In particular, people's knowledge of foreign foods has expanded greatly. Already in 1976 pizzas were known to eight out of ten people, chow mein, sweet and sour pork and ravioli to seven, though chilli con carne had then reached only four people, moussaka and Wiener schnitzel three.[3] A more recent survey between 1994 and 1996 investigated the numbers of people who had eaten in any kind of commercial establishment at least once during the year: 52 per cent had done so in a café or teashop, 49 per cent in a burger or other fast food restaurant and the same proportion in a pub with bar food, 41 per cent in a pizza house, 41 per cent in a pub restaurant, 33 per cent in an Indian and 29 per cent in a Chinese or Thai restaurant.[4] In view of such numbers, eating in more than 300,000 catering outlets, it is difficult to accept the judgement of Roy Ackerman that 'Eating out is not a meaningful part of our culture . . . the mass of people in Britain appears to be indifferent to quality food in any shape or form.'[5]

It might be expected that the increased interest in food would be reflected in an increased extent of eating out, but this has not been the case. The average number of meals eaten outside the home per person has hovered around three per week, and is slightly lower now than in the 1980s (see Table 10.1).

TABLE 10.1 ◆ *Average number of meals eaten out per person per week,*
1976–1996

	Midday meals	Other meals	Total
1976	1.72	1.25	2.97
1986	1.73	1.64	3.37
1995	1.77	1.17	2.94
1996	1.73	1.19	2.92

Note: Does not include meals eaten out, but from home supplies
Source: *National Food Survey, Annual Report*, The Stationery Office, 1996, p. 13.

The main reason for the decline is a fall in the number of meals eaten at
the workplace as manufacturing industry declined and the provision of
works canteens was reduced; additionally, school meals have also fallen
since the ending of compulsory local authority provision in 1980.[6] More
broadly, the extent of recreational eating has always been influenced by
the general state of the economy, which since the 1970s has experienced
an oil crisis, a three-day week, the return of high levels of unemployment, rapid price inflation and, most recently, sharp falls in the stock
market. A result has been a change in the pattern of consumption, with
fewer people eating in subsidised factory and school canteens, but more
in the purely commercial sectors. In 1975 meals at work were 40 per cent
of all eating-out occasions: by 1984 they had fallen to 25 per cent, while
meals in the commercial sector grew from 49 per cent to 63 per cent and
expenditure on them to 85 per cent of all spending on meals out.[7]

The average of three meals out a week is only a general indicator,
within which there are wide variations. In 1996/7 more meals were eaten
out in the north-west of England, followed closely by London and the
south-east: the fewest were eaten in the south-west, indicating that the
frequency of eating out is related to the degree of urbanisation and the
number of catering facilities. But despite the 'democratisation' of places
of refreshment and the spread of disposable earnings to broader bands of
the population, income still emerges as the main determinant of eating
out. In 1996/7 socio-economic Group A (weekly income of head of household £595+) ate 5.05 meals out a week, twice as many as Group D (£150
a week) with 2.46; old age pensioners ate the fewest at 1.42. Amongst
highest earners half the meals eaten out were at times other than
lunchtime, representing more recreational eating. It is also evident that

TABLE 10.2 ◆ *Numbers of meals eaten in commercial establishments, 1998/9 (millions)*

Pubs	345 (restaurants 248, bar meals 97)
Fish-and-chip shops	302
Burger houses	247
Chinese takeaways	245
Pizza places	159
Other restaurants	124
Cafés, Coffee shops	122
Indian takeaways	108
Hotels	58
In-store catering	57
Indian (on premises)	54
Chinese (on premises)	45
Fried Chicken outlets	42
Italian restaurants	41
Motorway services	17

Notes
1. The statistics relate to those classified as 'meals', not including snacks or sandwiches.
2. The statistics do not include subsidised meals in works or school canteens, or in public institutions, e.g. hospitals.
3. The statistics include takeaways since these are provided, and may be eaten, outside the home.
Source: Taylor Nelson Sofres, MealTrak – Out of Home, 364/950, 1999.

the habit is most strongly established among younger age groups – by age the most frequent eaters-out are those under 25 (3.81 meals a week), falling steadily to only 1.53 for those over 65.[8] The places where people eat show both the survival of traditional catering and the strong growth of ethnic restaurants and fast food outlets: Table 10.2 shows all the main sectors which served commercial meals in the year March 1998–February 1999 (a total of 2,088 million meals).

The numbers given in Table 10.2 represent a huge catering industry which had grown to employ to 1.26 million in the commercial sector and 1.12 million in institutional catering by 1990.[9] Inevitably, the consumer pays for these services – for the ingredients, the cooking and waiting, and the overheads and profits of the establishment – and the proportion of household food expenditure on meals out has now risen to almost one-third (Table 10.3). However, this growth has to be seen against a large fall in the proportion of spending on food generally. In the past, food was much the largest item in all household budgets, taking an average of more

TABLE 10.3 ◆ *Weekly household expenditure on all food and the proportion on food eaten outside the home, 1959–1995 (£s)*

Year		All food	Food eaten out	% on food eaten out
1959	Average	£5.01	£0.48	9.6
	Wealthiest group	£9.50	£2.70	28.4
1975	Average	£13.50	£1.85	13.7
	Wealthiest group	£22.80	£4.99	21.9
1995	Average	£50.43	£14.92	29.6
	Wealthiest group	£89.36	£33.70	37.1

Source: *Family Expenditure Survey*, 1957–9 and 1975, *Family Spending*, 1994–5, The Stationery Office.

than 30 per cent in the 1950s. As real incomes rose and household size declined, food absorbed an ever-smaller share – 22.4 per cent in 1975, 18.4 per cent in 1985 and 17 per cent in 1998; by then leisure and transport each took the same proportion of 17 per cent, closely followed by housing at 16 per cent.[10]

Before the 1970s eating out, except for 'necessity' eating associated with work, was a rare experience for the majority of the population despite the advances in standards of living. This became a matter of concern to the catering industry, and from 1965 onwards a series of National Catering Inquiries was sponsored by Smethursts Foods under the direction of Professor John Fuller. The first Report on *The British Eating Out* (1966) showed how uncommon the habit was at this time: only 3 per cent of people ate out for pleasure more than once a week and 34 per cent only once every few weeks,[11] usually for a special event such as a wedding, birthday or other celebration. On the other hand, 30,000 industrial canteens served 2,300 million meals a year (44 million a week), representing most people's experience of eating outside the home. Two-thirds of those interviewed said that they would like to eat out for pleasure more often, but gave their reasons for not doing so as, in order, cost (the average price for a restaurant meal was 13/2d. compared with 2/10d. for a canteen meal), family ties, dislike of the cooking and too great distance from home; their reasons for choosing a particular restaurant, also in order, were quality of the cooking, cleanliness and quick service. A Supplementary Report suggested that more people could afford to eat out more often, but did not give it priority over other entertainments such as the pub, the cinema, dancing or bingo. Eating out was more often the woman's choice than the man's, since it released her from kitchen tasks, but it was also said that going out for a meal was regarded as only part of an evening's entertainment: 'We never eat out just on its own – this wouldn't be good enough for the evening.' And when people did eat out they much preferred to do so in the company of friends for variety and conversation. A married couple said that on their own 'We wouldn't know what to talk about'.[12]

Thirty years on, the way we eat now has been reshaped by a series of social changes. A fundamental shift has taken place in household forma-tion towards smaller size, so that in 1999 the average household con-tained only 2.4 people – half what it was in 1900. In fact, 31 per cent of households now consist of only one person, and another 34 per cent of two. Meals which were formerly geared to a large number of mouths to be fed, especially in poorer families, are now adapted more to individual tastes, and where wives are also earners (72 per cent of women are now economically active) to eat out or buy takeaways is more convenient than cooking for one or two people. It has also been argued that a family meal in a restaurant for parents and children, as well as representing a treat, helps to promote family solidarity in a period when this is under threat.[13] Despite supposedly conservative tastes, many children have learned to enjoy once unfamiliar foods, not only burgers, pizzas and fried chicken, but also Chinese and Indian dishes, increasingly available in restaurants, ethnic food shops and as prepared meals in supermarkets.

An important influence on eating out is the increasing pressure on time experienced by many people. Working hours in Britain have not fallen significantly in recent years, and at an average of 45.7 hours a week for men and 40.7 for women in full-time work, are said to be the longest in any European country. To these have to be added the longer journeys to work as commuting from greater distances has become common, one response to which has been the growth of flexitime working. The former practice of a one-hour lunch break has often given way to a sandwich at the desk, and even over a restaurant meal people are less inclined to linger than formerly. Earning and leisure are major, interdependent prior-ities in modern lifestyles. Many leisure activities involve eating out, such as day visits to sporting events, tourist attractions and country houses, most of which provide catering facilities: in 1998 5.9 billion day leisure visits were recorded in Britain, an average of around 100 per person per year.[14] This is a huge expansion of the long-established habit of day excursions, now facilitated by the almost universal ownership of cars. But an even greater change has been the growth of holidays due to greater disposable incomes and employees' entitlement to up to four weeks of paid leave a year. In 1998 56 million holidays (defined as four or more nights) were taken in Britain, a third more than in 1971, and for the first time more were taken abroad (29 million) than at home (27 million). The most popular foreign destinations were, in order, Spain, France, the United States, Greece and Italy;[15] as recently as 1971 only 36 per cent of Britons had had a foreign holiday at some time. Holidays abroad have undoubtedly broadened British tastes: even though tourist hotels often adopt 'international' menus, regional dishes are usually available in restaurants and enjoyed as one of the pleasures of foreign travel.

These social changes have greatly influenced the ways we live and eat now. Lives are more fluid and mobile, relationships more stressful than when seemingly united families ate three cooked meals a day at regular times, at least two of which were at home. In 1958 59 per cent of men and 39 per cent of women ate a cooked breakfast: for the main meal of the day, midday 'dinner', six out of ten men returned home for a meat course followed by a pudding, while on Sunday the traditional roast and vegetables was enjoyed by 59 per cent of all families. The last meal of the day, described as 'tea', was eaten between 5 and 6 pm and was usually uncooked; only in the upper classes, and mainly in the south-east of England, was a later, cooked 'dinner' eaten.[16] Thirty years on, in 1988, much had changed, when Taylor Nelson Research investigated current food habits. They identified the main trends as a move away from formal meals towards snacks; increased reliance on convenience foods; greater demands for variety; and increased interest in the relationship between food and health.[17] Breakfast was now the meal most frequently eaten at home (29 per cent of all eating occasions), though its composition had greatly changed towards cereals, toast, fruit and yoghurt, and fried food only appeared at 9 per cent of breakfasts. Even so, many people left home without eating any solid food. A survey by Kellogg's found that 17 per cent of the population, representing nine million people, had either nothing at all or only a drink at this time: they included 500,000 children under 12 and a million teenagers.[18] The Taylor Nelson study also showed that the former primacy of the midday meal was much in decline. At

three-quarters of these meals at home only one or two people were present and formality had given way to a snack of canned soup, sandwiches,
pâté, cheese and the like: speed and convenience were the main criteria.
Another former British institution, 'tea', has also shrunk in importance,
and is now largely confined to the elderly and young children. The
evening meal is now the principal meal of the day and eaten later, usually
around 6.30–7.0 pm. There is generally something cooked – meat, poultry, pasta, pizza or a rice dish – often ready-made and suitable for the
microwave, while the takeaway comes into its own at this time. In summary, what has occurred is a fragmentation of the traditional pattern of
main meals towards lighter, more frequent snacking and 'grazing': it is
estimated that British people eat 6.5 times a day, in smaller amounts but
more frequently.[19] There is now a polarisation of meal times towards the
beginning and the end of the day, with lunch and tea increasingly
replaced by snacks, which account for 40 per cent of all in-home eating
occasions. In these respects Britain has been following trends set in the
United States, and while it would be premature to speak of the death of
the domestic meal, the occasions when several people sit together for a
meal are becoming ever fewer in what Roy Strong has described as 'the
post-table society'.[20] The dining-room – when it is still provided in
modern house design – has often become redundant as such, replaced by
an enlarged kitchen as the centre of social activity.[21]

All these changes in domestic life have impacted on eating out.
People who skimp or skip breakfast and are faced with long travelling
times feel the need for a mid-morning snack as well as something more
at lunchtime, while later home-coming and the later evening meal create
a gap in mid-afternoon. Neither women nor men are willing to spend
hours in cooking after a day's work, while traditional meals are in any
case inappropriate for small households. To eat out avoids labour and
relieves the monotony of too many packaged meals, and given the sufficient incomes which many now enjoy it is no longer a rare celebration
but a normal expectation of a leisure society. It may well be that with the
decline in formality in the home sociability has been removed to the
restaurant, representing a lingering desire for a ritualised occasion where
one is greeted, waited upon and served with food of one's choice, a
'restorative' experience which not only satisfies the appetite but also con-
duces to well-being and self-esteem.

Continuity: the enduring characteristics of eating out

The restaurant is the tank in the warfare of cookery because it has always been a major instrument in smashing old eating habits ... The competition of restaurants has been decisive in introducing new tastes.[22]

If so, it was an old, slow-moving vehicle which encountered heavy opposition. Restaurants, for good reason, generally respond to existing tastes rather than attempt to create new ones, and except in sophisticated circles where stylish innovations may become fashionable, competition is usually in terms of the cost, quality and service of long-established food preferences. Expectations have certainly risen somewhat since the 1960s when Derek Cooper's *Bad Food Guide* denounced caterers for serving uneatable meals and customers for meekly accepting them. He believed that there was an 'almost universal indifference' to good food in Britain, that customers 'don't mind what is put before them', and that bad food was encountered at all social levels. Cooper cited the experience of an American visitor who was entertained to lunch by a peer in a London club where he was regaled with oxtail soup, a tiny, burnt lamb chop with cabbage, carrots and boiled potatoes, followed by rice pudding: 'Nobody can seriously eat like this – I mean, it must be a kind of hoax?' Cooper later explained to him that it was exactly the kind of food the peer would have been served at his public school, and that 'as the food isn't very nice, there's no temptation to fall into a state of disgrace by actually enjoying it'. Near the other end of the social spectrum, Sunday lunch at Butlin's Holiday Camp at Clacton consisted of 'Romany Soup' (from a packet), roast beef with cabbage, carrots, roast and boiled potatoes, and (tinned) peaches and cream, while at seaside cafés throughout the land menus had remained 'uncannily the same' for the last forty years. One example from Hornsea must stand for the many (reproduced below).

SET LUNCH

Soup or Fruit Juice   :   Roast beef and 2 veg.

Fruit Pie and Custard   :   Cup of Tea. 6/0d.

OR

Bacon, egg and tomatoes	4/0d.
Baked beans and chips	2/6d.
Sausage and chips	4/0d.
Chicken and chips	5/0d.
Poached egg on toast	2/9d.
Steak and kidney pie, peas and chips	3/6d.
Cod and chips	3/6d.
Plaice and chips	5/0d.
Halibut and chips	5/6d.

All dishes included tea, bread and butter. Yet, continued Cooper, 'the food critics tell us that a revolution is sweeping across the country, and that it's all scampi now, and pâté and melon'.[23]

His criticisms may have contributed to a growing national concern about the state of British catering at this time and the initiation of a series of investigations directed by Professor John Fuller. The first Report on *The British Eating Out* (1966) commented about British tastes:

> One could argue endlessly about what people should eat, and nowadays considerable effort is expended in persuading them to try new kinds of food. But facts are inescapable, and tend to support the view that by and large people are still conservative in their food choice. National food habits take generations to establish, and a whole pattern of food manufacture and supply has been built on what generations of people have decided is good for them and what is within their financial reach.[24]

This conservatism was demonstrated by people's choices of their favourite restaurant menu, as Table 10.4 indicates.

This was all very traditional and, perhaps, predictable only a decade after the end of rationing: the British love of meat, soup and fruit pie was very evident, the dislike of fish – at least, as part of a restaurant menu – more surprising. Only in London was there some indication of more sophisticated tastes: here, soup fell in popularity while melon and hors

TABLE 10.4 ◆ *Favourite restaurant choices, 1966 (percentages)*

Course	Preferred dish	Per cent
First	Soup	65
	Hors d'oeuvres	9
	Melon	6
	Pâté	6
	Shellfish	5
Main	Meat	63
	Mixed grill	10
	Poultry	9
	Fish	1
Vegetables	Potatoes	66
	Peas	49
	Brussels sprouts	21
	Green beans	13
	Broccoli	6
	Asparagus	5
Dessert (in order of preference)	Fruit salad	*
	Fruit pie or tart	
	Cheese and biscuits	
	Ice cream	
	Fresh fruit	

* Not stated.
Source: Adapted from *The British Eating Out*, 1966.

d'oeuvres increased substantially, and for the main course fish or shell-fish rose to 8 per cent. A Supplementary Report the following year also showed that social class was a major influence on choice: within the same priced menu of 12/6d. the better-off groups chose less soup but more melon, much more chicken or duck, and preferred to end their meal with cheese rather than a sweet dessert.[25]

At various times over the next thirty years further surveys showed that, with few exceptions, British tastes remained stubbornly attached to long-established favourites. In 1973 Gallup Poll again asked a cross-section of people to select their favourite menu if price was no object, as they had first done in the dark days of 1947. The menu is reproduced below.

THE PERFECT MEAL, 1947 AND 1973

1947	1973
Sherry	Sherry
Tomato soup	Tomato soup
Sole	Prawn cocktail
Roast chicken	Steak
Roast potatoes, peas and sprouts	Roast or chipped potatoes, peas, sprouts, mushrooms
Trifle and cream	Trifle or Apple pie and cream
Cheese and biscuits	Cheese and biscuits
Coffee	Coffee
Red or white wine	Liqueurs or Brandy
	Red or white wine

A quarter of a century of revolutionary social change and rise in the standard of living had apparently resulted only in the substitution of prawns for sole and steak for chicken, by 1973 so commonplace as to have fallen in popularity. Alcoholic drinks during and after the meal were more often requested, but neither luxury foods nor the now increasingly common Indian or Chinese dishes appeared on the list.[26]

Sixteen years later, in 1989, some new trends were evident. The survey of the year now distinguished between overall preferences and those of customers in pub and Continental restaurants.[27] These choices are reproduced below.

BRITONS' TOP THREE FAVOURITE LUNCH FOODS, 1989 (IN ORDER)

Overall	Pub restaurants	Continental restaurants
Soup	Soup	Soup
Prawn cocktail	Prawn cocktail	Garlic mushrooms
Garlic mushrooms	Garlic mushrooms	Seafood or Melon
———	———	———
Fish	Steak	Pasta
Hamburgers	Pies	Pizza
Steak	Fish	Steak
Chips, salad	Chips, salad	Chips, salad
———	———	———
Ice cream	Ice cream	Ice cream
Apple pie	Gateaux	Gateaux
Gateaux	Fresh fruit	Sponge puddings [!]

Some new tastes were apparent here. What had been trendy foods in the 1970s – seafood, garlic mushrooms, side salads and gateaux (? Black Forest) had now passed into mass consumption, though had not displaced the soup (minestrone rather than tomato), the steak and chips, fish and chips and the ice cream. For restaurant critics the monotony of plebeian tastes was saddening, but as *The Caterer and Hotelkeeper* well understood, these were the popular dishes which could be easily prepared, often from ready-made materials, and marketed at affordable prices. Dishes which were only rarely requested, and which required more skilled cooking, were not usually found on such menus. In 2000 the *Radio Times* invited readers to nominate their ten favourite dishes from a list of 30, which included some more recent additions such as paella, chicken tikka, moussaka and tiramisu. Readers' choices were, in order: 1. Roast beef, 2. Apple pie, 3. Shepherd's pie, 4. Rhubarb crumble, 5. Fish pie, 6. Fried plaice and chips, 7. Spaghetti Bolognese, 8. Liver and bacon, 9. Salmon en croute, 10. Beef Wellington.[28] The English love of roast beef and various kinds of pie was as firmly ingrained as ever.

Familiarity was also a leading characteristic of the places where people chose to eat. For many decades the English public house had supplied little more than beer and spirits, the only food cheese and pickled onions to stimulate thirst. Attempts to revive the old traditions of the English inn by providing meals and leisure facilities which have been previously described – the 'reformed public house movement' of the late nineteenth century and the experiments of liquor control during the First World War – had few lasting effects, nor had the hopes in 1945 of a renaissance of family-friendly places of entertainment. At long last, these hopes have been in part realised since the 1970s, mainly by large brewery companies such as Bass and Whitbread which have transformed some of their tied houses into chains of family restaurants under such names as 'Beefeater', 'Harvester' and 'Vintage Inns'. So successful has this been that in 1999 pubs served 345.5 million meals (not including snacks), one in six of all commercial meals eaten out: they now represent the largest sector of the catering trade, well ahead of burger houses and three times as many as Chinese and Indian restaurants combined.[29] Their attractions are familiarity and informality, menus closely geared to popular choices, and low prices made possible by bulk purchase and the profits on drinks. 'We are giving the people what they want,' says Jeremy

FIGURE 10.1 ◆ *The true taste of Britain? A Toby Carvery, illustrating the enduring commitment of many English diners to traditional roasts and unadorned vegetables.*

Source: Courtesy of Mitchells & Butlers, Plc.

Spencer, who launched 'All Bar One': 'The principle of our branded chains, and why they are so successful, is that they have a formula, a decor, menu and style which people like.'[30] It is easy for critics to deride the formula – the themed decor of 'Olde England' with artificial log fires, agricultural implements and antique sporting equipment, the picture menus, salad cart and chirpily programmed waitresses, and Jonathan Meades hugely enjoyed his description (if not the food) of a 'Harvester', 'frequented by the unreconstructed, non-aspirational working class and by the retired... If you are keen to experience typical British food in 2000, then it is Harvester you should try rather than some effete joint with a skilled chef, proper ingredients and a foreign commitment to excellence.'[31] Of course, there is no shortage of bad pub food – of blackboards announcing 'home-made' steak and kidney pie which consists of tasteless mince with a separate, cardboard-like crust, and moussaka or lasagne direct from the supermarket – but there is currently a revival of real cooking from fresh, locally sourced materials encouraged by the publication of *The Good Pub Guide*. A recent innovation is the stylish 'gastropub' like 'The Eagle' in London, where meat for the steak sandwich is marinated overnight in red wine, olive oil, chillies, garlic and onion. Such consideration may not be suitable for the mass market, or even desired, but it has been persuasively argued that 'the battle for wholesome eating out at affordable prices must take place in the pub – the cultural parallel of Europe's cafés and bistros, and the environment best suited to Britain's incipient restaurant habit outside the capital'.[32]

Another long-established British institution, the fish-and-chip shop, has also survived despite sharp rises in fish prices and the strong competition of other fast foods. Described by Egon Ronay as 'Our most distinctive contribution to world cuisine',[33] in 1999 fish-and-chip shops sold 302 million meals, second only to pubs and around one in six of all meals out:[34] one in every ten adults visits a shop at least once a week.[35] This is in spite of a large fall in the number of shops from their peak of around 35,000 in 1927 to 8,600 today, though their unit size and turnover is considerably larger than it was then. The modern, hygienic shop has changed its back-street image, a trend initiated by Harry Ramsden who began selling from a hut in Guiseley, near Leeds, in 1928 but shortly opened a purpose-built restaurant with chandeliers, wall-to-wall carpeting and seating for 200.[36] Chains such as his are however still unusual in a trade characterised by independent proprietors. They have done something to dispel public concerns about the fat content of their products by increased use of vegetable oils for frying instead of dripping, and to promote fish as a healthy food providing significant quantities of proteins and vitamins as well as energy.[37] Fish and chips are no longer cheap food, and some shops have even moved into more expensive species for upmarket tastes such as red snapper, hoki, sea bass and shark – one London shop includes grilled lobster, caviar with blinis and swordfish with salsa.[38] Nevertheless, the original article apparently has devotees across the social classes, enjoyed by Tony Blair and John Major, stars like Liza

Minnelli, Mel Gibson and Halle Berry, while the late Queen Mother was known to dispatch a footman for an occasional fish and chip supper.

Two other long-established institutions, works and school canteens, have continued at rather reduced levels. In the years after the Second World War meals in the workplace were for many people the principal occasions for eating out; in the 1950s there were at least 25,000 'canteens' (for factory workers), 'restaurants' (for clerical staff) and 'dining-rooms' (for directors) provided and subsidised by employers, and still 21,000 in 1973. A *Report on the British Eating Out at Work* that year believed that 'the sandwich syndrome' (the traditional packed lunch from home) was declining except among older workers, and that most preferred a cooked two- or even three-course meal. Two-thirds of workers then had access to a canteen, of which about half used it regularly; of the other half, 56 per cent brought a packed lunch, 33 per cent went home and the remainder went to a pub or café. Most canteen users regarded it as their main meal of the day, choosing a substantial dish such as a roast, fish and chips, meat pies or sausages, though there was some sign of a trend towards a lighter meal, salads being chosen by 15 per cent. It was also noted that 'the days of Spotted Dick and Bread Pudding are fast disappearing'.[39] Since then, economic recessions, the decline in manufacturing industry and periodic high unemployment levels have reduced the scale of canteen provision, though in 1993 around 18,000 still remained. A survey in 1990 found only 15 per cent of the working population using a staff cafeteria daily, 55 per cent having a packed lunch and only 14 per cent of men going home, far fewer than in past times.[40] The heaviest users of canteens were the 16–24 age group, but their tastes have evidently shifted away from the hearty meals of the past, only 7 per cent now nominating roasts as their favourite meal, these having been replaced by pasta, jacket potatoes, salads and snacks.[41]

Many firms which are too small to operate their own staff restaurants have found a convenient alternative perquisite for their employees by the issue of free Luncheon Vouchers exchangeable at many catering outlets. They began in 1954 as rationing ended and there was uncertainty about the effects of a free market on the price of food for workers. The scheme has now expanded greatly to all categories of employees, who receive booklets of vouchers exchangeable at 33,000 places, including restaurants, cafés, sandwich bars and all the major supermarkets: vouchers are used by more than 100,000 people a month, giving them the choice of a regular snack or an occasional full meal.[42]

The feeding of children in school has changed radically since the Education Act 1944 made the provision of school meals a compulsory duty of local education authorities, and laid down minimum nutritional standards. First, free school milk for secondary school pupils was withdrawn in 1968, then in 1971 for primary schoolchildren under the age of 7: the argument was that this supplement was no longer necessary on nutritional grounds, and that there was a declining take-up of the service. School meals, however, continued to rise to a peak of 70 per cent of all pupils in 1975 until in 1980 the controversial Education Act made their provision optional except for the small minority who received free meals: it also allowed authorities to determine the form, content and price of meals. The Act proceeded from the Thatcherite philosophy of reducing government control and returning autonomy and choice to the consumer, but it also recognised that the eating habits of children were turning away from the traditional two-course school dinner towards more varied patterns. The senior Catering Adviser to the Department of Education commented: 'It could truly be said that the school meals service changed almost overnight from a social service to a quasi-commercial catering operation.'[43]

A few local authorities have discontinued a service except for children of parents receiving Income Support, who are still entitled to free meals. In 1997 these numbered 15 per cent while 27 per cent of children paid a subsidised price averaging £1.28 per meal:[44] the total take-up has, therefore, fallen substantially to 42 per cent of pupils. Most authorities now operate a choice, varying from a simple, two-course set menu to a cafeteria system with each item separately priced. Under this there can be little control of what children eat, and many local authorities have responded to nutritional concerns by introducing 'healthy eating' programmes which attempt to steer demand towards desirable foods. This has taken the form of salad bars, jacket potatoes, wholemeal breads and fresh fruit with selective pricing in which 'star' items are costed preferentially. There is, of course, no control over the 58 per cent of pupils who do not take school meals, most of whom bring a lunch box from home or, in the case of some senior pupils, eat out at lunch time in cafés, takeaways and fast food shops.

Change: a new dawn in eating out?

So far we have described some of the enduring aspects of eating out which still command popular appeal despite the social transformations of modern times. We must now sketch the outlines of recent changes, a complex picture which has many dimensions and no single focus. Even to ask a seemingly straightforward question – whether standards of catering have improved or declined – is to be met by a variety of opinions and prejudices, and no consensus about what constitutes a 'good meal'. According to an outside view, the Finnair guide to restaurants, London since the late 1980s has become 'the restaurant capital of the world, famous for its culinary diversity and worldwide cuisines'.[45] In 1997 the *Good Food Guide*, so often critical of standards in the past, believed that 'there has never been a more exciting time to eat out...unprecedented variety of food, of price, ambience, location and lots more', while for Kit Chapman the new dawn of gastronomy broke in 1987, 'the marvellous year' when Marco Pierre White, Simon Hopkinson and Rowleigh Leigh opened their restaurants.[46] Yet the acerbic critic, Michael Winner, is of the opinion that English cooking has not improved at all since 'the golden period of the 1950s, when food tasted like what it was meant to be, every vegetable and meat had not been over-purified, chemicalised and messed about... I think we should look back rather than forward.'[47]

Apart from this last, such views have, perhaps, little to do with the ways that most people eat out today. Different places offer different things to the customer in terms of cuisine and, most importantly, price, and in a recent survey most people expected to pay less than £10 for an everyday meal, up to £40 for a special occasion. The reasons given for choosing a particular restaurant were, in order, the quality of the food, value for money, range of the menu, attentiveness of the service, overall atmosphere, the welcoming of children and convenience of the location, of which the first two were much the most important.[48] Social class, or rather wealth, is still a principal determinant of where one eats, even in a society which is somewhat more egalitarian than formerly, and where, as Christopher Driver commented, 'At student level, in university cities, the unwaged punk and the heir to a Georgian mansion are equal before the kebab and the biriani.'[49] How far such equality extends up the age/prosperity scale is doubtful, and for the glitterati where you eat, and are seen, may be more important in defining status than what you eat. The three million or so people described as 'the Affluentials', with average incomes of £91,700 a year, spend £10,000 on leisure activities, including three holidays and £1,800 a year on other dining out. Anthony Worrall Thompson has observed that the yuppy extravagance of the 1980s has now given way to more careful spending: 'When I sold Ménage à Trois in 1988 the average cheque per head was £44. Now [2001] it is £30.'[50] This is a far cry from the six Barclays investment bankers who ran up a bill of £44,000 for wine at Gordon Ramsay's Petrus restaurant (they were not charged for the food).[51] The old aristocracy who once patronised the 'best' hotels and restaurants have been largely replaced by a meritocracy of financiers, fashion gurus, pop stars and media 'celebrities': in the words of Roy Strong, 'Class snobbery and social division are still firmly in place, but tempered by the possibility of Everyman gaining admittance ... the shared table continues to exert its power as an index of social aspiration, privilege and acceptance.'[52]

The simple division between luxury and everyday eating out has been elaborated by Joanne Finkelstein into a typology of restaurants representing a hierarchy of wealth and fashionability. At the summit are places of great renown chosen for a 'fête spéciale', which establishes the diner as cultured and civilised. These are 'spectacular' on account of their luxurious or dramatic decor, their famous cuisine and international reputation. The 'bistro mondain' is smaller in scale but also fashionable for its gourmet cuisine, usually associated with a celebrity chef; it may merge with the 'parodic' restaurant which deliberately sets out to amuse by its ambience and eclectic style of menu, a reconstruction of reality into an emotional experience. Below these are the essentially 'convenience' restaurants for a casual meal, including cafés, ethnic restaurants and fast food places. She argues that these different places convey different 'meanings' – the 'spectacular' restaurant denotes power, affluence and fashionability, the bistro suggests romance, the 'parodic' is for fun and McDonald's is for family unity. But she further suggests that free choice in any of these types is an illusion: the diner is controlled by the restaurant, which transforms expectations into commodities like other consumer goods, mediated by a financial transaction.[53]

Luxury or elite restaurants – Finkelstein's first two categories – represent only a very small proportion of all catering establishments. Of the

2,088 million meals served in commercial premises in 1999, restaurants other than ethnic provided 124 million and hotels 57.6 million, together well under one in ten of all meals even in the unlikely event that all would qualify for the top categories; the most famous places, whose names and chefs were internationally renowned, numbered only two or three score. Here, in the 1970s, French 'haute cuisine' derived from Escoffier was still the dominant style, but outside London only a handful attained an outstanding reputation (exceptions included the Roux brothers at Bray-on-Thames, Miller Howe on Lake Windermere and the Box Tree Cottage at Ilkley). Soon after this time, however, classic French cooking began to be challenged by '*nouvelle cuisine*', the origins of which are traced to Henri Gault and Christian Millau, French food writers who supposedly coined the term in 1973.[54] It began as a reaction against Escoffier's 'partie' system in which the compilation of a dish was divided between a brigade of specialist chefs: it could produce very high quality in each component, but it came to be seen as too regimented and offering little scope for individual creativity. In *nouvelle cuisine* the complete dish, or 'plate', including the meat, poultry or fish together with the vegetables and sauces, is assembled in the kitchen by, ideally, one chef: the waiter merely delivers it to the table. It therefore gives the chef much more scope for originality and invention, elevating him to an artist and by adroit image creation and media publicity, the status of a superstar.[55] As *nouvelle cuisine* spread to lower strata of the catering trade in the 1980s, it was easy to deride some of the offerings as 'A child's portion served to a man', and 'Not enough on your plate and too much on your bill', but properly employed it stood for sound principles – an accent on purity, freshness and natural ingredients, authentic flavours not masked by heavy, flour-based sauces: it also stood for the importance of the visual, aesthetic appearance of the 'plate', very suitable for colour photography in cookery books and magazines. In the hands of Anton Mosimann at the Dorchester, Raymond Blanc at Le Manoir aux Quat' Saisons or Anton Edelman at the Savoy, *nouvelle cuisine* was an important, timely innovation which has had some enduring effects on English cooking, much more than a passing, fashionable fad.

A more general reaction against French styles, however, subsequently emerged in the movement for Modern British Cooking, a counterculture which rediscovered the virtues of native meats, fish, game and poultry unpretentiously presented, of seasonal vegetables and fruits from local sources, and of traditional pies and puddings. It has also reclaimed products once regarded as inferior, such as trotters, tripe, knuckles, shins, tongues, ham shanks, ox-tail and a wide variety of flavoured sausages and pig meats. Key figures in this renaissance include Gary Rhodes, Fergus Henderson, Paul Heathcote and Shaun Hill.[56] All these changes mean that there is now no single cuisine in England which can claim superiority: indeed, since the 1990s there has arisen a deliberately 'Eclectic' style which attempts to fuse the culinary traditions of many lands, European, Asian, African and American, into what has been described as 'a glorious mix'. If the architectural analogy for Modern British Cooking is the vernacular styles, that of the Eclectic is the astylar. It remains to be seen whether this particular cooking pot, into which anything goes, is more than a flash in the fashion pan.

Faced with such variety, the diner's choice of a perfect meal will depend, as it has always done, on personal taste and the experience of a particular restaurant at a particular time. Chefs, managers and staff change frequently, and places which once served outstanding food may long trade on past reputations. Nevertheless, a few names consistently command wide respect. In 1989 Clement Freud selected Le Gavroche, Grosvenor House and the old-established Rules for special approval, and outside London the Carved Angel (Dartmouth), Sharrow Bay and Miller Howe (Lake District), Le Manoir aux Quat' Saisons (Oxfordshire) and Hintlesham Hall (Suffolk).[57] In the early 1990s the *Ackerman Guide* gave its highest, Four Clover Leaf awards to the Dorchester, the Ritz, the Savoy, Claridge's, Le Gavroche, Bibendum, Le Caprice, Sharrow Bay, Miller Howe and Cliveden (Taplow, Bucks).[58] In 2000, Michael Winner also believed that the best hotels were the Dorchester and Claridge's and the best restaurant the Ivy, but, independent as ever, placed Cliveden and the Waterside Inn (Bray-on-Thames) which others had praised, among his worst experiences.[59]

Descending the scale, those places described as 'cafés and coffee shops' sold 121.7 million meals in 1999, and if the similar in-store cafeterias are added, they represent one in twelve of all meals sold.[60] 'Café' was always an indeterminate category (the Café Royal was one of the leading restaurants), but it generally referred to places serving light refreshments and beverages, and was especially associated with Lyons or other similar chains of teashops. Lyons' great catering empire never fully recovered after the war, and through the 1960s their once-famous shops were in decline as tastes changed away from cooked lunches and after-noon tea: by 1969, their number had fallen to 120 and many were now loss making. An attempt to revive them as 'Jolyon Restaurants' (after the popular TV series, 'The Forsyte Saga') also failed, and the one successful innovation, Wimpy Bars, were soon in competition from other fast food chains. Lyons' first teashop (in Piccadilly, 1894) closed in 1976, the year that Wimpy was sold to United Biscuits, and in 1981 all their remaining teashops ended; meanwhile, the equally famous Corner Houses also dis-appeared, the last, the Strand, in 1977. It seemed that the magic touch, which had made Lyons a household name, had lost its power when one of their last initiations, the 'Upper Crust', proved to be only 'a burst of madness'. The scheme was to convert a London bus into a 24-seater restaurant touring historic landmarks in a three-hour trip during which a four-course meal would be served on board with champagne, smoked salmon and Scotch beef fillet steak. The intention, for obvious reasons, was to serve the meal while the bus was at a standstill, but it was discov-ered that this infringed legal restrictions as the bus then became a 'restau-rant' and required a liquor licence: otherwise, it had to be on the move at 15 miles an hour, hardly comfortable for dining in the London traffic. The experiment was abandoned after a few trips. Lyons continued some busi-ness as contract caterers at airports and museums, echoing their original enterprise at exhibitions, but the Lyons name disappeared in 1994 when they merged with Allied Domecq PLC, a wine and spirit business, ironi-cally for a firm which had begun life with temperance motives.[61]

By contrast, small, independent tea- and coffee-shops have flourished in recent years, and now abound in towns and in villages which attract a tourist trade: they have benefited from the growth of snacking at any time of day as well as some revival of the traditional afternoon tea – even extending to tea dances in some larger hotels. There are now Guides to good teashops, one listing more than 500 places, most of which have home-made cakes, scones and sandwiches as well as varieties of Indian, China and other leaf teas.[62] Upmarket teashops like 'Ch'a', a Brooke Bond enterprise, offer exotic, spiced blends and frappés made from iced tea, fruit and yoghurt, while at the Savoy the set tea now costs £24 ('booking advisable'). The broad category of 'cafés' also extends to a recent innovation of gourmet soup-kitchens like 'Soup Opera' where a dozen freshly made soups are offered each day: with wholemeal bread and a piece of fruit these are suggested as a healthy alternative to sandwiches and may be eaten in or as takeaways for the office.[63] Health concerns have had a considerable impact on eating habits, particularly since the 1980s, evidenced by a marked growth of fish and vegetarian restaurants. In 1978 there were estimated to be only 52 of the latter in London and 80 elsewhere, but ten years later 750 throughout the United Kingdom, giving them a rate of growth comparable with any fast food chain.[64]

Few people in 1970 could have foreseen the phenomenal growth of Chinese and Indian restaurants which in 1999 served more than one-fifth of all commercial meals – see Table 10.5.

Indian restaurants grew from 2,000 in 1970 to 8,500 in 1998, and Chicken Tikka has been pronounced the most popular restaurant dish in Britain with a sale of 23 million portions a year.[65] The attractions of Indian and Chinese restaurants in terms of taste, price, speed and late opening hours were discussed in the previous chapter: they now occupy a wide niche in the catering market between fashionable, expensive restaurants and fast food outlets, and have lost the taint of inferiority with which some were at first received. Most striking is the size of the takeaway trade, formerly dominated by fish and chips. Many people evidently prefer to eat in the comfort of their own homes with the entertainment of television or videos and without the inconvenience of travel or child-minding. The range of ethnic foods has now extended to other south-east Asian cuisines, including those of Thailand, Indonesia, Singapore and Japan; the first Japanese restaurant, the Hiroko, opened in 1967: sushi bars are now common in many cities.

But although ethnic foods, suitably modified for British tastes, are now a normal part of eating out, the most remarkable change in recent years is the growth of fast foods, in which Britain follows trends set in America rather

TABLE 10.5 ◆ *Numbers of Indian and Chinese meals sold, 1999 (millions)*

	Restaurant	Takeaways	Total
Indian	53.6	107.9	161.5
Chinese	44.5	244.6	289.1
Total	98.1	352.5	450.6

Source: from Taylor Nelson, *MealTrak*, op. cit.

than Continental Europe. Ready-to-eat foods have, of course, a long history from medieval cookshops to the sandwich and the pork pie which stemmed the pangs of Georgian card-players and fox-hunters, and to the great variety of comestibles purveyed by Victorian street-sellers. And, arguably, bread is the oldest of all fast foods. However, the modern use of the term is mainly associated with the rapid growth of chains of restaurants selling hamburgers, pizzas and fried chicken for consumption on the premises or as takeaways: their characteristics are standardised products, speed of delivery, predictable quality, low prices and a clean, family-friendly environment. This is mass production for a mass market, the manufacturing techniques of Fordism applied to catering: as described by Claude Fischler, the processes are broken down into component parts, there is a limited number of menu items requiring only simple cooking skills, while in the cafeteria system the customer himself is put to work by queueing and self-service.[66] Fast food restaurants positively wish to appear ordinary and familiar 'homes from home': the products have easily recognisable names ('Big Mac', 'Large Fries'), the servers wear uniforms, ask set questions and work from detailed schedules of regulations. For Margaret Visser the 'Big Mac' is a cultural construct: its round shape, composed of bread, meat, salads and dressings symbolises a complete meal which can be eaten in the hand,[67] (though a 'square meal' derives from the square shape of early wooden platters). Fast food is easy to eat, comforting and time saving for the demands of work or leisure: it 'reproduces the taste sensations of childhood, a kind of regression coupled with transgression'.[68]

Spending on fast food grew from 5 per cent of catering expenditure in 1982 to 14 per cent ten years later and Britain leads the field in Europe.[69] But although chain restaurants are the most visible part of the fast food

TABLE 10.6 ◆ *Numbers of fast food meals served, 1999 (millions)*

Fish-and-chip shops	302.1
Burger houses	246.7
Chinese takeaways	244.6
Pizza houses	159.1
Indian takeaways	107.9
Fried chicken	42.3
Total	1,102.7

Source: Taylor Nelson Sofres Research, *MealTrak – Out of Home*, 364/950, 1999.

trade on our high streets, they are not the largest part. Table 10.6 provides a summary of the fast food trade.

The fast food meals included in Table 10.6 therefore represent half of the 2,088 million meals sold or, if we exclude takeaways and fish and chips (though a proportion of these are eaten outside the home) then around a quarter. Surprisingly, fish and chips are still ahead of 'the McDonald revolution', and the modern takeaways in smart carrier-bags may be considered as merely an extension of the old newspaper-wrapped packets. But the statistics quoted in Table 10.6 may be complicated by the question of what constitutes a 'meal'. For many people sandwiches have long been a standard midday meal: convenient, hand held and widely available with a large variety of fillings, they ideally fit the pattern of lunchtime requirements – speed (the average time spent at lunch today is 36 minutes), variety of taste and low cost (the average expenditure on lunch is £1.69, very close to the price of many sandwiches). From the producer's point of view they are also very profitable as they have high added value from the cheap basic ingredient. Taking this broader definition of fast food to include sandwiches, MSI calculate the total value of the fast food market as £7,447 billions, of which sandwiches alone comprise almost 40 per cent, as Table 10.7 shows.

The success of the sandwich has been partly due also to its perception as healthy eating, particularly promoted by caterers such as 'Prêt À Manger' (118 branches) who claim to use only fresh ingredients free from preservatives and other additives. The long-term decline in bread consumption has been halted by sandwiches, which take 30 per cent of bakery output: they

TABLE 10.7 ◆ *UK market shares for fast foods, 2000*

	Value (£ billion)	% share
Sandwiches	2,856	38
Hamburgers	1,513	20
Pizza and Pasta	935	13
Fish and chips	649	9
Chicken	562	7
Chinese	436	6
Indian	345	5
Mexican	86	1
Soup	65	1
	£7,447	100

Source: *Fast Food UK*, Report by MSI, Market Research for Industry, 2002, Tables 5 and 6, pp. 15, 17.

are eaten by 30 per cent of workers every day, and by 80 per cent at least once a week. Other bakery products such as rolls, buns, baps, brioches, bagels and muffins account for another 25 per cent of the bread market.[70]

While the sandwich revolution has been occurring almost unnoticed, public perception of fast food is dominated by the iconic images of the chain restaurants. In 2000 Kentucky Fried Chicken had 600 UK outlets, Pizza Hut 446, Burger King 400 and Pizza Express 286, but these are over-shadowed by McDonald's who, after their late entry to Britain in 1974, reached 1,000 branches in 1999 (the one-thousandth at the ill-fated Millennium Dome): worldwide they then numbered 23,000. The ham-burger of minced beef (not pork) of German origin, probably made its first appearance at the St Louis World's Fair in 1904, but the first chain was launched by E. W. Ingram in 1921 as the 'White Castle' drive-in service on the new American highways. The McDonald brothers began with a similar drive-in chain in 1955 from their base near Chicago and the great stockyard trade.[71] McDonald's now serve 2½ million meals a day in Britain. Initially they appealed particularly to the youth market, but now after a generation the burger has moved up the age range: the largest con-sumers are now those aged 30–39 years (27 per cent), followed by those 20–29 (25 per cent) and 15–19 (22 per cent), but falling to only 7 per cent of those aged 50–55. Lunchtime has the largest number of users, closely followed by evening meals, but breakfast, which is very popular in America, has so far attracted few here. McDonald's patrons are by no means among the under-privileged. Their research shows that their largest market is in the socio-economic groups B and C (junior mana-gerial, clerical and skilled workers): 38 per cent of customers have GCE A levels or the equivalent, and 29 per cent claim to be graduates or post-graduates.[72]

Fast food caterers have been at pains to counter accusations of unhealthiness and to distinguish their products from 'junk foods' of little nutritional value. In 2002 McDonald's reported losses in Britain and began closing some of their branches; they have decided to introduce bags of fresh fruit which can replace chips in their Happy Meal menus.[73] Particular concern has been about the levels of fats and sugars and the effects these may be having on the undoubted increase of obesity in chil-dren and young adults, but a direct relationship has not yet been proven: obesity is likely to be the result of wider cultural changes of which fast food is only part.[74] More serious anxiety concerns the category of 'junk foods' such as sweets, snacks and fizzy drinks particularly targeted at children, whose annual consumption is estimated at 17.6 kg of chocolate, 6.4 kg of savoury snacks, 6.3 kg of chilled desserts and 4.5 kg of biscuits: an investigation by the Food Commission of 358 such products concluded that only one in ten could be regarded as healthy while 77 per cent contained excessive levels of saturated fat, sugar and salt.[75]

Throughout this book we have referred to the connection between eating out and travel, and this has continued to increase with the escalation of journeys by road, rail and air. From the introduction of the Pullman dining-car in 1879 railway chefs performed miracles to cook meals at modest prices – in 1903 the London and North-Western Railway served lunch of Boiled Haddock and Parsley Sauce, Roast Beef with Potatoes and Cabbage, and Apple Pie and Custard for 2/6d., while the menu for a special race meeting excursion from London to Aintree in 1913 included plovers' eggs, quails, salmon, asparagus and caviar. Pullman restaurant-cars were suspended in the 1970s and re-launched in 1985, though by then quicker journeys and lighter appetites were halving the demand for meals from its peak of 3.5 million served in 1973. British Rail's 'Travellers Fare' responded with more informal provision such as Cafeteria Cars, Griddle Cars and Mini-Buffet Trolleys, and even ventured into some bistro-style station buffets with continental dishes.[76] But by then much more traffic was on the roads and motorways, and caterers quickly seized the opportunities for all-day services, much as the coaching inns had done two centuries before. Charles Forte opened the first motorway restaurant at Newport Pagnell in 1960, the year after the first section of the M1 was developed, and later established Motor Chef on other new routes. The virtual monopoly which motorway restaurants enjoyed led to considerable criticism of their prices and quality, publicly voiced in the Prior Committee of Inquiry into Motorway Service Areas in 1978, which compared many unfavourably with their counterparts in Europe.[77] Eating on the move has also been given a new dimension by the rapid growth of air travel. Between the wars, when flying was still a privileged mode of travel, meals were served on flower-decorated tables by white-coated stewards, and on long-haul journeys passengers alighted for more elaborate meals in the shadow of the plane. Package holidays and 'Economy' flights have produced the miniature meal on a tray, described by Margaret Visser as 'a technological miracle. People hurtling through the air in a metal tube, both uneasily aware of what could go wrong and stupefied with boredom, are deemed to require solace.'[78] At least, they are kept occupied in managing the intricacies of the tray, which attempts to reproduce a complete meal with an hors d'oeuvre, main course and a dessert – this is truly fast food in a fast environment.

Eating literally 'out', in the open air, which was characterised by Victorian street-food, has revived after a period when street-eating was frowned upon by the respectable classes. In the 1930s children licked ice creams from the 8,000 Walls 'Stop Me and Buy One' tricycles, but this and other street food disappeared under the wartime restrictions. The revival of street food dates especially from the 1980s, when Theodore Zeldin noted that 'The street vendor is coming back to the West... the counterpart of the jeans revolution in clothes'.[79] The range now extends to burgers, hot dogs, pizza and chicken and even to packaged risotto, paella and curries: it is now apparently 'cool' to eat such things and to drink from a can in city streets or on park benches, a trend perhaps stimulated by the response of foreign tourists to high restaurant prices. Meanwhile, the English love of the picnic has continued unabated with the increased mobility of the population and easier access to the countryside, the coasts and sporting events. Its popularity cuts across age and class: it can be a simple affair of sandwiches or a gourmet alfresco meal at Glyndebourne or Henley. For a luxury picnic at Ascot in 1971 Beryl Gould-Marks noted that 'Not many years ago, chicken would have been an obvious choice', but this was now too commonplace; she suggested salmon, beef with foie gras in a pastry case, fish in aspic, avocadoes, fresh fruit and a variety of cheeses.[80] But a recent significant trend has been the growth of eating in domestic gardens, no longer a sedate ceremony of afternoon tea on the lawn, but a hot meal barbecued on the patio by adult Boy Scouts. It makes a popular entertainment for friends and children, representing, as Mary Douglas suggests, a half-way stage of intimacy between an indoor dinner and a mere invitation to a drinks party.[81] The barbecue is 'a vivid display of strength, a confirmation of manhood, a reminder to all females observing the ritual that this ordinary guy... is not many steps from the loin-cloth clad hunter-gatherer who he imagines to be the man of their dreams.'[82] And for their added pleasure on chilly evenings he even lights the outdoor heater.

Notes and references

1 The Guild of Food Writers, Newsletter, November/December 2002.

2 Reay Tannahill, *Food in History*, Harmondsworth, Middlesex, Penguin Books, Revised edn, 1988, p. 80.

3 *Birds Eye Annual Review*, 1976, p. 3.

4 Alan Warde and Lydia Martens, 'Eating Out and the Commercialisation of Mental Life', *British Food Journal*, vol. 100 (3), 1998, Table 1, p. 150.

5 Roy Ackerman, *The Ackerman Martell Guide to the Best Restaurants and Hotels in the British Isles, 1991–1992*, Alfresco Leisure Publications, 1991, Introduction, p. 10.

6 G. Heald, 'Trends in Eating Out', in Richard Cottrell (ed.), *Nutrition in Catering*, Carnforth, Lancashire, Parthenon Publishing Group, 1987, p. 76.

7 ibid., Table 4.4, p. 80.

8 *National Food Survey, Annual Report*, 1996, The Stationery Office, Table B.3, p. 97.

9 Alan Warde and Lydia Martens, *Eating Out. Social Differentiation, Consumption and Pleasure*, Cambridge, Cambridge University Press, 2000, p. 26.

10 *Social Trends 30*, The Stationery Office, 2000, p. 107.

11 *The British Eating Out*, A Report from Britain's National Catering Inquiry, sponsored by Smethursts Foods Ltd., 1966, p. 5 passim.

12 *Food Choice and Price*, National Catering Inquiry Supplementary Report prepared by John McKenzie, 1967, pp. 2–4.

13 Peter Cullen, 'Time, Tastes and Technology. The Economic Evolution of Eating Out', *British Food Journal*, vol. 96 (10), 1994, pp. 4–9.

14 *Social Trends 30*, 2000, op. cit., p. 216.

15 ibid., p. 217.

16 Geoffrey C. Warren (ed.), *The Foods We Eat*, Cassell, 1958.

17 *The Changing Structure of Meals in Britain, A Report* by Taylor Nelson Research Ltd., 1988.

18 *Who Eats Breakfast?*, Breakfast Research Study by John Birmingham for the Kellogg Company of Great Britain Ltd., 1976.

19 Ben Fine and Ellen Leopold, *The World of Consumption*, Routledge, 1993, p. 165, citing a Key Note Report, 1989.

20 Roy Strong, *Feast. A History of Grand Eating*, Jonathan Cape, 2002, p. 311.

21 John Burnett, 'Time, Place and Content. The Changing Structure of Meals in Britain in the Nineteenth and Twentieth Centuries', in Martin R. Schärer and

Alexander Fenton (eds), *Food and Material Culture*, East Lothian, Scotland, Tuckwell Press, 1998, pp. 116–32.

22 Theodore Zeldin, *The Listener*, 15 April 1982, quoted Christopher Driver, *The British at Table, 1940–1980*, Chatto & Windus, 1983, p. 147.

23 Derek Cooper, *The Bad Food Guide*, Routledge & Kegan Paul, 1967, pp. xvi, 8, 19, 21–2.

24 *The British Eating Out*, op. cit., p. 12.

25 McKenzie, *Food Choice and Price*, op. cit., pp. 9–14.

26 'Meals in the Mind', *Daily Telegraph Magazine*, 14 Dec. 1973, inquiry conducted by Social Surveys (Gallup Poll) Ltd.

27 'Britons' Favourite Foods', *Caterer and Hotelkeeper*, 14 Sept. 1989, inquiry by Gallup Poll Surveys Ltd.

28 *Radio Times*, 8–14 July and 9–15 Sept. 2000.

29 Taylor Nelson Research Ltd., *MealTrak – Out of Home*, 364/950, 1999.

30 'The Inn Thing', *The Times Magazine*, Saturday 29 April 2000, pp. 56–8.

31 Jonathan Meades, *The Times Magazine*, Saturday 30 Sept. 2000, pp. 65–6.

32 Kit Chapman, *Great British Chefs*, Mitchell Beazley, 1995, p. 8.

33 *Fish the Dish*, Factsheet published by the Sea Fish Industry Authority, 2000.

34 Taylor Nelson Research Ltd., *MealTrak*, op. cit.

35 Alan Coxon and Kathy Sykes, *Ever Wondered About Food?*, Milton Keynes, The Open University, 2002, p. 15.

36 John K. Walton, *Fish and Chips and the British Working Class, 1870–1940*, Leicester, Leicester University Press, 1992, p. 34.

37 Analysis of an average-sized portion of fish and chips showed 38.7g of fat, similar to a quarter-pound burger with fries, but less than a portion of sweet and sour pork with rice at 48.2g: the fish and chips also provided 34% of daily recommended allowance of protein for a man: Cottrell, *Nutrition in Catering*, op. cit., pp. 104–5. This analysis was done in Leeds, where dripping was then (1980s) widely used for frying; vegetable oil would yield considerably less fat.

38 'Why fish'n'chips is the new caviar', *Sunday Times Style Supplement*, 14 April 2002.

30 *The British Eating Out at Work, A Report from Britain's National Catering Inquiry*, 1973, pp. 13–17.

40 *The Compass Lunchtime Report*, 1990, Tisbury, Wiltshire, E=Mc^2.

41 *The Compass Lunchtime Report*, 1998, Tisbury, Wiltshire, E=Mc^2.

42 *Luncheon Voucher Factsheets*, kindly supplied by Accor Services, London.

43 T. A. Bull, 'The Impact of Nutritional and Health Concepts on Catering Practice Within the School Meals Service', in Cottrell (ed.), op. cit., p. 115.

44 *School Meals*, Education and Employment Committee, First Report, 1999, The Stationery Office, p. viii.

45 Mikko Takula, *London: Restaurant Capital of the World*, Helsinki, Finland, Finnair, Blue Wings, Helsinki Media Co., June–July 2000.

46 Kit Chapman, *Great British Chefs*, op. cit., pp. 10, 13.

47 Michael Winner, *Winner's Dinners*, Robson Books, 2000, p. xi.

48 Alan Beardsworth and Teresa Keil, *Sociology on the Menu. An Invitation to the Study of Food and Society*, Routledge, 1997, p. 117.

49 Christopher Driver, *The British at Table, 1940–1980*, Chatto & Windus, 1983, p. 176.

50 'The Affluentials who spend £10,000 a year on fun', *Daily Mail*, Wednesday 20 June 2001, citing a survey by Barclays Premier Banking.

51 *Sunday Times*, 15 July 2001.

52 Strong, *Feast*, op. cit., pp. 308, 312.

53 Joanne Finkelstein, *Dining Out. A Sociology of Modern Manners*, Cambridge, Polity Press, 1989.

54 Roy C. Wood, 'The Shock of the New. A Sociology of Nouvelle Cuisine', *Journal of Consumer Studies and Home Economics*, vol. 15(4), 1991, pp. 327–38.

55 Cailein H. Gillespie, 'Gastrosophy and Nouvelle Cuisine. Entrepreneurial Fashion and Fiction', *British Food Journal*, vol. 96(10), 1994, pp. 19–23.

56 For a fuller account, see Colin Spencer, *British Food. An Extraordinary Thousand Years of History*, Grub Street, 2002, pp. 342–3.

57 Clement Freud, *The Gourmet's Tour of Great Britain and Ireland*, Boston, USA and London, Little, Brown and Co., 1989.

58 Ackerman, *The Ackerman Martell Guide*, 1991–2, op. cit.

59 Michael Winner, *Winner's Dinners*, op. cit.; *Sunday Times Style Supplement*, 12 November 2000.

60 Taylor Nelson Research, 1999, op. cit.

61 Peter Bird, *The First Food Empire. A History of J. Lyons & Co.*, Chichester, West Sussex, Phillimore, 2000, pp. 200–3, 340–4.

62 For example, Patricia Rose Cress, *That Tea Book*, HHL Publishing Group for Brooke Bond Foods Ltd, 1992; *The Tea Set. Fifty Great Places for Afternoon Tea*, Times Magazine in association with 'Bonne Maman', 2002.

63 '*Soup Opera*', Press release, London, 2000.

64 Colin Spencer, *The Heretic's Feast. A History of Vegetarianism*, Fourth Estate, 1993, p. 322n. citing Annabel Whittet, *Where to Eat if you Don't Eat Meat*, Whittet Books, 1988.

65 Alan Coxon and Kathy Sykes, op. cit., p. 9.

66 Claude Fischler, 'The McDonaldization of Culture', in Jean-Louis Flandrin and Massimo Montanari (eds), *Food. A Culinary History from Antiquity to the Present*, New York, Columbia University Press, 1999.

67 Margaret Visser, *The Rituals of Dinner*, Harmondsworth, Middlesex, Penguin Books, 1993, pp. 208, 346–8.

68 Fischler, in Flandrin and Montanari, op. cit., p. 546.

69 David Duffill and Hugh Martin, 'The U.K. Chain Restaurant Market. Developments in this Evolving Industry', *British Food Journal,* vol. 95(4), 1993, pp. 12–16.

70 *The British Bread and Bakery Snacks Market*, Factsheet No. 3, Federation of Bakers, 2002, p. 6.

71 Tom Hudgins, 'Burgers and Fries. From White Castles to Golden Arches', in Harlan Walker (ed.), *Public Eating. Oxford Symposium on Food and Cookery*, Prospect Books, 1991, pp. 142–5.

72 *McDonald's Fact File, 2000*, and additional demographic data supplied by the Corporate Affairs Department, McDonald's Restaurants Ltd, London.

73 *The Times*, Saturday 1 March 2003.

74 Eric Schlosser, *Fast Food Nation*, Harmondsworth, Middlesex Penguin Books, 2002, p. 242.

75 'How Kids are turned into Junkies', *The Times Weekend*, Saturday 8 July 2000.

76 Neil Wooler, *Dinner in the Diner. The History of Railway Catering*, Newton Abbot, Devon, David & Charles, 1987.

77 On motorway catering generally, see David Lawrence, *Always a Welcome. The glove compartment history of the motorway service area*, Twickenham, Between Books, 1999.

78 Visser, op. cit., pp. 205–6. And see generally K. Hudson and J. Pettifer, *Diamonds in the Sky. A Social History of Air Travel*, Bodley Head, 1979.

79 Theodore Zeldin, *The Listener*, 15 April 1982, quoted Driver, op. cit., p. 147.

80 Beryl Gould-Marks, *Eating in the Open*, Faber and Faber, 1971, p. 105.

81 Mary Douglas, *Implicit Meanings. Essays in Anthropology*, Routledge & Kegan Paul, 1975, ch. 16, 'Deciphering a Meal', pp. 256–7.

82 'Burning Question. Why do men BBQ?', *The Times Weekend*, Saturday 3 July 1999.

Conclusion

It remains to identify and analyse the principal trends and changes in eating out, to suggest explanations for these, and to set the phenomenon of eating out within the broader context of modern society.

1 Although statistical evidence is only available for recent years, it is probable that the total volume of eating out in England has not significantly increased over the whole period of this book. What has changed is the balance between eating out from necessity which has always been closely associated with work, and eating out from choice and for pleasure, that is, as a leisure activity. Eating at work has necessarily continued though the cooked midday lunch, which was often the main meal of the day, has usually been replaced by a light snack, while recreational eating out has moved towards the evening, especially at weekends.

The extent and type of eating out was determined by financial constraints – the affordability of commercial meals provided for a profit in relation to other demands on consumers' budgets. In particular, the frequency and form of pleasure eating was, and is still, directly related to social class as defined by income, occupation and education. For much of the nineteenth century the subsistence earnings of the working classes precluded such pleasures except for rare, celebratory occasions. The spread of recreational consumption was predicated on the growth of national wealth and changes in its distribution, processes in which two periods stand out as especially significant. From being the prerogative mainly of the rich and powerful, eating in public for pleasure began to be adopted by the bourgeoisie in the years 1880–1914, part of the wider changes in cultural values and conspicuous consumption of the rising middle classes. The second major change dates from the

1960s – the democratisation of eating out for pleasure to all classes, made possible by rises in disposable incomes and the emergence of new types of catering outlets with wide popular appeal.

By contrast, charity was a significant provider of meals outside the home for the poor. As we saw, such activities included extensive soup-kitchens in times of national distress, school feeding of 'necessitous' children, Harvest Homes for farmworkers and annual outings provided by employers for their staff. The gift relationship so created was often the means of promoting deference and dependence through the medium of food and drink. Factory canteens, which began as a semi-philanthropic provision, grew rapidly in times of war as aids to health and productivity, again having instrumental motives: until recently, they were a principal occasion of eating in public for many workers. The role of the state has also been important in familiarising both adults and children with eating out. Communal feeding in British Restaurants and emergency feeding centres was a valuable supplement to the restricted rations of civilians, while for children the Education Act of 1944 extended school meals to a national welfare service, providing at its peak in the 1970s a main midday meal for three-quarters of all schoolchildren.

Previous chapters have argued that demographic changes have had major impacts on eating out. Smaller family and household sizes in the twentieth century much reduced the proportion of income required for domestic food, releasing more spending for entertainment, travel and holidays, which frequently involve eating outside the home. The sharp increase in one- and two-person households has tended to reduce the amount of home cooking and increased the use of ready-made meals, takeaways and restaurants as convenient alternatives to traditional home-cooked meals needing lengthy preparation. This is especially the case since it has become normal for married women to be employed, and for couples to enjoy the material benefits of double incomes, including greater sharing in leisure activities. In the nineteenth century eating outside the home was predominantly a male activity, often associated with their work: men ate at clubs and pubs, in chop-houses and cookshops, bought snacks from street-sellers or brought food from home, but respectability codes did not normally allow women of any social standing to eat in public places. The change began towards the end of the century with the rise of luxury hotels and smart restaurants which deliberately aimed to encourage a new fashion of mixed dining among the upper and middle classes. Subsequently, the development of chains of clean, comfortable teashops, of in-store cafés and more modest restaurants and hotels familiarised women of all classes with eating in the public sphere, with or without male companions, a significant aspect of their social liberation in the twentieth century. For juveniles to eat out except as members of family groups is a more recent phenomenon, dependent on their higher earnings, greater independence, and especially on the development of fast food restaurants having strong fashionable appeal to young consumers.

The growing affordability of eating out was, therefore, paralleled by the establishment of a wide variety of places to do so, though it is not always obvious how the forces of supply and demand operated in the catering industry. In some instances supply anticipated and contributed to creating demand, entrepreneurs recognising a potential market and creating appropriate outlets to satisfy it. This was the case, for example, with Ritz and Escoffier and their imitators in the late nineteenth century, whose innovations virtually established the habit of fashionable dining with ladies; with Joseph Lyons who democratised the teashop for office workers and shoppers; and with Butlin who invented the holiday camp as a mass leisure entertainment. More recently, the explosion of fast food restaurants was predicated, at least partly, on the belief that British consumers could be persuaded by heavy advertising to follow the American lead. This contrasts with the spread of ethnic restaurants, mainly by independent proprietors, who built on a small demand already established in London and some areas of immigrant population, to supply modified versions of Indian, Chinese and other cuisines to suit English palates.

Frequent reference has been made to eating out for pleasure as a form of entertainment – both for the enjoyment of the food itself and for the music, dancing and cabarets which sometimes accompanied the dining experience. Restaurants were often located close to public entertainments such as theatres, cinemas and exhibitions or were even integral to them, while country hotels included pleasure grounds, tennis courts, swimming pools and golf courses. This close association between eating out and other leisure activities, and especially with holidays, has been evident throughout the period, but much increased in the post-war years with the provision of longer, paid holidays and the greater mobility of people by road and air travel. Holidays abroad widened opportunities to sample different foods and cuisines, and in turn, stimulated the popularity of ethnic restaurants in Britain. There is no doubt that over the period covered by this book consumers became more interested in and more knowledgeable about matters to do with food and about places to eat out. Restaurant guides, from the few that existed in the later nineteenth century, mainly recommending luxury establishments for visitors, proliferated between the two world wars and even more after the end of rationing in the 1950s.Today, the public is bombarded with restaurant guides, newspaper columns and magazine articles, while television demonstrations by 'superstar' chefs rival the popularity of soap operas. Yet the stubborn attachment of so many consumers to tried and trusted English dishes, unadorned save by the sauce bottle, may suggest that both share the common ingredient of fantasy.

2 So far, we have considered a range of factors which allowed or encouraged eating out, but they do not in themselves explain why people chose to do so rather than eating possibly similar meals at home, or spending time and money on some other form of entertainment. To answer this takes us into a realm of social and psychological desires in which physical needs are subordinate to mental and emotional satisfactions. In choosing to eat out for pleasure, people expect to enjoy the experience, and the overwhelming majority evidently do so. Recent research showed that 81 per cent of a cross-section sample of people said that they enjoyed their last meal out 'a lot', while only 5 per cent disliked it a little or much. Similarly high proportions said that they had enjoyed the food, the company, the conversation and the atmosphere, though somewhat fewer people gave top rating to the service (65 per cent) or the decor of the restaurant (56 per cent).[1]

The main reasons given for enjoyment were experiencing something different from the everyday, a break from domestic meal preparation, a liking for the different foods available, the socialising with other people and a sense of celebration, of participating in a 'treat'.[2] It is clear that the degree of enjoyment is almost always directly related to the presence of others at table – the pleasures of social intercourse, conversation, observation of the surroundings and of other diners. It seems that some people can be almost indifferent to the food itself: the essence of the occasion is the sociability and companionship with friends, colleagues or kin. Eating out alone does not satisfy these requirements: it is likely to be 'necessitous' eating of a simple meal, quickly consumed.

The 'meanings' which underlie food, and which food conveys, have received much scholarly attention from social scientists in recent times. Food is seen as a language, a medium of communication which is socially and historically determined. For Roland Barthes it is 'a body of images' to which the consumer brings certain acquired expectations. What Barthes wrote about wine – that 'it is, above all, a converting substance, capable of reversing situations and states... [a] power to transmute'[3] – might apply almost equally to the restaurant meal, especially where alcohol accompanies the food. It has long been recognised that different foods carry different associations of festivity, celebration, friendship, family solidarity and so on: the choice of expensive fashionable dishes in a restaurant may suggest sophistication and 'savoir-faire', that of caviar or foie gras evokes images of Edwardian luxury, while to choose game or roast meat may symbolise the survival of an idealised rural past.[4] Similarly, the choice of where to eat 'speaks volumes': for a host to take guests to a cheap restaurant may seem insulting, to one too famous or expensive, ostentatious.[5] Restaurants are artificial constructs, deliberately different from the home environment and aiming to change the mood of the diner. This is especially true of the 'spectacular' and 'parodic' restaurants, as Finkelstein shows,[6] but it can also apply to modest ethnic restaurants, to reconstructions of the 'traditional' English inn and the 'country kitchen' tearoom. Decor is a necessary part of the total aesthetic experience of eating out, whether carefully contrived or understated.

Diners usually respond to the symbolic aspects of the restaurant in their behaviour and dress, thereby themselves contributing to the sense of occasion and change of consciousness. Although dress codes are now much less formal than when ladies wore elaborate hats and men tail coats or dinner jackets at top places, it is not long since women in trousers were not admitted and some restaurants still keep a supply of ties for men with open-necked shirts. Formal dining was a marker of bourgeois admissibility to what had once been a preserve of aristocracy and wealth, and even in our democratic age women still expect to 'dress up' for evening dining. The restaurant has been described as 'a stage where people play a variety of rôles'.[7] In an environment which is more anonymous than the home, people may feel less inhibited about interacting and 'playing up' to the occasion than, for example, at a domestic dinner party. Yet the restaurant carries its own rituals of deference – the greeting, seating, ordering from the menu and the presentation and serving of the food and drink. These involve formalities now largely absent at home and which may be valued as reassurances of order and stability. The ability to command the services of restaurant staff may be felt as a reminder of the formerly widespread employment of domestic servants.

Eating out for pleasure is not, then, merely a substitute for eating at home. It is an important aspect of the modern culture of leisure and entertainment, offering a sense of other worlds, desires and fantasies in which people can imagine themselves more empowered, fashionable and sophisticated, more accustomed to superior standards than in their everyday lives. Ultimately, of course, eating out is a commercial transaction in which desires and feelings are commodified for money – in the restaurant we buy and are fed a menu of satisfactions.

Consumer surveys indicate that most people consider eating out represents good value, and would like to eat out more often if their circumstances allowed. Eating out is now a firmly established habit in our affluent society, and in the long run its growth is likely to continue. Like other forms of leisure, however, eating out is sensitive to a wide range of economic, social and political factors, including fears about recession, job security, levels of taxation, terrorism and international conflict. More specifically some concerns about current trends in food supply and consumption could well impact on eating out. Recent food scares such as salmonella in the 1980s and BSE in the 1990s dented public confidence in the purity of what we eat, and notified cases of food poisoning rose dramatically from 10,000 a year in the mid-1960s to 90,000 a year in the late 1990s.[8] These occurrences cannot, of course be laid solely, or even principally, at the doors of the commercial catering industry, though the increased use there of processed foods, inadequate cooking by microwave ovens and, in some places, poor standards of hygiene may be significant causes. A similar verdict holds for the recent increase in obesity: estimated proportions of English adults classified as obese almost trebled from 6 per cent of men and 8 per cent of women in 1980 to 17 per cent and 21 per cent respectively in 1998.[9] Given the declining energy intake of British diets in recent years, the reasons for the rise in obesity are somewhat puzzling, but the high levels of saturated fats and sugars in many fast foods, snacks, confectionery and soft drinks, often consumed outside the home by both adults and children, may be important contributory causes of overweight and the diseases of affluence.

3 Viewed more broadly, the democratisation of eating out is an important aspect of the growth of consumption which has characterized modern society and was greatly stimulated by Britain's emergence as 'the first industrial nation'. The period around 1830 was taken as the starting point for this book, the time when England was passing from an agrarian, rural society to a predominantly industrial, urban one in which new sources of wealth and new class structures were rapidly developing. The early beneficiaries of this process were the middle classes, but ultimately almost all levels of society came to share, if unequally, in increased prosperity: even in post-industrial Britain, when many of the traditional manufacturing sources of wealth have declined or disappeared, new employment opportunities have continued to raise the standards of living of the majority of the population.

   The great expansion of trade which accompanied the Industrial Revolution brought Britain into closer contact with European and more distant markets: in some of these the flag followed trade, and during the nineteenth century Britain acquired the largest empire in history. English diet was enriched by many products, including sugar and spices, tea and coffee, which became important ingredients of both domestic and commercial catering, but in terms of cooking style the greatest influence was that of our nearest neighbour, France. English versions of 'haute cuisine' were developed by French chefs who emigrated during and after the French Revolution and were employed in noble households and gentlemen's clubs; subsequently the taste was spread by English visitors to the Continent as travel became easier and quicker, and French, Swiss and Italian resorts became fashionable with the bourgeoisie. Easier travel had effects both outward and inward. In the later nineteenth century French and Italian immigrants established modest cafés in Soho, some of which developed into high-class restaurants, while following decolonisation after the Second World War, Asian migrants became responsible for the rapid spread of Indian and other ethnic restaurants. China was a somewhat different case, since with the exception of Hong Kong it had not been a British possession, though in fact many of the Chinese restaurants in England, despite their claims to superior, regional cuisines, were established by immigrants from this single Territory.

Yet despite its wealth, it could not be said that England was an eating-out nation until the latter half of the twentieth century. English social life remained strongly domestic and private. The aristocracy and wealthy in their country mansions and town houses served by skilful, often French, chefs, had little need to eat out for luxury food or social intercourse, while the home-loving, family-centred middle classes, except on holiday, rarely ventured out for gastronomic delights: among many of them there long persisted the relics of a puritanical view that to be too much interested in food was impolite, if not actually sinful. For the working classes the male-dominated public house was the natural social centre – for drink and company, not food. There was, therefore, no equivalent of Continental café culture, or of the evening outing to a restaurant 'en famille'. The change to eating out as popular leisure dates principally from the Second World War and accelerated in the following years of prosperity. The war itself, with its shared privations, rationing and communal feeding programmes, contributed to major social changes towards greater egalitarianism, subsequently reinforced by the construction of the Welfare State, policies of full employment and free access to secondary and further education. Years of austerity were followed by a boom in holiday-making and leisure activities generally: new levels of spending power, with incomes no longer taken up by expenditure on basic necessities, went into more comfortable homes, domestic appliances, fashion clothes, travel and entertainment. In these trends, the model was more transatlantic than European. In America, in a more open, democratic and classless society, a consumer revolution was already well under way, and mass-production methods, originated in vehicle manufacture, were being applied to food, drink and catering services. The 'Americanisation' of British diet had begun earlier with breakfast cereals and a wide range of canned foods, but the post-war innovations of burger, chicken and pizza bars and cola drinks, eventually a global phenomenon, influenced English eating-out habits more quickly and deeply than in most other countries.

Until the later nineteenth century the English catering industry had consisted of small, independent units, but it then quickly began to take advantage of limited liability legislation for the construction of grand hotels, the formation of brewery companies and chains of restaurants. Today, catering is one of Britain's largest industries, and international capital lies behind the familiar names in English high streets and shopping malls. Although excellent quality, individually cooked meals from fresh ingredients are still to be found, at a price, much of modern catering depends on technology to put food on the plate within minutes – freeze-dried, pre-prepared ingredients, factory-made flavourings and microwave cooking.[10] A mass market is, by definition, not a highly discerning one, but the evidence suggests that most people like what they get, and like what they pay for it. The burger and the biriani may be almost identical in Swindon and in Sunderland, and in that sense it may be argued that there are diminishing differences in English diet, but many people like the familiarity of the predictable, and, in any case, they now have a much greater choice of places to eat out than in the past.

Notes and references

1 Alan Warde and Lydia Martens. *Eating Out. Social Differentiation, Consumption and Pleasure*, Cambridge, Cambridge University Press, 2000, Table 8.1, p. 173.

2 ibid., pp. 47ff.

3 Roland Barthes. *Mythologies* (1972), quoted Simon Rae (ed.), *The Faber Book of Drink, Drinkers and Drinking*, Faber and Faber, 1991, p. 6.

4 See generally, Stephen Mennell. *All Manners of Food. Eating and Taste in England and France from the Middle Ages to the Present*, Oxford, Basil Blackwell, 1985, p. 6 passim.

5 Reay Tannahill. *Food in History*, Harmondsworth, Middlesex, Penguin Books, Revised edn., 1988, p. 80.

6 Joanne Finkelstein. *Dining Out. A Sociology of Modern Manners*, Cambridge, Polity Press, 1989.

7 Gerald Mars and Michael Nicod. *The World of Waiters*, George Allen & Unwin, 1984, p. 50.

8 Derek J. Oddy. *From Plain Fare to Fusion Food. British Diet from the 1890s to the 1990s*, Woodbridge, Suffolk, The Boydell Press, 2003, p. 213.

9 ibid., p. 221, citing the National Audit Office, Report by the Comptroller and Auditor General, *Tackling Obesity in England*, HC 220, Session 2000–2001, 2001, Executive Summary, p. 1.

10 Adel P. den Hartog. 'Technological Innovations and Eating Out as a Mass Phenomenon in Europe: A Preamble', in Marc Jacobs and Peter Scholliers (eds), *Eating Out in Europe*, Oxford, Berg, 2003, pp. 263–80.

Select bibliography

The place of publication is London unless otherwise stated.

Books and chapters in books

Ackerman, Roy. *The Ackerman Martell Guide to the Best Restaurants and Hotels in the British Isles, 1991–1992*, Alfresco Leisure Publications, 1991.

Adburgham, Alison. *Shops and Shopping, 1800–1914*, Barrie and Jenkins, 2nd edn, 1989.

Adburgham, Alison. *Silver Fork Society*, Constable, 1983.

Agar, Nigel E. *The Bedfordshire Farm Worker in the Nineteenth Century*, Bedford, Bedfordshire Historical Record Society, vol. 60, 1981.

Anderson, R. E. *Gastronomy as a Fine Art, or The Science of Good Living*, Chatto & Windus, New edn, 1889. Translation of Brillat-Savarin, J. A. *Physiologie du Goût*, (1825).

Anon. *The Epicure's Year Book for 1869* (Second Year), Bradbury, Evans and Co., 1869.

Anon, *London At Dinner. Where to Dine in 1858*, Facsimile of 1858 edn, Newton Abbot, Devon, David & Charles, 1969.

Baden-Powell, Lieut.-General R. S. S. *Scouting for Boys. A Handbook for Instruction in Good Citizenship*, C. Arthur Pearson, revised edn, 1909.

Baedeker, K. *London and its Environs. Handbook for Travellers*, Dulan and Co., 2nd edn, 1879.

Baedeker, Karl. *London and its Environs. Handbook for Travellers*, Leipzig and London, 1908.

Bailey, Peter. *Leisure and Class in Victorian England. Rational Recreation and the Contest for Control, 1830–1885*, Methuen University Paperbacks, 1987.

Banks, J. A. *Prosperity and Parenthood. A Study of Family Planning among the Victorian Middle Classes*, Routledge & Kegan Paul, 1965.

Barker, T. C., Oddy, D. J. and Yudkin, John. *The Dietary Surveys of Dr Edward Smith, 1862–3*, Queen Elizabeth College, University of London, Occasional Paper No. 1, Staples Press, 1970.

Barnett, L. Margaret. *British Food Policy During the First World War*, George Allen & Unwin, 1985.

Bateman, Michael. *Cooking People*, Leslie Frewin, for the Cookery Book Club, 1967.

Batterberry, Michael and Batterberry, Ariane. *On the Town in New York. The Landmark History of Eating, Drinking and Entertainments from the American Revolution to the Food Revolution*, New York and London, Routledge, 1999.

Battiscombe, Georgina, *English Picnics*, The Harvill Press, 1949.

Beardsworth, Alan and Keil, Teresa. *Sociology on the Menu. An Invitation to the Study of Food and Society*, Routledge, 1997.

Beeton, Isabella, *The Book of Household Management* (1st edn, 1861). Facsimile edn by Jonathan Cape and Times Newspapers, 1968.

Beveridge, Sir William H. *British Food Control*, Humphrey Milford, 1928.

Bird, Peter, *The First Food Empire. A History of J. Lyons and Co.*, Chichester, West Sussex, Phillimore, 2000.

Birds Eye Annual Review, 1976.

Birmingham, John. *Who Eats Breakfast?* Breakfast Research Study for the Kellogg Company of Great Britain Ltd, 1976.

'Bon Viveur', *Where to Dine in London*, Geoffrey Bles, 1937.

'Bon Viveur' in London. (Fanny and John Cradock). H. A. and W. L. Pitkin, for the *Daily Telegraph*, n.d. (1953).

Booth, Charles. *Life and Labour of the People in London. Final Volume. Notes on Social Influences*, Macmillan, 1902.

Borer, Mary Cathcart. *The British Hotel through the Ages*, Guildford and London, Lutterworth Press, 1972.

Bowden, Gregory Houston. *British Gastronomy. The Rise of Great Restaurants*, Chatto & Windus, 1975.

Bramah, Edward. *Tea and Coffee. A Modern View of Three Hundred Years of Tradition*, Hutchinson, 1972.

Branson, Noreen. *Britain in the Nineteen-Twenties*, Weidenfeld & Nicolson, 1975.

Brears, Peter. 'The Waning of a Long Tradition', in C. Anne Wilson (ed.),

Luncheon, Nuncheon and other Meals. Eating with the Victorians, Stroud, Gloucestershire, Alan Sutton Publishing, 1994.

British Bread and Bakery Snacks Market, Factsheet No. 3, Federation of Bakers, 2002.

British Eating Out. A Report from Britain's National Catering Inquiry, sponsored by Smethursts Foods Ltd., 1966.

British Eating Out at Work. A Report from Britain's National Catering Inquiry, sponsored by Smethursts Foods Ltd., 1973.

Broad, Richard and Fleming, Suzie (eds). *Nella Last's War. A Mother's Diary, 1939–1945*, Bristol, Falling Wall Press, 1981.

Brodrick, George C. *English Land and English Landlords* (1st edn 1881). Republished New York, Augustus M. Kelley, 1968.

Buckley, M. K. *The Feeding of School Children*, G. Bell and Sons, 1914.

Bull, T. A. 'The Impact of Nutritional and Health Concepts on Catering Practice Within the School Meals Service', in Cottrell, Richard (ed.), *Nutrition in Catering*, Carnforth, Lancashire, Parthenon Publishing Group, 1987.

Burke, Thomas. *Out and About. A Note-Book of London in War-Time*, George Allen & Unwin, 1919.

Burke, Thomas. *The English Inn*, Longmans, Green and Co., 1931.

Burke, Thomas. *London in My Time*, Rich and Cowan, 1934.

Burnett, John (ed.). *Destiny Obscure. Autobiographies of Childhood, Education and Family from the 1820s to the 1920s*, Allen Lane, 1982.

Burnett, John. *Plenty and Want. A Social History of Food in England from 1815 to the Present Day*, 3rd edn, Routledge, 1989.

Burnett, John. 'Coffee in the British Diet, 1650–1990', in Ball, Daniela U. (ed.), *Coffee in the Context of European Drinking Habits*, Zurich, Switzerland, Johann Jacobs Museum, 1991.

Burnett, John. *A History of the Cost of Living* (1st edn, 1969). Republished Aldershot, Hampshire, Gregg Revivals, 1993.

Burnett, John (ed.). *Useful Toil. Autobiographies of Working People from the 1820s to the 1920s*, Routledge, 1994 (1st edn, 1974).

Burnett, John. *Idle Hands. The Experience of Unemployment, 1790–1990*, Routledge, 1994.

Burnett, John. 'The Rise and Decline of School Meals in Britain, 1860–1990', in Burnett, John and Oddy, Derek J. (eds), *The Origins and Development of Food Policies in Europe*, Leicester, Leicester University Press, 1994.

Burnett, John. 'Time, Place and Content. The Changing Structure of Meals in

Britain in the Nineteenth and Twentieth Centuries', in Schärer, Martin R. and Fenton, Alexander (eds), *Food and Material Culture*, East Lothian, Scotland, Tuckwell Press, 1998.

Burnett, John. *Liquid Pleasures. A Social History of Drinks in Modern Britain*, Routledge, 1999.

Caird, James. *English Agriculture in 1850–51.* Longman, Brown, Green and Longmans, 1852.

Calder, Angus. *The People's War, 1939–1945*, Pimlico, 1992.

Carter, Henry. *The Control of the Liquor Trade in Britain. A Contribution to National Efficiency during the Great War, 1915–1918* (2nd edn), Longmans, Green and Co., 1919.

Cecil, Robert. *Life in Edwardian England*, B. T. Batsford, 1969.

Chamberlin, E. R. *Life in Wartime Britain*, Batsford, 1972.

Chapman, Kit. *Great British Chefs*, Mitchell Beazley, 1995.

Clark, Peter. *The English Alehouse. A Social History, 1200–1830*, Longman, 1983.

Cobbett, William. *Rural Rides* (1st edn, 1830). Edited and Introduced by George Woodcock, Harmondsworth, Middlesex, Penguin Books, 1981.

Coburn, Oliver. *Youth Hostel Story. The First Twenty Years*, National Council of Social Service, 1950.

Compass Lunchtime Reports, 1990, 1998, Tisbury, Wiltshire, E = Mc^2.

Cooper, Derek. *The Bad Food Guide*, Routledge & Kegan Paul, 1967.

Cottrell, Richard (ed). *Nutrition in Catering*, Carnforth, Lancashire, Parthenon Publishing Group, 1987.

Coxon, Alan and Sykes, Kathy. *Ever Wondered About Food?*, Milton Keynes, The Open University, 2002.

Crawford, Sir William and Broadley, H. *The People's Food*, William Heinemann, 1938.

Cress, Patricia Rose. *That Tea Book*, H.H.L. Publishing Group, for Brooke Bond Foods Ltd., 1992.

Curle, Virginia. *A History of Stone's Chop House*, Stone's Chop House, n.d., *c*.1960.

Curtis-Bennett, Sir Noel. *The Food of the People, being the History of Industrial Feeding*, Faber and Faber, 1949.

Dale, Frances and Cradock, John. *Around Britain with Bon Viveur*, John Lehmann, 1952.

David, Elizabeth. *A Book of Mediterranean Food*, Harmondsworth, Middlesex, Penguin Books, revised edn, 1955.

David, Elizabeth. *Harvest of the Cold Months. The Social History of Ice and Ices* (ed. Jill Norman), Harmondsworth, Middlesex, Penguin Books, 1996.

Davidoff, Leonore. *The Best Circles. Society, Etiquette and the Season*, Croom Helm, 1973.

Davies, David. *The Case of Labourers in Husbandry Stated and Considered* (1st edn, 1795). Facsimile edn, Fairfield, New Jersey, Augustus M. Kelley, 1977.

Davies, Margaret Llewelyn (ed.). *Life as We Have Known It, by Co-operative Working Women* (1st edn, 1931), Virago, 1977.

Day, Ivan (ed.). *Eat, Drink and Be Merry. The British At Table, 1600–2000*, Philip Wilson Publishers, 2000.

Deghy, Guy. *Paradise in the Strand. The Story of Romano's*, The Richards Press, 1958.

Deghy, Guy and Waterhouse, Keith. *Café Royal. Ninety Years of Bohemia*, Hutchinson, 1955.

Delgado, Alan. *The Annual Outing and Other Excursions*, George Allen & Unwin, 1977.

Denes, Gabor. *The Story of the Imperial. The Life and Times of Torquay's Great Hotel*, Newton Abbot, Devon, David & Charles, 1982.

Dickens, Cedric. *Dining with Dickens. Being a Ramble through Dickensian Foods*, Goring-on-Thames, Elvendon Press, 1984.

'Diner-Out'. *London Restaurants*, Geoffrey Bles, n.d., *c*.1924.

Dodd, George. *The Food of London*, Longman, Brown, Green and Longmans, 1856.

Donnelly, Peter (ed.). *Mrs Milburn's Diaries. An Englishwoman's Day-to-Day Reflections, 1939–1945*, Abacus, 1995.

Douglas, Mary. *Implicit Meanings. Essays in Anthropology*, Routledge & Kegan Paul, 1975.

Dreiser, Theodore. *A Traveller at Forty*, Grant Richards Ltd., 1914.

Driver, Christopher. *The British at Table, 1940–1980*, Chatto & Windus, 1983.

Drummond, J. C. and Wilbraham, Anne. *The Englishman's Food. A History of Five Centuries of English Diet*, Jonathan Cape, 1939.

Dunlop, John. *The Philosophy of Artificial and Compulsory Drinking Usages in Great Britain and Ireland*, Houlston and Stoneman, 1839.

Escoffier, Auguste. *Memories of My Life*, Translated by Laurence Escoffier, New York, Van Nostrand Reinhold, 1997.

Escoffier, G. Auguste. *A Guide to Modern Cookery* (1st edn, 1903). Hutchinson, 1957.

Evans, David M. *City Men and City Manners, with Sketches on 'Change and at the Coffee Houses*, Groombridge and Sons, 1852.

Fast Food UK. Report by MSI, Market Research for Industry, 2002.

Fernandez-Armesto, F. *Food. A History*, Macmillan, 2001.

Fielding, Daphne. *Duchess of Jermyn Street*, Eyre and Spottiswoode, 1964.

Fine, Ben and Leopold, Ellen. *The World of Consumption*, Routledge, 1993.

Finkelstein, Joanne. *Dining Out. A Sociology of Modern Manners*, Cambridge, Polity Press, 1989.

Fischler, Claude. 'The McDonaldization of Culture', in Flandrin, Jean-Louis and Montanari, Massimo (eds), *Food, A Culinary History from Antiquity to the Present*, New York, Columbia University Press, 1999.

Forrest, Denys. *Tea For The British. The Social and Economic History of a Famous Trade*, Chatto & Windus, 1973.

Fothergill, John. *An Innkeeper's Diary* (1st edn, 1931). Faber and Faber, 1987.

Francatelli, Charles Elmé. *A Plain Cookery Book for the Working Classes* (1852). Reprinted by the Scolar Press, 1977.

Fraser, W. Hamish. *The Coming of the Mass Market, 1850–1914*, Hamden, Conn., Archon Books, 1981.

Freeman, Sarah. *Mutton and Oysters. The Victorians and their Food*, Victor Gollancz, 1989.

French, R. K. *The History and Virtues of Cyder*, Robert Hale, 1982.

Freud, Clement. *The Gourmet's Tour of Great Britain and Ireland*, Boston, USA, and London, Little, Brown and Co., 1989.

Frewin, Leslie (ed.). *Parnassus Near Piccadilly. The Café Royal Centenary Book, An Anthology*, Leslie Frewin, *c.*1965.

Gallati, Mario. *Mario of the Caprice. The Autobiography of a Restaurateur*, Hutchinson, 1960.

Gilbert, Bentley B. *The Evolution of National Insurance in Great Britain*, Michael Joseph, 1966.

Gould-Marks, Beryl. *Eating in the Open*, Faber and Faber, 1971.

Gourvish, T. R. and Wilson, R. G. *The British Brewing Industry, 1830–1980*, Cambridge, Cambridge University Press, 1994.

Granville, A. B. *The Spas of England and Principal Sea-bathing Places*, 2 vols. (1841). Facsimile edn, Bath, Somerset, Adams and Dart, 1971.

Graves, Robert and Hodge, Alan. *The Long Weekend. A Social History of Great Britain, 1918–1939*, Faber and Faber, 1940.

Grey, Edwin. *Cottage Life in a Hertfordshire Village* (1st edn, 1934). Harpenden, Herts., Harpenden and District Local History Society, 1977.

Griffiths, James. *Pages from Memory*, J. M. Dent, 1969.

Hall, E. Hepple. *Coffee Taverns, Cocoa Houses and Coffee Palaces. Their Rise, Progress and Prospects*, S. W. Partridge, 1878.

Halliday, Andrew (ed.). *The Savage Club Papers for 1868*, Tinsley Bros, 1868.

Hammond, R. J. *Food: The Growth of Policy* (Vol. I, 1951); *Food: Studies in Administration and Control* (Vol. II, 1956, Vol. III, 1962), the Official History of the Second World War, HMSO and Longmans, Green and Co.

Hardyment, Christina. *Slice of Life. The British Way of Eating Since 1945*, BBC Books, 1995.

Hartley, Dorothy. *Food in England*, Little, Brown and Co., 1999.

Hayward, A. *The Art of Dining, or Gastronomy and Gastronomes* (1st edn, 1852). New edition, John Murray, 1883.

Heald, G. 'Trends In Eating Out', in Cottrell, Richard (ed.), *Nutrition in Catering*, Carnforth, Lancashire, Parthenon Publishing Group, 1987.

Heath, Francis George. *The English Peasantry*, Frederick Warne, 1874.

Heath, Richard. *The English Peasant. Studies Historical, Local and Biographic*, T. Fisher Unwin, 1893.

Hembry, Phyllis. *The English Spa, 1560–1815. A Social History*, Athlone Press, 1990.

Hembry, Phyllis. *British Spas from 1815 to the Present. A Social History*, Edited and Completed by Cowie, Leonard W. and Cowie, Evelyn E., Athlone Press, 1997.

Hewett, Edward and Axton, W. F. *Convivial Dickens. The Drinks of Dickens and his Times*, Athens, Ohio, Ohio University Press, 1983.

Hooper, Mary. *Little Dinners. How to Serve Them with Elegance and Economy*, C. Kegan Paul, 1878.

Horn, Pamela. *The Rural World, 1780–1850: Social Change in the English Countryside*, Hutchinson, 1980.

Hudgins, Tom. 'Burgers and Fries. From White Castles to Golden Arches', in Walker, Harlan (ed.), *Public Eating. Oxford Symposium on Food and Cookery*, Prospect Books, 1991.

Hudson, K. and Pettifer, J. *Diamonds In the Sky. A Social History of Air Travel*, Bodley Head, 1979.

Jackson, Stanley. *The Savoy. The Romance of a Great Hotel*, Frederick Muller, 1964.

Jacobs, M. and Scholliers, P. (eds). *Eating Out in Europe*, Oxford, Berg, 2003.

James, Robert Rhodes (ed.). *Chips. The Diaries of Sir Henry Channon*, Weidenfeld & Nicolson, 1967.

Johnston, Moira (ed.). *London Eats Out. 500 Years of Capital Dining*, Philip Wilson and Museum of London, 1999.

Jones, Gareth Stedman. *Outcast London. A Study of the Relationship between Classes in Victorian Society*, Harmondsworth, Middlesex, Penguin Books, 1976.

Jones, Stephen G. *Workers at Play. A Social and Economic History of Leisure, 1918–1939*, Routledge & Kegan Paul, 1986.

Journeyman Engineer (Thomas Wright). *Some Habits and Customs of the Working Classes*, (1867). Reprinted New York, Augustus M. Kelley, 1967.

Journeyman Engineer (Thomas Wright). *The Great Unwashed* (1868). Reprinted New York, Augustus M. Kelley, 1970.

Kaye-Smith, Sheila. *Kitchen Fugue*, Cassell, 1945.

Langley, Andrew. *The Selected Soyer. The Writings of the Legendary Victorian Chef, Alexis Soyer*, Bath, Avon, Absolute Press in conjunction with the Reform Club, 1987.

Lawrence, David. *Always a Welcome. The glove compartment history of the motorway service area*, Twickenham, Between Books, 1999.

Lawrence, D. H. *The Rainbow* (1915), quoted Allen, Brigid (ed.), *Food. An Oxford Anthology*, Oxford, Oxford University Press, 1994.

Layton, T. A. *Dining Round London*, Noel Carrington (2nd edn), 1947.

Leach, Alison (ed.). *The Savoy Food and Drink Book*, Pyramid Books, 1988.

Leeson, R. A. *Travelling Brothers. The six centuries' road from craft fellowship to trade unionism*, George Allen & Unwin, 1979.

Leoni, Peppino. *I Shall Die On The Carpet*, Leslie Frewin, 1966.

Levenstein, Harvey A. *Revolution At The Table. The Transformation of the American Diet*, New York, Oxford University Press, 1988.

Longmate, Norman. *The Way We Lived Then. A History of Everyday Life During the Second World War*, Hutchinson, 1977.

Longmate, Norman. *The Hungry Mills. The Story of the Lancashire Cotton Famine, 1861–5*, Temple Smith, 1978.

Lowerson, John and Myerscough, John. *Time to Spare in Victorian England*, Hassocks, Sussex, Harvester Press, 1977.

MacClure, Victor. *Good Appetite My Companion. A Gourmand At Large*, Odham's Press, 1955.

McDonald's Fact File 2000, McDonald's Restaurants Ltd.

McDouall, Robin. *Clubland Cooking*, Phaedon Press, 1974.

McKee, Francis. 'Ice Cream and Immorality', in Walker, Harlan (ed.), *Public Eating, Oxford Symposium on Food and Cookery*, Prospect Books, 1991.

McKendrick, N., Brewer, J. and Plumb, J. H. *The Birth of a Consumer Society. The Commercialization of Eighteenth Century England*, Europa Publications, 1982.

Mackenzie, Compton. *The Savoy of London*, George G. Harrap, 1953.

McKenzie, John. *Food Choice and Price*, Supplementary Report from The National Catering Inquiry, sponsored by Smethursts Foods Ltd., 1967.

Mackray, Robert. *The Night Side of London* (1st edn, 1902). Reprinted Bibliophile Books, 1984.

Mars, Gerald and Nicod, Michael. *The World of Waiters*, George Allen & Unwin, 1984.

Mars, Valerie. 'Service à la Russe. The New Way of Dining', in C. Anne Wilson (ed.), *Luncheon, Nuncheon and other Meals. Eating with the Victorians*, Stroud, Gloucestershire, Alan Sutton Publishing, 1994.

Martin, Geoffrey. Introduction to Granville, A. B. *The Spas of England*, op. cit.

Mason, Laura. 'Learning How to Eat in Public: School Dinners', in Walker, Harlan (ed.), *Public Eating, Oxford Symposium on Food and Cookery*, Prospect Books, 1991.

Masterman, C. F. G. *The Condition of England*, Methuen and Co., 2nd edn, 1909.

Masterman, C. F. G. *The Heart of the Empire* (1st edn, 1901). Brighton, Sussex, The Harvester Press, 1973.

Masters, Anthony. *Rosa Lewis. An Exceptional Edwardian*, Weidenfeld & Nicolson, 1977.

Mayhew, Henry. *London Labour and the London Poor. Vol. 1, The London Street-Folk*, Griffin, Bohn and Co., 1861.

Memoirs of a Stomach. Written by Himself, that All Who Eat May Read: Edited by a Minister of the Interior, Chapman and Hall, 5th edn, n.d., *c*.1855.

Mennell, Stephen. *All Manners of Food. Eating and Taste in England and France from the Middle Ages to the Present*, Oxford, Basil Blackwell, 1985.

Mingay, G. E. *The Transformation of Britain*, 1830–1939, Routledge & Kegan Paul, 1986.

Mitchell, B. R. and Deane, Phyllis. *Abstract of British Historical Statistics*, Cambridge, Cambridge University Press, 1962.

Money, L. G. Chiozza. *Riches and Poverty* (1st edn, 1905). Methuen and Co., 11th edn, 1914.

Montizambert, Elizabeth. *London Discoveries. Shops and Restaurants*, Women Publishers Ltd, 1924.

Morgan, Bryan. *Express Journey, 1864–1964. A Centenary History of the Express Dairy Co. Ltd.*, Newman Neame Ltd, 1964.

Morris, Helen. *Portrait of a Chef. The Life of Alexis Soyer*, Oxford, Oxford University Press, 1980.

Newnham-Davis, Lieut. Col. N. *Dinners and Diners. Where and How to Dine in London*, Grant Richards, 1901.

Oddy, D. J. 'The Changing Techniques and Structure of the Fishing Industry', in Barker, T. C. and Yudkin, John (eds), *Fish in Britain. Trends in the Supply, Distribution and Consumption During the Past Two Centuries*, Department of Nutrition, Queen Elizabeth College, University of London, Occasional Paper No. 2, 1971.

Oddy, D. J. 'Food, Drink and Nutrition', in Thompson, F. M. L. (ed.), *The Cambridge Social History of Britain, 1750–1950*, Cambridge University Press, 1990.

Oddy, Derek J. *From Plain Fare to Fusion Food. British Diet from the 1890s to the 1990s*, Woodbridge, Suffolk, The Boydell Press, 2003.

Oliver, Basil. *The Renaissance of the English Public House*, Faber and Faber, 1947.

Orr, Sir John Boyd and Lubbock, David. *Feeding the People in Wartime*, Macmillan, 1940.

Owen, David. *English Philanthropy, 1660–1960*, Cambridge, Mass., Harvard University Press, 1964.

Pankhurst, E. Sylvia. *The Home Front. A Mirror to Life in England during the World War*, Hutchinson, 1932.

Patten, Marguerite. *Century of British Cooking*, Grub Street, 1999.

Patten, Marguerite, *Post-War Kitchen*, Oxford, Past Times, 2001.

Peel, Mrs. C. S. *A Hundred Wonderful Years. Social and Domestic Life of a Century, 1820–1920*, (1926). Cheap Edition John Lane, The Bodley Head, 1929.

Peel, Mrs C. S. *The Way We Lived Then, 1914–1918*, The Bodley Head, 1929.

Petrie, Sir Charles. *Scenes of Edwardian Life*, Eyre and Spottiswoode, 1965.

Pigache, Captain D. Nicols. *Café Royal Days*, Hutchinson, 1934.

Pimlott, J. A. R. *The Englishman's Holiday. A Social History*, Faber and Faber, 1947.

Playne, Caroline E. *Society At War, 1914–1916*, George Allen & Unwin, 1931.

Playne, Caroline E. *Britain Holds On, 1917–1918*, George Allen & Unwin, 1933.

Porter, G. R. *The Progress of the Nation in its Various Social and Economical Relations*, John Murray, 1847.

Postgate, Raymond (ed.). *The Good Food Guide, 1961–1962*, Cassell, 1961.

Postgate, Raymond. *The Good Food Guide, 1969–1970*. Revised edn by Christopher Driver, Consumers' Association and Hodder & Stoughton, 1970.

Preston, Sir Harry. *Leaves From My Unwritten Diary*, Hutchinson, 1936.

Price, Stephen. 'Eating Out in London: A Social History, 1900–1950', Brunel University Dissertation, 1986.

Prunier, Madame. *La Maison. The History of Prunier's*, Longmans, Green and Co., 1957.

Read, Jan and Manjón, Maite. *The Great British Breakfast*, Michael Joseph, 1981.

Reeves, Mrs Pember. *Round About a Pound a Week* (1st edn, 1913). Republished Virago, 1979.

Rey, J. *The Whole Art of Dining, with Notes on the Subject of Service and Table Decorations*, Carmona and Baker, n.d., *c.*1914.

Roberts, Robert. *The Classic Slum. Salford Life in the First Quarter of the Century*, Manchester, Manchester University Press, 1971.

Routh, Guy. *Occupations of the People of Great Britain, 1801–1981*, Macmillan, 1987.

Rowntree, B. Seebohm. *Poverty. A Study of Town Life*, Macmillan and Co. (1901), 4th edn, 1902.

Royal Institution. *The Nation's Larder and the Housewife's Part Therein* (text of lectures), G. Bell and Sons, 1940.

Sala, George Augustus. *Twice Round the Clock* (1st edn, 1859). Republished Leicester, Leicester University Press, 1971.

Samuel, Raphael (ed.). *Village Life and Labour*, History Workshop Series, Routledge & Kegan Paul, 1975.

Schlosser, Eric. *Fast Food Nation*, Harmondsworth, Middlesex, Penguin Books, 2002.

Selby, Charles. *See* Tickletooth, Tabitha.

Shaw, Charles. *When I Was A Child* (1st edn, 1903). Introduction by John Burnett, Firle, Sussex, Caliban Books, 1980.

Shaw, D. ('One of the Old Brigade'). *London in the Sixties*, Everett and Co., 1908.

Sheridan, Dorothy (ed.). *Wartime Women. An Anthology of Women's Wartime Writing for Mass Observation, 1937–1945*, Mandarin, 1991.

Simon, André L. *The Art of Good Living*, Constable and Co., 1929.

Simon, André L. 'From Esau to Escoffier, or The History of Gastronomy', in Golding, Louis and Simon, André L. (eds). *We Shall Eat and Drink Again. A Wine and Food Anthology*, Hutchinson, n.d., *c*.1948.

Simon, André. *Food*, Burke Publishing Co., 1949.

Sims, George R. *My Life. Sixty Years' Recollections of Bohemian London*, Eveleigh Nash, 1917.

Sissons, Michael and French, Philip (eds). *Age of Austerity*, Hodder & Stoughton, 1963.

Slater, Gilbert. *Poverty and the State*, Constable and Co., 1930.

Smith, Albert. *The English Hotel Nuisance*, David Bryce, 1856.

Smith, Edward. *Practical Dietaries for Families, Schools and the Labouring Classes*, Walton and Maberly, 1864.

Soyer, Alexis. *A Shilling Cookery for the People*, Geo. Routledge and Co., 1855.

Spang, Rebecca L. *The Invention of the Restaurant. Paris and Modern Gastronomic Culture*, Harvard University Press, 2000.

Spencer, Colin. *The Heretic's Feast. A History of Vegetarianism*, Fourth Estate, 1993.

Spencer, Colin. *British Food. An Extraordinary Thousand Years of History*, Grub Street, 2002.

Spencer, Edward ('Nathaniel Gubbins'). *Cakes and Ale. A Dissertation on Banquets, etc.* (1st edn, 1897). Stanley Paul and Co., 1913.

Stenton, F. M. *Norman London. An Essay*, G. Bell and Son, 1934.

Stevenson, John. *British Society, 1914–1945*, Allen Lane, 1984.

Stone, J. Harris. *Caravan and Camp Cooking Recipes*, The Caravan Club of Great Britain and Ireland, n.d., *c*.1925.

Strong, Roy. *Feast. A History of Grand Eating*, Jonathan Cape, 2002.

Takula, Mikko. *London, Restaurant Capital of the World*, Helsinki, Finland, Finnair, Blue Wings, Helsinki Media Co., June–July 2000.

Tannahill, Reay. *Food in History*, Revised edn, Harmondsworth, Middlesex, Penguin Books, 1988.

Taylor, Derek. *Fortune, Fame and Folly. British Hotels and Catering from 1878 to 1978*, IPC Business Press, 1977.

Taylor Nelson Research Ltd. *The Changing Structure of Meals in Britain. A Report*, 1988.

Taylor Nelson Sofres Research Plc, *MealTrak – Out of Home*, 364/950, 1999.

Thompson, Flora. *Lark Rise to Candleford* (1st edn, 1939). Harmondsworth, Middlesex, Penguin Books, 1976.

Thompson, F. M. L. *English Landed Society in the Nineteenth Century*, Routledge & Kegan Paul, 1963.

Thorne, Robert. 'Places of Refreshment in the Nineteenth-Century City', in King, Anthony D. (ed.), *Buildings and Society. Essays on the Social Development of the Built Environment*, Routledge & Kegan Paul, 1980.

Thorne, Robert. 'The Movement for Public House Reform, 1882–1914', in Oddy, Derek J. and Miller, Derek S. (eds), *Diet and Health in Modern Britain*, Croom Helm, 1985.

Tickletooth, Tabitha (Charles Selby). *The Dinner Question. Or How to Dine Well and Economically* (1st edn, 1860). Facsimile edn, Totnes, Devon, Prospect Books, 1999.

Timbs, John. *Clubs and Club Life in London*, John Camden Hotten, 1872.

Tressall (Noonan), Robert. *The Ragged Trousered Philanthropists* (1914). Quoted Allen, Brigid (ed.), *Food. An Oxford Anthology*, Oxford, Oxford University Press, 1994.

Unwin, Mrs Cobden. 'Introduction', in *The Hungry Forties. Life under the Bread Tax*. Descriptive letters and other testimonies from contemporary witnesses, T. Fisher Unwin, 1905.

Veal, Irene. *Recipes of the 1940s*, John Gifford, 1944.

Visser, Margaret. *The Rituals of Dinner*, Harmondsworth, Middlesex, Penguin Books, 1993.

Walton, John K. *The Blackpool Landlady. A Social History*, Manchester, Manchester University Press, 1978.

Walton, John K. *Fish and Chips and the British Working Class, 1870–1940*, Leicester, Leicester University Press, 1992.

Walton, John K. *The British Seaside. Holidays and Resorts in the Twentieth Century*, Manchester University Press, 2000.

Ward, Colin and Hardy, Dennis. *Goodnight Campers. The History of the British Holiday Camp*, Mansell Publishing, 1986.

Warde, Alan. 'Continuity and Change in British Restaurants, 1951–2001. Evidence from The Good Food Guide', in Jacobs, M. and Scholliers, P. (eds), *Eating Out in Europe*, Oxford, Berg, 2003.

Warde, Alan and Martens, Lydia. *Eating Out. Social Differentiation, Consumption and Pleasure*, Cambridge University Press, 2000.

Warren, Geoffrey C. (ed.). *The Foods We Eat. A Survey of Meals ... Conducted in Great Britain by the Market Research Division of W. S. Crawford Ltd*, Cassell, 1958.

Weir, Robin. 'Penny Licks and Hokey-Pokey. Ice Cream before the Cone', in Walker, Harlan (ed.), *Public Eating, Oxford Symposium on Food and Cookery*, Prospect Books, 1991.

White, Arthur. *Palaces of the People. A Social History of Commercial Hospitality*, Rapp and Whiting, 1968.

Wilson, C. Anne. 'Eight Centuries of the English Restaurant', in *The Good Food Guide*, Hodder & Stoughton/Consumers' Association, 1986.

Wilson, C. Anne (ed.). *Food for the Community. Special Diets for Special Groups*, Edinburgh, Edinburgh University Press, 1993.

Wilson, C. Anne (ed.). *Luncheon, Nuncheon and Other Meals. Eating with the Victorians*, Stroud, Gloucestershire, Alan Sutton Publishing, 1994.

Winner, Michael. *Winner's Dinners*, Robson Books, 2000.

Wood, Roy C. *The Sociology of the Meal*, Edinburgh University Press, 1995.

Wooler, Neil. *Dinner in the Diner. The History of Railway Catering*, Newton Abbot, Devon, David & Charles, 1987.

Wright, Thomas. *See* Journeyman Engineer.

Wroth, Warwick. *Cremorne and the Later London Gardens*, Elliot Stock, 1907.

Zweiniger-Bargielowska, Ina. *Austerity in Britain. Rationing, Controls and Consumption, 1939–1955*, Oxford, Oxford University Press, 2000.

Articles in Journals

Anon. 'London Eating Houses', *Chambers Edinburgh Journal*, 24 June 1837.

Anon. 'A Cup of Coffee', *Household Words*, 1852.

Anon. 'London Coffee Houses Past and Present', *Leisure Hour*, March 1863.

Anon. 'Inns Old and New', *All the Year Round*, 23 June 1866.

Booth, Charles. 'Occupations of the People of the United Kingdom, 1801–1881', *Journal of the Statistical Society*, vol. XLIX, 1886.

Bowley, A. L. 'Changes in Average Wages (Nominal and Real) in the United Kingdom between 1860 and 1891', *Journal of the Statistical Society*, vol. LVIII, 1895.

Collins, Edward and Oddy, Derek J. 'The Centenary of the British Food Journal, 1899–1999', *British Food Journal*, vol. 100(10/11), 1998.

Colmore, G. 'Eight Hundred A Year', *Cornhill Magazine*, New Series, vol. X, Jan.–June 1901.

Cullen, Peter. 'Time, Tastes and Technology. The Economic Evolution of Eating Out', *British Food Journal*, vol. 96(10), 1994.

Duffill, David and Martin, Hugh. 'The U.K. Chain Restaurant Market. Developments in this Evolving Industry', *British Food Journal*, vol. 95(4), 1993.

Elliott, Sir Charles. 'State Feeding of School Children in London', *Nineteenth Century and After*, vol. LXV, Jan.–June 1909.

Gallup Poll Surveys Ltd. 'Britons' Favourite Foods', *Caterer and Hotelkeeper*, 14 Sept. 1989.

Gillespie, Cailein H. 'Gastrosophy and Nouvelle Cuisine. Entrepreneurial Fashion and Fiction', *British Food Journal*, vol. 96(10), 1994.

Greg, W. R. 'Life At High Pressure', *Contemporary Review*, March 1875.

Layard, G. S. 'A Lower-Middle Class Budget', *Cornhill Magazine*, New Series, vol. X, Jan.–June 1901.

Lyons, Joseph. 'Chats with Caterers'. Interviewed by S. J. Adair Fitz-Gerald in *Caterer and Hotelkeepers Gazette*, 15 June 1904.

McKenzie, J. C. 'Recipes and the Housewife', *Home Economics*, March 1963.

Pearce, John. 'Chats with Caterers'. Interviewed by S. J. Adair Fitz-Gerald in *Caterer and Hotelkeepers Gazette*, 16 Jan. 1905.

Simon, André (ed.). *Wine and Food. A Gastronomic Quarterly*, Nos 33, Spring 1942 and 34, Summer 1942.

Titmarch, M. A. (William Makepeace Thackeray), 'Memorials of Gourmandizing, in a Letter to Oliver Yorke, Esq.', *Fraser's Magazine*, June 1841. In George Saintsbury (ed.), *The Works*, Oxford, Oxford University Press, vol. III, 1908.

Warde, Alan and Martens, Lydia. 'Eating Out and the Commercialisation of Mental Life', *British Food Journal*, vol. 100(3), 1998.

Wood, Roy C. 'The Shock of the New. A Sociology of Nouvelle Cuisine', *Journal of Consumer Studies and Home Economics*, vol. 15(4), 1991.

Official Publications

PP = Parliamentary Papers.

1824	Labourers' Wages. Report from the Select Committee on the Rate of Agricultural Wages and on the Condition and Morals of Labourers in that Employment. PP (392), vol. VI.
1831–2	Report of the Select Committee on Factory Children's Labour. PP, vol. XV.
1862	Report Relative to the Grievances Complained of by the Journeyman Bakers. PP (3027), vol. XLVII.
1904	Report of the Inter-Departmental Committee on Physical Deterioration. PP, Cmd. 2175, vol.1.
1918	Report of the Sumner Committee on the Working Classes' Cost of Living. PP, Cmd. 8980.
1943	Wagner, Gertrude. 'Food During the War. A Summary of Studies', Central Office of Information, Wartime Social Survey, TS, undated.
1946	*How Britain Was Fed in Wartime, Food Control, 1939–1945*, HMSO.
1956	Consumers' Expenditure on Meals and Other Food Eaten Outside the Home. The Social Survey, Central Statistical Office.
1999	*School Meals*. Education and Employment Committee, First Report. The Stationery Office.

Annual Reports. The Stationery Office.

Family Expenditure Survey (now *Family Spending*).

National Food Survey.

Social Trends.

Index

The index includes the Introduction; Chapters 1 – 10 (and associated footnotes); and the Conclusion. Titles of books, official reports and legislation are shown in *italic*. References to footnotes are indicated by *n* and the number after the page reference, definitions and explanations by *def'n,* black and white illustrations and menus by *illus.*, and illustrative tables by *table*. Colour plates do not have page references but are indicated by their numbers eg. coffee stall Plate 1. Filing order is word-by-word; numbers file as if spelled out.